The Missing Dimension

THE MISSING DIMENSION

Governments and Intelligence Communities in
the Twentieth Century

Edited by
CHRISTOPHER ANDREW
and
DAVID DILKS

University of Illinois Press
Urbana and Chicago

First published in 1984 in the United States of America by
University of Illinois Press, Urbana and Chicago
Manufactured in Great Britain

Library of Congress Cataloging in Publication Data
Main entry under title:

The Missing dimension.

  Includes bibliographies and index.
  1. Intelligence service–History–20th century–
Addresses, essays, lectures.   I. Andrew, Christopher M.
II. Dilks, David, 1938–
UB250.M57   1985   327.1′2   84–2513
ISBN 0–252–01157–0
ISBN 0–333–36864–9   (UK edition, Macmillan)

Contents

Introduction

CHRISTOPHER ANDREW
and
DAVID DILKS

SECRET intelligence has been described by one distinguished diplomat as 'the missing dimension of most diplomatic history'.[1] The
same dimension is also absent from most political and much military
history. Academic historians have frequently tended either to ignore
intelligence altogether, or to treat it as of little importance. The
distinguished editor of a major volume of military diaries published in
1972 failed to realise that the references to 'C' and 'C's information'
referred to the head of the Secret Intelligence Service (SIS); the
author of an important political history published in 1979 confused
the head of the Special Branch with the head of the Security Service
(MI5). A. J. P. Taylor's brilliant 875-page survey of *English History
1914–1945* finds space (quite rightly) for George Robey and Nellie
Melba but none for heads of the intelligence community. In this
respect at least, Mr Taylor merely follows long-established precedent
among modern historians.

The great danger of any missing historical dimension is that its
absence may distort our understanding of other, accessible dimen-
sions. The Franks Committee clearly felt it impossible to produce a
balanced assessment of the 1982 Falklands conflict without access to
the intelligence files, even though they, of course, contain only part of
the story. As some of the articles in this volume show, balanced
accounts of earlier twentieth-century conflicts also require access to
intelligence files. Since 1973 the revelation of 'the Ultra secret' has
changed our understanding of the Second World War. It is now clear
that intelligence played a major, perhaps decisive, part in – notably –
the turning of the tide of war in North Africa, the winning of the long
drawn-out naval battle of the North Atlantic, and the preparations for
the D-day landing. Professor F. H. Hinsley, the official historian of

1

British intelligence in the Second World War, has hazarded the estimate that the superiority of Allied intelligence shortened the war by three years.[2] Intelligence is, of course, not usually so influential. During many modern crises it has been misunderstood, not used or simply wrong. But the historian of national or international politics can never afford to ignore it.

Historians have a general tendency to pay too much attention to the evidence which survives, and to make too little allowance for what does not. Intelligence has become a 'missing dimension' first and foremost because its written records are so difficult to come by. Despite the revelations about Second World War intelligence over the last decade, the official veil which shrouds the past history of the intelligence community has been only slightly raised. First, although some of the intelligence supplied to government departments has now been released to the Public Record Office, all the records of the intelligence services themselves remain completely closed. The government refuses even to set some far distant date for their release. Secondly, what has been officially released so far is curiously lop-sided. A three-volume official history of British intelligence in the Second World War is in course of publication but there is no present prospect of an official peacetime history.[3] The secretary of the cabinet explained to a Commons select committee in February 1983 that peacetime intelligence records are still considered much more secret than wartime records.[4] This odd distinction, which seems to reflect a traditional embarrassment at admitting that Britain collects intelligence at all in peacetime, has produced a series of curious anomalies in the records so far made available. Thus, although many thousands of intercepted German wartime telegrams of the early 1940s have been released, Soviet peacetime telegrams intercepted twenty years earlier have not. Most scholarly research published over the last decade in Britain has therefore concentrated on wartime rather than peacetime intelligence. The interwar history of the intelligence community is far less well known than its record in the Second World War.

The yawning gaps in the history of British intelligence left by academic historians have to some extent been filled by more adventurous non-academics. The important contributions of such writers as David Kahn, Ronald Lewin and Patrick Beesly are well grounded in publicly available source material. The contribution of those writers who rely largely on inside information from the intelligence community, past and present, is much more difficult to assess. The two authors who claim most inside information, Chapman Pincher and 'Nigel West', disagree about such essentials as whether Sir Roger Hollis, director-general of MI5 from 1956 to 1965, was or was not a Soviet agent.[5] Our sympathies on this issue lie with Nigel West and the much maligned Sir Roger Hollis. But Mr West, the most prolific recent writer on British intelligence history, himself poses severe problems for other historians. His best-selling books contain much new information but almost no footnotes or references; even when free to divulge a source, he seems reluctant to do so. The reader is thus bound to gauge the reliability of what he cannot check against the reliability of what he can. When Mr West repeatedly asserts that the prime minister in 1921 was Ramsay MacDonald (and not, as previously believed, Lloyd George) or claims that Sir Horace Wilson (previously believed to be Chamberlain's chief industrial adviser and confidant) was in fact head of Indian political intelligence, the historian's confidence in other parts of his often interesting narrative is bound to be shaken.[6]

As well as being deterred from considering the intelligence dimension by the gaps in the archives and the difficulty in evaluating the 'inside information' of Mr West and others, academic historians have also been repelled by the evident absurdity of many best-selling publications on the subject. The treatment of intelligence by both mass media and publishers often seems ideally calculated to persuade the academic world that it is no subject for scholars. The problem is not a new one. The most successful and prolific spy novelist before the First World War, William Le Queux, allegedly Queen Alexandra's favourite writer, claimed that many of his books were thinly-disguised documentaries and that he himself had 'imperturbably risked his life in countless exploits' as an unofficial British secret agent. His fraudulent 'documentary' work *German Spies in England*, published early in the First World War, purporting to describe *inter alia* how he had obtained the text of a vital (and in fact non-existent) secret speech by the Kaiser only to have it stolen by German intelligence, went through six editions in three weeks and contained enthusiastic endorsements from five gullible peers, two MPs, the Lord Mayor of London, Sir Arthur Conan Doyle, five national and four provincial newspapers.[7]

Echoes of the Le Queux school of intelligence fantasy linger on. The most expensive intelligence production shown on British television up to the time of writing is the twelve-part Thames Television drama 'documentary' series first broadcast in the autumn of 1983 on 'Reilly – Ace of Spies'. It features: 'Sidney Reilly. A rogue. A womaniser. An adventurer. A man whose skill and audacity changed the face of world history.' According to Thames Television the series is 'the true story of a man whose exploits defied belief'.[8] They do indeed; some of them are fiction in the grand Le Queux tradition. There is probably no other historical series in which ITV has tolerated the same degree of dramatic licence. The lapse is significant. Intelligence is commonly treated as a subject exempt from normal critical standards on which accuracy may be readily sacrificed to box-office appeal. One TV critic counted in the first episode of 'Reilly': 'two murders, two executions, one earthquake, two strip-tease performances (difficult with all that Victorian corsetry), one whorehouse scene, one seduction and an endless amount of double-dealing, betrayal and international intrigue.'[9] Reilly's main female box-office rival is probably 'Cynthia', a British agent in the United States during the Second World War. The publishers, if not the author, of a biography detailing her 'Conquests on a Satin Battlefield' choose to begin the story of Britain's 'Most Seductive Secret Weapon' thus:

> Cynthia sprang from the couch in the darkened Embassy corridor, and began unbuttoning her dress: 'What are you doing?' gasped the bewildered man who had been on the couch with her. Now she was naked. 'Your turn!' she hissed.[10]

At least in their professional lives, academic historians are curiously ill at ease in such situations. They share the bewilderment of Cynthia's companion on the couch when faced with a surfeit of imaginative prose and a shortage of documentary evidence. Alexandre Dumas once said of a woefully inaccurate history of the French Revolution that it had 'raised history to the level of a novel'. Many writers on intelligence have achieved the same feat.

But historians have been far more put off the subject of intelligence than they need have been. One of the purposes of this volume is to show what can be reliably based on existing archives and published source material. Though the articles published here deal in greatest detail with British Intelligence history in the twentieth century, they also draw on American, French, German, Irish, Japanese, Polish and Russian experience. Historians of twentieth-century Western societies are so used to the vast (and often excessive) files generated by modern bureaucracies that they tend perhaps to be more easily deterred by gaps in the archives than historians of, say, Anglo-Saxon England or Stalinist Russia who face evidential problems of at least equal magnitude. In Britain at least, the source material now available, for all its many gaps and defects, is sufficient to fill in both the general outline of the missing intelligence dimension and much of its operational detail. Whitehall has been dismayed to discover how much Duncan Campbell, the most articulate left-wing critic of the intelligence community, has been able to deduce about very recent intelligence operations from published sources.

Even the two most secret sections of Britain's interwar intelligence community, the espionage agency SIS (also known as MI6) and the codebreakers, used non-secret organisations as cover – the network of Passport Control Offices and the Government Code and Cypher School. The Foreign Office and Treasury files on these two organisations, which have lain virtually undisturbed in the Public Record Office since the introduction of the Thirty Year Rule, though heavily 'weeded', contain the names and salaries of most interwar cryptanalysts and SIS station chiefs.[11] A significant number of private papers and other archives contain intelligence documents which Whitehall would never willingly have released but it is nowadays reluctant to make itself conspicuous by reclaiming them.[12] Even the censored files of the Public Record Office contain a surprising amount of both raw intelligence and intelligence analysis. 'This telegram should be burnt when read', reads one secret Foreign Office communication to the legation at Belgrade in 1939, 'together with the figures, and you should keep no copy of any reply which you may send.' Happily, the Foreign Office copy of this telegram was not burned. Nor, perhaps surprisingly, has it been weeded.[13] The PRO contains a remarkable variety of improbable intelligence material which has still to be researched, among it – to take only one example – papers which suggest that H. St J. Philby (father of Kim) was, like his son, responsible for a serious leakage of secret documents.[14] The articles in this volume draw heavily on the files available in public archives.

The main concern of this volume is with the primary function of intelligence: to obtain by covert means, and then to analyse, information which policy-makers cannot acquire by more conventional methods. The boundary between public information and secret intelligence is usually arbitrary, is constantly shifting, and varies

widely according to time and place. Thus in Moscow the head of the
intelligence community is publicly identified but accurate street maps
are classified; in London the reverse is true. Secret intelligence never
makes sense in isolation. It has always to be considered together with
other sorts of information.

It is unfortunate that in contemporary English usage 'intelligence'
collection should have become so linguistically distinct from 'information' gathering, of which it is but one variety. It was not always so.
The English word 'intelligence', when not referring to brainpower,
formerly meant simply 'news' or 'information'. Other major languages wisely avoid a sharp distinction between 'intelligence' and
'information'. The French *renseignements*, the German *Nachrichten*, and
the Japanese *jōhō* have both meanings.[15]

Intelligence communities have, of course, frequently been concerned with more than intelligence collection and analysis. Most, if
not all, have in varying ways and to varying degrees been drawn into
covert operations other than information-gathering. Like many
others, Allen Dulles found the intelligence community 'an ideal
vehicle for conspiracy'.[16] It is difficult for any non-pacifist to reject
entirely the idea of covert operations. One may feel a certain
sympathy with the suggestion of Colonel Mason-Macfarlane, military attaché in Berlin in 1938, that he shoot the Führer during his
birthday parade, even if his confidence that he 'could pick the bastard
off as easy as winking' fails to carry complete conviction.[17] The
majority of peacetime covert operations, however, have probably
been either crimes or mistakes or both. Under Stalin and Pol Pot, to
take but two examples, intelligence services became involved in
mass murder. Most of the CIA's much more limited range of dirty
tricks have backfired. Even when successful in the short term they
have discredited American policy in the long term. And as Harry
Ransom persuasively argues, they have served to divert the CIA from
its primary functions of intelligence collection and analysis.

Two major themes emerge from the articles which follow: the
gradual and erratic professionalisation of intelligence communities in
the West, and the equally gradual and erratic way in which
governments have learned to cope with them. Intelligence at the
beginning of this century was in general far less professional than
either diplomacy or the planning of military operations. Sir Edward
Spears, the British liaison officer with the Deuxième Bureau at the
outbreak of war in 1914, marvelled at the 'wonderful smoothness' of

Anglo-French arrangements for mobilisation and concentration which worked 'practically without a hitch'. But the British Intelligence Corps, responsible for field intelligence at the Front, was not set up until the day after war was declared.[18] Though the German army had led the world in the development of the general staff, pre-war Germany – like Britain and the United States – had no codebreaking unit at all. The most professional intelligence community in 1914 was, unsurprisingly, in Russia, where it had long been one of the mechanisms by which the Tsarist autocracy (like its Bolshevik successor) preserved its hold. Tsarist Russia probably led the world both in cryptanalysis and in intelligence penetration of 'subversive' movements. One of Lenin's closest associates, Roman Malinovsky, once charged by Lenin with looking for police spies in the Bolshevik organisation, was discovered after the Revolution to have been a police spy himself.[19] But Tsarist intelligence had a primitive as well as a sophisticated side. Ian Nish shows that in battle-order and field intelligence during the Russo-Japanese War the Russians were probably less efficient than the Japanese who drew on traditions of the Tokugawa shoguns as well as learning from European experience.

Western intelligence before the First World War was a curious mixture of old and new. The old tradition of 'intelligence rides' by cavalrymen along enemy frontiers was reinforced both by the problems of defending the *Raj* and by the scramble for Africa.[20] Though intelligence collection on India's north-western frontier was sometimes a hazardous business, at other times the 'Great Game' was literally a game. In both Africa and Asia the natives were sometimes willing to join in. As Assistant Director of Military Operations and Intelligence from 1907 to 1911, Lord Edward Gleichen discovered when surveying Moroccan fortifications that:

Oddly enough, the natives raised no objection. On the contrary they took much interest in my doings, and several of them willingly assisted me in 'shooting' angles and slopes.[21]

Gleichen's plans and maps were later given to the French to assist them in the military 'pacification' of Morocco. Colonel (later Lord) Robert Baden-Powell similarly emphasised the 'sporting value' of his various intelligence missions before the First World War. 'For anyone who is tired of life', he wrote, 'the thrilling life of a spy should be the very finest recuperator.' Baden-Powell staunchly defended the amateur tradition against those who supported the foundation of a professional espionage network. 'The best spies', he insisted, 'are unpaid men who are doing it for the love of the thing.'[22] The Secret Service Bureau founded in 1909 did not deviate much from Baden-Powell's advice. Until the First World War its Foreign Department (the forerunner of SIS) employed only 'casual agents'.[23]

But while Baden-Powell, disguised as an eccentric butterfly-collector, was travelling the Balkans secretly concealing maps of fortifications in elaborate drawings of butterfly wings, cryptanalysts in France and Russia were simultaneously developing a much more advanced system of intelligence collection. Franco-Russian successes in decrypting German telegrams during the Moroccan crises of 1905 and 1911 and Japanese telegrams during the Russo-Japanese War[24] foreshadowed the two most important intelligence achievements of the Second World War: the breaking of the German 'Enigma' machine ciphers by the British and the breaking of the Japanese 'Purple' and armed services codes by the Americans. Until the emergence of the spy satellite in the 1960s cryptanalysis was the single most important twentieth-century intelligence source. Despite Japan's success in the Russo-Japanese War, her failure to learn cryptanalysis from the West as successfully as she had imitated the earlier tradition of 'intelligence rides' thereafter condemned her intelligence community to second-class status.

Although the First World War underlined the failings of 'casual agents' as well as the importance of cryptanalysis, the intelligence community continued to find room for gentlemen as well as players. Admiral 'Blinker' Hall, Director of Naval Intelligence from 1914 to 1919 and the most influential British intelligence chief of the First World War, personifies both traditions. He is best known as the presiding genius of Room 40, the first British codebreaking agency since the closure of the Foreign Office's Decyphering Branch in 1844. But Eunan O'Halpin reveals another, less professional side of Hall as the organiser of the comic-opera *Sayonara* cruise in the autumn of 1914 and the purveyor of inaccurate rumours of a German-Sinn Fein plot in 1918.

From 1923 the codebreakers of the Government Code and Cypher School (GC&CS) and the SIS espionage network were both commanded by the newly appointed Head of the Secret Service, Admiral 'Quex' Sinclair. But the two organisations, though under a single head, represented very different attitudes to intelligence. From the moment of its foundation in 1914 Room 40 had depended on graduate recruits. Its ablest cryptanalyst was 'Dilly' Knox, Fellow of King's College, Cambridge. Two other King's dons recruited to Room 40, Frank Adcock (later knighted) and Frank Birch, were to lead a recruiting drive in Cambridge for Bletchley Park on the eve of the Second World War.[25] As Jean Stengers shows, the breaking of the Enigma machine cipher depended on the achievements of brilliant mathematicians from Poznan and Cambridge universities, assisted by French espionage.[26]

SIS, however, shunned higher education. Partly in a misguided attempt to preserve itself from Bolshevik contagion, SIS restricted its interwar recruiting drive to men with 'minds untainted by the solvent force of a university education'.[27] Most SIS recruits had a service background. Apart from some basic instruction in communications and accounts, they were given no training. When Leslie Nicholson joined SIS in 1930 he was told 'there was no need for expert knowledge'. When he asked for 'tips on *how* to be a spy', he was referred to Captain Kendrick, the station chief in Vienna. 'You'll just have to work it out for yourself', Kendrick told him: 'I think everyone has his own methods and I can't think of anything I can tell you.'[28] Robert Cecil's article on the Cambridge Comintern is a reminder that Soviet intelligence, via its Comintern subsidiary, began recruiting in Cambridge and Oxford some years ahead of SIS. MI5 began a little earlier than SIS though later than Comintern. Its first Oxford recruit, Dick White, taken on in 1936, was later to play a leading part in tracking down Philby, recruited three years earlier by the Russians. Later, as head of SIS from 1956 to 1969, White was to complete the professionalisation of an agency still tinged with the sometimes casual amateurishness of the interwar period.

The structural weaknesses of Western intelligence communities up to (and in some cases beyond) the Second World War reflect the slow and fitful development of government interest in them. In most Western states the armed services, police force and foreign ministry independently developed their own intelligence systems less as a result of any decision by central government than through a process of creeping bureaucratic growth. The development of twentieth-century intelligence systems has been repeatedly confused by the domestic rivalries between these separate systems. Christopher Andrew's article shows how the development of cryptanalysis was complicated in a variety of remarkable ways by interservice rivalry in Britain and

the United States and by the antagonism of the Quai d'Orsay and the
Sûreté in France. Eunan O'Halpin documents the confusion caused
during the final years of British rule in Ireland by the simultaneous
operations of no less than five distinct intelligence systems. The
reorganisation of the intelligence community after the First World
War produced only a limited improvement. Wesley Wark and David
Dilks illustrate the grave problems encountered by Whitehall in
assessing the German menace on the eve of the Second World War
caused by the diffuse and ill-coordinated machinery of intelligence
collection and assessment. The British intelligence successes of the
Second World War owed much to the greatly improved coordination
and direction provided by the Joint Intelligence Committee and the
Joint Intelligence Staff. By contrast, David Kahn picks out the
fragmentation of the German intelligence community as one of the
reasons why, despite successes such as those analysed by Jürgen
Rohwer, it was less successful than its Allied opponents.

Ever since the Second World War the most special part of the
'special relationship' between Britain and the USA has been the
intelligence relationship. The wartime agreement to divide sigint
(signals intelligence), with Bletchley Park concentrating on German
communications and the Americans concentrating on the Japanese,
formed the basis of the secret post-war UK-USA pact. During the war
Britain had been the senior partner in the intelligence alliance. Under
the UK-USA pact she became the junior partner. The truth was that
she could no longer afford to take the lead. A system of Communications Intelligence based on a growing complex of computers (the first
of which was invented at Bletchley Park), intercept stations around
the globe and sigint personnel eventually running into six figures,
required a massive investment of which only the United States could
provide the lion's share.[29] The age of the spy satellite which dawned in
the 1960s confirmed American leadership of the intelligence alliance.
The virtual monopoly of spy satellites enjoyed by the USA and the
Soviet Union has since given their intelligence services a major
advantage over all others. By the end of the 1980s that monopoly may
well have been successfully challenged.

Nothing has so disturbed the Anglo-American special intelligence
relationship as the discovery of Britain's Soviet moles. That the
moles were able to do so much damage was due chiefly to alarming
gaps in British security. David Dilks reveals failings in pre-war
Foreign Office and embassy security which now seem scarcely

believable. Robert Cecil shows how limited the Foreign Office response was to the revelation of some of those failings, and aptly compares the contest between the KGB and British security until the 1950s to 'a football match between Manchester United and the Corinthian Casuals' in the declining years of amateurism.

The Central Intelligence Agency founded in 1947, though heavily influenced by British experience, was intended to mark a new departure. The original role of the CIA and its Director was, as Harry Ransom emphasises, first and foremost to coordinate intelligence collected chiefly by other agencies for the President and the National Security Council. The Cold War, however, diverted its energies into covert operations. During Allen Dulles's term as Director of Central Intelligence (1953–61) the ascendancy of covert operations over intelligence analysis became so complete that the CIA's own analysts were not consulted in planning the disastrous Bay of Pigs invasion. Following a half-hearted attempt under John McCone (DCI 1961–5) to reaffirm the CIA's original objectives, the Agency's main energies were diverted once again under Presidents Johnson and Nixon into covert operations. Both Presidents viewed the CIA 'primarily as an instrument for the execution of White House wishes by secret methods'. Intelligence coordination went by the board. The intelligence community at the time of Watergate was a series of overlapping agencies, competing for the attention of policy-makers, each feeling, in the words of Richard Helms (DCI 1966–73) that 'it's got to have a publication that arrives in the White House every morning'.[30]

For all its failings (indeed partly because of them), the CIA has acquired an importance in American policy-making which would have been unthinkable between the wars. Half a century ago it was still possible for the governments of Western democracies virtually to ignore their diminutive intelligence communities. Henry Stimson became American Secretary of State in 1929 believing that governments, like gentlemen, should not 'read each other's mail', with consequences for American Sigint described by Christopher Andrew. Arthur Henderson, Stimson's teetotal contemporary as British Foreign Secretary, similarly preferred to have no dealings with either SIS or GC&CS: 'His simplicity was great. He rated Secret Service like hard liquor, because he knew, and wanted to know, nothing of it.'[31] Such attitudes are inconceivable today. The importance of intelligence communities in relations between the superpowers was symbolised during 1983 by the meeting at Brezhnev's funeral between his

short-lived successor, Yuri Andropov, formerly head of the KGB, and
Vice-President Bush, formerly Director of Central Intelligence, as
well as by the American's use of intercepted Soviet transmissions
during the crisis which followed the shooting down of the South
Korean airliner. The importance of intelligence in the world's main
present trouble-spot, the Middle East, was similarly underlined in
1983 when the former Israeli intelligence officer, Yitzhak Shamir,
became his country's prime minister.

During and since the post-Watergate investigations the problems
of the CIA have been examined more fully and more openly than the
affairs of any intelligence community have ever been discussed before.
That discussion has served to focus attention on three issues in
particular which are – or ought to be – of major concern to all
intelligence communities. The first is the age-old problem of intelligence coordination. The information explosion produced by the
modern technology of collection – described by one analyst as 'an
all-source glut' – has further complicated the traditional problem of
distinguishing really important intelligence from background 'noise'.
Deputy Secretary of Defense Clements told the Defense Panel on
Intelligence in 1975: 'In every instance I know about when there was
a horrendous failure of intelligence, the information was in fact
available to have averted the problem.'[32] But the really important
intelligence was not distinguished in time from the mass of often
contradictory evidence. That seems to have been true of a whole series
of recent crises including the Yom Kippur War of 1973, the Turkish
invasion of Cyprus in 1974, and the Russian invasion of Afghanistan
in 1979. The Franks Committee in England concluded that the
invasion of the Falkland Islands in 1982 could not have been foreseen
because of the late date at which the order was given and the shortage
of satellite and other intelligence on Argentinian military movements.
But it nonetheless criticised the Joint Intelligence Organisation for
inadequately collating the secret and non-secret sources, and giving
too much weight to the former: 'The changes in the Argentine
position were, we believe, more evident on the diplomatic front and in
the associated press campaign than in the intelligence reports.'[33]

All systems of intelligence assessment have now to cope with one
very difficult dilemma. Unless the 'all-source glut' of information is
collated and reduced to an assessment of manageable length, the
policy-maker is likely to be confused rather than assisted by it. But
this very process of assessment carries with it the danger that it will

emphasise intelligence which conforms to the conventional wisdom of the time (which is invariably afterwards discovered to have contained at least some false assumptions) and exclude or underplay apparently eccentric information which points in other directions. Wesley Wark's article lends support to Michael Handel's persuasive argument that: 'Most intelligence failures occur because intelligence analysts and decision makers refuse to adapt their concepts to new information.' The serious United States intelligence miscalculations of Soviet strategic missile strength and accuracy during the 1960s and 1970s derived far less from weaknesses in intelligence collection than from the false assumptions of the assessment staff. In an extraordinary, but almost unheeded, speech of 1965 even Leonid Brezhnev warned 'the intelligence services of the imperialist states' that they were greatly underestimating 'Soviet rocket and nuclear might'. Not until President Ford established the so-called 'B Team' of outside analysts under the Harvard historian Richard Pipes did the full scale of previous errors become clear.[34]

Even the best intelligence analyst cannot hope to avoid being regularly surprised by the movements of global politics just as no economic analyst can hope to predict all the movements of the stock market. But the articles in this volume and studies of the recent experience of the CIA suggest that considerable scope for improvement remains. The ideal intelligence assessment is one which produces a coherent overall analysis for the policy-maker while at the same time drawing attention to the flaws in its own arguments and assumptions. Perhaps the nearest approach to that almost impossible ideal is the Israeli system adopted after the surprise of the Yom Kippur War. The most important Israeli intelligence assessment is 'The Estimate' – a twice-yearly assessment of the Middle Eastern situation and the potential threats to Israel. In 1974 the office of the 'Devil's Advocate' was established to look for flaws in 'The Estimate' and challenge its conclusions. In the case of other intelligence assessments where there is serious dissent among the assessment staff, the dissenter (however junior) is allowed as much space as those whose views he challenges.[35] The Franks Committee recommended giving the British Joint Intelligence Committee, chaired since 1939 by a member of the Foreign Office, an outside chairman appointed by the prime minister in order to develop 'a more critical and independent role'.[36] It might perhaps usefully have gone further still and considered the Israeli experience.

The second great issue raised in the United States by the post-Watergate investigations of the intelligence community is its constitutional position. Harry Ransom shows how the movement for a new intelligence charter defining the functions and authority of the CIA lost momentum as Soviet–American relations worsened. But Intelligence Committees survived from the post-Watergate reform era in both the Senate and the House of Representatives and preserved the principle of Congressional oversight of the intelligence community. The result, according to the former DCI William Colby, has been 'to spread the concept of Intelligence working under the law and not outside it'.[37]

The establishment of Congressional oversight inevitably has repercussions on the other side of the Atlantic. To all British governments, whether Labour or Conservative, the idea of exposing the intelligence community to parliamentary accountability has traditionally been anathema. Sir Harold Wilson's chapter on 'The Prime Minister and National Security' in his book *The Governance of Britain* is barely a page long – perhaps the shortest chapter ever written by a British Prime Minister. It concludes thus:

> The Prime Minister is occasionally questioned on security matters. His answers may be regarded as uniformly uninformative. There is no further information that can usefully or properly be added before bringing this chapter to an end.[38]

The Callaghan government reaffirmed the traditional constitutional doctrine that in matters concerning the intelligence community, 'Parliament accepts that accountability must be to Ministers rather than to Parliament, and trusts Ministers to discharge that responsibility faithfully'.[39] By the late 1970s, however, that traditional doctrine appeared rather frayed at the edges. The establishment of Congressional oversight in the United States coincided with, and helped to encourage, growing curiosity about the intelligence community within the Mother of Parliaments. In 1977 Sir Harold Wilson, disregarding the recent advice of his own book, began voicing suspicions of an improbable plot against him by MI5.[40] There followed a period of thirties nostalgia in which defunct or ageing Oxbridge moles, some real (like Anthony Blunt), others imaginary (like Sir Roger Hollis) hit the headlines and Parliament briefly joined the public hue and cry.

As Foreign Secretary from 1976 to 1979, and responsible during those years for both SIS and GCHQ, David Owen came to favour the creation of an Intelligence Select Committee in the Commons composed of 'senior Members of Parliament, trusted on all sides' (probably Privy Counsellors) with the right to question *in camera* both the Foreign Secretary and intelligence chiefs: 'People have got to feel confident that a secret service has democratic accountability and that its powers and secrecy could never be abused'. By the 1983 election Owen's views were broadly shared by the majority of Labour and Alliance MPs, and a handful of Conservatives.[41] The Thatcher administration, however, resolutely defended the constitutional doctrine of its Labour predecessor. The Franks Committee of Privy Counsellors appointed to carry out the Falkland Islands Review marks, nonetheless, a potentially important breach in that doctrine. The six Privy Counsellors included four members of the Lords and one of the Commons. They were subject to 'no reservations' in seeing 'intelligence assessments and reports' and taking oral evidence from intelligence officers. They were in other words allowed, so far as the Falklands conflict was concerned, privileges at least as extensive as those of American Congressional Intelligence Committees. Having accepted the recommendations of the Franks Committee on changes in the Joint Intelligence Organization, the government is now ill-placed to argue that a standing committee is either undesirable or unworkable.

The third great issue raised on both sides of the Atlantic by the post-Watergate investigation of the American intelligence community concerns the issue of secrecy. The traditional British doctrine is that enunciated by Austen Chamberlain in 1924:

> It is of the essence of a Secret Service that it must be secret, and if you once begin disclosure it is perfectly obvious . . . that there is no longer any Secret Service and that you must do without it.[42]

As Alasdair Palmer shows, the secrecy of the secret service has traditionally been protected not merely by the Official Secrets Act but also by the D-notice system under which journalists and editors have voluntarily censored themselves in the national interest. During the 1970s the consensus on which the D-notice system depended began visibly to disintegrate. A new consensus has yet to emerge. What has become clear is the simplistic nature of the traditional argument that on intelligence matters total disclosure is the only alternative to total secrecy. Intelligence communities necessarily require a high degree of secrecy about their current operations but they no longer require, for example, the withholding of files on British intelligence operations in Tsarist Russia. The efficiency of the intelligence community, like other branches of government, can be harmed by too much secrecy as well as by too little. It emerged while this volume was going through the press that the Prime Minister and her closest advisers had concluded by 1981 that industrial disruption at GCHQ posed so serious a threat to vital intelligence operations that union membership among its staff could no longer be allowed. But because they could not yet bring themselves to admit publicly that GCHQ had an intelligence function, they felt unable to take action for the next three years. Incredibly, the government thus sacrificed what it judged to be the requirements of national security in order to preserve an official secret which it knew to be no longer secret.

Whitehall has sadly failed to heed the advice proffered to the Cabinet Defence Committee by the lowly Ministry of Supply in 1947: 'If too many documents or equipments are classified as Top Secret, the results are (i) that administration is impeded and (ii) that the security safeguards are weakened by being spread too widely.'[43] Overclassification does one further disservice to the intelligence community. It tends to bring into disrepute the official secrecy on which the success of their current operations depends. While the government refuses to set a date for the release of the records of the intelligence community even for the period before the First World War, its definition of the level of secrecy required by national security lacks sufficient credibility to gain public respect.

1. Japanese Intelligence and the Approach of the Russo-Japanese War[1]

IAN NISH

SINCE the Meiji Restoration of 1868 Japan had learnt some of the military arts at the hands of Europeans. Such war-making techniques as were used at the time of the Franco-Prussian War were imparted to the Japanese army at its military staff college by such tutors as Major (later General) Jacob Meckel in the 1880s.[2] Similarly, knowledge about the navy was taught to Japanese naval officers at Greenwich and in Japan by British naval instructors. Although, so far as is known, these courses did not cover training in intelligence, in this area also Japan was influenced by European example.

European expansion in Asia and Africa established a tradition of information-gathering by scouts and spies, and of 'intelligence rides' by cavalrymen on imperial frontiers who made journeys either alone or with a group of soldiers into remote parts and wrote reports which were often elaborate. Occasionally the exploits of the soldier might be matched by those of the journalist-adventurer like Archibald Colquhoun who in the 1880s and 1890s wrote of the Yunnan route into China, or George Ernest Morrison, the Australian who journeyed early in 1894 from Shanghai to Rangoon dressed as a Chinese and wrote up his experiences in *An Australian in China* (1895). Japan too had her 'intelligence rides' and her adventurers who amassed information about neighbouring countries in Asia for the state. Though influenced by Europe, Japanese intelligence-gathering also looked back to the Tokugawa period (1603–1868) when the shogun, trying to control the recalcitrant daimyo and samurai, had undertaken quite sophisticated spying and intelligence operations.

In this chapter we shall concentrate on intelligence about Russia and things with Russian connections. To be sure, the Japanese were gathering intelligence about other countries, notably Germany and Britain and British India. But Russia was the contemplated enemy of the Japanese army by the time of the Russo-Japanese War, and in practice Russia had been at least under close observation from 1890 or thereabouts. As well as observing Russia herself, Japan was also keeping watch on Russian activities in China, Korea, Manchuria, Siberia and even Central Asia. Since for most of the 1890s and 1900s China and Korea were treated in Japan as puppet states of Russia and regarded as being hostile to Japan, they were placed under special scrutiny. At a further remove Russia's activities in Siberia were associated with the Trans-Siberian railway, while her activities in Manchuria were linked to the Chinese Eastern Railway (from the Russian frontier to Harbin and thence to Port Arthur) which was being built between 1897 and 1903. This railway was looked upon as a military artery, rather than a commercial one. Since relations between Japan and Russia were so tense, the railway was seen as the engine of an encroachment on Japan's interests – and even of a possible invasion of Japan's islands themselves. The object of her intelligence was to keep tabs on the developments along the line and to estimate (after 1903) the number of troops who could be carried to the East from Europe and how long it would take.

The centrepiece of Japan's intelligence method appears to have been connected with the training of military and naval officers abroad. Since the Meiji restoration in 1868 there had been a tradition of sending military/naval officers abroad for training to legations overseas. Connected with the attaché's office was often to be found a group of language officers who also undertook intelligence work. In the case of the navy, the trend was to send these trainees, such as Admiral Tōgō, to Britain. But there were cases where they were sent elsewhere. Such were Admiral Yamamoto Gonnohyōe, Navy Minister from 1898 to 1906, who was seconded to the German navy in the 1870s while Prince Fushimi, Chief of the Navy General Staff from 1932 to 1942, also served in Germany before 1904. In the case of the army the officers were more commonly sent to Germany for training. But the practice seems to have developed after the Sino-Japanese War of sending some for language training and other purposes to Russia. We are told that the young Japanese officers were initially reluctant to go on *ryūgaku* to Russia because they regarded a posting to Germany as a sign that they were marked out for a distinguished career whereas St Petersburg was regarded as a second-rung posting.[3] As it eventually turned out, the reverse was true. Those who were sent to Russia and had the opportunity of attachment to Russian units were at a premium for their inside knowledge when war broke out in 1904.

While these military/naval activities may not have been fully known to the diplomats, they too were expected to have an intelligence function. Thus, Akizuki and Makino, the Japanese Ministers in Stockholm and Vienna at the time of the Russo-Japanese War, are known to have been paying agents from diplomatic funds, and often asked Tokyo for more cash for these purposes. Foreign Minister Mutsu wrote to Kurino at the height of the Sino-Japanese War: 'If use of money can facilitate your work, I will supply you with reasonable funds' (probably for the purpose of bribing politicians and newspapers).[4] At a lower level it was the responsibility of consuls at outlying ports to report *inter alia* on the movement of naval craft on a fairly regular basis.

The use of foreign paid agents by the Japanese was, according to the fragmentary evidence which survives, probably less common in Europe than in the Far East. In Europe one who boasted of his service to Japan was the German, Alexander von Siebold (1846–1911). In the decade following the Sino-Japanese War, he was back in Europe, busying himself in good causes for the Japanese. In the main his influence was exerted on the press in London, Berlin and Paris, and on politicians. He began the journal *Ostasien* (Tō-A) in 1899. Through this and through contributions to the press, both newspapers and journals, he tried to improve the public image of Japan. For the Japanese government he regularly prepared 'A report on the European press coverage of Japan'; and there are indications that he also played a deeper intelligence role both for diplomats and for the army.[5]

We should also refer here to one of the most important figures in the history of intelligence in Japan, General Baron Fukushima Yasumasa, who emerged during the Russo-Japanese War as the senior staff officer in Manchuria charged with special intelligence responsibilities. Fukushima (1852–1919), a native of Matsumoto, entered the army in 1878 and was posted to China as military attaché to the Japanese legation in Peking. He then led an 'intelligence ride' to India. Returning home from a spell as military attaché in Berlin (1887–92), he spent about 15 months crossing Siberia alone on

horseback. His route took him over Siberia, Mongolia and Manchuria and ended with the Amur river and Vladivostok. His reports
on his journey were the raw material for the anti-Russian party
already forming in Japan as a result of Russia's decision to embark on
the building of the Trans-Siberian railway. Lieutenant Colonel
Fukushima was probably the pioneer in Japan of the 'intelligence
ride' already widely practised by Russian and British officers in Asia.
His reports reached General Yamagata Aritomo, for three decades
the most influential elder statesman in military matters. Though we
do not have Fukushima's observations, we have a memorandum from
Yamagata of October 1893 in which he admits the weight they carried
in his strategic thinking.[6]

Reviewing the situation in east Asia, Yamagata saw as one of the
causes of instability the strategies and policies of three European
powers, Russia, France and Britain. He gave pride of place to 'Russia's
eastern policy and aggressiveness'. In a memorandum, he wrote

> Fukushima Yasumasa has crossed Russia's territory and inspected
> the situation. According to his account on his return, he said that
> the contruction of the said [Trans-Siberian] railway had pro-
> gressed very rapidly. Before ten years have elapsed, there is no
> doubt that we shall see its completion. When I asked him about
> Russia's military strength, he said that, when he visited the various
> camps, the lower ranks appeared to be well-organized and
> obedient. When we survey the position in Mongolia, the people are
> few in number and their customs are deteriorating. The Ching
> government is extremely inactive in protecting her and almost
> appears to be without resources to face an emergency. If Russia
> were to send some soldiers, she could defeat China, take possession
> of a wide area of north China, and then extend to the south and
> attack Peking.
>
> . . . But Russia up till now has not extended herself because the
> transportation links are still incomplete and communication is
> lacking. Ten years from now when the Siberian railway is
> complete, Russia will probably advance into Mongolia, or by
> extension penetrate into China herself.[7]

Yamagata used this intelligence to argue for increases in the size of the
Japanese army and navy, which over ten years were gradually
achieved.

Fukushima for his part served as Chief-of-Staff of the 1st Army during the war with China. After that he embarked on further travels in Europe and Asia (Turkey, Poland, Arabia, Central Asia, the Caucasus and India) and reported extensively. In 1900 he was to become commander of the Japanese expeditionary force sent to China at the time of the Boxer uprising.

It is clear that the building of the Trans-Siberian railway and the Three-Power intervention of April 1895 had a profound effect on the Japanese official mind and generated a suspicion about Russia's long-term intentions in east Asia. In 1896 there was a suggestion from General Uchiyama, the military attaché in Russia, that the Japanese army should send there some *ryūgakusei*, officers on study leave abroad.[8] After the China crisis of the early months of 1898 it was hardly surprising that this proposal should be taken up as a matter of urgency. In consequence two of the most promising officers from the academies were sent to St Petersburg in this capacity.

Hirose Takeo (1868–1904), a native of Bungo province in Kyushu, had been a distinguished graduate of Tokyo Naval College. He was appointed to Russia as a *ryūgakusei* in 1898 and served there for five years under the naval attaché to the Japanese legation, acquiring a first-rate knowledge of the internal state of Russia through his intimate friendship with Russian officers and officials. His reports to Tokyo about this period of Russian naval building were well-informed and significant.[9] Hirose had a special regard for his army opposite number, Captain Tanaka Giichi (1864–1929) who was born in Chōshū and graduated from the military academy in 1892. After distinguished service during the Sino-Japanese War, he joined first the general staff and then the military academy as instructor. In May 1898 he was sent by General Kawakami to Russia to study abroad, being attached to the military attaché's staff, and was specially charged to investigate the state of the Russian army. His biography tells us that he performed this function with enthusiasm, daring and skill.[10]

After being briefed en route by General Uchiyama in Paris, Captain Tanaka reached the Russian capital on 6 August 1898 and was attached to the office of military attaché (first Major Itō and then Colonel Murata). The studies which he had to undertake were defined as the condition of the Russian army, its operations, mobilisation, organisation, education and weapons; the general state of Russia; and, by looking at its social structure, the relations between the army and the people. It was hoped that as 'students' Hirose and Tanaka would be attached to Russian units, but since this had never been allowed before it was not easily achieved. Like Hirose, Tanaka identified himself with the country, studying the language intensively, learning to dance, and (it is said) professing belief in the Orthodox faith.[11]

As his knowledge of the language improved, Tanaka made extensive journeys throughout European Russia. When his Russian became adequate in March 1900, he asked to be posted to a unit; but this was not granted till June. His experience in barracks and on manoeuvres was quite exceptional; and he recorded it carefully in his diary for almost a year. Tanaka, who had become a major in 1900, also had deeper schemes (*Bōryaku*) to exploit internal unrest. The stability of Russia deteriorated steadily in 1900–1 because of strikes organised by the revolutionary movement, notably at Odessa. Tanaka observed this and saw what a weakness this could be to the Russian war effort. Another subject of study by Tanaka was the movement for Polish independence led by Pilsudski, and he attended functions in Warsaw. Though Tanaka did not stir up sedition, he appears to have built up a network of contacts which was to prove useful in 1904.[12] His researches made him increasingly apprehensive about Russian ambitions. When Marquis Itō visited St Petersburg in November 1901 to have discussions with the leaders, Tanaka, then a mere stripling of 37, had the effrontery to tell the great man that he was wasting his time in seeking a formula for peace with Russia, since war was necessary. Itō, furious, threatened to arrange his recall;[13] and Tanaka was indeed recalled in 1902. But this was perhaps due less to Itō than to the conviction of military circles in Tokyo that there was a distinct possibility of war with Russia for which contingency plans should be made. Tanaka returned feeling that he might be required to leave the army.

Before he left Europe, Tanaka was instructed by the general staff to linger on the return journey in Siberia and Manchuria, being one of the first officers to travel by the railway. He had been most active in advocating that Japanese visitors should return to Japan by this route for reconnaissance purposes, and was among those who recommended to Prince Kanin (1865–1945), one of the royal princes, who was touring in Europe in 1900, that he should return to Japan with his entourage by the Trans-Siberian railway. Kanin, it should be noted, had received his military training in France in the 1880s and was already influential in Japanese army circles. The Tsar encouraged the proposal, saying that it would be of great benefit to the reputation of the railway to be used so soon after its opening by a Japanese prince. The opening was still only partial. However, by the time Kanin was about to travel home in July, the Boxer turmoil had broken out in China and he eventually went home by sea, after visiting the ordnance works at Kronstadt.[14] Tanaka did succeed in persuading Lieutenant Hirose, his naval opposite number in St Petersburg, to return to Japan by the route across Siberia.[15]

Tanaka himself left St Petersburg on 24 April 1902, and travelled by the Siberian railway as far as Karymskoye, where he changed to the Chinese Eastern railway and went to Harbin. He sailed down the Sungari and Amur rivers, visited Khabarovsk, travelled onwards by the Ussuri railway and went south to Vladivostok. He then returned to Harbin and, switching to the southern artery of the Chinese Eastern railway, made his way to Port Arthur whence he sailed to Nagasaki. On 30 June he reached Tokyo on the completion of more than two months' journey of reconnaissance, justifying it on the ground that Russia's attitude to Japan had deteriorated since the signing of the Anglo-Japanese alliance and it was essential to examine the progress of the Chinese Eastern railway and its carrying capacity, the motives of the Russian armies in that area, and the possible lines of their planning for the future. These would all be vital pieces of information for the formulation of a strategic plan against Russia. In Tokyo he prepared a detailed report on his journey, entitled *Zuikanroku* (Miscellaneous notes), which was passed to the deputy chief of the general staff, General Tamura Iyozō. Its purpose was to promote the formulation of a strategic plan against Russia. When the Trans-Siberian and Chinese Eastern railways were completed in early 1905, he asked, how could Japan's field army of 13 divisions cope? Japan had no practical operational plan. Every department of the general staff was working away on something but there was hardly a document which could be passed over to the commander of an expeditionary force if mobilisation was declared.[16] With chapter and verse from his own experience, Tanaka drew up the ground rules for war preparations.

To his intense surprise, Lieutenant Colonel Tanaka was appointed on his return to the general staff. As head of the Russian section he became responsible in 1903 for formulating the operational plan against Russia. His journeys in Russia had stood him in good stead for this. He was also one of the inner circle who founded the *Kōgetsukai*, an organisation combining diplomats, military and naval men which acted as a lobby of bureaucrats stressing the need for stopping Russian encroachments by making war on her.[17] He was, in short, displaying the political energy which ultimately led him to become prime minister in 1927.

The Japanese military believed by 1903 that war was inevitable. But Russia was a vast country, with a large army which Japan could not match. Moreover when the Trans-Siberian railway overcame its teething troubles, it would be of immense strategic advantage for Russia. Hence Japan must fight without too much delay and attempt to subvert the Russian empire as much as possible. These were the views of General Fukushima, who by the summer of 1903 had reached the rank of vice-chief of the general staff.

The vulnerable points in Russia were Finland and Poland. In Finland, since the First Repression which had started around 1899, a group of radicals who opposed Tsarist rule had sprung up. They were to create a sensation in 1904 by assassinating the governor of the province. These were predominantly urban people who admired Japanese modernisation and industrialisation, and saw in Japan a possible ally in assisting Finland to escape from Tsarist tyranny.[18] For their part, the Japanese military saw the advantages of capitalising on Finnish resentment by subverting the war effort of the Russians. Could Russia be persuaded to retain her crack troops in Europe for the eventuality of a Finnish uprising?

Representative of Finnish willingness to seek Japanese help was Konrad (Konni) Zilliacus (1855–1914), a lawyer, editor and political activist who had stayed over two years in Japan at the time of the Sino-Japanese War. Zilliacus, no starry-eyed romantic in his view of Japan, considered that his country had no alternative but to obtain support wherever it could. The Japanese received through the Stockholm legation an unceasing flow of requests from him for arms and money.[19]

Poland too had a record of persecution at the hands of the Russians throughout the nineteenth century. Young Poles like Pilsudski were boiling over the policy of Russification and the ruthless repression. Here was the seedbed for the labour movement which spread in the 1890s to the Russian heartland, challenging Tsarist rule by strikes.

Tanaka delayed his departure from St Petersburg to write a note briefing his successor, Colonel Akashi Motojirō (1864–1919),[20] who became military attaché in August 1902. He had always specialised in intelligence work, having been trained in the Intelligence Branch of the Army General Staff. He had been military attaché in Paris from January 1901 and was instructed to go to Russia to study the army. From October 1903 he came under General Kodama, the single-minded Vice-Chief of Staff, who in preparing the way for war with Russia was determined to leave no stone unturned to exploit the weaknesses of the Russian empire. Though initially very inexperienced, Akashi set about a multitude of tasks which are defined by his biographer, Kurobane Shigeru, as follows:

> assistance to the Russian revolutionary party; confusion of [Russian] intelligence by purchasing a news gathering organization; purchase of Russian agents and their use; promotion of discord on the Black Sea; support for independence of states on the Baltic Sea coast; disruption of the transport of arms to Siberia; close relations with the British and German governments; improvement of European public opinion towards Japan.[21]

While these are mainly activities which came to fruition during the war years, preparations had been made in the pre-war period. It is understandable that Professor Kurobane should end this catalogue by commenting: 'Fact is stranger than fiction'.[22]

After war broke out, Akashi was evacuated from Russia to Sweden with other members of the legation. The Minister to Russia, Kurino Shinichirō, left the functions of the Swedish legation to be carried on by Akizuki, while he concentrated on helping Akashi with his activities.[23] The main objective was to disrupt the Russian war effort by promoting internal disorder and opposition in Russia, and thereby to make the Tsarist government reluctant to send its top regiments into battle in the East. From neutral Stockholm Akashi kept in touch with the Russian Revolutionary Socialist party and other anti-Tsarist groups in the Russian borderlands and elsewhere in Europe. He found them to be a motley group and helped to organise two conferences, one in Paris (October 1904) and the other in Geneva (April 1905) in order to contrive some unity between them. By way of encouragement to these groups, he distributed funds to them which are estimated to have cost Japan around one million yen (some £120,000).[24]

Information about Akashi's secret activities leaked out at the end of the war when he returned to Japan to join the general staff briefly before being posted to Berlin. His report on his actions to the chief of the general staff has come down to us in a manuscript (now published in some 50 pages) entitled *Rakka ryūsui* (literally, 'the flowers are fallen; the water flows on'), a rather poetic title for a paper written in January 1906 of a factual and down-to-earth kind. Indeed, the book, which exists in several different versions, resembles a sort of intelligence manual. Starting with a potted history of Russia, its land and agrarian systems and the institution of the *zemstvo*, it proceeds to discuss the origins of nihilism, anarchism and socialism and the activities of their Russian supporters. This is followed by a discussion of the nature of the disruptive parties in Russia and the key figures connected with them. He closes with an account in modest vein of his enterprises during the war and some of the consequences of them.[25] Sufficient of the story was allowed to leak out to win a great reputation for Akashi for his contribution to Japan's victory. It could, however, be argued that without the *Tanaka kōsaku* there could have been no *Akashi kōsaku*. In short, Tanaka was the true pioneer and deserves some of the credit.

While Akashi was a moving spirit in most of Japan's subversive manoeuvres during the war, there were other channels by which anti-Russian forces made themselves known. Through various legations in Europe, notably London and Vienna, arrangements were made for Roman Dmowski of the Polish People's Democratic party and Josef Pilsudski of the Polish Socialist party to be invited to Japan during the early months of the war. Dmowski visited Tokyo in May 1904 and Pilsudski two months later; indeed, they had their first meeting there. So far as we can tell, the Japanese government was not entirely happy to leave the Polish question in the hands of Akashi: it was not Tokyo's policy to support the forces of nationalism or revolution, even in the border territories of Russia. Rather, Japan's prime purpose was to subvert the war effort within Russia. This was the determination of the War Ministry. But the Foreign Ministry could see the perils of dealing with these anti-government elements and was cautious overall. Thus, while constructive talks did take place with the Polish visitors over the treatment of Polish prisoners of war found on the Manchurian front the Japanese government did not accept the proposal that it should not enter into peace talks with the Tsarist government.

What effect did the campaign of subversion have on the course of the war? Certainly the campaign seems to have been massive; according to one estimate, the amount expended between April and September 1905 was 730,000 yen (£75,000).[26] But ultimately the test has to be the number and quality of troops which the Tsarist government detained in Europe because of anti-Russian activities or revolutionary threats in the future. It is true that the Russians did not send their best troops to the East in the early months of the war; but this was probably due to the unexpectedness of the Japanese attack and Russia's propensity to underestimate the fighting qualities of the Japanese. When Akashi's activities were at their peak in the spring of 1905, the Russians did send their crack troops to the Manchurian battle-front. There is not, therefore, the direct correlation between Japan's subversive actions in Europe and the despatch of troops to the East, for which the Japanese might have hoped. This does not detract from Akashi's achievement. Nor did it damage his reputation: he died in 1919 as a full general.

It was not only Russia in Europe but also Russia in east Asia which had to be the concern of Japanese intelligence. In Asia one focus of the Japanese effort was on China which was assumed to have been a Russian puppet since 1895. The first thing that needs to be said is that for most of the decade down to the war with Russia, Japanese intelligence had been able to intercept messages between Chinese diplomats in Japan and their home government and to break the Chinese codes.[27] The institution which gets the credit for this is the telegraph section of the Foreign Ministry, which had at its head Satō Aimarō and later Ishii Kikujirō. Whether there were also agencies for interception in the military domain is not clear.

There is no evidence, however, that the Japanese managed to crack the European codes at this period. As against that, the Japanese believed that Russia had broken their codes in 1901. Hence a senior Japanese official from the London legation was sent to Russia in November to show Marquis Itō the text of the draft British alliance and himself decoded the message in St Petersburg. In 1903 General Bezobrazov, teasing a Japanese official, told him that he knew what his code-name was in the Japanese telegrams. Sergei Witte, the Russian statesman then out of office, told the Japanese Minister in 1904 that he was ready to speak confidentially to him provided he reported it by the diplomatic bag and not by telegraph, since the Russian Secret Cabinet was able to decode most messages to foreign governments.[28] As Christopher Andrew shows elsewhere in this volume, the French also broke the Japanese diplomatic code in 1904 and gave copies of the decrypts to the Russians later in the Russo-Japanese War.

The part of China which most concerned Japanese intelligence was what the Chinese call the 'Three Eastern provinces' (or 'Manchuria' to the Japanese), effectively under Russian military occupation from the autumn of 1900. This excited the wrath of a group which might be described as 'the China adventurers', Japanese who were close to the Chinese revolutionary movement. This group in 1901 founded the Kokuryūkai, an association to keep Russia beyond the Kokuryū or Amur river. It had a multitude of objectives and activities. Most important for our purposes were the schools for training Japanese in the Russian language; the drawing and circulation of maps of the area; and the organisation of a force of agents to keep track of Russia's doings in Manchuria. The head of the organisation, Uchida Ryōhei (1874–1937), a native of Fukuoka, developed close contacts with the army from 1903. Clearly many of its activities were ancillary to those of the army in the intelligence field. It operated in many respects like a secret society, promising to spy on Russian troop movements and cut lines of communications. Since the parent body was never affluent, it is not improbable that this civilian body of patriotic adventurers planted around China received large subventions from the army.[29]

It goes without saying that the Kokuryūkai and its like were an immense asset in the preparation of war. They contained a nucleus of Japanese residents overseas whose loyalty was entirely dependable. They had the ability to pose as Chinese with a fair chance of getting away without detection. In this way they were a more effective intelligence force than army officers themselves, of whom there seem to have been not a few at work; but they were more vulnerable to detection as in the notorious later case of Captain Nakamura, apprehended and murdered by the Chinese in 1931, while on a spying mission. Both before the outbreak of war and afterwards, the army general staff learnt a great deal from these civilian enthusiasts who were ready to collect intelligence information on the side.

The army also had its own arrangements in Manchuria. It appears to have employed characters like Ishimitsu Makiyo (1868–1942), a reserve service (*yobi-eki*) officer, who went to Harbin and set up a photographer's studio. He conscientiously photographed the Russian railways and the Port Arthur base. He claims in his publication, *Kōya no hana* (Flowers of the Open Country), to have been the frequent companion of Russian officers and soldiers. He returned to Japan on the outbreak of war and was called up for war service.[30] How representative his pre-war activities were is hard to say. But there is at least the possibility that they were replicated in key centres like Vladivostok.

Japan's great worries concerned Russia's capacity for moving troops and the movements of her ships. It would appear from the Japanese documents that a crucial role in ferreting out information about troop movements was played by the Japanese consul at Niu-ch'uang (Yingkow). He reported not only about the estimated movements of Russian troops from European Russia but also about those moving south from Harbin to Mukden and Port Arthur. Presumably his job was that of coordinator of material received from others; but their identities were not disclosed in the messages to Tokyo.[31] Niu-ch'uang was presumably chosen because there was no official Japanese representation in Port Arthur (Lushun) or Dalny (Talienwan), the dual seat of the Russian viceroy for the Far East. The lack of official observers there was also an impediment to obtaining intelligence about the movement of ships to Port Arthur. There were communities of Japanese merchants in each port who doubtless kept their eyes open. But the prime source of information about movements of naval ships in and out of Port Arthur was the Japanese consulate at Chefoo, from which steamers plied regularly to Port Arthur until the outbreak of war.

Another factor which became more important after the war with Russia began was the appointment as Japanese military attaché in Peking in December 1903 of Aoki Nobuzumi (1859–1924).[32] After leaving the military academy in 1879, he became a China specialist. After a brief spell of *ryūgaku* in Belgium in the late 1890s, he seems to have oscillated between the general staff and posts in China. For three spells spanning 12 years he was military attaché in Peking. During the war he liaised with the Chinese military leaders such as Yuan Shih-k'ai, and organised Chinese resistance to the Russians. Using Peking as a base, Major Aoki set up units for spying (*chōhō*) and sabotage (*hakai*) behind the enemy lines in Manchuria. These exploits are claimed to have been a great success, though they are not (so far as I am aware) admitted by the Russians.

In this area of China, Manchuria and Siberia the Japanese were operating in one of the vastest areas of Asia, and it is correspondingly hard to estimate their success. Many of their writings are in the heroic mould and make exaggerated claims for which there is not much confirmatory evidence by neutral observers. However, one such piece is to be found in a letter of George Ernest Morrison who, as *The Times* correspondent, knew the country well. He relates how in November 1903 Lieutenant Colonel C. M. Ducat, the military attaché to the British legation in Peking,

> with the help of *the Japanese who have agents at every railway station in Manchuria*, has just completed an accurate summary of all the Russian troops from Lake Baikal eastwards.[33]

If Ducat was able to get this information, it is a fair deduction that the Japanese, who were more numerous on the ground, had access to fairly accurate assessments of Russian strength in the East.

Turning to the other area of Russo-Japanese conflict, Korea, outside observers were very impressed by the standard of Japanese intelligence coverage. The British Minister, J. N. Jordan, wrote that the Japanese had 'a large and fully trained Intelligence Staff at their disposal'[34] in Seoul. Of course many of the trouble zones in Korea were remote frontier areas without modern communications, or at best with communication by boat or horse. The result was that rumours about the doings of the Russians on the Yalu river in 1903 circulated wildly. They could only be verified by a boat journey up the Korean coast or by intelligence rides. Colonel Ducat, mentioned earlier, visited the Yalu frontier on horseback at this time in order to throw more light on the uncertain activities of the Russian timber company.[35] The Japanese were also sending reconnaissance parties to the area and were by far the best informed of the foreign representatives. Jordan considered Japanese intelligence to be detailed, thorough and penetrating and their intelligence network to be the most accurate procurer of information which had operated there since 1900. By contrast, the standard of Russian intelligence was surprisingly weak in Korea, considering the size of Russian interests in the peninsula. Jordan could only conclude that 'the defective intelligence of the Russian Legation' in Seoul was due to the fact that 'the Russians, one and all, absolutely declined to entertain the idea that Japan would venture to take the offensive'.[35]

It is not easy to make a concluding estimate of Japan's intelligence work. There were points of weakness as well as points of strength. Plainly, Japanese cryptoanalysis was inferior to that of France or

Russia. A further weakness lay in lack of cooperation before the outbreak of the Russian war between army and navy intelligence. We do not have detailed information on the naval side, but the impression left by surviving documents is that each service acted separately in the intelligence field.[37] When war was declared, however, a general headquarters was established for the duration of the war and coordination developed. Nevertheless, army–navy tension was to be a feature of the relationship down to 1945, and as other contributors to this book show, such problems were not confined to Japan. Another weakness was that Japan's intelligence depended on a highly personalised type of information-gathering by such idiosyncratic personalities as Tanaka, Akashi, Ishimitsu and Aoki. Since the historian is left in the dark about the Tokyo organisation, his material tends to be biographical, making excessive claims about its hero's contribution to Japan's ultimate victory.

The Japanese succeeded, however, in collecting reliable information by field officers of imagination and talent and in using it to create anxiety on the home front in Russia on account of both Finnish and Polish resistance. Intelligence on the China side too was ingeniously collected and skilfully processed and circulated, despite all the problems of poor communications. So far as we know, the information was closely studied by the general staffs in Tokyo.[38] Japan was thus able to compensate for her lack of manpower and resources by shrewd application of intelligence, and to use a wide variety of clever methods of field intelligence as an essential preparation for the battle. Japan's decision to go to war with Russia represented a calculated gamble. She saw herself as the underdog both on land and sea who had to employ every means of counter-intelligence and subversion if she was to win the early victory which she sought.

Since this chapter has focused upon military officers, let us in conclusion relate the story of the most famous language officer of the war, Lieutenant-Commander Hirose Takeo. He was in command of the *Hokoku-maru* during the second attempt to blockade Port Arthur in March 1904. When it was hit by a torpedo, he was slow to evacuate his ship because of his efforts to rescue a member of the crew who was trapped. Hirose was himself hit and died instantly. His activities as a selfless patriot were praised in the children's songs of the day which were prescribed for use in all schools. He was recognised as a naval hero of the war and became a national legend. We saw him earlier in his career as a lieutenant engaged in intelligence work in St

Petersburg, where he loved the country and the work. There is an interesting twist in the Hirose story: it was not revealed to his juvenile admirers that a letter was discovered among his possessions which told of his love of Russia as a second home. It was, he wrote, his hope, when the blockade had been accomplished, to get approval to leave his ship and visit the Russian viceroy in Port Arthur, Admiral Alekseyev, and convince him of the need to surrender. He intended by this expedient to secure the dual objective of serving his own country while at the same time paying his debt to the Russians.[39]

It was a vain aspiration. Hirose died. But he had acquired in the strange career of intelligence officer a specialised understanding of an alien society with which the Japanese – and he himself – were destined to fight.

2. Codebreakers and Foreign Offices: The French, British and American Experience

CHRISTOPHER ANDREW

LIKE other major foreign ministries, the Quai d'Orsay, the Foreign and Commonwealth Office and the State Department nowadays receive much of their most valuable intelligence from cryptanalysts: from the Groupement des Contrôles Radio-électriques in France, from the Government Communications Headquarters in Britain, and from the National Security Agency in the United States. The historical origins of these three secret agencies are very different. In France there is an almost continuous history of diplomatic codebreaking stretching back to the *cabinet noir* founded by Cardinal Richelieu. In Britain the Foreign Office inherited an official 'decypherer on its foundation in 1782 but abolished the post in 1844 and abandoned codebreaking altogether for the next seventy years. The United States lived in a state of cryptographic innocence until its entry into the First World War prompted the creation of its first 'Black Chamber' (so named in honour of the French original). Despite these national differences, however, there are three striking similarities in the twentieth-century experience of diplomatic codebreaking in France, Britain and the United States. In each country the development of codebreaking has been severely hampered by chronic interdepartmental rivalry; some of the most valuable diplomatic intelligence has been compromised by spectacular indiscretions; and each foreign office has learned only slowly and painfully how to cope with cryptanalysis. Good intelligence has often been badly used.

I

By the early 1890s the *cabinet noir* at the Quai d'Orsay was able to decrypt substantial numbers of Italian, Spanish, English and Turkish diplomatic telegrams (then transmitted by overland cable).[1] In the course of the decade it also began to have more limited success with German diplomatic traffic.[2] Many officials in the ministry were unaware of the *cabinet noir*'s existence.[3] Those senior officials privy to the secret tended to look on cryptanalysts less as bureaucrats like themselves than as practitioners of suspiciously black arts. As late as 1914 Maurice Paléologue, the *directeur des affaires politiques*, still spoke of the *cabinet noir* as a place 'where perspicacity, clairvoyance, penetration, flair, the strange instinct which lays bare enigmas and hieroglyphics, border on magical divination'.[4] At least until the early twentieth century both senior officials and their ministers, most of whom must have been amazed to discover the success of the codebreakers when they took office, were apt to suspend their normal standards of judgement when presented with the products of this almost 'magical divination'.

In fact the diplomatic decrypts produced by the Quai d'Orsay merited a cautious treatment which they did not receive. Its leading cryptanalyst, Commandant Etienne Bazeries, an army officer on secondment, was a codebreaker of genius. But he was also an alcoholic, a compulsive gambler, ill-educated, ignorant of foreign languages, and altogether 'un singulier bohème'. Bazeries had 'barely to be told the probable subject of a [coded] message for him to begin erecting hypothesis upon hypothesis with a vertiginous rapidity'.[5] Some of Bazeries's hypotheses were brilliant. Others were wrong. For more than a decade the Quai d'Orsay sometimes failed to distinguish between the two.[6]

Perhaps the most tragic of Bazeries's errors occurred during the Dreyfus affair. On 1 November 1894 news of the arrest of Captain Alfred Dreyfus was published in the French press along with allegations that he had been spying for both Germany and Italy. Next day Panizzardi, the Italian military attaché in Paris, sent a telegram to Rome. On 6 November the *cabinet noir* handed military intelligence a decrypted version of that telegram which was substantially correct save for the final phrase. Instead of the correct conclusion 'in order to avoid press comment', the decrypt ended with the words 'Our emissary has been warned'. Four days later the *cabinet noir* produced a corrected – and accurate – version. The correct version was not shown to Dreyfus's judges. But the incorrect version, which appeared to hint at contacts with the Italians via an 'emissary (who) has been warned', was.[7]

Another partially inaccurate decrypt probably produced by Bazeries added notably to the complications of the Anglo-French crisis caused by the arrival of the Marchand expedition at Fashoda on the Upper Nile in the summer of 1898, the most serious crisis in Anglo-French relations since the battle of Waterloo. The crisis began in earnest when news of Marchand's meeting with Kitchener at Fashoda reached Europe on 26 September. Four days later, at a critical point during the crisis, an intercepted telegram from the Italian ambassador to his government, incorrectly decrypted by Bazeries, gave the news that the British ambassador in Paris had received instructions to deliver a formal ultimatum demanding Marchand's immediate withdrawal and to threaten war if France refused. The news of the ultimatum was wholly wrong but Delcassé, the new French Foreign Minister, was wholly deceived by it. When Monson, the British ambassador, called at the Quai d'Orsay later the same day, 30 September 1898, he found Delcassé in an emotional mood. Before Monson could utter a word, Delcassé began an impassioned plea begging him not to ask for the sacrifice of French national honour. When Monson, after this performance, failed to deliver an ultimatum which he did not possess, Delcassé believed he had achieved one of the great triumphs of French diplomacy. 'Posterity', he told his wife, might well consider 30 September 1898 'an historic day'. And he added melodramatically: 'It is at times like this that a man realises the full meaning of patriotism.'[8]

After several further contretemps produced by faulty decrypts, Octave Homberg at last made it a rule, on becoming head of the *cabinet noir* in 1903, never to pass on to the Foreign Minister decrypts whose accuracy was uncertain.[9] The Quai d'Orsay was remarkably well supplied with good intelligence during the two major international crises of the next few years – the Russo-Japanese War of 1904–5 and the first Moroccan crisis of 1905–6. Some of that intelligence, however, came not from the *cabinet noir* of the Quai d'Orsay but from the Sûreté. Though the Sûreté did not establish a full-time cryptographic unit until 1907, it had become involved in codebreaking when intercepting coded correspondence between anarchists in the 1890s and employed Bazeries as a part-time consultant on a 300-franc monthly retainer. By the turn of the century the Sûreté had moved on to monitor some diplomatic traffic also. Early in 1904, at the beginning of the Russo-Japanese War, agents of the Sûreté succeeded in obtaining fragmentary information on the Japanese diplomatic code. Bazeries was summoned to examine the Japanese material but after a week's work declared it impossible to reconstruct the code. One of the Sûreté's own part-time cryptanalysts, Commissaire Haverna, then gained permission to try his hand where Bazeries had failed. After two months work Haverna and an assistant had achieved the remarkable feat of reconstructing almost the entire Japanese code book, 1600 pages long with a hundred lines to the page. For the remainder of the Russo-Japanese War all diplomatic telegrams exchanged between Tokyo and the Paris embassy were decrypted at the Sûreté and copies sent to the Quai d'Orsay.[10]

The *cabinet noir* at the Foreign Ministry simultaneously achieved one major success of its own. The Sûreté never succeeded in breaking any German diplomatic code.[11] The Quai d'Orsay did. From 1904 onwards, its knowledge of German code and cypher systems, though probably still incomplete, was sufficient to produce a regular flow of German decrypts.[12] These decrypts assumed a particular significance during the first Moroccan crisis. The most dramatic of the German intercepts during the crisis was one of 26 April 1905 which revealed to Delcassé that Rouvier, the Prime Minister, had secretly offered to dismiss him as a peace offering to the Germans. The only revenge which Delcassé allowed himself after his forced resignation on 6 June was to hand Rouvier a selection of the intercepts most likely to embarrass him.[13]

The failure of some other ministers to preserve similar standards of discretion goes far to explain the decline of diplomatic cryptanalysts before the First World War. Another major reason was rivalry between the *cabinets noirs* of the Sûreté and the Quai d'Orsay. In October 1905 cooperation between the two teams of cryptanalysts came to an abrupt conclusion. The responsibility for this breach was Rouvier's. Soon after succeeding Delcassé as caretaker Foreign Minister, Rouvier received from the Russian ambassador a copy of a German telegram to the St Petersburg embassy deciphered by the Russian *cabinet noir*. In return Rouvier ordered the Sûreté to pass on to the Russians copies of intercepted Japanese telegrams. But the telegrams containing these intercepts, sent to St Petersburg by the

Russian secret police in Paris, were themselves intercepted by the *cabinet noir* at Quai d'Orsay. Unaware of the instructions given by Rouvier, the officials of the Foreign Ministry jumped to the conclusion that the Sûreté had been guilty of a serious breach of security. Bazeries was sent to Cavard, director of the Sûreté, to seek an explanation. Cavard, for his part, could not reveal that the Japanese intercepts had been shown to the Russians on secret orders from the Prime Minister. Instead he was reduced to insisting rather lamely that there had been no breach of security. Bazeries, already rather jealous of Haverna's success, was convinced of the contrary. In October 1905 he was ordered to end all contact with the Sûreté and henceforth to work exclusively for the Quai d'Orsay. For the next eight years the two rival *cabinets noirs* independently decrypted a substantial amount of diplomatic traffic – sometimes the *same* diplomatic traffic – without showing each other their results. Since during this period the Prime Minister was usually also Minister of the Interior (and thus responsible for the Sûreté), he and the Foreign Minister were frequently in the extraordinary position of receiving decrypts of the same intercepted telegrams from different sources.[14]

The last in the series of pre-war Franco-German crises over Morocco – the Agadir crisis of 1911 – provides a curious parallel with the first. Once again the Prime Minister, this time Caillaux, made secret contact with the German embassy, though on this occasion only to offer better terms to end the crisis. Once again, the Foreign Minister, this time de Selves, learned of the Prime Minister's action through decrypted German telegrams. This time, however, the dénouement was very different. Both de Selves and Caillaux were far less discreet than Delcassé and Rouvier six years earlier.

On 28 July 1911 de Selves confronted Caillaux with the decrypt of a German telegram sent the previous day. Immediately after the stormy encounter between them, Caillaux told Hyacinthe Fondère, a businessman he had used as intermediary in his dealings with the Germans, what had happened. Though there is no evidence that Caillaux told Fondère to warn the German embassy, there was clearly the danger that he would do so. Fondère in fact lost no time in telling the embassy counsellor, Oskar von der Lancken, that German telegrams were being decrypted by the French. The Germans, predictably, changed their codes. Save on a few isolated occasions, the *cabinet noir* at the Quai d'Orsay was able to decrypt no further German diplomatic telegrams from August 1911 until the outbreak of war three years later. France had lost its single most valuable intelligence source.[15]

Even had Fondère not warned the Germans directly, it seems likely that leaks from the Quai d'Orsay would have done so indirectly. De Selves and his officials used the German intercepts as the basis of a whispering campaign accusing Caillaux of treacherous dealings with the Germans. Caillaux responded by taking the extraordinary step of calling on Lancken and asking to see the original text of the decrypted telegrams. Raymond Poincaré, who succeeded Caillaux as Prime Minister, told him he had acted with 'inexcusable thoughtlessness': 'Your imprudence provided the Germans with proof of our decrypts'. 'I was wrong', replied Caillaux, 'but I had to defend myself.'[16]

During the first Moroccan crisis German decrypts had warned the Foreign Minister that the Prime Minister was planning to dismiss him. After the Agadir crisis they helped the Foreign Minister bring down the Prime Minister. The Senate commission responsible for considering the Franco-German treaty ending the crisis met on 9 January 1912 in the presence of both Caillaux and de Selves. Caillaux declared that no unofficial negotiations had taken place with Germany. Georges Clemenceau, who had heard rumours of the intercepts, turned to de Selves and asked sarcastically if he could 'confirm the declaration of the Prime Minister'. De Selves requested 'the permission of the commission not to reply'. Uproar followed. The chairman suspended the commission meeting; there was a violent altercation between Prime Minister and Foreign Minister; de Selves left for the Elysée to proffer his resignation, and brought down the government.[17]

The internecine warfare which characterised many Third Republic cabinets hampered the *cabinet noir* at the Sûreté even more severely than that at the Quai d'Orsay. In the spring of 1913 Haverna and his assistants decrypted three telegrams from Tittoni, the Italian ambassador, to Rome, suggesting that both Stephen Pichon, the Foreign Minister, and Poincaré, now President of the Republic, were engaged in secret manoeuvres to restore diplomatic relations with the Vatican – an enormously sensitive issue in the anti-clerical atmosphere of the pre-war Third Republic. Louis-Lucien Klotz, who as Minister of the Interior was responsible for the Sûreté, brought these intercepts to the attention of the cabinet on 6 May 1913. There was an immediate uproar. The Foreign Minister's personal indignation was further fuelled by the growing resentment of the Quai d'Orsay at the

Sûreté's meddling with diplomatic intelligence. Pichon threatened to resign unless the Sûreté was immediately denied access to diplomatic telegrams. Though Klotz defended the Sûreté, Pichon's view prevailed. From May 1913 until the eve of the First World War the Sûreté was no longer supplied by the post-office with copies of telegrams sent and received by Paris embassies.[18]

Though the French government by now received almost no current German intercepts, the intercepts of the Agadir crisis returned to plague it on the eve of war. In the winter of 1913–14 *Le Figaro* embarked on a series of daily attacks on Joseph Caillaux, now leader of the Radical party. During January 1914 the editor Gaston Calmette returned to the theme of 'secret negotiations' during the Agadir crisis of 1911, suggesting that Caillaux was working in the German interest. Among the documents in Calmette's possession were copies of three of the German intercepts. Caillaux believed, probably correctly, that he had obtained them from another journalist named Albin who had in turn received them from de Selves' *chef de cabinet*, Maurice Herbette. Indeed Caillaux himself had copies stolen from Albin's desk drawer.[19]

On 14 January Caillaux called on Poincaré and warned him that *Le Figaro* was about to publish the intercepts. At Poincaré's request the former Prime Minister Louis Barthou went to see Calmette and persuaded him, in the national interest, not to go ahead. Caillaux, however, had already taken devious precautions of his own. During a week as caretaker Minister of the Interior in December 1913 he had raided the Sûreté archives (Pujalet, the Sûreté director, indignantly described the raid as 'burglary') and removed copies of the Italian intercepts which had embarrassed Poincaré the previous spring – no doubt as a potential means of putting pressure on the President. Caillaux also removed copies of Spanish intercepts which showed that Calmette had been bribed by the Spanish government to support some of its territorial claims in North Africa. Not content with that, he succeeded in acquiring by means unknown copies of German intercepts of 1905–6 decrypted at the Quai d'Orsay which revealed potentially embarrassing contacts between some French ministers and the German embassy; they may well have included the telegram which contained Rouvier's secret offer to dismiss Delcassé during the first Moroccan crisis.[20]

The whole extraordinary affair took a new and sensational twist on the afternoon of 16 March when Madame Henriette Caillaux walked into Calmette's office, drew a revolver from her muff, and shot him dead. Her immediate motive for committing murder was to prevent *Le Figaro* publishing love letters exchanged between herself and Caillaux while he was still married to his first wife. It was quickly rumoured, however, that Calmette had been killed to prevent the publication not of the love letters but of the German telegrams intercepted during the Agadir crisis. The German ambassador called at the Quai d'Orsay and made clear that his government would regard the publication of the telegrams as a public insult. If that happened, said the ambassador menacingly, 'a bomb would explode'.[21]

Until the eve of the First World War the French government lived in dread of a major international scandal when Madame Caillaux's trial opened on 20 July. On 28 May Caillaux called on Poincaré and threatened that if the Agadir decrypts were referred to during his wife's trial, he would retaliate by 'divulging plenty of others' from the *cabinets noirs* of both the Sûreté and the Quai d'Orsay. However, he added, he would not need to do so if the government would formally declare that it possessed no documents which cast aspersions on his honour or patriotism. Poincaré described this suggestion as attempted blackmail. After several weeks of indecision, however, the government gave way to it. Despite Poincaré's initial insistence that the government could not interfere in the judicial process, René Viviani, the Prime Minister, informed Caillaux on 25 June that the *procureur-général* would be authorised to declare at the trial that the Quai d'Orsay possessed no document which put in doubt his honour or his patriotism.[22]

That was not the end of the affair. When the trial opened on 20 July both the President and the Prime Minister were on a state visit to Russia. Poincaré notes in his diary that Viviani remained preoccupied by the trial throughout the visit, fearful that it would somehow erupt into a major political scandal.[23] Indeed the government as a whole was far less concerned by the prospect of war with Germany, which it was blithely unaware was only a fortnight away, than by the Caillaux trial. On the second day of the trial came the allusion to the German decrypts which the government had dreaded. Louis Latzarus, a journalist on *Le Figaro*, blurted out the allegation that Calmette had possessed 'horrifying documents' which 'every good Frenchman who read them would have thought established the infamy and treason of a certain person', but had declined to publish them 'because their publication might be dangerous to the country'. The identity of the 'certain person' was clear to all in the courtroom. Caillaux immediately demanded that the question of the alleged documents be settled 'once and for all'.[24] Bienvenu-Martin, the Minister of Justice and acting Prime Minister, consulted a few of his colleagues and drew up a draft statement asserting that the documents referred to at the trial were forgeries and repeating that the Quai d'Orsay possessed no document reflecting on Caillaux's honour and patriotism. The text was telegraphed to the President and Prime Minister in Russia. Though Poincaré insisted that Caillaux was still engaged in 'blackmail', Viviani – fearful that Caillaux would otherwise proceed with his threat to produce intercepts from both *cabinets noirs* – gave his consent. Poincaré noted in his diary:

> From the moment he received the news from Paris, Viviani was overcome with gloom. He is becoming more and more nervous and sullen, and his increasing bad temper is noticed by everyone who approaches him.[25]

By the time Viviani's formal consent arrived in Paris, the *procureur-général* had already made a statement in the courtroom. As Abel Ferry, the Under Secretary for Foreign Affairs, noted in his diary, his 'fantastic declaration' deceived no one: 'We declared non-existent documents which were only too real'.[26] But though no European diplomat had been deceived, the primary purpose of avoiding a major international scandal had been achieved. On the evening of 28 July Madame Caillaux was found not guilty of the murder she had committed by a gallant all-male jury. Almost as the jury returned their verdict, the news passed around the courtroom that Austria–Hungary had declared war on Serbia. Six days later France was at war.

During the final weeks of peace, when the government had greatest need of diplomatic intercepts to provide intelligence on the growing crisis, it was virtually deprived of them. Instead it spent much of its time trying to prevent an international scandal over earlier decrypts. The numerous indiscretions which preceded Madame Caillaux's trial had alerted all major foreign ministries to the activities of French codebreakers. As a result they changed either the keys to their cyphers or the codes and cyphers themselves. The Quai d'Orsay suddenly found itself on the eve of world war unable – for the first time in a generation – to decrypt the telegrams of any power of importance. On 27 July its *cabinet noir* appealed for help from the Sûreté and an interministerial commission on cryptography, founded in 1909, which it had hitherto boycotted. It was too late. The flow of decrypts did not resume until after the outbreak of war.[27]

During the years before the war the diplomatic intercepts supplied by the *cabinets noirs* of the Sûreté and the Quai d'Orsay were thus worse than useless. Because of the incompetence and indiscretion with which they were handled, they did more to distract French policy-makers than to inform them. Those who cannot handle secret intelligence are better off without it.

II

After the abolition of the Foreign Office's deciphering branch in 1844, Victorian Britain rapidly returned to a state bordering on cryptographic innocence. Gladstone found it difficult to believe that even the French were capable of such infamous behaviour as to open his correspondence during his foreign travels. When finally persuaded that they were, he proved hopelessly naïve in his efforts to outwit them. On one occasion, when writing to the Foreign Secretary, Lord Granville, from Cannes, Gladstone asked a friend to write the address for him, confident, he told Granville, that if the French authorities failed to recognise his handwriting on the envelope they would not bother to open it. As Granville replied in some exasperation, the fact that the letter was addressed to the British Foreign Office was, in itself, sufficient to attract the attention of the *cabinet noir*. 'You would,' he told Gladstone, 'have been a good clergyman, a first-rate lawyer and the greatest of generals, but you would have been an indifferent Fouché in dealing with the post office.' When Lord Lansdowne became Foreign Secretary in 1900, he proved almost as incautious as Gladstone. 'I think it right to tell you,' wrote his ambassador in Paris 1902, 'that your recent letters by post have been palpably opened by the *bureau noir* . . .'[28]

After further revelations of ungentlemanly French behaviour the Foreign Office began to take more precautions. It acknowledged in 1911 that its traditionally amateurish approach to code and cypher production and security had 'really broken down'. Henceforth there was to be, for the first time, 'a permanent man in charge of the business', 'more frequent issue of new cyphers', and 'closer supervision . . . over the custody of cyphers abroad'.[29] The Foreign Office still showed no inclination, however, to revive the ancient office of decypherer. In the years before the First World War, British diplomacy remained such a byword for probity that the Cambon brothers, French ambassadors in London and Berlin, fearing to entrust their private correspondence either to the French post office or the Quai d'Orsay, regularly corresponded via the British diplomatic bag instead.[30]

In August 1914, under the pressure of war and after a break of seventy years, Britain began once again to intercept – and attempt to decrypt – foreign governments' communications. The initiative came not from the Foreign Office but from the Admiralty.[31] In the first days of war Admiral H. F. Oliver, the Director of Naval Intelligence, was sent copies of a series of German signals intercepted by an Admiralty wireless-telegraph station, by the Marconi Company, and by the Post Office. Oliver had at first little idea what to do with them. Over lunch one day with his friend, Sir Alfred Ewing, the Director of Naval Education, it suddenly occurred to him that Ewing was the very man to deal with this 'unknown and unexpected occurrence'. Ewing had 'a very good knowledge of the German language, an expert knowledge of radio-telegraphy and very great brain power'. He had, however, little knowledge of codes and cyphers. He spent the next few days delving into all the code books he could find at Lloyds, the British Museum, and the GPO, and enlisted the help of several friends and colleagues. One of his first recruits, Alastair Denniston, a languages teacher at Osborne naval college, later became the operational head of British cryptanalysis. But in 1914 Denniston, like the other new recruits, had no experience of cryptography. Indeed, as he wrote later, [British] cryptographers did not exist, so far as one knew'.[32] When Captain (later Admiral) 'Blinker' Hall succeeded Oliver as DNI in November 1914, he was quick to see the potential value of Ewing's inexperienced team. So too was the First Lord of the Admiralty, Winston Churchill. With their support, the codebreakers of Room 40 in the Admiralty Old Building revived with remarkable speed the tradition of British codebreaking abandoned by the Foreign Office in 1844. Hall did not confine his activities to naval intercepts. In the summer of 1915 he established a political branch of Room 40 to deal with diplomatic traffic. Hall acted with such vigorous independence (as, for example, over the celebrated Zimmermann telegram in 1917) that by the end of the war there were moves within the Foreign Office to suppress the post of DNI altogether.[33]

The revival of British codebreaking was hampered as in France, however, by interdepartmental rivalry. In the early days of the war the War Office set up its own crypytanalytic unit, MI1b, and proposed cooperation with Room 40. Ewing agreed and sent two of his own staff (Denniston and Anstie, another German teacher from Osborne) to provide liaison with the War Office. Cooperation soon broke down. According to Denniston: 'It is said that a climax was reached when the all highest on one side of Whitehall was told [of an intercept] of great interest (actually, proposals for treatment of Indian prisoners) by his opposite number before his own section had managed to get the information through to him.' Room 40's representatives were withdrawn from the War Office and all contact with the less successful military cryptanalytic unit was ended until the spring of 1917. 'Looking back over the work of those years,' wrote Denniston later, 'the loss of efficiency to both departments caused originally by mere official jealousy is the most regrettable fact in the development of intelligence based on cryptography.'[34]

The post-war coordination of cryptography proceeded more smoothly in its early stages than the bitter wartime service rivalries might have suggested. On the recommendation of its Secret Service Committee in 1919, the Cabinet instructed Admiral 'Quex' Sinclair, Hall's successor as DNI, to form a cryptographic unit, known as the Government Code and Cypher School (GC&CS), from 'the remnants of Room 40 and MI1b'. The publicly announced function of the school (like that of its present-day successor GCHQ) was 'to advise as to the security of codes and cyphers used by all Government departments and to assist in their provision'. But it was also given a secret directive 'to study the methods of cypher communications used by foreign powers'. Initially GC&CS came under the Admiralty, which had been the main wartime supplier and consumer of signals intelligence (sigint), but by far the most numerous and important peacetime sigint turned out to be diplomatic rather than naval and military. The Foreign Office was eventually embarrassed into assuming direct responsibility for GC&CS on 1 April 1922 after its codebreakers had decrypted a telegram from the French ambassador in London reporting a secret conversation with the Foreign Secretary,

Lord Curzon, in which Curzon had opposed the views of the rest of the cabinet.[35]

The single most valuable Russian intelligence source available to the British government during the decade after the Bolshevik Revolution was the diplomatic traffic of the Soviet government decrypted by the codebreakers of GC&CS. The Bolsheviks suffered initially from two serious cryptographic handicaps. The first was their fear of relying on the relatively sophisticated Tsarist codes and cyphers which they inherited and their consequent use of less secure systems based at first on simple transposition. The second was the dispersion of the Tsarist codebreakers who had given pre-revolutionary Russia the world lead in message interception. Worst still, some of the best defected to the opposition. Fetterlein, the head of the Russian section at GC&CS between the wars, had been one of the leading cryptanalysts of Tsarist Russia.

Despite the early complications caused by forgeries, the governments of Lloyd George and Bonar Law received a remarkable flow of intelligence on Soviet Russia, 'revolutionary' movements in Britain and the links between the two. All intelligence consumers have, of course, to face the recurrent dilemma that to act on information received may betray a source which will then dry up. The governments of the early 1920s found no solution to it. The first cabinet crisis caused by Soviet intercepts came during talks on an Anglo-Soviet trade agreement in the summer and autumn of 1920. Most of the subversion revealed by the intercepts – for example, the Soviet sale of Tsarist diamonds to subsidise the *Daily Herald* – now seems of minor importance. That was Lloyd George's view at the time. But his intelligence chiefs, the service chiefs and most of his cabinet disagreed. Men who would subsidise the *Daily Herald* were, in their view, men who would stop at nothing. By cabinet decision, a selection of the Soviet intercepts was published to alert the British public to the peril in their midst. The attempt made to disguise their source was quite inadequate, *The Times* beginning its story with the words: 'The following wireless messages have been intercepted by the British Government'. Oddly, the Russians did not at first deduce that their codes had been broken. But at the end of the year they devised new codes which for a few months defeated the codebreakers of GC&CS.[36]

In April 1923 Bonar Law's cabinet decided to publish another set of intercepts in order to warn the Soviet Union to mend its ways or risk the cancellation of the trade agreement. In an extraordinary diplomatic note approved by the cabinet, Curzon repeatedly taunted the Russians with Britain's successful interception of their communications:

> The Russian Commissariat for Foreign Affairs will no doubt recognise the following communication dated 21st February 1923, which they received from M. Raskolnikov . . . The Commissariat for Foreign Affairs will also doubtless recognise a communication received by them from Kabul, dated the 8th November 1922 . . . Nor will they have forgotten a communication, dated the 16th March 1923, from M. Karakhan, the Assistant Commissary for Foreign Affairs, to M. Raskolnikov . . .

Once again the Russians changed their codes (though not for some time); once again GC&CS cracked them within a few months.

Curzon provides a classic example of a minister suddenly introduced to sigint in the later stages of his career who was emotionally incapable of coping with it. French as well as Russian decrypts were capable of driving him to distraction. The celebrated occasion in 1922 when he had to be led weeping from discussions with Poincaré, now the French Prime Minister, in a state of nervous collapse, panting 'I can't bear that horrid little man', is probably to be explained by Curzon's sense of outrage at what he judged the perfidious references to himself contained in French intercepts. In 1923 he denounced the 'treachery' revealed by them as 'the worst thing that I have come across in my public life'.[37]

The most serious lapse of security in the use of Soviet intelligence came in the spring of 1927. Having decided to break off diplomatic relations with the Soviet Union and having failed to find much incriminating evidence in a Special Branch raid on the London premises of Arcos (the All-Russian Cooperative Society), Baldwin's cabinet decided to fall back on the appalling precedent of the Curzon ultimatum and use Russian decrypts to justify its charges of subversion. The first public reference to the intercepted Soviet telegrams was made by the Prime Minister on 24 May 1927 in a Commons statement on the Arcos raid. Baldwin read out four Russian telegrams which had, he drily observed, 'come into the possession of His Majesty's Government'. An opposition MP challenged Baldwin to say how the government had obtained the telegrams, but there was uproar (or as *Hansard* put it, 'interruption') before he could finish his question. The Speaker intervened and deferred further discussion until the debate two days later on the decision to end diplomatic relations with the Soviet Union.

That debate, on 26 May, developed into an orgy of governmental indiscretion about secret intelligence for which there is no parallel in modern parliamentary history. Both Chamberlain and the Home Secretary, Joynson-Hicks ('Jix'), followed Baldwin's bad example by quoting intercepted Russian telegrams. Chamberlain also quoted intercepted Comintern communications in order to show that 'the Zinoviev letter was not the only or the last [such document]'. Jix became quite carried away while accusing the Soviet trade delegation of running 'one of the most complete and one of the most nefarious spy systems that it has ever been my lot to meet'. 'I happen to have in my possession,' he boasted, 'not merely the names but the addresses of most of those spies.' He stopped short of actually reading out the names and addresses.

On the day of the debate Chamberlain informed the Russian chargé d'affaires of the decision to break off diplomatic relations because of 'anti-British espionage and propaganda'. Chamberlain gave his message an unusually personal point by quoting an intercepted telegram from the chargé d'affaires to Moscow on 1 April 'in which you request material to enable you to support a political campaign against His Majesty's Government'. Baldwin's government was able to prove its charge of Soviet dabbling in British politics. But the documents seized in the Arcos raid and the intercepted telegrams published in a White Paper contained only a few cryptic allusions to the much more serious sin of espionage. The government contrived in the end to have the worst of both worlds. It compromised its most secret and most valuable intelligence agency, GC&CS. And yet at the same time it failed to produce public evidence to support Jix's dramatic charges of 'one of the most nefarious spy systems that it has ever been my lot to meet'.[38]

The effect of the government's publication of the Soviet intercepts on the intelligence services was traumatic. The Soviet Union responded by adopting the theoretically unbreakable 'one-time pad' for its diplomatic traffic. Between 1927 and the Second World War GC&CS was able to decrypt no high-grade Soviet communications (though it continued to have some success with Comintern messages). Alastair Denniston, the operational head of GC&CS, wrote bitterly that Baldwin's government had 'found it necessary to compromise our work beyond question'.[39] New entrants to GC&CS over the next decade were told the story of the loss of the Russian codes as a warning of the depths of indiscretion to which politicians were capable of sinking.[40] They were not, however, told the full story. What Denniston probably did not know was that pressure for the publication of Soviet intercepts had begun not with the politicians but with the intelligence chiefs themselves. Admiral Sinclair, who became head of SIS (with responsibility also for GC&CS) in 1923, had argued as DNI in 1920 that 'even if the publication of the telegrams was to result in not another message being decoded, then the present situation would fully justify it'.[41] In the course of the 1920s Sinclair learned greater discretion. But Baldwin's government did no more in 1927 than follow the earlier advice of the head of its secret service.

III

Before the First World War the United States' cryptographic innocence exceeded Britain's. The State Department employed what the first head of the American Black Chamber later dismissed as 'schoolboy codes and ciphers'.[42] Even during the First World War Woodrow Wilson displayed an innocence in intelligence matters almost worthy of Gladstone himself. Anxious to ensure the secrecy of his own personal communications, Wilson spent 'many hours of many nights', sometimes assisted by his wife, laboriously encoding and decoding telegrams to and from Colonel House, his confidential agent to the capitals of Europe. In one of his two main codes, the word he employed for 'secretary of war' was 'Mars'. The reader may test his skill as a codebreaker by attempting to deduce Wilson's code word for 'secretary of the navy'.[43] European codebreakers doubtless found the few hours required to decrypt Wilson's most secret communications unusually diverting. The great champion of open diplomacy was splendidly unaware of the degree to which he was practising it himself.

   American cryptanalysis owed its origins not to the government but to an eccentric piece of private enterprise by George Fabyan, a wealthy textile merchant and honorary Kentucky colonel with private laboratories in his 500-acre Riverbank estate in the Chicago suburbs. 'Colonel' Fabyan convinced himself that hidden in Tudor and Stuart literature was a secret cypher proving that the work ascribed to Shakespeare and others had been written by Francis Bacon. Having arrived at that eccentric conclusion, he set up a team of codebreakers to prove it at his Riverbank laboratories. In 1916 Fabyan patriotically offered his codebreakers' service to the government; thereafter intercepted messages in a variety of codes and cyphers were sent intermittently to Riverbank by the War, Navy, State and Justice Departments. The head of Fabyan's wartime team, also director of the Riverbank Department of Genetics, was William F. Friedman, later to become famous as 'the man who broke Purple', the greatest American cryptanalyst of modern times.[44]

The founder of American official cryptanalysis in 1917, however, was Herbert O. Yardley, a 28-year-old code clerk in the State Department who disconcerted his superiors by cracking one of the President's supposedly unbreakable codes. Soon after the American declaration of war in April 1917, Yardley persuaded the War Department to found a codebreaking unit, MI8, with himself as head. After leading a similar unit at the Paris peace conference in 1919, he persuaded the Departments of State and War to fund jointly a peacetime codebreaking unit, the Cypher Bureau, better known as the Black Chamber. By August 1919 the Black Chamber was operating at a secret address in New York. Its early priorities were the diplomatic traffic of Japan, Britain and Germany (in that order). In May 1920 Yardley was able to report that the Black Chamber had broken four Japanese and two German codes. The section of Yardley's report dealing with his work on British codes is still classified under the terms of an Anglo-American intelligence agreement which require the United States to apply the same exaggerated degree of censorship to British intelligence material as the Whitehall weeders.[45]

The Black Chamber's main success was with Japanese traffic. At the Washington naval conference in 1921 the decrypted telegrams of the Japanese delegation gave the State Department a vital negotiating advantage which it turned into diplomatic victory. The intercepts revealed that, if no better settlement proved possible, the Japanese would reluctantly accept a 6 to 10 naval ratio with the United States. Having seen their opponents' hand, the Americans stuck it out until the Japanese negotiators gave way. Yardley received a Christmas bonus of $998 to distribute among his staff. During 1922, however, the Black Chamber began a gradual decline. Its main problem was not the difficulty of foreign codes and cyphers, but a shortage of intercepts. The cable companies were reluctant to supply copies of the cables passing over their lines and the flow of radio intercepts from the Army Signal Corps dwindled. In the course of the 1920s American cryptanalysis was almost crippled by legal restrictions imposed by the Radio Communications Acts. According to a secret office history:

> The effect of the Act of 1912 was to hamper, and that of the Act of 1927 to forbid, the interception of radio traffic of any kind, either in time of peace or time of war, though this could hardly have been the intention of Congress in enacting these two laws.

In 1927 the Black Chamber received a total of 428 Japanese intercepts in over ten different codes, but because of shortage of telegrams in some of the codes it was able to decrypt only 150. During the decade up to 1929 the Black Chamber produced a total of about 10,000 decrypts, 1600 of them during the Washington conference.[46]

After a gradual decline for most of the 1920s the Black Chamber came to an abrupt end in 1929. Following the inauguration of President Herbert Hoover in March 1929, Henry Stimson became Secretary of State. In view of Stimson's well-advertised insistence on high ethical standards in public affairs his officials decided not to bring the existence of the Black Chamber to his attention until he had had some weeks to acclimatise himself to the lower moral tone of day-to-day diplomacy. In May the State Department decided, with some trepidation, to place a few Japanese intercepts on Stimson's desk. According to a later account by William Friedman:

> His reaction was violent and his action drastic. Upon learning how the material was obtained, he characterised the activity as being highly unethical and declared that it would cease *immediately*, so far as the State Department was concerned. To put teeth into his decision he gave instructions that the necessary funds of the State Department would be withdrawn *at once*.

'Gentlemen', explained Stimson later (though probably not at the time), 'do not read each other's mail.' It was only with difficulty that Stimson was persuaded to allow the Black Chamber two months to close down and hand its files to the Army Signal Corps, and to give the six sacked cryptographers (none with pension rights) a three-month gratuity.[47]

Yardley took a terrible revenge. It is probable that he sold the secrets of the Black Chamber to the Japanese for $7000.[48] His revenge, however, was public as well as private. In 1931, still short of money, he published his memoirs first as a sensational series of articles in *The Saturday Evening Post*, then as a book entitled *The American Black Chamber*. There was an immediate diplomatic row with the Japanese Foreign Minister publicly accusing the United States of 'a breach of faith' at the Washington conference ten years earlier. With a research assistant Yardley wrote a sequel entitled *Japanese Diplomatic Secrets*. It was never published. Instead it became the first manuscript in the history of American publishing to be impounded for reasons of national security. To prevent any further revelations a bill was hurried through Congress in 1933 'For the Protection of Government Records' which prohibited all government employees, past and present, revealing their knowledge of either American codes 'or any matter which was obtained while in the process of transmission between any foreign government and its diplomatic mission in the United States'.[49]

Writing in June 1942, William Friedman believed that the effect of Yardley's revelations could still 'hardly be estimated':

I refer here to the jolt which his book gave the Japanese cryptographers, leading them out of their blissful ignorance, and causing them to develop really complex methods which are now giving us many difficulties. The same is true probably as regards the German and Italian cryptographers – their education has been entirely at Uncle Sam's expense and the final consequences of Yardley's work cannot yet be foreseen. They may well turn out to be disastrous.[50]

Friedman believed that a subsidiary reason for Yardley's revelations after the closure of the Black Chamber was his conviction that American codebreaking had come to a complete halt. Yardley was mistaken. His work was continued and developed by an even abler cryptanalyst, Friedman himself. In 1921 Friedman had been appointed Chief Cryptanalyst at the War Department but until the demise of the Black Chamber his work had been far more concerned with codemaking than with codebreaking. In 1929, however, he was made head of a new military Signal Intelligence Service with a staff of six whose duties now included cryptanalysis.[51]

The Navy Code and Signal Section had begun to interest itself in cryptanalysis in 1924. That interest was strengthened when naval intelligence captured a copy of one of the Japanese naval codes early in 1929.[52] In 1930 the Army Signal Intelligence Service and the Navy Code and Signal Section collaborated for three months at the request of the Chairman of the House of Representatives Committee investigating communist activities in an attempt to decrypt Russian cablegrams exchanged between Moscow and the Amtorg Trading Corporation in New York. The attempt failed. Only later was it discovered that the messages were all sent in 'one-time pad'.[53]

There followed a period of acute and damaging rivalry between the army and navy signal services. Like the Sûreté and the Quai d'Orsay from 1906 and 1914, like Room 40 and MI1b from 1914 to 1917, the Signal Intelligence Service and the Code and Signal Section of the navy were not on speaking terms. By attempting to crack independently the same diplomatic codes and cyphers, each strove 'to gain credit for itself as the agency by which the information obtained was made available to the Government'. Their rivalry was eventually contained, though not resolved, by a compromise of memorable absurdity:

> It was agreed after lengthy negotiations that the Army and Navy would exchange all diplomatic traffic from their intercept facilities, and that both services would work on this traffic. But in order to avoid as much duplication of effort as possible it was agreed that the Army would receive all traffic of days with an even date and the Navy all traffic of days with an odd date. This arrangement was [intended] ... to give both services equal opportunities for training, 'credit', and so on.[54]

In Friedman's admittedly biased view, the damaging interservice cryptanalytical competition was won by the army:

> ... For each dollar the Army was able to obtain for cryptanalytic and cryptographic work the Navy was able to obtain three to five dollars, until by 1939, as far as concerned numbers of officers and civilian personnel engaged in these activities, amount of equipment on hand, and funds available for research, the Navy had considerably outstripped the Army. However, it may be said with some justifiable pride perhaps, that while they were ahead of us in

quantity we were ahead in quality, for all the important developments in both the cryptographic and the cryptanalytic fields must be credited to Army personnel.[55]

A secret history of American cryptanalysis prepared in 1946 concluded that the two main interwar problems had been the 'lack of unified control' and the 'extremely limited' funding of the Signals Intelligence Service.[56]

The greatest codebreaking success before Pearl Harbor – the breaking of the Japanese 'Purple' diplomatic cypher machine in the late summer of 1940 – was due, at least in part, to improved funding and interservice cooperation after Major General Joseph Mauborgne became Chief Signal Officer in October 1937. While Friedman with an increased staff concentrated on Purple, the navy passed on what it learned from its attack on other, less complex Japanese diplomatic codes (notably the 'Red') which provided useful clues on Purple also.[57] Friedman himself pinned the blame for the weaknesses of interwar American cryptanalysis squarely on the Federal Government. He wrote six months after Pearl Harbor:

It would be of utmost value to the winning of this war if the Government were now in a position to read the codes and ciphers of all the foreign powers whose actions and probable intentions are of interest and importance in our prosecution of the war. *It could have been in this fortunate position had it given to cryptanalytic studies the attention which it* [sic] *deserves during peace time and had provided funds for their continuity on a scale sufficient for the purpose for which they are intended.*[58]

In the event the wartime achievements of both British and American cryptanalysts exceeded all pre-war expectations. The greatly increased flow of both men and money into signals intelligence, combined with German and Japanese overconfidence in code and cypher security, enabled Britain and the United States to make good the damage done by interwar neglect with remarkable speed. Ironically, the Secretary of War who presided over the reform and expansion of American signals intelligence after Pearl Harbor was Henry Stimson, who had closed down Yardley's Black Chamber twelve years before. Stimson explained that in 1929, at a time of international 'good will' he had felt obliged to deal 'as a gentleman' with the representatives of foreign powers.[59] He did so no longer.

3. British Intelligence in Ireland, 1914–1921

EUNAN O'HALPIN

I

THE purpose of this chapter is to discuss the organisation and performance of British intelligence in Ireland from the outbreak of the First World War to the cessation of hostilities between the authorities in Ireland and the Irish separatists. This seven-year period is best divided into three phases, from 1914 to the Easter rebellion in 1916, from the rebellion to the end of the war in 1918, and from then onwards to the Irish treaty in 1921. These phases are quite distinct, but in each can be seen the same problems of obtaining, organising and evaluating intelligence which characterised the British effort to maintain order and political control in Ireland.

Prior to the war, intelligence was provided principally by the two Irish police forces, the DMP (Dublin Metropolitan Police) and the RIC (Royal Irish Constabulary). These had long experience of dealing with unrest in Ireland, and elaborate if old-fashioned procedures had been developed over the years to report to Dublin Castle information and assessment of all occurrences of a political or subversive nature. The DMP's detective unit, the G division, contained a number of officers who specialised in political work; the RIC, responsible for all of Ireland outside Dublin City, had few detectives as such, but in each county certain men were assigned to concentrate on political matters, and their reports were forwarded to the RIC Special Crime Branch in Dublin Castle. This small office was staffed by a county inspector, a district inspector and a few clerks; its function was to keep in touch with political crime throughout the country and to furnish an overall assessment of the state of affairs for the use of the Irish executive. As well as reports from around the country, it received information from RIC officers based in Glasgow, Liverpool, Holyhead and the United States, and in addition it served as a liaison office with the DMP, whose headquarters were located close by. There was continuous consultation between the two forces on political matters, and cooperation seems to have been complete. There were, however, certain differences in the kind of material which they provided: the DMP's detectives (of whom less than a dozen were concerned with political matters) concentrated on shadowing suspects, attending political meetings and keeping premises under observation, whereas the RIC, a force developed specifically in response to political and agrarian crime, were better able to find out what was going on in each area and to detect changes in the political climate. Unionist politicians frequently complained that the Irish police had been deprived of funds for 'secret service' work since the advent of Liberal rule in 1906, but in fact the Irish authorities were kept reasonably well informed of the state of the country and of the various separatist organisations which were active. However, the onset of war brought with it the new danger and complication of German espionage and intrigue in Ireland, as well as problems of maritime security with which the civil authorities were not equipped to deal. Consequently a number of steps were taken in 1914 to counter the wartime threats.

On the outbreak of hostilities, an RIC officer, Inspector Ivon Price, was appointed intelligence officer to the army's Irish Command with the rank of major.[1] As such he saw all the relevant information supplied by the two Irish police forces, and he also dealt with Colonel Kell of MI5 at the War Office in London. In addition to this, he received 'material obtained from the Postal and Cable Censors, the Admiralty, Ministry of Munitions, Chief Constables, and other sources' in Ireland, Britain and abroad.[2] Although military intelligence officers were appointed in each of the three military districts in Ireland, their reports were of little consequence.[3] As Kell put it in 1916, 'the County Inspectors are the people who can give full and reliable information regarding their own districts': it was they, and Major Price, who counted.[4] The Admiralty maintained a separate intelligence network in the Irish ports under the direction of W. V. Harrel, a former assistant commissioner of the DMP.[5] It reported to the admiral commanding at Queenstown, the principal naval base, and its activities were limited to 'Admiralty matters' and touched on more general questions only in relation to the loyalty of dockyard employees.[6] What evidence there is suggests that it had virtually no contact with naval intelligence in London. This was of considerable significance, as the Admiralty's naval intelligence division dominated the British intelligence community during the war, and its chief, Captain Reginald Hall, wielded a great deal of power. He did not wield it wisely where Ireland was concerned.

II

The civil authorities and the naval and military forces in Ireland were faced with a number of tasks once war broke out. The navy's principal concern was to protect British shipping in the seas around Ireland, and in particular to detect and destroy enemy submarines.[7] The army was obliged to help the civil powers to maintain order if required, but saw its primary wartime job as the recruitment and training of men for military service. In so far as it took a direct interest in security policy, the army pressed for action against separatist agitators on the grounds that they affected recruitment rather than because they represented a serious threat to British rule.[8] The police forces and the Irish administration which they served had somewhat more complex problems to deal with.

The Ulster crisis had posed a dilemma which neither the authorities in Ireland nor the cabinet in London had been able to resolve, and in consequence a large number of arms had been imported into Ireland without hindrance from the government. Although the loyalty of Ulster and of the great majority of the National Volunteers was not in doubt, it was inevitable that some arms would come into the possession of extremists, and that they might be tempted to use them. Furthermore, it was plain that Germany would do what she could to stir up trouble in Ireland, whether by political agitation through Irish American organisations, or by direct military aid to Irish separatists. The Irish authorities had long experience of the machinations of Irish American secret societies, but they had none at all of intrigue and subversion by a foreign power.

Shortly after war was declared, all enemy aliens of military age known to the Irish authorities were arrested, an obvious precaution justified by the circumstances of the time.[9] The police were instructed to watch out for signs of German naval activity around the coast, especially the landing of arms, and to keep all foreigners under observation. Similar steps were taken in Britain, but in neither case were leading Unionists satisfied with what was done. Scare stories abounded, and Walter Long, who had a great deal of influence in Irish affairs, complained in November that 'as to invasion and spies, nothing can in my judgement be worse than the position of affairs' prevailing in the United Kingdom.[10] In December a *Morning Post* journalist visited Ireland, and prepared a secret report which stated that there were 'many spies of German nationality in the north and west of Ireland prior to the outbreak of war. Not all of these have left the country or been interned', and 'more drastic measures' than the police were willing to apply were 'urgently called for'. There was 'very strong presumptive evidence that the money remitted from America' to separatist organisations 'is really German money', while 'mysterious strangers have been seen on several occasions, particularly during the month of October, on the shores of Sligo Bay'. It was 'believed that mines were conveyed on board trawlers which subsequently proceeded north. The mines were said to have been packed in sections, placed inside boxes . . . [and] the sections . . . screwed together and the mines thus made ready to be launched. These may have been the mines which caused a disaster off the northern coast of Ireland at the end of October.'[11] A more precise tale reached Captain Hall of naval intelligence in December: a 'confidential source' informed him that in April 1914 Sir Roger Casement had, while motoring in Connemara with a German visitor, lost an overcoat containing secret correspondence. It transpired that the 'confidential source' was the Unionist MP Sir John Lonsdale, who had got the story from the driver of Casement's car, and that the coat full of documents was nothing more than a fiction invented by an RIC man to trick the driver into disclosing what places Casement had visited.[12]

Despite the vagueness and evident unreliability of such reports, Captain Hall appeared to heed them rather than the more prosaic account of affairs provided by the Irish authorities, who month after month found no trace of German intrigue in Ireland. There were two reasons for Hall's attitude: firstly, he had an outstanding and unimpeachable source of information on German plans for Ireland, as his staff had broken the telegraphic code in which messages were passed between the German Foreign Office and its embassy in Washington; secondly, he had no time for the conciliatory – or dilatory – approach taken by the Irish administration under the Liberals, and he was prepared to by-pass them altogether. A striking instance of this in the first year of the war was the cruise of the yacht *Sayonara* in the autumn of 1914, an episode of which he was unaccountably proud.[13] Alarmed by the talk of German submarines gaining shelter along the west coast of Ireland, and aware that Casement was seeking German aid for a rebellion and might attempt to return to Ireland, Hall and Basil Thomson of Scotland Yard hit upon the idea of sending the *Sayonara* to investigate. An American yacht, it was crewed by three Royal Navy officers with American accents, and by fifty ratings who had been taught the rudiments of American slang. It was hoped that, by adopting an anti-British attitude, the men of the *Sayonara* might gain the confidence of disloyal Irishmen and thus learn where submarines were hiding and even perhaps discover when Casement was expected to arrive. Neither the Irish authorities nor the admiral commanding at Queenstown were informed of the yacht's mission, and they had reported nothing which would have justified it. The expedition aroused the suspicions of the regular naval patrols, and spent some time under arrest. This may have substantiated its authenticity for the separatists it sought to hoodwink, but it uncovered nothing at all of substance. Its most tangible effect was to add to the scare stories which had prompted its dispatch – the Marquess of Sligo, always on the look out for subversion, dashed over from his home in County Mayo to tell Hall of the sinister craft.[14] Casement remained a prime target of British intelligence, and Hall was able to keep a fairly close track of his movements by intercepting German communications.[15]

The Irish authorities went about their business in a less exotic manner, using their traditional methods of observation of suspects and collection of information. These had worked adequately in the past, but the political circumstances of the war made it difficult to act against troublemakers even when they had been clearly identified.[16] The Irish Volunteers, the Citizen Army and the IRB (Irish Republican Brotherhood) were correctly regarded as the most dangerous organisations, but the police failed to infiltrate them. This was a marked change from earlier times: it was, perhaps, due partly to the efficiency of the separatists, but was at least as much because of police slackness. The public statements made in the wake of the 1916 rebellion that the police had few 'friends' in these bodies were deceptive, in that early in 1916 the DMP did get quite detailed information from two sources, 'Chalk' and 'Granite', which prompted one official to comment that 'we seem at last to be getting *some* information'.[17] However, as events were to prove, this was too late in the day. After the rebellion Basil Thomson reported that the RIC had a total of only £400 a year with which to pay informants, but the permanent head of the Irish administration said that 'there was no difficulty' about funds for such purposes.[18] On balance, it appears that it was a lack of initiative, rather than a shortage of cash, which hampered the RIC and the DMP in their investigation of separatist organisations. Furthermore, criticism of their failures must be qualified by the reflection that the plans of the inner circle of conspirators who initiated the Easter rebellion were unknown not only to the authorities but to the chief of staff of the Irish Volunteers, Eoin MacNeill.[19]

The outbreak of the rising on Easter Monday 1916 came as a complete surprise to the Irish authorities, who had assumed that the events of the previous days had made any attempt at insurrection unlikely. As already mentioned, the DMP in March had belatedly secured information which indicated that some action was being contemplated. On 17 April news reached Dublin Castle that a ship carrying arms for a rebellion had left Germany for Ireland some days previously, and that these would be landed on the south-west coast. This information came in a letter to the army commander, General Friend, from General Stafford, the officer commanding in Cork. Stafford had apparently learnt this 'not officially, but casually', in a conversation with the admiral commanding at Queenstown, Admiral Bayly.[20] Bayly had received this information from Hall's Naval Intelligence Division, which did not attempt to warn the Irish authorities formally either through him or through Major Price. This 'very extraordinary fact' was touched on briefly by the commission of inquiry into the rebellion, but no conclusions were drawn from it.[21] It is now clear that Hall was anxious above all to avoid disclosing his source, decrypted German messages; in so doing he jeopardised the security of Ireland, although Bayly's remarks to Stafford were obviously intended to alert Dublin Castle.[22] In this they succeeded: on 21 April the German arms ship *Aud* was captured by the navy off the coast of Kerry, while an RIC patrol detained one of three men who had been landed from a German submarine in Tralee Bay. It was only the next day, Easter Saturday, that this prisoner was identified as Roger Casement. He was immediately sent to London for interrogation, and the Irish authorities therefore had no chance to question him closely. On Easter Sunday he arrived in London, where Hall refused his request that news of his arrest be published in Ireland together with his appeal that no rising be attempted.[23] Given Hall's outlook and general behaviour, it is quite possible that he intended the rebellion to take place, knowing that it would be crushed and that the government would be obliged to follow a policy of repression in its wake. In fact, the military council of the IRB (Irish Republican Brotherhood) already knew of Casement's arrest, though not that he had come to Ireland specifically to stop the rising taking place, and they were firmly committed to action.[24] Eoin MacNeill, the Volunteers' chief of staff, was not, and when he learnt of the capture of the arms ship he issued an order cancelling the manoeuvres and parades which had been arranged as cover for a mobilisation and uprising.[25] This, together with the arrest of Casement, convinced the Irish authorities that the immediate crisis was over.[26] On Easter Monday Sir Mathew Nathan and Major Price were actually discussing plans for the arrest of the leaders of the conspiracy when Dublin Castle was attacked, the shooting of a DMP man at the gate being the first intimation they received that a rebellion was in progress.[27] General Friend, who had left Ireland on Good Friday after learning of the capture of the *Aud*, later expressed the bewilderment of the Irish authorities in speaking of 'this unexpected rising which took place without any warning, so far as I could see it was quite unforeseen by anyone'.[28]

The commission of inquiry set up to enquire into the causes of the rebellion laid the blame squarely on the political head of the Irish administration, the chief secretary Augustine Birrell.[29] In so doing they concluded that the outbreak was the consequence not of a lack of intelligence but of political resolve: both Irish police forces were specifically exempted from any criticism. No allusion was made in their report to the dilatory manner in which the Irish authorities were warned of the *Aud*'s mission, although one member of the commission commented on it during the proceedings.[30] That this omission was not dictated simply by security considerations is shown by the faith which both the British government and the Irish authorities continued to repose in Hall and Basil Thomson.[31] In September Thomson reported on the organisation of intelligence in Ireland. He found 'overlapping, lack of co-ordination, and unnecessary expense', pointing out that

Intelligence in Ireland is obtained by no less than five public bodies, viz:– The Admiralty, War Office (M15), Irish Command, Royal Irish Constabulary, and Dublin Metropolitan Police, and in America by the Home Office, War Office, Foreign Office and Royal Irish Constabulary, and . . . although all the material reports may reach the Irish Executive, there is certainly a danger that from lack of co-ordination the Irish Government may be the last Department to receive information of grave moment to the peace of Ireland.

He was particularly critical of the provision of information from America, where 'there is much overlapping', but he made no mention of naval intelligence, which was by far the most important agency where Ireland was concerned. He recommended some changes in the organisation of the Crimes Special Office of the RIC, called for 'a judicious expenditure of money for information' as 'it is always cheaper and more effective to reward very liberally one person in a prominent position than a number of persons who are on the fringe of a movement', and advocated the creation of a covert intelligence service, staffed by RIC men who 'would ostensibly be working in the Crimes Special Office', which would take over the political work of the DMP after Home Rule had been granted.[32] Few of these measures were in fact adopted, although two years later Thomson told Lord French that they were 'now the working system' in Ireland. The idea of a secret RIC unit based in Dublin was resurrected late in 1919, and something on those lines was eventually established in the summer of 1920.[33]

Thomson's observations were reasonable in themselves, but they obscured the fact that the greatest weakness of the organisation of intelligence in Ireland lay not in the multiplicity of agencies involved – after all, the RIC, the DMP and the military were closely linked through Major Price, who also had direct access to the permanent head of the Irish administration – but in the unwillingness of intelligence chiefs in London either to share vital information with the Irish authorities or to accept what they said about the state of the country. As will be seen, Hall in particular was determined to act as he saw fit, even to the extent of apparent distortion of evidence to force Dublin Castle into repressive action against the separatist movement.

III

The defeat of the rebellion was followed by the arrest and deportation of over 1800 suspected activists from throughout the country. This was successful in that almost all the leading separatists were detained. However, politically it proved very unpopular, and the government soon began to release those detained without trial. This was done in a characteristically haphazard fashion, so that dangerous men were freed along with harmless ones. The police and military in Ireland protested at this, believing it an encouragement to disloyalty, but they were confident that no serious disorder could occur.[34] That confidence was tested in September, when the War Office sent to the army commander in Ireland information 'which may be accepted as coming from the highest source and [is] in every respect reliable'.[35] This was that two members of the 'Control Committee' of Sinn Fein had escaped detection and were organising another rising, that ample funds were available to them, and that arms had already been smuggled into the country.[36] This report caused great alarm in the Irish administration, but Major Price wrote that 'I cannot consider this information reliable': although popular sentiment had swung in Sinn Fein's favour since the Easter rebellion, the separatists were completely disorganised and most of the leaders were in jail. There was no evidence that arms had been smuggled in, and the bulk of the money sent to Ireland from America had undoubtedly been used for legitimate purposes, while 'the number of troops in Ireland renders all hope of a rising vain, unless there was a German invasion in force'.[37] Events proved him right, and the War Office subsequently passed on a correction of the original information which qualified it considerably.[38]

The warning to Dublin Castle was based on documents seized by the American authorities in the office of a Clan na Gael organiser in San Francisco, and on decrypts of telegrams by naval intelligence in which Bernstorff, the German ambassador in Washington, told Berlin of his dealings with Clan na Gael, the most important Irish-American society. These messages were eventually published by the British government in 1921, along with other evidence 'proving the intrigue between Sinn Fein and Germany'; what they in fact disclosed was that Clan na Gael's 'Revolutionary Directorate' had virtually no contact with active separatists in Ireland, and little idea of conditions in the country.[39] They were pressing for a German commitment to send arms and men to support another rising, whereas in Ireland no such action was contemplated. Hall faced a genuine dilemma in his handling of information since the secrecy of his sources was his paramount consideration, and this frequently made it difficult to give the Irish authorities sufficient material to allow them to evaluate the dangers for themselves. Nevertheless, it is quite clear that he made use of the inviolability of his sources to foist upon Dublin Castle alarming information which they could not test and upon which they were obliged to act. This happened again in February 1917, when a warning was received from London that an arms landing was imminent. That warning was based partly on further decrypts of German telegrams, from which it appeared that Clan na Gael was again seeking the dispatch of troops and arms; there was no indication that anyone in Ireland knew of the plans, but this was not made clear to the Irish authorities.[40] As a result they were forced to deport a number of prominent Sinn Feiners, against whom no charge could be proved, and the political consequences were unfortunate.[41]

Diplomatic relations between the United States and Germany were broken off in February 1917. This deprived Hall of his principal source of information. However, his influence was unimpaired, since the provenance of his material was secret. Thus anything he said concerning Ireland continued to be treated with the utmost respect although most of it was in fact based on the flimsiest of evidence and the stories of spy-conscious Unionists. In the summer of 1917 an informant within the Irish administration began sending reports to London, using the editor of a Belfast newspaper and St Loe Strachey of the *Spectator* as intermediaries. Referred to in Strachey's correspondence only as 'Z', his reports made up in colour what they lacked in accuracy: the Germans had landed machine guns and other arms on the west coast, Sinn Fein was preparing another rebellion, and 'communications between the Sinn Feiners and Germany are kept up largely through Maynooth and the Vatican'.[42] Strachey passed on this material to Basil Thomson, who in turn gave it to Hall, and who also 'transmitted his information on occasion to Mr Duke', the Chief Secretary for Ireland. 'This was really unavoidable'.[43] Thus the political head of the Irish administration was in the extraordinary position of hearing from an authoritative source alarming stories which in fact derived from the gossiping and fantasies of one of his own subordinates. It is plain from the reports of the Irish police forces, the military and the navy that there was no substance in these tales – it was not as though 'Z' was communicating material which had been suppressed within the administration for political reasons. 'Z' was ultimately 'blown to pieces' through an indiscretion, but two of his colleagues, 'JK' and 'Lt Col Retd', continued the work.[44] They had nothing of any importance to report, merely relaying as fact the wild rumours of the day. Such talk greatly increased the difficulties of the Irish administration: Walter Long believed it implicitly and demanded action accordingly, while its endorsement by Hall and Thomson in London gave it a spurious authenticity which was impossible to challenge.[45]

In the White Paper on links between Germany and Sinn Fein which appeared in 1921, the government stated that communications between the two, interrupted by America's entry into the war, 'were again opened up in June 1917'. No evidence of this was offered, but telegrams from the German embassy in Madrid of August and September 1917 were quoted which discussed the possibility of sending arms to Ireland from South America, and asked whether 'warehouses, etc., on Argentine soil' might be attacked by an exiled Sinn Feiner.[46] These inconclusive trivia were the best proof that Hall's cryptanalysts could provide of continued contact between Sinn Fein and Germany; it is likely therefore that the White Paper's further claims – that in the autumn of 1917 'communications were taking place . . . by means of U-boats off the West Coast of Ireland and German propaganda leaflets and pamphlets were thus disseminated in Ireland', that by 1918 'arms and ammunition were being landed' from submarines, and that Sinn Feiners were sending 'messages in code' to offshore U-boats – were based largely on the stories of rumourmongers such as 'Z' and 'JK'.[47] They certainly did not tally with the reports furnished by the organisation which knew Ireland best, the RIC.

Despite the shock of the 1916 rebellion, the Irish police forces plodded along as they had done for years. They failed to penetrate the higher councils of Sinn Fein or of the Irish Volunteers, but they at least provided realistic assessments of political feeling and of the state of the country upon which the administration could rely. The trends they discerned were not encouraging: separatist sentiment had grown since the rising, and, while there was no immediate danger of another insurrection, the country was increasingly disaffected. From time to time Sinn Fein appeared to be on the wane, but overall it was a growing threat to the established order.[48] Military intelligence officers reached broadly the same conclusions.[49] Neither they, the navy nor the police found much sign of German activity in Ireland, or of the submarine landings so often reported in London.[50] Because of this, the sudden discovery in April 1918 of the 'German plot' came all the more as a shock to the Irish authorities.

The 'German plot' is the most notable illustration of the apparent manipulation of intelligence by Hall and his cronies in order to prod the Irish authorities into action against Sinn Fein. Following the German military offensive in March 1918, the cabinet took a sudden decision to apply conscription to Ireland, a step they had hitherto avoided because of its probable political consequences.[51] It had precisely the result feared: nationalist Ireland united in opposition to the measure, Sinn Fein gained immensely, and in the end the government were forced to back down. In the midst of the political turmoil which followed the cabinet's decision, the RIC, acting on a warning from naval intelligence, on 12 April arrested a man on the coast of County Clare. This was Corporal Joseph Dowling, who as a prisoner of war in Germany had joined Casement's Irish brigade.[52] Under interrogation in London, he admitted that he had been brought from Germany by U-boat to make contact with Sinn Fein leaders in order 'to ascertain the true state of affairs' in Ireland and to settle details for a landing of 'arms, artillery, machine guns and German troops'.[53] He was to spend a fortnight in Ireland before making his way back to Germany – according to one account he would summon a U-boat by waving his handkerchief from the shore.[54] Dowling was demonstrably ignorant of Irish affairs – he had planned to get in touch with John Dillon and John Redmond, neither of whom supported Sinn Fein and the latter of whom was dead – and it is hard to believe that the Germans reposed much faith in him.[55] Initially his arrest and confessions found a varied reaction amongst the authorities: Major Price and the police were seriously alarmed, whereas Lord French, who was about to become viceroy, wrote on 21 April that 'I didn't believe a word' of Dowling's claims that the Germans were about to land arms and men.[56] French was confirmed in this by conversations with Admiral Bayly and Mr Harrel, the head of the Admiralty's Irish intelligence network. Harrel said that 'it might be *possible* but gave very good reasons why it is not in the least probable' that the Germans would risk any submarines 'in order to land arms which in all probability would never be used for the purpose for which they were intended. He does not think that much has been done in this way & I am inclined to agree with him'.[57] Yet within two weeks, French accepted the lord lieutenancy 'on the understanding that I was to go to Ireland for the purpose of *restoring order* and combating German intrigues'.[58] To understand this change of attitude, the events of April 1918 must be examined in some detail.

The capture of Dowling was followed four days later by the discovery of two men named Cotter, one of them said to be a brother-in-law of de Valera, early in the morning 'in a sailing boat' in Dublin Bay. It was surmised that they were attempting to make contact with an enemy submarine previously reported in the area, 'and calculations as to wind and tide make it possible that they even did so'.[59] This seems most unlikely.[60] Their arrest, together with Dowling's capture and various rumours of arms landings, convinced Price that Hall was correct in believing that 'it is more than probable' that the Germans were about to send arms and troops, 'even though on quite a small scale'.[61] The inspector general of the RIC thought the situation warranted the arrest of 'the Sinn Fein leaders without delay'.[62] Additional information received early in May increased the anxiety of Irish officials: there were further rumours of impending arms landings, and the Admiralty on 3 May passed on a report received from Copenhagen that 'on the evening of April 26th, seven closed Railway Cars were put into pier at Cuxhaven alongside two large submarines. After dark their contents which were supposed to be rifles and machine guns with munitions' were loaded on board the submarines. 'From various rumours received it is considered that they are destined for Ireland'.[63] The Irish authorities had no means of evaluating such reports – they were dependent on Hall, especially as their own knowledge of the state of feeling in Ireland for once tallied with what he maintained. The decision to impose conscription had produced more uproar and unrest in Ireland than any German-inspired agitation could have hoped to achieve.

For most ministers, the condition of Ireland, however grave, was only one of many urgent problems to be faced, as Germany seemed on the verge of victory in France. On 2 May Walter Long complained that his cabinet colleagues had not 'properly realised the dangerous state of things in Ireland – especially the prevalence of German intrigue'.[64] In fact this worked to his advantage, since he was allowed to proceed unhindered on the government's behalf with the elaborate arrangements which culminated in the unmasking of the 'German plot', despite the doubts which his own party leader had already expressed: 'we have nothing I am told which would be proof in a Court of Law. Midleton thought the Irish Office had proof but Duke tells me they have nothing except what comes from Hall and which I am told is not proof'.[65] Long had the full support of the Irish authorities and of the new lord lieutenant Lord French in preparing for action against Sinn Fein, but the principal advisers upon whom both he and they depended were Hall and Thomson.[66] The course agreed was that on the night of 17–18 May the police would arrest a large number of Sinn Fein activists, and that Lord French would then issue a proclamation declaring that the government had uncovered evidence of a Sinn Fein–German conspiracy.[67] Although some ministers expressed reservations about the plan – Smuts warned that 'there was a danger of discrediting the government if they made a great deal of pro-German activities in Ireland, and then found out that the evidence was not very considerable or convincing' – the cabinet on 10 May endorsed Long's scheme as part of a new policy of firmness towards Ireland in the wake of the conscription débâcle.[68] This they were soon to regret.

The wave of arrests went remarkably well. Lord French commented that 'the seizures . . . were entirely unexpected', without however drawing the inference that this was because the people seized were innocent of the charges made against them.[69] Ironically, one of the few to escape arrest was Michael Collins, who was tipped off by a DMP detective. He had received a message from the Germans promising support for another rising, but thought such an idea impractical though he did want weapons to be sent.[70] It rapidly became clear that the government could produce no real evidence of a plot, certainly nothing to substantiate the existence of any conspiracy between those detained and Germany. Long had hoped to do this by arranging for publication in the United States of what material there was, as this would disguise the fact that it came from Hall's cryptanalysts. But the Americans refused either to publish the documents themselves or to give 'public sanction to their publication in England'. Initially Long made little of this reverse, but he came to see it as significant.[71] In this he was probably mistaken, as the information available was so inadequate: on 21 May the cabinet secretary found Lloyd George

rather low about the Irish proclamation issued last Saturday, to the effect that a plot had been discovered between the Sinn Feiners and the Germans. There has since been an outcry for the . . . evidence, and Walter Long and the Irish Executive (who forced the Cabinet to approve the proclamation by putting a pistol to their head) have only produced evidence of the most flimsy and ancient description. So the Government are put in a hole, as I expected they would be.[72]

When Hall appeared before the cabinet a day later, ministers were scathing about his material, which 'provided ample evidence of German designs, but not of Sinn Fein complicity', especially 'having regard to the very strong statement that had been published to the effect that we had evidence of a German plot', and the chief secretary for Ireland complained of 'the circuitous system of communication of information' between the naval authorities and Dublin Castle.[73] A few days afterwards the outgoing army commander in Ireland remarked that 'there were no proofs of the German Sinn Fein plot', and implied that he had been removed for saying so.[74] Most nationalists saw the arrests as a form of retribution for the country's opposition to conscription, as no conspiracy was ever proved and as none of those detained were tried for dealing with the enemy.[75] This was slightly simplistic: the Irish authorities were certainly convinced that a plot was afoot.[76] So too was Long. Whether Hall believed this is an open question: if his admirers are to be trusted, he was never wrong.[77] If so, then he deliberately misled politicians and officials over the supposed conspiracy.

Two days after the arrests French wrote that 'I have roused up the Detective Dept. with a view to getting at more of these intrigues. I know there *are* more'.[79] Over the next two years he was frequently to complain of the inadequacy of the police forces, but not until the end of 1919 did he or anyone else do much about it. Neither the RIC nor the DMP showed any inclination to change their ways: this was partly because of inertia, since they expected that the end of the war would bring with it Home Rule and an inevitable reconstitution of the two forces. Besides this, the chiefs of the two forces had little time for new methods of collecting intelligence. In July they both complained that a new agency, referred to only as 'Q', was 'really useless; that all the information Major Price had, was derived from them as distinct from Q'. It was agreed that the advice of MI5 should be sought 'as to the best means of improving Q'.[80] What exactly 'Q' was is unclear: it may have been the covert organisation suggested by Basil Thomson, but it seems more likely that it was a branch of military intelligence, since it was the responsibility of the commander in chief.[81] Towards the end of 1918 the inspector general of the RIC indicated that he had a valuable informant within Sinn Fein, but one who appears to have provided political rather than military – or criminal – intelligence.[82]

Ireland was quiet throughout the remaining months of the war. A succession of labour disputes in the summer and autumn caused some anxiety, although the RIC concluded that the interests of unionised workers and of middle-class supporters of Sinn Fein were incompatible and would prevent an effective alliance between socialists and separatists. There was no sign of further German activity, but Walter Long was nevertheless disturbed by the growth of labour unrest throughout the British Isles, seeing in it 'the hand of Germany . . . all this is due to German intrigue and German money'. What was needed was a reorganised intelligence service to 'cope with the Bolshevik, Syndicalist and the German spy. I am satisfied that these three are still actively pursuing their infernal practices'.[83] Even after Germany's collapse he continued to fret about the dangers of Bolshevism in Ireland, and early in 1919 he dispatched an agent to Belfast, where 'a Soviet had been established'. The agent 'finally formed the opinion that a display of force was the only method of ending this Soviet threat', and the subsequent appearance of troops on the streets 'did the trick!'.[84] In fact, as events were to show, the threat to British rule in Ireland was based entirely on nationalism. It was one with which the Irish authorities proved unable to deal, though the failure was less theirs than the government's whom they served.

IV

The end of the war brought no relief for the Irish administration. The election of December 1918 saw a clear victory for Sinn Fein, which won 73 of the 105 Irish seats. Neither the cabinet in London nor Lord French in Ireland were prepared to adjust their policy in the light of this. Sinn Fein they continued to regard as a temporary phenomenon which would quickly lose support in the face of firm government. The sporadic attacks on police which began on 21 January 1919 with the shooting of two constables in Tipperary only confirmed them in this belief. Their view did not go unchallenged within the administration: General Byrne of the RIC argued that Sinn Fein had become a

majority party and could no longer be treated simply as an armed
conspiracy by a handful of fanatics. In the course of 1919 he became
increasingly estranged from the dominant clique in Dublin Castle,
until in December he was finally disposed of by being sent on
indefinite leave.[85] As head of the RIC he was well aware of the state of
feeling in the country, and he argued that the only policy that offered
any hope of success was to separate the politicians from the physical
force section, the Irish Volunteers or IRA (Irish Republican Army)
as they became known. Such a policy required considerable conces-
sions from the government, and these were not forthcoming. Instead
Sinn Fein was treated as a hostile and subversive organisation
indistinguishable from the IRA. This further alienated public opinion
and made it all the harder for the police to get to grips with political
crime. Although raids for arms and documents occasionally brought
results, Lord French's policy of firm government was ineffective and it
served only to strengthen the extremists within the separatist
movement.[86] It also led to divisions within the administration, which
made effective reorganisation of the police forces difficult to achieve.

In the early months of 1919 concern grew about the capacity of the
police to deal with political crime, but as usual little was done. In
January Major Price returned to ordinary RIC work, and no
successor emerged to replace him as co-ordinator and effective
director of intelligence in Ireland.[87] Furthermore, the army were
anxious to reduce their commitments in Ireland as elsewhere, while
Harrel's Admiralty network had been wound up after the Armistice.[88]
While the Crown forces were being cut, the IRA was increasing its
activities. In 1918 and 1919 its director of intelligence, Michael
Collins, secured the services of four men in RIC headquarters and in
the DMP. These were able to provide a great deal of information on
police operations, and they also disclosed the identities of informers
and undercover agents who then became targets for 'the Squad', a
group of gunmen working under Collins' orders.[89]

Discussion within the administration of how to improve intelligence in the face of increased violence was complicated by the dispute
about policy: General Byrne came in for fierce criticism about the
'state of affairs' in the RIC, whereas no complaints were made about
the DMP.[90] This made little sense: although the RIC's capacity to
collect intelligence was impaired by its increasing isolation from the
community, it remained a formidable and competent force which
could provide reliable information on the state of the country. The

DMP, by contrast, became almost a neutral body: of the ten or so detectives engaged on political work, five had been killed or wounded by the end of the year, and the chief commissioner was reduced to petitioning London to find a safe job in Britain for his best detective before he too was shot.[91] In December Lord French and his closest advisers decided to take action. Having concluded that almost no one in Dublin Castle could be trusted, they set up a secret committee to 'place matters in Dublin and the country on a proper footing'.[92] It consisted of the chief commissioner of the DMP, the acting inspector general of the RIC, the assistant under secretary Sir John Taylor, and Alan Bell, a resident magistrate and former RIC officer with many years' experience of political crime.[93] Their report 'has not been typed as the matter is of too confidential a nature to allow out of the hands of the Committee'.[94] They found that 'an organised conspiracy of murder, outrage and intimidation has existed for some time past with the object of . . . rendering useless the Police Forces'. While 'the ramifications extend all over the country, Dublin City is the storm centre and the mainspring of it all'. It was 'absolutely essential that all the resources of Government should be used in the Metropolis to break down and destroy' the IRA, which 'contemplates further murders during the winter months'. The DMP could no longer rely on 'even loyal and respectable people' for information, which must in future

> come from the inside. This might be speedily obtained if an accredited agent, already closely connected with the organisation in America were to come to this country and ingratiate himself with the extreme section here and learn their plans. Such a person should not be known to any member of the Police Forces in Ireland. He ought to be able to give . . . information which would lead to the capture of intending assassins and the breaking up of the criminal organisation. It might also be possible to find men skilled in trades who could be sent to Dublin, being engaged for a regular salary, to ply their trade, join their appropriate Union and mix with the artisans who would be their fellow workers. Such men should be capable of gaining valuable information.

The report said also that 'at present the Sinn Feiners know all the detectives in the "G" Division, but the "G" Division have not the same intimate knowledge of them. This is a great handicap.' It

recommended the appointment of an additional assistant commissioner who would 'devote his full time' to G Division's political
work, and suggested

> sending to Dublin a dozen members of the RIC, young active men
> of courage and determination, good shots and preferably men
> accustomed to city life. These men should be lodged in pairs in
> various localities in the City. Their presence should not be made
> known to either the DMP or the RIC. Having made themselves
> acquainted with the members of the 'G' Division as regards their
> appearance they might very occasionally follow at a distance
> behind them so as to be ready to take action should anything occur
> . . . We are inclined to think that the shooting of a few would-be
> assassins would have an excellent effect. Up to the present they
> have escaped with impunity. We think that this should be tried as
> soon as possible.

The selection of men to become secret agents 'from the lists of
candidates before they join the RIC and become policemen' was also
suggested.[95]
    This report was notable in several respects. It acknowledged what
had long been apparent: it was the DMP, not the RIC, which was in
most danger of collapse. Secondly, it illustrated the fear of betrayal
which pervaded the administration: General Byrne was only the first
of a number of senior policemen to fall under suspicion.[96] Furthermore, some of its recommendations were acted upon. Within a
fortnight a 'very able' RIC officer from Belfast, Inspector Redmond,
was made assistant commissioner of the DMP to 'take care of political
crime'.[97] It appears also that some covert agents were put to work
under the direction of Alan Bell, who reported that 'in the course of
their moving about my men have picked up a good deal of useful
information which leads to raids'.[98] In addition, some months later
the authorities did organise an undercover squad of RIC men in
Dublin – the army already had their own plain clothes men operating
in the city – which became known to its enemies as the 'Murder
Gang'. Their task was not the protection of DMP detectives, who
had by then ceased to matter, but the capture or elimination of
wanted IRA men. Finally, the idea of infiltrating trade unions was
evidently not forgotten: in July 1921 Collins warned a union leader
that 'Dublin Castle is selecting men from the Military there to go . . .

anywhere there is a Trade Union . . . supplied with faked union badges and forged instructions . . . in order to find out the class of men attending meetings and anything else that would matter in their eyes. . . . Their intention to do this is beyond doubt.'[99]

The steps taken in the wake of the report did not have any immediate effect. On 19 December gunmen narrowly failed to assassinate Lord French near Ashtown in County Dublin. A month later the newly appointed assistant commissioner Redmond was shot dead. This was a particular blow to Alan Bell, as 'through him I was able to make inquiries which I should not care to entrust to the "G" Division', of which he was justifiably suspicious.[100] Bell himself was taken off a tram and shot in March 1920 by men of Collins's 'Squad', the usual explanation being that he was 'investigating the Republic's secret bank accounts'.[101] In fact the evidence suggests that he was doing rather more: he led secret inquiries into the attempt on Lord French and the killing of Redmond, and appears to have been an unofficial head of intelligence for the administration.[102] By the time of his death, the regime which had sponsored his activities was on its last legs. In May the organisation of Dublin Castle was radically altered on the orders of the British government, and following this a determined effort was made to get to grips with terrorism in Ireland. This led to an escalation in violence, but it also saw occasional victories for the intelligence services over their IRA opponents. Thenceforth the antagonists were distinguishable less by their methods than by their efficiency.

The reform of the civil administration was accompanied by changes in the conduct of intelligence operations. At the suggestion of the army commander, General Macready, the cabinet appointed an officer to supervise the work of all the intelligence agencies in Ireland.[103] He was to perform the coordinating function carried out by Major Price up to 1919, but he would have greater authority to direct the efforts of the various organisations. Unfortunately for the British, the man chosen was not up to the job: Brigadier General Ormonde de l'Epee Winter, or 'O' as he preferred to be known, was a colourful figure, but his fondness of cloak and dagger methods could not conceal his incapacity for effective organisation. Macready complained of him in 1921 that he 'has not got the right method, and we here very much doubt whether he will ever get it'.[104] With the exception of military intelligence in Dublin, the collection and analysis of information remained a haphazard business.[105] In the second half of 1920 there was an influx of 'sleuths' into Dublin, undercover and plain clothes agents who roamed the streets in search of the IRA and the Republican leaders: besides the army's own people, the RIC and Basil Thomson's directorate of intelligence also had men engaged on such work.[106] Some were army officers of Irish extraction, others men on loan from the Indian secret service.[107] These agents were not under adequate control – for example, they spied on a senior Dublin Castle official whose brief was to build up contacts with Sinn Fein.[108] In the violent circumstances of the time they did not operate within the law: suspects were sometimes shot, and prisoners tortured. The political repercussions of such behaviour probably outweighed the results gained, though it must be said that they made life a great deal harder for the IRA and scored some successes against them.

It is difficult to assess the effectiveness of the contending intelligence services in the most intense period of disorder. The success of Michael Collins in infiltrating Dublin Castle and in neutralising the DMP has been lauded *ad nauseam*, and like all good stories has acquired gloss after gloss over the years.[109] The attacks in 1919 on DMP detectives were successful and they severely shook the administration, but it should be said that the victims were men who had been doing political work openly for years and who were well known to their assailants.[110] Their killing required not a masterstroke of intelligence work but rather ruthlessness and efficiency. The systematic shooting of officers which took place on 21 November 1920, Bloody Sunday, was in a different category. Although it is still not clear whether all those killed were in fact intelligence officers, some were undoubtedly members of the 'Cairo gang', a network which had been operating in Dublin since the summer. This action has been described as marking 'the defeat of the police and the nullification of their intelligence services', but while it certainly was spectacular it did not bring the operations of British intelligence to a halt.[111] After all, seven IRA men were subsequently hanged for their part in the killings, while an eighth was convicted but escaped from prison.[112] A few weeks after the shootings, a Dublin Castle official wrote that 'O' would 'I'm sure . . . regard peace now as a tragedy', and on balance Bloody Sunday appears to have dispelled the 'amateurish attitude' of intelligence officers towards their work, not to have intimidated them into retreat.[113] Furthermore, the fact that the IRA continued to kill suspected informers indicates that Collins at least believed that the intelligence services still posed a serious threat, whatever Bloody

Sunday had achieved.[114] It is true to say that the IRA held the upper hand in intelligence during the war of independence – without it they could not have survived. They had the considerable advantage of popular support for their aims if not always for their methods, and their intelligence work was efficiently conducted. But there is also strength in numbers: the British had many thousands of troops and police to hand, and although the swarms of undercover agents in Ireland achieved little, the lack of adequate information could partly be remedied by large-scale sweeps and searches.[115] This was how most IRA men were captured and worthwhile intelligence gathered. By the time of the truce in July 1921 the rebels were under extreme pressure as a result of such operations, although the prospects for a decisive British victory were as slim as ever. The IRA had won by not being defeated.

V

British intelligence in Ireland from 1914 to 1921 failed in its primary objective of ensuring that the government had adequate information on the activities and intentions of the separatist movement. It was a failure on the one hand of collection and analysis of intelligence, and on the other of security.

The two police forces never succeeded in obtaining worthwhile material from within separatist organisations, in previous decades notoriously easy to penetrate, and they seem barely to have tried. The DMP was badly led and inefficient, but until the autumn of 1919 the RIC did provide reliable information on the state of the country. Thereafter its progressive isolation from the community, and the political fixations of its new commanders, made it ineffective as a police force. Furthermore, by 1920 the IRA had well-placed informants within both the DMP and the RIC, the Dublin police being particularly affected. These informants did a great deal of damage, yet efforts to neutralise them were half-hearted and inept. Furthermore, security precautions were remarkably casual: one of Collins's informants in the DMP was able to read the notes made by detectives investigating political crime, while another agent in RIC headquarters, a confidential typist, simply took an extra carbon of each document which he handled.[116] Even Alan Bell, who appreciated the danger and who knew that there were spies within the administration,

helped his killers by taking the same route into Dublin each morning
and by travelling unarmed. As late as November 1920 security was
sufficiently slack to enable the IRA to kill on Bloody Sunday about a
dozen newly arrived intelligence officers.[117] This laxity was not
confined to the police: as late as the autumn of 1922 the Republican
side in the civil war had an agent within British military headquarters, while it is said that the IRA received much information from a
secretary of the army commander in Cork, General Strickland.[118] The
security defects of the Admiralty's network in Ireland should also be
noted.[119]

The army in Ireland took little part in intelligence operations until
the war with Germany had ended, but in the course of 1919 military
intelligence officers set up a fairly efficient organisation in the Dublin
military district. It is the impression of this writer that the army was
thereafter somewhat more successful than its civilian counterparts in
intelligence work, perhaps because its officers were better organised
and were able to deal systematically with a large volume of low-grade
information. Despite the appointment of 'O', coordination with other
bodies seems to have been inadequate, due partly to mutual rivalry
and partly to mistrust of the police.

Basil Thomson, the director of intelligence at Scotland Yard,
dabbled in Irish affairs throughout the period without displaying the
least grasp of what was happening, while other departments took an
interest from time to time. Of these the most important was Hall's
naval intelligence division, which was predominant in intelligence
matters throughout the First World War. Whether through incompetence or otherwise, Hall on occasion seriously misrepresented
information available to him in such a way as to push Dublin Castle
into repressive action which had serious political consequences and
which was not justified by the situation. His part in the events leading
up to the 1916 rising is somewhat obscure; what however is clear is
that in 1918 he misled both Dublin Castle and the British cabinet
about the 'German plot'. If he believed that the scrappy and
inconclusive information which he held was definite proof of an actual
plot then he was a fool; if he did not, then he deliberately deceived his
political masters on the matter. While the war lasted Hall was a law
unto himself, but his influence disappeared with the Armistice and
naval intelligence ceased to count.

In addition to the various agencies involved in procuring information, the British government or members of it often received material

from private individuals concerned at the state of affairs in Ireland. This was particularly the case during the First World War, when there were frequent warnings from Irish Unionists that the country was on the verge of anarchy and that rebellion could be expected at any time. They distrusted the Irish administration almost as much as they did Sinn Fein, and so they made their complaints directly to London. Some politicians took such information seriously, in particular Walter Long, the most important minister where Ireland was concerned, and this affected the cabinet's approach to Irish questions. The Irish authorities in general were not given a full account of such warnings and where they came from, receiving at most a cryptic message from one or other of the London intelligence organisations. Coming from such a source Dublin Castle had to accept this material at face value. Here again the suspicion arises that the intelligence people in London, in particular Hall, deliberately misled the Irish authorities.

British policy towards Ireland in the 1914–21 period was inept, and consisted largely in refusing to take difficult decisions until forced to by events. It would be wrong to lay the blame for what happened at the door of the intelligence services alone: for the most part their performance reflected rather than created the incoherence and confusion of the cabinet's Irish policy. But there was one instance where a failure of intelligence seems in retrospect to have been decisive: the 1916 rebellion. The dilatory attitude of the Irish authorities in the months leading up to the outbreak was in itself deplorable; worse still however was the approach of naval intelligence in London. Whether or not Hall deliberately withheld information and allowed events to take their course, having ensured that any rebellion would take place without German arms and without Casement, remains a matter of opinion. His part in the 'German plot' two years later, and his behaviour as an MP in the 1920s, do not give a favourable impression either of his integrity or of his judgement.

In conclusion, it should be asked whether there are any lessons to be learnt from the history of British intelligence in Ireland in this period. If the case of Ireland is any guide, intelligence organisations require firm political supervision, especially when producing information upon which vital political decisions will be based. The more compelling and authoritative the intelligence, the more closely it must be examined. Intelligence agencies tend to be mistrustful of politicians; politicians in turn should not trust them unreservedly.

4. British Military and Economic Intelligence: Assessments of Nazi Germany Before the Second World War

WESLEY K. WARK

THE term 'intelligence' is often taken to mean covert operations to gather information, conducted by a (literally) Secret Service. However, for most of the interwar period, the Secret Service proper (MI6 or SIS) was a small, fringe organisation. It was understaffed, underpaid, and could run few agents abroad, while the cryptanalysts of GC&CS provided a disappointingly limited access to the coded radio traffic of both Hitler's Germany and Stalin's Russia. The main work of intelligence assessment was conducted by a wider bureaucracy, which utilised both covert and public sources of information. Military intelligence work was done by the three service departments, each concentrating in an independent fashion on the rearmament of its German opposite number. Economic intelligence was gathered by the Industrial Intelligence Centre (IIC). A limited coordination of this material was achieved by the Chiefs of Staff (COS). But this took the form, for most of the decade, of an accumulation of the details provided by the three service departments and the IIC, rather than an attempt at a synthesis.

The image of German power upon which successive British cabinets based their foreign policy was, in large measure, a composite product of this wider intelligence bureaucracy. Given the fragmentary nature of intelligence reporting, it is hardly surprising that each part of the bureaucracy evolved its own picture of developments in Nazi Germany, not only to fit the available facts but to blend with its own preconceptions and policy interests. In only one case was anything like a 'mirror image' adopted: this was an important aspect of the Air Ministry's earliest response to the creation of a German air force. But with the two other services and the IIC, it happened that British concepts were grafted on to intelligence facts. Sometimes German propaganda was an essential part of the grafting; at other times mere wishful thinking or a lack of pertinent information played a part. The actual mixture which went into the images of German power makes them doubly revealing. Preconceptions were fitted with intelligence facts laboriously culled from a stream of often contradictory and always incomplete information. Occasional intelligence 'coups' blended with received propaganda. The construction of these images illustrates the problems associated with intelligence work in a peacetime era when its importance was not understood, proper finances were lacking and no special sources (such as Ultra) were available. More importantly, they offer a unique insight into service attitudes, especially to the major events in the history of the pre-war Nazi state.

I   AIR INTELLIGENCE

Widespread concern about the German air menace and fear of the devastation which aerial bombardment would entail transformed the air intelligence directorate from a wholly minor appendage of the Air Ministry into one of its most vital bureaucratic parts. Great pressure was put on the intelligence branch by senior Air Ministry officials, the Foreign Office and cabinet ministers to come up not only with accurate contemporary estimates of the size of the German air force (a job to which they were accustomed and which they performed reasonably well), but to make accurate predictions about the future.[1] Long-range predictions necessitated some kind of relevant image of a force which, in the early days of Nazi rule, was secret, relatively small and in some cases technologically backward. The Air Staff employed, during the first three years of their study of the German air force, what was essentially a mirror image and on this basis proceeded to make long-range predictions with an unwarranted degree of confidence and surety. In fact, the RAF looked at the German air force and saw itself a decade earlier, struggling to build an independent force and to lay secure foundations for the future. The only difference was that the German air force seemed to enjoy unlimited finances and enthusiastic political backing.

The use of a mirror image was legitimised by the acquisition of what was regarded as first-class intelligence during 1934–5. This information, derived from SIS and *Deuxième Bureau* sources, was not invention, but neither did it tell the whole story and by the time it reached the West it tended to be out of date.[2] The figures indicated that the German air force would be built up in stages, to a maximum of 1500–2000 planes. The two senior officers in the Air Ministry, Air Marshals Ellington (the Chief of the Air Staff) and Ludlow-Hewitt (the Deputy Chief), used this data to argue that the German air force would be restrained in its expansion by the dictates of what they called 'efficiency'.[3] As late as 1936, the Air Staff stuck to the view, against mounting evidence, that the German air force would have to slow down its expansion once a force of 1500 first-line aircraft had been reached, and begin to consolidate its strength.[4]

What the available intelligence could not throw light upon was the kind of thinking going on inside the German Air Ministry. The early German programmes were designed to create, at the first possible moment, a 'risk fleet', under cover of which Germany could proceed to full-scale rearmament. Industrial targets were set at maximum figures, even though this would involve producing large quantities of trainers and obsolescent aircraft, in order to build the production basis of even more formidable programmes later on.[5] The adequate use of such slices of reality as were in the possession of the Air Staff in London would have required a further, intuitive understanding of the Nazi state. Unhappily, the kind of breakneck progress in air force strength demanded by Hitler and Goering was far from the minds of British intelligencers during the first half of the decade.[6]

The mirror image eventually cracked under the force of contradictory intelligence. A wholesale discarding of the previous assumptions about the German air force finally occurred in October 1936. In a restricted circulation paper for the Committee of Imperial Defence, the Air Staff announced: 'it would appear that Germany is intending to provide for the greatest possible expansion'.[7] The Air Staff's new understanding of the Luftwaffe put the emphasis on the complementary features of numerical superiority (particularly in bombers) and the potential Germany possessed to deliver a knock-out blow. Some side-effects of this image were beneficial, others not.

The liberating effect on air intelligence predictions was soon felt. Estimates spiralled, and ultimately gained in accuracy. Figures circulated in October 1936 put German air force strength in 1939 at 2500 first-line aircraft. By June 1937, the estimate had risen to 3240 first-line planes in 1939. The last pre-war prediction, ventured in October 1938, estimated German strength at 5000 first-line aircraft by the end of 1940.[8] RAF programmes were accelerated to match the new intelligence estimates, so far as finances and production allowed, though the attainment of numerical parity was, even as early as September 1936, regarded as impossible.[9]

The benefits which accrued after 1936 from the abandonment of the mirror image, in the field of predictions of numerical strength, were destined not to be repeated in the study of German aerial doctrine. Ironically, in the one area where their use might have proved beneficial, mirror images were never employed. While, as a result of detailed planning during 1937–8, the Air Staff began to lose faith in their own ability to conduct a strategic air offensive, they still believed that one might well be launched by the Luftwaffe.[10] What looks like a paradox is partly explained by the fact that such an offensive was predicted upon nothing more than the possession of a large number of bombers and a sufficiently vulnerable target. While the RAF lacked both, the Luftwaffe apparently did not. The first-line strength of the German air force in September 1938 was estimated at 927 long-range bombers.[11] For a target they had London. This elementary differentiation was at the heart of air power calculations during the Munich crisis.

What sustained the fear of a German knock-out blow was a set of calculations about the tonnage of bombs which the German air force might deliver on London and the casualties which would ensue. The Air Staff's arithmetic was based on imperfect intelligence and inflated by application of a worst case logic (see Table A, overleaf). An exaggeration of the order of 80 per cent (945 tons versus 531 tons) in the figures for bomb delivery was allied to a supposition that the German air force could make a maximum of 720 sorties against England in one day. The 945 tons of bombs this represented, when matched with the 50 casualties per ton estimate used by the Air Raid Precautions department, resulted in a figure of c. 50,000 casualties in a 24-hour period.[14] Even the Air Staff did not entirely

TABLE A

German bomber type	British intelligence[12]		Reality[13]	
	Range (full tanks) (miles)	Bomb load (lbs)	Range (miles)	Bomb load (lbs)
Dornier 17 (EI)	765	1650	985	1100
Heinkel 111 (BI)	700	4400	744	2200
Junkers 86 (E+G)	830	2200	900–1200	2200
(Note – few in service)				
Bomber force making 720 sorties could deliver:	945 tons		531 tons	

believe in their own 'calculus of destruction'. Such a strong concentration of bombers against England, some 75 per cent of the total German force, seemed doubtful in the context of the Czech crisis. Moreover, the plans branch reminded their superiors that all the intelligence estimates were based on the worst case practice of taking the highest available estimate.[15] The Chief of the Air Staff told his own staff to prepare for a limited German strike only and informed the Secretary of State for Air, Sir Kingsley Wood, on 10 September 1938, that he could not visualise the possibility of a 'bolt from the blue'.[16] A solitary communication of this kind was not enough, however, to overturn a conception of the future air war which had been ingrained by two decades of Air Staff and civilian rhetoric.[17]

When a major change of policy was enacted by the government in the last days of March 1939, the Air Staff suddenly found that its assessment of the strategic situation in Europe was no longer of much relevance. The knock-out blow no longer figured at the top of the government's list of anxieties, as a current of military optimism swept through Whitehall and as a higher degree of fatalism about an Anglo-German clash took root. The Director of Plans, Group Captain (later Air Chief Marshal) John Slessor, remembered:

I was unhappy about what I thought was an unduly optimistic report by the DCOS on the military implications of a pact with Poland. We also had an uneasy feeling that the Intelligence Staff in the War Office were being unduly optimistic about the number of German divisions that would be required in the East.[18]

To gather evidence for the case against a British commitment to the Eastern front idea, the air attaché made a quick visit to Poland in early April. On his return to Berlin he wrote to his superiors at the Air Ministry that the outlook for Poland in a war with Germany 'is pretty desperate'. Wing Commander Vachell concluded that 'it must be decidedly to our advantage to avoid being involved in war during the summer months'.[19]

The Air Staff grew somewhat keener on a policy of deterrence as the summer months passed, initiating a project to invite some highly placed German official to Britain for a tour of British aircraft factories and air force establishments. Such 'Lindbergh' tactics were ultimately vetoed by the embassy in Berlin, with Foreign Office concurrence. The reason advanced was that:

> If British output of aircraft is now considered highly satisfactory and equals or perhaps even exceeds Germany's output, we feel convinced that a display of this fact (already doubtless well known to Goering) would not deter Hitler from going to war if he decided that war would suit his policy.[20]

Such a high confidence in the ability of German military intelligence to make itself heard at the top of the Nazi hierarchy, given the personalities involved and the fractured nature of the Nazi bureaucracy, was unwarranted. The embassy's judgement that Hitler would not be deterred by isolated military facts was, surely, more accurate. Hitler, not without a moment of indecision, did perform to these expectations in September 1939.

The Air Staff's vision of the future balance of power swung, during the 1930s, on a pendulum – from optimism (1933–6) to pessimism (1936–8) and back towards optimism (1939). Their image of the German air force's knock-out blow intentions and capabilities may have been permanently divorced from reality, but this was not true to the same extent in regard to comparative strengths.[21] The onset of pessimism after 1936 was timed to the loss of air parity. Not until 1939 was there any sign that, if not air parity at least a reasonable chance of air power deterrence and, if it came to it, successful defence against air attack, was attainable. A similar pattern can be perceived in the reactions of the War Office to the growth of the German army. The significant difference was that the War Office never had any opportunity to use a mirror image. They were struggling to equip a 5-division expeditionary force while the German army expanded towards a figure of 100 divisions.

II WAR OFFICE INTELLIGENCE

War Office intelligence estimates, like those of the Air Ministry, suffered in accuracy from an early misunderstanding of the dynamism of German rearmament. The first paper in a bi-annual series of War Office–Industrial Intelligence Centre reports on the German army, circulated in July 1935, contained the prediction that Germany would expand her forces at a maximum rate of 8–9 divisions per year. By 1943 the army was expected to peak at a strength of 90–100 divisions.[22] The calculation was based on extrapolation and on official German statements. Neither proved dependable. One wrong assumption was that the performance of the Nazi regime in the first two years of its rearmament programme would be a reliable guide to the future. A second assumption, to be proved equally erroneous, was that the tempo of arms production would remain fairly constant. Any dramatic increase was thought unlikely because of difficulties in the supply of raw materials and the competing demands of the air force and the navy. The 8–9 division estimate of annual German expansion did not remain the standard for long, but succumbed to higher and higher figures as deductions from the early period of Nazi rearmament were modified by evidence of the continued growth of the arms industry.

The early War Office predictions, which proved to be such drastic underestimates, had the further effect of fostering a complacent attitude towards German rearmament inside the department. The team of General Dill, Colonel Paget and Major Whitefoord, collectively responsible for German intelligence in the War Office during 1933–6, were prepared to be accommodating towards the rebirth of the German army for two reasons. The first was that they perceived the results of the Röhm putsch in the summer of 1934 as a victory of the army over the Nazi party: one which legitimised the traditional, semi-autonomous role of the army in the German state.[23] The second reason was that the War Office accepted Hitler's pronouncement that the German army would not exceed a peacetime strength of 36 divisions.[24] Such a strength was not regarded as excessive by the War Office, who gave some space in their internal correspondence to complaints about the 'anti-German' attitude of the Foreign Office.[25] General Dill summed up the War Office's outlook in a report of an amiable visit of inspection to the German army in September 1935: 'it [the army] appears to have escaped the danger of political infection . . . and is now probably the most important factor in stabilising conditions inside Germany'.[26] Three years later, when the Munich crisis approached, the War Office still placed some residual faith in the role of the German high command as a rational brake on the wilder foreign policy impulses of Hitler and the party 'extremists'.[27] In the meantime, however, the complacent image of German rearmament had been shattered by the announcement in September 1936 that the 36–division army limit had been exceeded. Current estimates of German army strength in the summer of 1938 indicated that it had attained a size which the War Office had originally thought could not be reached before 1943.

TABLE B

	German army strength[28] predicted by 1943 (July 1935) (divisions)	Estimate of current[29] German army strength (July 1938) (divisions)
Regular army	36 (3 armoured)	46 (3 armoured)
1st Line reserve	30	18–20
Landwehr	30	24
Total	96	88–90

When it became clear, in the summer of 1938, that Nazi Germany might be preparing for a war against Czechoslovakia, all the independent ingredients of the War Office's image of the German army rapidly coalesced. A large army, built at an astonishing pace, looked about to launch itself into a war in Eastern Europe. The War Office's response was to regard the military outcome as an inevitable and swift victory for the German army. Their pessimism about the

Czech powers of resistance was, in any case, of long standing. As early as November 1933, military intelligence predicted that if ever Germany absorbed Austria, a subsequent attack on Czechoslovakia would be the end of that 'ramshackle republic'.[30] The same conclusion was reached in further studies in July 1935, June 1936, in the Chiefs of Staff paper of March 1938, once in August 1938, and twice in September 1938.[31] Scarcely any heed was paid in any of these studies to the possibility of effective Czech resistance.[32] No thought was given to the effect that the neutralisation of the Czech armed forces might have on the European balance of power. The combination of the War Office's inflated image of German military power and a physically encircled Czechoslovakia was enough to decide the issue. The Director of Military Operations and Intelligence, General Pownall (who, extraordinary as it seems, was not recalled from his holidays until the crisis was four weeks old), believed that the Munich crisis was neither the right time nor the occasion for a showdown with Nazi Germany. In a situation report dated 27 September, he wrote:

> But from the military p.o.v. the balance of advantage is definitely in favour of postponement. This is probably an exception to the rule that 'no war is inevitable', for it will almost certainly come later. Our real object is not to save Czechoslovakia – that is impossible in any event – but to end the days of the Nazi regime. This is not our selected moment, it is theirs; we are in a bad condition to wage even a defensive war at the present time; the grouping of the powers at the moment makes well nigh hopeless the waging of a successful war.[33]

Pownall was not alone in arguing for postponement. Similar views were expressed by General Gort (the Chief of the Imperial General Staff), General Ironside (the British Expeditionary Force commander-designate) and by Colonel Ismay (the secretary of the Committee of Imperial Defence).[34] They were all prepared to wait and see what the future would hold, in the expectation that things could not get any worse than they were at Munich.[35] However, in material terms, the military balance grew more, rather than less, disadvantageous in the months after Munich. The German army continued to expand at a rate greater than that allowed for by the intelligence estimates. The balance of power on land, with the disappearance of the Czech forces after March 1939, swung ominously, for the first time in the 1930s, towards outright German numerical superiority.

Despite the fact that intelligence provided little objective good news during the remaining eleven months of peace after Munich, a revolution occurred in the War Office's image of Nazi German power. To be more precise, the image was turned almost inside-out. Instead of warning about the dangers of any British involvement in Eastern Europe, as they had done on many occasions before 1938, the War Office, in March 1939, lent their support to the idea of forming an 'Eastern front'.[36] They also began to shift their attention from the sheer size of the German army and its remarkable rate of growth to a probing of its war readiness and efficiency. The climax came in February 1939, in a moment of calm between the Holland war scare of January 1939 and the ones to come in March concerning first Roumania and then Poland. The War Office grew suddenly bold in their assessment of German army deficiencies. On 22 February, MI3(b) reported that German rearmament, coupled with vast public expenditure, had 'taxed the endurance of the German people and the stability of the economic system to a point where any further effort can only be achieved at the risk of a breakdown of the whole structure'.[37] The next day, MI3(b) recorded its opinion that the German military machine was not ready to undertake more than an *'attaque brusqée'* against a first-class power – 'a far different proposition', they commented, 'to a protracted war'.[38] Four days later, 27 February, the War Office described the German army of 100 divisions as 'an imposing façade of armaments behind which there are very little spares and reserves'.[39]

The relative optimism displayed by this series of reports pointed the way to the War Office's support for the hasty construction of an Eastern front in March 1939. The military intelligence directorate acted as the principal analyst for the cabinet on the Polish crisis; the events of which had been primed by the military attaché in Berlin.[40] Contrary to what has sometimes been written, the War Office was entirely consistent in its reporting on the Polish crisis. The Deputy Director of Military Intelligence's conclusion, made available to the cabinet, was that Germany was putting pressure on Poland by military and diplomatic means, with the intention either of launching a limited coup over Danzig or of keeping Poland out of the arms of the West.[41] In the light of the War Office reports of 30 March, the British guarantee to Poland can be explained not so much as a deterrent to an expected German invasion, but rather as a reaction to German attempts at intimidation of a potential ally and important member of the prospective Eastern front – an idea which rapidly took shape and gained favour in the aftermath of the German occupation of Prague.

Besides priming the Polish war scare, the British military attaché in Berlin, Colonel Mason-Macfarlane, became the most extreme advocate of an aggressive Eastern front policy. He was, surely, the only man to see a silver lining in Germany's occupation of Czechoslovakia. Concentrating less on the enormous war booty which the Germans secured and more on the shock administered to Germany's neighbours and the disruption caused to the army's training programme, Mason-Macfarlane urged, on 23 March, that the situation was ripe for the encirclement of Germany. He based his argument on three points: that in the aftermath of Prague, Britain would be able to find adequate allies in the East; that Russia was now more likely to side with Britain; and that the German home front was 'incapable of sustaining an effective blockade for any length of time'.[42] Even normally cautious men such as Sir Alexander Cadogan, the Permanent Under-Secretary at the Foreign Office, were influenced by the attaché's message. In an important diary entry for 26 March 1939, Cadogan defined his own change of thinking after Prague, and revealed the part played in it by Mason-Macfarlane's analysis (and, of course, by Vansittart):

> I must say it is turning out at present as Van predicted and as I never believed it would. If we want to stem the German expansion, I believe we must try to build the dam now. Of course, as to whether, if Germany really does gobble up South East Europe, she will *really* be stronger than us, I still have some doubts. But Mason-Macfarlane thinks she will and he ought to know more about it than I.[43]

Six days after his first despatch, Mason-Macfarlane went much further. He advocated a preventive war against Germany. This time, no one could be found to agree with this extremist prophet of the Eastern front and the economic blockade. In the Foreign Office, Cadogan called it a 'rather hysterical outpouring'.[44] The Air Ministry was incensed that such an analysis should have been circulated at all.[45]

Prior to 1936 the War Office viewed the German army as a useful stabilising factor in German politics and refused to see it as a potential menace to European peace. Once the 36-division limit was broken, in the autumn of 1936, their attitude changed profoundly. This change was noticed, incidentally, by the German military attaché in London, who found his telephone tapped and his movements watched.[46]

From 1936 to the Munich crisis, the War Office seem to have been held spellbound by the rapid expansion of the German army and the modernity of its equipment. Although they arrived at no coherent vision of a German *blitzkrieg*, the War Office did manage to identify some of its elements – including the emphasis placed on offensive training, the striking power of the tank, and the possibility of air operations in support of ground forces.[47] During the Munich crisis itself, War Office valuations of the striking power of the German army prevailed over order-of-battle facts, which showed that the German army was badly outnumbered on its French flank and possessed only a limited numerical superiority against the Czechs.[48]

After Munich, the War Office was seduced by reports of German economic difficulties into supposing that the construction of an Eastern front would be the best solution to either peace or war. A psychological factor was also at work, as War Office attitudes to Nazi Germany hardened with the experiences of 1938–9 – first the military humiliation of Munich, then the Kristalnacht, finally the blatant occupation of Prague. The Director of Military Operations and Intelligence's comment in his diary on 29 August 1939, was perhaps typical of this new attitude: 'Last September we might have lost a short war. Now we shouldn't, nor a long war either. But that the [Nazi] regime must go I am convinced'.[49]

III   NAVAL INTELLIGENCE

The last of the service departments to reach such a resolution was undoubtedly the Admiralty. The Naval Intelligence Directorate (NID) was the least well integrated and most out-of-step Service intelligence department in Whitehall in the 1930s.[50] Partly this was a feature of a department in eclipse nursing memories of better days. After some spectacular codebreaking successes during the First World War, the NID had suffered badly from financial cutbacks in the 1920s, the loss of parts of its intelligence 'empire' and the lower

priority attached to such work in peacetime.[51] One War Office
intelligence officer, who took his job seriously, commented:

> As far as the Admiralty were concerned, a legend had built up
> around a mysterious Room 40 and the highly secret operations of
> Admiral 'Blinker' Hall in World War One. Perhaps as a result
> there was a tendency for naval intelligence to feel itself superior, in
> efficiency and influence, to the Intelligence departments of the
> other two Services; in fact, there was no justification at all for this
> attitude.[52]

Eccentric posturing of this kind would hardly have made any
difference had it not been for the fact that the NID and the Admiralty
as a whole found themselves increasingly at odds with the Foreign
Office and the other service departments in their depiction of the
threat posed by Nazi Germany.

Admiralty perceptions of Nazi Germany were given a relatively
early, and what was to prove lasting, form in the Anglo-German
Naval Agreement (AGNA) of June 1935.[53] From that date onwards,
in the midst of a growing Whitehall pessimism about the European
military balance, the Admiralty stuck to their conviction that the
German navy was the product of *Gleichberechtigung* (roughly, equality
of status) and a desire to rule not Britannia, but the Baltic. Why did
the Admiralty accept a German fleet strength of the magnitude of 35
per cent, the proportion allowed by AGNA, without any show of
anxiety? Winston Churchill was, after all, right to think that 'what
had in fact been done was to authorise Germany to build up to her
utmost capacity for five or six years to come'.[54] The answer lies partly
in the contemporary state of naval intelligence and the deductions
which the Admiralty had already drawn about the future role of the
German navy.

Intelligence shortcomings concerning both the capital ship position and submarine construction made AGNA attractive.[55] It
promised greatly to simplify the tasks of information-gathering and
analysis. This was particularly so, in that it was assumed that
Germany would build a 'normal fleet' within the 35 per cent ratio: a
fleet consisting of roughly the same proportions and types of ships
that the Royal Navy contained.[56] On its own, of course, the intelligence
factor was not enough to propel the Admiralty into a naval agreement
with the Germans. The Admiralty regarded it as a panacea for a much

wider range of difficulties, and could see it in this light because they had accepted the repeated assertions of Admiral Raeder and his staff that the German navy would never again be built as a threat to the British. The Tirpitz concept of a 'risk fleet' was, the British were assured, renounced forever.[57] Plans division came to the conclusion that the German navy was designed for action in the Baltic Sea, to secure communications in support of land operations eastwards – the *Drang nach Osten*.[58] With such a reassuring strategic picture, the Admiralty could look to the political benefits of AGNA: it would prevent a naval arms race in the European theatre; provide support for the navy's case that the needs of imperial defence (especially in the Far East) should take precedence; and offer a simple basis of calculation for the desired two-power naval standard.[59]

Until it was denounced by the Germans in April 1939, AGNA was consistently defended by the Admiralty as the key to Anglo-German relations.[60] Such a partisan degree of commitment, by no means shared in Berlin, did have its costs. The naval intelligence effort slackened as even greater reliance was placed on official German pronouncements. The result was that, in the words of the Director of Naval Intelligence, the Admiralty was 'hoodwinked' concerning the size of the major German capital ships – the battlecruisers *Gneisenau* and *Scharnhorst* and the battleships *Bismarck* and *Tirpitz*.[61] Little attempt was made, at least before Admiral Godfrey took over as DNI in January 1939, to broaden the intelligence sources available and the possibilities of naval sigint (signals intelligence) went unexplored.[62] Under the leadership of Admiral Chatfield, the Chief of the Naval Staff from 1933–8, the navy developed its own vision of 'limited liability' in Europe. Their 'private' foreign policy was based on the twin assumptions that Germany was not antagonistic towards Great Britain and that the Nazi regime could not be prevented from carrying out an expansion to the East.[63]

Grave intelligence and foreign policy misjudgements were matched by an equally serious misreading of the threat which the German navy might prove to British commerce in a future war. The possession of Asdic and the modest size of pre-war German submarine construction helped to blunt anxieties about a U-boat menace. Ignorance of the fact that German warships were being built in considerable excess of their announced tonnage and armament blended together with the long-running assumption that the German navy's primary mission was operations in the Baltic Sea. Because of these factors, prior to 1939, studies of Anglo-German naval conflict had an academic character. The NID's German navy handbook, completed in August 1936 and unrevised before the outbreak of war, provides a good example.[64] Of the three offensive strategies sketched out for the German navy, the NID thought unrestricted submarine warfare to be the least likely and raids by armed merchant cruisers relatively harmless. This left the option of commerce warfare undertaken by 'composite naval forces', whose striking power was to be provided by Germany's three pocket battleships. The idea was by no means without merit, but it was not tuned to German strategic thought and did not result in any serious attention, on the British side, to the problems of convoy defence.[65]

The Admiralty had neither the staff nor the resources to make any consistent study of German naval publications. Not until 1939 did they investigate Admiral Wegener's *Seestrategie des Weltkriegs* (1929), and then only at the prompting of the Foreign Office. Wegener's book was a highly influential critique of Tirpitz's First World War strategy and the Foreign Office had heard it referred to as Hitler's 'naval bible'. Wegener argued that the German fleet should have pursued a more aggressive trade war against the Allies from the outset and should have occupied Denmark in order to challenge the British control of the vital North Sea.[66] The review of *Seestrategie*, eventually produced by the British naval attaché in Berlin, Captain Troubridge, became the centrepiece for a remarkably prescient account of Germany's inclination towards a strategic naval offensive. Troubridge pointed to the high radius of action of German capital ships and cruisers, the concentration of manoeuvres in the Kattegat and Norwegian coast areas, and the navy's activity off the coast of Spain, as indications that the German navy realised that a sea war against Great Britain could only be won in the Atlantic. One of Troubridge's observations, in the context of a potential German naval offensive, was especially prophetic. He wrote: 'The capture of Bergen and Trondheim would not prove of insuperable difficulty and would make our task harder. The possibility of such operations to improve the "geographic position" should not be overlooked.'[67] Admiral Godfrey, the DNI, minuted his agreement: 'reports of German intentions to seize Skagen and Lacso and the Norwegian fears concerning Stavanger aerodrome give colour to the views expressed'.[68] These ideas were formulated only three months before the outbreak of war and had little chance to take root. Nevertheless, they were part of the painful adjustment of its thinking that the Admiralty had to carry out in 1939 after the German denunciation of AGNA. Germany now had to be regarded as a potential naval enemy, added to the ranks of Japan and Italy. A crop of war scares underlined the fact. These included more or less fantastic stories of a surprise attack on the fleet in harbour, the maritime bush-whacking of the king on his way to Canada, the German spring cruise of 1939 as a cover for war dispositions in the Atlantic, and above all the 'submarine bogey' – the reporting of a shoal of U-boats on patrol in the South Atlantic.[69] After four years of fervent belief in the guarantee of peace provided by AGNA, the Admiralty could do little in the remaining months of peace, beyond taking various *ad hoc* measures to improve their readiness.

The isolation of the NID from the other services, which was reinforced not only by differing attitudes but by the lack of any effective bureaucratic machinery to link the intelligence departments together, helped to sustain the Admiralty in their egocentric vision of peaceful relations between Britain and Germany. Not until 1939 arrived was the Admiralty forced to draw the conclusion that, even though the German navy was by no means ready, a conflict between the two powers was nonetheless likely. The realisation came late; some three years after the RAF and the army had been forced to make their own reappraisals of the German threat. Whether these years could have been better used by the Royal Navy in their material preparations is a matter for speculation. Financial pressure from the Treasury and industrial limitations on production would have been constant factors, in any case.[70] But naval intelligence would certainly have benefited enormously from an earlier injection of realism about the German threat.

IV THE INDUSTRIAL INTELLIGENCE CENTRE

Alongside the three service intelligence departments a fourth, civilian body existed whose task was to monitor German economic preparations for war. Established in March 1931, the IIC (Industrial Intelligence Centre) was made the responsibility of an officer on loan from the Secret Service, Major Desmond Morton. The activities of Morton's Centre were very broadly defined to include the study of the vulnerability of foreign countries' industries to land and air attack, the potential expansion of munitions industries in war and the possibility of uncovering war preparations through 'the continuous study of imports of raw materials, machinery etc.'[71] Russia was selected as the first test case for the IIC and remained so until at least 1934. But even before the arrival of a Nazi government, the IIC had begun to report on German industrial activities and concentrated more and more upon this country after 1934.

Although Germany became the focus, the IIC did not report regularly on the German economic system.[72] There were several reasons for this. One was the strength of the IIC's own preconceptions. They assumed from the beginning of their study that the German economy was being designed for total war. As a result, they failed to place any question marks beside the goals of German rearmament in the industrial sphere. There was thus no apparent need to report on the nature of the economy. Priorities, bureaucratic situations and resources also had an effect. The mainstream of the IIC's work was a detailed analysis of the German arms industry and the raw materials position. Study of the economic system was meant to provide only a backdrop for this work. Bureaucratic structures mitigated against more general reporting by the IIC. Although it had a centralised intelligence function – to report on all aspects of economic rearmament – the IIC had to respect the traditional jurisdictional boundaries between Whitehall departments.[73] It acted as a full partner with the service departments in the preparation of reports, but these were on the individual industrial positions of the three branches of the German armed forces. The result was a piecemeal and specialised knowledge. The IIC was a unique and modern-looking agency, but it cannot be said that the government used it very intelligently. Lastly, it should be noted that even had there been a greater demand for an overall picture of the Nazi economy, the task would have been a difficult one and could not have been met, on any regular basis, by the IIC's existing peacetime staff.[74]

The two papers which the IIC did manage to compose during the 1930s on the German economic system reveal the consistency of the Centre's image of the Nazi economy. This image influenced every aspect of their more specialised reporting on German rearmament. The first, written in March 1934, constituted a warning about German industrial potential; while the second, circulated four years later in May 1938, involved a retrospective analysis of German achievements.[75]

The March 1934 paper, written in conjunction with the Air

Ministry, provided the IIC with its first opportunity to report directly to the Committee of Imperial Defence. The picture of the Nazi regime's war economy drawn by the IIC in March 1934 had three key elements: enormous potential industrial capacity; carefully laid plans for industrial mobilisation; and a centralised structure permitting a large degree of government control.[76]

During the four years which elapsed between their March 1934 and May 1938 papers, the IIC's totalitarian economic image of Nazi Germany found widespread acceptance – especially after the inauguration of the Four-Year Plan in 1936. The strongest overall proof, as far as the IIC was concerned, for the correctness of their view, was the 'incredible rapidity' of German rearmament.[77] The single piece of evidence which seems to have excited the IIC most was a semi-official publication entitled *Industrielle Mobilmachung*, a copy of which came into their possession in May 1937. *Industrielle Mobilmachung* was full of telling statements, as for example: 'the country which can develop its striking power the quicker, easily seizes the initiative . . . the work of preparation to that end is correspondingly essential in peacetime'.[78] The German text perfectly matched the IIC's vision of the primacy of economic preparations for war. And if such was the theory, the IIC expected that the practice must follow, given the centralised power and totalitarian dogma of the Nazi state.

Morton's IIC was the originator of an intelligence message which, by its nature, was propaganda for recognition of the importance of industrial mobilisation and, implicitly, for the necessity of greater British preparations, in order to match the German strength. A chance occurred for the IIC to drive home its message to the government in early 1938. The Inskip defence review, which suggested that British rearmament had to be conducted within fixed financial limits in order to preserve economic resources for a long war, had been circulated and was proving controversial.[79] The Foreign Office were preparing to align themselves with the service departments and Chiefs of Staff to prevent any cutbacks to the defence programmes. Seeking ammunition for a potential battle with Inskip and the Treasury, the Foreign Office approached the IIC for a paper outlining the reasons why Germany seemed able to follow a massive rearmament programme and export arms as well.[80] The IIC's answer was to take the form of the most extensive analysis of the German system of arms production circulated during the 1930s.

The IIC paper, begun in January, was printed for the Committee of

Imperial Defence in early May 1938.[81] Their analysis concentrated on two features to explain German rearmament successes: full-scale planning before rearmament commenced; and the exercise of the powers of a totalitarian state. Both features had been highlighted in the March 1934 essay and were now given a retrospective treatment covering the period 1933–8. A relatively detailed history of German industrial planning was provided, to illustrate the IIC's claim that the arms output achieved by the Hitler regime was based on preparations made during the Weimar era – they 'would not have been possible without extensive plans for mobilisation of industry already in existence'. Once rearmament was under way, the powers exercised by a totalitarian state were 'chiefly responsible' for Germany's ability to find rapid solutions to the problems of labour, raw materials and finance connected with a great rearmament effort. The coercion of labour by the state was complemented by what the IIC termed the 'remarkable progress in techniques of armament manufacture' achieved by the Germans. In the area of finance, the Germans had managed to overcome their foreign exchange problem through the use of clearing arrangements and had paid for rearmament at home by extensive and unorthodox borrowing. The raw materials situation was considered by the IIC the most intractable problem facing the Germans and therefore illustrated the workings of the Nazi system with the greatest clarity. The Nazi regime was credited with having introduced five measures: (1) strict rationing of the supply of raw materials; (2) the sacrifice of the home market for consumer goods; (3) the careful collection of waste and scrap; (4) intensive development of domestic sources of raw materials and substitutes; and (5) the control of foreign credit and its utilisation in the best interests of import requirements of the rearmament plan. These measures were characterised as 'normally associated with a state in war'. None of them could operate without the 'rigid, centralised, government control of everything which forms the foundation of the totalitarian state'. To block any inferences being drawn about popular dissent, the IIC commented that the Nazis had correctly appraised the psychology of their countrymen and that the system was founded on the 'broad, general consent of the nation'.

The Foreign Office, while finding Morton's paper 'instructive', clearly had difficulty in drawing lessons from it.[82] Lord Halifax, the Secretary of State for Foreign Affairs, did raise the matter at a cabinet meeting in May 1938.[83] On the practical question of what measures might be taken in imitation of Nazi Germany to speed up British rearmament, ministers had few ideas. The more abstract question of whether the economic systems of the two countries were at all comparable provoked a livelier discussion. The most significant intervention came from the Prime Minister himself, who told his colleagues that he had 'examined this document with some care'. Chamberlain rejected the idea that the British state could intervene in the economy in the way that the Nazi state had done. There could be no imitation of the 'tremendous measures' for control over labour; of the 'elaborate measures' for control of raw materials; or of the 'drastic technical devices and strategems in the region of finance'.[84] The language applied to all three 'totalitarian' solutions to rearmament was hyperbolic and suggestive. The implication of the Prime Minister's statement was clear – Britain was significantly behind Germany in rearmament, could not imitate the Nazi system and, therefore, could not hope to rival the German rearmament effort. Totalitarianism, in an economic perspective, was seen as an efficient means to an end – the end being industrial mobilisation for total war purposes. Democratic regimes, by contrast, possessed no comparable means to this end. The Chancellor of the Exchequer, Sir John Simon, put the matter more bluntly to the Committee of Imperial Defence. Industrial mobilisation, as the Germans practised it in peacetime, was possible only with a Hitler. Britain could adopt such practices only 'if we had a "Hitler" and a population prepared to accept a "Hitler" '.[85]

The IIC's attempt to make the government aware of the dangers of the German lead in industrial mobilisation ended in the establishment of an ideologically-oriented and exaggerated dichotomy between the conditions of rearmament in Germany and in Britain. To a certain extent the IIC became a victim of its own reporting. Morton's bureau adopted a very cautious attitude to reports of German economic shortcomings and closed their minds to alternative explanations of the German economy's performance (which were, in any case, almost non-existent).[86] One criticism offered by the Berlin embassy to an IIC paper on German industrial mobilisation is illuminating: 'We would suggest that the report shows rather too much tendency to attribute to Germany in every respect the sort of Machiavellian super-intelligence which is easier to imagine than to create'.[87]

While the IIC did ultimately over-rate the success of the German drive towards total war readiness, what they did see from the beginning of their study of the German economic system was that the country possessed great industrial potential and that this potential would be utilised for the creation of a formidable military machine.[88] In this sense, the 'threat perception' of the IIC was both prescient and accurate. But the distortions built into the IIC picture did help to distort the British foreign policy response. Exaggeration of the German rearmament achievement, a feature of intelligence reporting for most of the 1930s, was an important element in the pursuit of appeasement. Equally, the first signs that the arms race gap was being closed, during 1939, helped to foster that unreal atmosphere of confidence which was the background to the fateful British guarantees to the states of Central and Eastern Europe.[89]

V THE CHIEFS OF STAFF – A CONCLUSION

The images of Nazi Germany entertained by the various branches of British intelligence were never static and remained, before 1939, as independent as those bureaucratic structures which created them. Each intelligence directorate evolved its own specialised vision of German power, modified by events relevant only to that part of the German military machine under study. This diversity of response was a product, in part, of the traditional boundaries of authority inside Whitehall, which helped to keep intelligence reporting uncoordinated, and of a myopic approach to their subjects taken by the service departments and the IIC. Diversity was also a reflection of the difficulties and fears created for Great Britain by the advent of a militaristic German regime. Worst case assumptions and obsessions were never far from the surface. The Air Ministry (after 1936) concentrated on the problem of a German knock-out blow, without any serious consideration of the practicality, from the German point of view, of such an offensive. The War Office experienced the shock effect of German army expansion, which greatly exceeded their predictions, in such a way as to overestimate its war readiness, equipment and training standards during the crises of 1938. The IIC, impressed by the acceleration of arms production achieved by the Nazi regime, became even more convinced about the effectiveness of totalitarian measures of rearmament. The Admiralty's treatment remained the exception to this grim picture of German power, understandably in so far as the German navy was not sufficiently strong to challenge the Royal Navy single-handedly. Instead, the Admiralty regarded the German threat as a distraction and sought to keep some part of Britain's defence policy focused on the problems of imperial communications and the situation in the Far East.

The most successful attempt made to give these disparate images some coherence in an overall picture of the German threat occurred in the Chiefs of Staff's 'Strategical Appreciation' of February 1939. This paper was the fourth and last in a pre-war series of appreciations of a possible Anglo-German war drafted by the Joint Planning Committee (JPC).[90] Earlier studies had either been censored or gone uncirculated, largely because of their unpromising picture of the military balance or the European political situation.[91] The February 1939 JPC draft was the only one to win full acceptance from the Chiefs of Staff and to be given a wide circulation through the ministries and Service echelons. This change in fortune was the result of the Joint Planners more robust depiction of the European balance of power. The chief impression given by the 1939 Strategical Appreciation, in comparison with its predecessors, was that Britain's military position was beginning to offer a greater degree of security and some confidence as to the future. A dramatic shift of perspective, rather than any real improvement in the numerical ratio of forces, was at work. While the actual balance of military forces had not changed in Britain's favour (and was in some cases worsening), the COS now gave greater emphasis to such comparative factors as air defence, popular morale and 'latent' economic strength. The expansion of the radar chain, increase in anti-aircraft armaments, and the delivery of modern fighter aircraft into home squadrons had greatly improved Britain's capability to meet a knock-out blow. The great gap between British and German aircraft production appeared to have been eliminated. Intelligence reports from the Munich crisis, on the indifference of the German population to the Czech issue, were taken to mean that Hitler's hold over the populace might be on the wane. At the same time, a new confidence was expressed in British solidarity and public resolve, even under the imagined conditions of all-out aerial bombardment. Lastly, the 'long war' hypothesis was asserted. The British economy could survive a lengthy military contest, better able to tap emergency resources than its German counterpart, which was already mobilised and would be subjected to the rigours of an economic blockade.[92]

The impact of the Chiefs of Staff paper on the cabinet was a matter of timing. Sent to the Committee of Imperial Defence in late February, the month of the 'curious lull' in diplomatic tensions, the Strategical Appreciation reinforced a mood in government circles of confidence in the European situation.[93] However, some signs already existed that the COS paper was an inaccurate guide to a fast-changing situation. One of the main messages of the COS study was that British defences would improve dramatically by 1940 and that war could be postponed with advantage. Even as early as February 1939 it was not clear, given the series of war scares that had already occurred, that such a postponement would be possible. Moreover, the kind of war which the COS described, with Germany engaged only in the West, was soon to be called into question by the guarantees which Britain gave to Poland, Roumania and Greece.

That forcing Hitler to face a war on two fronts, the strategic rationale behind the guarantees, might not be enough to deter the German dictator or even to ensure an Allied victory, was made all too apparent in the course of the Allied staff talks during the summer of 1939.[94] The most brutal blow to such illusions came with the announcement of the Nazi–Soviet pact in August 1939. Yet scarcely any military pressure was put on the government either to strengthen its Eastern commitments or to withdraw from them at any time after March 1939.[95] Instead, military optimism became tempered by a fatalism about the approach of war. This sense was induced by the repetitious pattern of events in 1939 – German action over Poland inevitably recalled the Czech crisis – as well as by the nervous strain imposed on all Whitehall departments by the almost continuous stream of war scares. In some circles, there was even a sense of relief when war broke out. Group Captain Slessor, the Air Ministry representative on the Joint Planning Committee, recalled: 'many dreary months were to pass before we were severely attacked; but at least that awful period of indecision and uncertainty was over'.[96] By September 1939 the Chiefs of Staff were prepared to confront Nazi Germany, the power which had been at the heart of their strategic anxieties since 1934. From the moment of their appraisal of the February 1939 'Strategical Appreciation', they possessed a re-arranged and cohesive military image of that power to accord with this new resolution.

5. Flashes of Intelligence: The Foreign Office, The SIS and Security Before the Second World War

DAVID DILKS

> No mask like open truth to cover lies
> As to go naked is the best disguise
> > Congreve, *The Double Dealer*

> As for his secret *Spials*, which he did employ both at home and abroad, by them to discover what *Practices* and Conspiracies were against him, surely his *Case* required it: He had such *Moles* perpetually working and casting to undermine him. Neither can it be reprehended. For if *Spials* be lawful against lawful *Enemies*, much more against *Conspirators* and *Traytors*.
> > Francis Bacon, *The History of the Reign of Henry VII*

> With the Russians stealthily and cunningly pulling the strings behind the scenes to get us involved in war with Germany (our Secret Service doesn't spend all its time looking out of the window). . . .
> > Neville Chamberlain to his sister, 20 March 1938

I

IF the unveiling of hitherto secret material about British penetration of the enemy's communications during the Second World War finds no precise parallel in the documents released for the period between the wars, the Public Record Office nevertheless offers a good deal of material about the 'intelligence' of those days. Admittedly, the records of the intelligence services themselves (a loose but convenient term to cover a number of agencies which gathered material in or about foreign countries, or carried out covert operations there, or resisted attempts to penetrate British secrets) are still withheld, as are the papers of committees which dealt with the intelligence services. Probably the pre-war archives of the intelligence services are but patchily preserved, though assurances have recently been given[1] that such material is not wilfully destroyed, and will be kept in case its release ever becomes possible. But since the various services had to provide the fruits of their work to departments of state, and the Foreign Office controlled, under the direction of the Permanent Under-Secretary, the Secret Intelligence Service, material relating to SIS had occasionally to be incorporated in the records of that Office.

Peculiar difficulties attend the interpretation of such material. While we have no means of knowing how much of it has been extracted from particular files, or what proportion of files has been withheld altogether, we can sometimes confirm that particular papers, sufficiently secret to be entered 'green' with restricted circulation inside the Office, are not available in the PRO; their former existence can be established because the Office kept for its own purposes a separate 'green index', and it seems clear that some of them have been destroyed. Nor, needless to say, is that the end of the story. There must have been many occasions when it was quicker or safer to transact such business by word of mouth. Ministers vary widely in their receptivity to 'intelligence' and Secretaries of State perhaps liked to possess the fruits of intelligence operations without enquiring too precisely how those materials had been gained; for they had to deal constantly with envoys whose secrets the British were trying to penetrate, or whose servants they were trying to suborn, and whose own governments were doing the same thing against the British. Care was taken not to give away tricks on the files. For example, there was a standing instruction that the Government Code and Cypher School should not be mentioned.

Individual officers of SIS and other services were seldom named on Foreign Office papers. Occasionally, those who dealt with arcane subjects in 'Room 8' or 'Room 14', or the Communications Department of the Foreign Office itself, can be identified; but in all these instances common sense suggests that there will have been many similar instances not recorded in released papers.

We do not know how frequently the head of SIS, or some other officer of that Service, saw the Foreign Secretary or the Prime Minister, or how much material derived from secret sources was placed before ministers; nor can we tell whether it was heavily filtered and interpreted by intelligence officers or by the Foreign Office itself. However, a comparison of the sources in the PRO with the published material does at least enable an informed guess; the probability on the present evidence is that 'C', as successive chiefs of SIS were known, saw ministers very rarely, but the Permanent Under-Secretary at the Foreign Office commonly, especially in times of crisis. The security service operating within Britain, MI5 and its off-shoots, also had direct connections to the Foreign Office, and would sometimes provide timely intelligence about subjects in which, on the face of it, SIS had a greater interest: when the Permanent Under-Secretary received firm but belated intelligence of the impending German stroke against the remnant of Czechoslovakia in the second week of March 1939, it came in the first instance from MI5.[2] The Private Secretary to the Permanent Under-Secretary, Mr Clifford Norton in Sir Robert Vansittart's time, and then Mr Gladwyn Jebb (later Lord Gladwyn) for the first part of Sir Alexander Cadogan's tenure, acted as the point of liaison between the Permanent Under-Secretary, SIS and other parts of the official machine. Both Vansittart and Cadogan paid serious attention to intelligence. Of the two, Vansittart wrote and spoke the more about the subject; but he wrote and spoke more about everything.

Foreign Office papers do not normally refer to intercepts or decrypts; occasionally, however, some such phrase as 'our best source' or 'most secret and reliable indications' was employed in telegrams. To some missions, SIS reports were sent directly; to most of the main posts which had an SIS man under diplomatic cover on the staff, such documents were not sent because the information could be passed directly to the British ambassador or Minister. All the same, it is hard to imagine that the security of SIS's own papers, as distinct from Foreign Office papers containing material derived from SIS, was wholly preserved during the 1930s. In the early part of that decade, SIS reports were sent in original from the Foreign Office to Berlin, with instructions that they should 'only be seen by responsible members of the staff and should not be handled by archivists etc.', be kept out of embassy's files, and burnt after perusal. A letter from SIS to Clifford Norton remarked in 1931, 'I see no reason why a limit should be set on what is sent out, *provided* its absolutely safe handling at the other end is ensured'. Special arrangements obtained in the Foreign Office whereby such SIS reports were preserved, but did not become part of 'the archive'[3] and therefore do not appear in the Public Record Office. It may be added that although a few sensitive items may have crept into the public domain by accident, the majority have been deliberately released; in many cases, names or references have been deleted.

Given the need to protect sources, whether in the form of the well-placed agent or intercepted communications, much valuable material could either not be used at all in the execution of policy, or only in an oblique way. The information reaching the Service Departments about German rearmament in 1933 provides a particularly telling example of the problem. 'All these departments' says a memorandum of July, 'were insistent upon the impossibility of our using their secret information, even in the most disguised form, in any communication which we may make to the German Government. The War Office were particularly strong on this point and it was for this reason that it was decided, for the present at any rate, to confine our representations to the aviation issue, where we can rely on official statements.' 'Of course we cd. never use our secret stuff' minuted Vansittart. 'We have ourselves taken that line all along.'[4] In well-attested instances, however, other powers made free use of material gained by clandestine means. Apart from the exploitation by Italy of such sources, which was done in a way which certainly put those sources at risk, the German government gave Chamberlain texts of intercepted telephone conversations to prove the ill-faith of the Czechs during the negotiations of September 1938; and on 31 August 1939, Goering did not hesitate to show intercepted Polish messages to the Swedish intermediary Dahlerus, for transmission to the British ambassador in Berlin, Sir Nevile Henderson; who had himself on at least one occasion, and apparently without rousing German suspicions, arranged for the transmission of an important message in a cypher which he knew the Germans could read. The ambassador in Rome, Sir Percy Loraine, used the same tactic in August 1939. As Cadogan remarked, it seemed unlikely to deceive the astute Italians; but Loraine may have calculated that they would believe a confiden-

tial telegram to have been sent by mistake in a less than secure cypher.
At all events, he reported Count Ciano as markedly more cordial after
this ruse had been employed.[5]

From time to time the files also bear notes about the security of the
Foreign Office and SIS papers: for example, the loss of confidential
documents loaned to those attending the Imperial Conference of
1930, which produced a severe minute from the new Permanent
Under-Secretary, Vansittart, about 'these slipshod, irresponsible –
and therefore untrustworthy – representatives of the Dominions',
whose actions had apparently exposed the British cyphers to serious
risk;[6] and an incautious act by the British Minister in Tehran, who
showed a Persian politician the actual text of a document obtained
from Moscow, and provoked a polite protest from SIS asking that in
future permission should be sought before any such action was taken.
The Foreign Office minute on this paper refers to the large amount of
secret information regularly forwarded to Tehran, adding 'We cannot
be too careful about the Russian documents'.[7] Occasionally, the
reverse happened: a British diplomat or service attaché abroad would
be shown the text of a telegram and, if he had a particularly retentive
memory, might be able to reconstruct sufficient of the document to
allow the other power's cypher to be broken.[8] In other instances of
leakage, it seemed more than likely that the fault lay with members of
the cabinet, to whom Foreign Office despatches and telegrams
circulated each day; as the old saying is, a cask usually leaks from the
top.

II

With these limitations in mind, let us turn to three sets of documents
released in the British archives which bear upon connected aspects of
intelligence: the security of documents (or rather, the lack of it) in the
British embassy in Rome, the Legation to the Holy See, the embassy
in Berlin and the Foreign Office itself; the recommendations for
British policy tendered by SIS in the third week of September 1938,
just before Chamberlain's second visit to Hitler; and the assessment
within the Foreign Office of machinery for the handling and collation
of intelligence as war drew near in 1939. Taken together, these papers
raise issues about 'intelligence' in several senses; espionage and
counter-espionage, the balancing of material obtained from secret

sources against that from open sources, the use of such material as a basis for policy, and, to take the word in its strict sense, the understanding of the issues as distinct from the acquisition of facts.

In *The Mist Procession*, Vansittart remarks that he discovered Mussolini to be obtaining British documents and, suspecting a leak in the Foreign Office, '– set about spy-hunting and drew blank. Then he must be getting the goods from our Embassy in Rome'.[9] (We may note in passing that these are not simple alternatives; the Italians might be getting British secret papers neither by leakage nor by theft, but by interception and decyphering.) The ambassador dismissed the idea of leakage in the embassy, we are further told, but Vansittart 'sent out the head of our Secret Service who soon got ample confirmation'. Still the ambassador could not believe Italian members of his staff guilty of treachery until, 'returning from a ball, he locked his wife's tiara in an official box, found empty next morning'. To Italy's knowledge of British weakness and indecision Vansittart attributed the failure to reach a compromise over the Abyssinian crisis in 1935. The impression left by this account, then, is that although serious damage was done, the leakage was stopped after investigation.

Unhappily, this proves to be a good deal less than the truth. Certainly Mussolini was obtaining a great deal of secret British material in 1935.[10] Indeed, Professor Toscano, who had access to the documents in original, ascribed a good part of Italian policy to the effect upon the Duce of the constant flow of British communications. Copies of the intercepts are presumably preserved in the Italian archives, for Toscano describes how Mussolini wrote marginal comments upon them; scanning the messages between London and units of the Mediterranean fleet in 1935, he knew of the acute shortages of anti-aircraft ammunition, which doubtless brought as much comfort to him as anxiety to British ministers. It is fair to add that the British were in their turn reading a good deal of Italy's traffic; one of the reasons for which Chamberlain as Prime Minister was willing in 1937 and 1938 to pursue the prospect of an agreement with Italy lay in his knowledge from intercepted Italian communications of the fact that most of the information given by Italy about troop movements in Libya and naval dispositions in the Mediterranean was broadly true.[11]

The documents in the Public Record Office make it almost certain that Vansittart's memory played him false in several important respects. It may be that the 'head of our Secret Service' made an investigation in 1935; if so, it proved ineffective, for a full-scale enquiry was carried out, as we shall see, in 1937. The report[12] shows that in January a necklace vanished from a locked red box in the ambassador's quarters; and it seems somehow improbable that Lady Drummond's stock of jewellery should have been depleted twice in this fashion. This report, and other papers from Foreign Office archives, reveal a state of affairs which would be dismissed as incredible were it not so painstakingly recorded. After the loss of the necklace, local enquiry had produced no result; and the only agreed deduction from the facts, as the investigator expressed it, 'was to the effect that a "inside" agent, probably carrying out a regular routine in searching the Ambassador's Red Box for papers, had come upon the necklace and was unable to resist temptation.'

The calm tone of the reference to a routine searching of the box, and the statement elsewhere in the document that the writer had been concerned with investigations into leakages from the embassy in Rome and other government offices for a decade are not the least surprising parts of this affair. It becomes, alas, clear – as Robert Cecil's article in this book demonstrates in greater detail – that many senior members of the diplomatic service took 'security' far too casually. We do not know by what means, or when, Vansittart learned that Mussolini was receiving secret British documents; but an event of 1936, coupled with what we now learn to be a long history of leakage from the embassy, should have stimulated the most thorough search and reform.

In the early stages of the Abyssinian crisis, a committee of officials under Sir John Maffey of the Colonial Office had looked at Britain's material interests in Abyssinia and the adjacent territories, concluding that they were not great enough to warrant British opposition to an Italian conquest. The report was completed in the third week of June 1935 and submitted to the new Foreign Secretary, Sir Samuel Hoare. All the copies were printed in, and sent out from, the Foreign Office. In the last week of February 1936, at a moment when the British government was talking of an oil sanction against Italy, the League Council was about to hold a crucial meeting, the Italian forces in Abyssinia were at last making rapid progress, and the French were deeply anxious not to commit themselves against Italy unless Britain would undertake to support them against Germany, Mussolini published the Maffey Report in the *Giornale d'Italia*. Two versions of the paper had been circulated, one with a covering memorandum by

Hoare to his colleagues in the cabinet, and the other without the memorandum, distributed by the Foreign Office to a number of posts abroad; including, needless to say, the embassy at Rome.[13] It is likely that the Italian copy came from the latter batch. If the Italian intelligence service had possessed a copy of Hoare's note to the cabinet, the temptation to publish that also might have proved irresistible; but this is not conclusive, for the Italians might well have followed the same line of reasoning. Moreover, Professor Toscano states explicitly that the rash act of publishing the report indicated Mussolini's resentment at British condemnation of an Italian action, the invasion of Abyssinia, which had been 'taken in part on the strength of the conclusions reached by a commission of British experts'. Without further access to the Italian archives, we cannot assess the truth of this statement; it implies that the Italian government received a copy of the Maffey Report very shortly after it was written. Even then, the hypothesis is doubtful; for Italian preparations for war against Abyssinia were far advanced by the third week of June 1935. The same authority avers that Mussolini's policy throughout the campaign was based largely on interception of British material;[14] and since British policy contained an element of bluff, we must presume that Mussolini was sufficiently well informed to call it at all stages.

When the Italian newspaper published the Maffey Report, to acute British embarrassment, urgent searches began in the Foreign Office and the embassy at Rome. The Office could account for all its copies; while Sir Eric Drummond reported that both copies sent to the embassy remained in the file.[15] In each instance, therefore, the authorities were expecting outright theft of the text; whereas it is more probable that whether the report was obtained in London or in the embassy, a photocopy had been quickly taken before the original was returned to lie innocently in its place. A greater success of the Italian intelligence services in 1936 is so well documented that it need not be recounted here; the securing of Mr Anthony Eden's cabinet paper about 'The German Danger', a paper which, ironically, carried a special warning about secrecy because of leakages of information obtained by the British ambassador in Berlin. This document was used with marked effect by Mussolini, who told a visiting German minister that from Eden's memorandum it was clear that 'England intends to live with Germany only insofar as it will give her time to achieve rearmament', a judgement which had at least a grain of truth;

and by Ciano, who presented the documents to Hitler. However, we have no reason to think that the British authorities were aware of the loss of this memorandum; whereas they knew, and took seriously, the activities of Italian employees of the Marconi company in Egypt, who had access to highly confidential telegrams and had passed copies of some to the Italian authorities in Egypt.[16] Although it was hoped that telegrams to the Residency in Cairo, and to the British army and air force commands, had not been compromised, it is likely enough that they had, as the authorities in the Foreign Office realised. Once again, they were begged not to disclose the source of their information; minutes on the paper rightly record that 'our cyphers are based on the assumption that the cyphered text may be available to foreign govts.', and in spite of the restraint that the Marconi company undertook what the paper delicately calls 'special services' on the British government's behalf, there should have been enough in this file, which reached the Permanent Under-Secretary, to enforce a renewed heartsearching about those activities and areas where Britain and Italy clashed with increasing frequency.

To go back to the events at the embassy in Rome, the Foreign Office's copy of the report[17] does not bear the name of its author; and if this was indeed the enquiry to which Vansittart refers, we must take with a grain of salt his statement about the 'head of our Secret Service'. Indeed, the document, clearly written by an officer of long experience, begins with the startling remark, 'I do not believe that such a thing as an expert in security measures exists, and I make no pretensions to being one . . .'; it is based on an investigation of four or five days in mid-February 1937, undertaken on direct instructions from Vansittart, who asked that the general conclusions should be so framed that as many as possible might be applied to other missions.

The report starts from the proposition that in certain countries – especially Italy, Germany, Russia and Japan – the intelligence services would have established

the most complete arrangements for taking advantage of every opportunity afforded by (a) Venality or openness to pressure on the part of Embassy personnel, (b) Inadequacy of watch and ward arrangements, (c) Occasional or habitual carelessness in the handling of keys, and (d) Imprudent handling of various categories of papers.

It follows that, if an Embassy Staff contains natives of the country or persons belonging to the British community domiciled in the country, the task of the 'enemy' Intelligence will be obviously much simpler and the danger to State secrets much greater. Where the Staff too, habitually carry important keys and papers to their private quarters, the danger will again be increased, since we must assume that all private servants will have been pressed into the service of the Intelligence.

At HM embassy in Rome, where the subordinate staff included many Italians or domiciled British subjects: 'there are ample indications among the instances of leakage since 1925 to suggest that there is at least one traitor among them'. A recently published volume of *Documents on British Foreign Policy* states that a Signor Constantini, employed in the embassy since 1914, had been recruited by the Italian intelligence services, and was able to pass to them documents and cyphers, which were taken away, photographed and returned promptly. These authorities also possessed duplicate keys to the safes.[18] In the report of 1937, we find that the four servants in the Chancery at the embassy had all been locally recruited; among them

S. Constantini is an Italian subject and has been employed in the Chancery for twenty-one years. He might, therefore, have been directly or indirectly responsible for any, or all, of the thefts of papers or valuables which have taken place, or are thought to have taken place, from this Mission. He was, I understand, not quite free of suspicion of being himself concerned in a dishonest transaction for which his brother, then also a Chancery servant, was dismissed a short while ago. Moreover, though the Diplomatic Staff at the time did not connect him with the matter, I am clear in my own mind that the circumstances of the loss of two copies of the 'R' Code from a locked press in the Chancery in 1925 point towards S. Constantini, or his brother, or both, as the culprits.

The investigation showed that the Chancery servants were always there during working hours, and must have had many opportunities for removing papers or taking wax impressions of carelessly left keys. During the embassy's 'dead' periods (from 1 p.m. to 5 p.m., and 8.15 p.m. until 10 a.m. the following morning), opportunity for use of such keys would have been limitless. Even if treachery were discounted, the Chancery servants represented the only system of vigilance against intrusion; and the Italian policeman at the gate should, as the report expressed it, 'be regarded as a menace rather than a safeguard'. The investigator, together with Mr Noble (then Head of Chancery at the embassy in Rome) determined to put matters to the test. Entering by the lodge gates, Mr Noble and his companion were seen by a member of the lodge-keeper's family, who would presumably have challenged them had she not recognised Mr Noble. However, this did not prove that someone else could not have slipped in unobserved, or with permission obtained from the lodge-keeper under a pretext. Arriving in the ambassador's compound, they discovered that the window of Mr Noble's own room, notwithstanding orders to the contrary, stood unlocked and invitingly open. The two accordingly made their way all round the Chancery, with no effort to reduce noise, but were left completely undisturbed for about half an hour before one of the servants came to investigate.

Much of the report, dealing with wooden presses, obsolete filing cabinets and the safeguarding of keys, need not concern us; in general many of the arrangements showed a laxity wholly unsuitable in an 'enemy' country. The combination-lock safe, used as a repository for cyphers, and in future to house most of the keys of the embassy, left nothing to be desired; unhappily, a former First Secretary had thoughtfully made a note of the combination and then left it in a red box, where it was found after his departure. The combination was thereafter changed. The doors of some of the presses could be removed by the simple use of a screwdriver, and the wooden filing cabinet in the room of the Press Officer, described as 'rather inclined to retain for longish periods' confidential papers, could be opened by the removal of six screws. The same key fitted the whole series of red boxes; in the past at least six such keys had normally accompanied their owners to their private residences 'and in the course of time must have been at the disposal of native servants'. Moreover, the ambassador's private quarters were readily accessible to servants. From the revelations of a defector, it was highly probable that leakages had been taking place from the embassy from 1924 at least until 1930, chiefly from the confidential print regularly sent out from the Foreign Office to missions abroad and containing a great deal of current material; the part of the 1937 report which describes the handling of the print indicates little difficulty in removing copies. Although the embassy already acted on the assumption that outside telephone conversations would be tapped, the switchboard was operated by one of the Chancery servants, and internal calls might well be heard by the Italian authorities. None of the staff of the embassy had realised that telephones might have been adjusted to transmit conversations taking place within the building: 'in this connection, it was observed in Rome, in the course of discussing the point, that the cypher Officers were working at a table on which stood a brand-new instrument, which, if activated, would no doubt be conveniently supplying the Italian authorities with code and clear versions of all telegrams reaching and issuing from the Embassy.'

A visit was also paid to the British legation to the Holy See; its premises, entertainingly enough, were located in the quarters of a branch of the Italian military forces. The report tersely remarks: 'They are entirely unoccupied at night, are quite unsuitable for their purpose and afford no protection whatever for the documents they house.' The legation received the confidential print and sections of telegrams from the Foreign Office, and presumably possessed cyphers. Entering the premises at night, the investigator unlocked a red box left on a table; there he found, on top of a pile of documents, the keys of the legation, giving access to all the steel and wooden presses though not to the safe where the cyphers were kept.

A little later in the year, the same investigator visited the embassy in Berlin. Though there is no proven history of leakage from that embassy, his separate report[19] indicates a most serious risk to security; for the porter was a German, the residence of the ambassador was not properly guarded, and for two months of each year, during the ambassador's leave, the British embassy in Berlin lay, outside working hours, at the mercy of the solitary porter.

> This means, in fact, that the Gestapo could, if they were so minded, introduce nightly and for a practically unlimited period each night any number of lock-smiths and experts in safe-breaking, thereby having continuous access to current papers, telegrams and prints without leaving any trace. . . .
>
> There is, of course, no evidence that the porter has admitted Gestapo agents, but, having in view the situation in Berlin and the German mentality, it would be sheer lunacy not to act on the assumption (a) that the porter is in the pay of the Gestapo, (b) that the latter have at their disposal as expert lock-pickers as the criminal world can produce.

The first report recommended strongly that the four Chancery servants in Rome should be replaced at once and the same principle followed in other embassies. So far as Rome was concerned, Sir Robert Vansittart marked against this recommendation 'Essential'. Presumably because the cost would have been a few hundred pounds a year the recommendation was not executed; the leakages continued until the embassy closed on the declaration of war in 1940. Nothing was done, it appears, about the report's clear identification of Signor Constantini as the likely culprit; and this despite the fact that for a quite separate reason, the Foreign Office again reviewed security at the embassy in Rome in that same spring of 1937.

The Italian Foreign Minister, in coversation with a diplomat, said that he knew Prince Paul of Yugoslavia had given Sir Ronald Campbell (British Minister in Belgrade) an assurance that he would conclude only a meaningless agreement with Italy.[20] This came a few weeks after Britain and Italy had themselves negotiated what is infelicitously known as the Gentlemen's Agreement. The Italian government had told Yugoslavia that they wanted an alliance; and if Yugoslavia refused, it would be war to the knife. Sir Ronald Campbell enjoyed close relations with the Prince Regent, who had sought British advice and let the Minister see confidential papers. For obvious reasons, the British wished to support Prince Paul's own desire not to go far in meeting Italian wishes. Campbell was accordingly instructed to lose no opportunity of ensuring that Yugoslavia resisted any Italian attempt to form an exclusive alliance between the two countries. Eden's despatch to Belgrade set forth the British government's information at some length, and dwelt on his lack of confidence in Italian policy.[21] From intimate knowledge of the Italian records, Professor Toscano judged that the collapse of the 'Gentlemen's Agreement' could be traced to Mussolini's desire to spite the British after he had read Eden's instructions to the British missions. While this may well exaggerate the effect of a particular episode – for the despatch of Italian 'volunteers' to Spain probably did more than any other factor to undermine whatever modest chance the Gentlemen's Agreement ever had – it is highly probable that the bitterness of the Italian government's hostility towards Eden, evident from the days when he was identified with the League's condemnation of Italian aggression in Abyssinia, was enhanced by this continual leakage.

At all events, Ciano's incautious remarks could have given the game away. The Prince Regent summoned Campbell and said that he could think of only three explanations: 'either there must have been a leakage from the British Embassy in Rome, or from the Foreign Office in London, or the Italians must have our cypher. I said', Campbell recorded, 'that I could not believe that any of those explanations was the true one and that there must be some other.'[22] He was hardly to know that two of the explanations were certainly true, and quite possibly all three. Plainly, Campbell knew nothing of leakages in Rome going back ten and twelve years; understandably, Prince Paul felt that this failure of security had made matters much more difficult for him. At one point he said with dejection, 'You must not forget that Italy can do Yugoslavia such infinite harm and that you are not in a position to give her any material help.'[23]

The minutes of officials on these papers disclose a state of affairs as startling as that revealed in the report just summarised. Alone of those dealing with the issue in the Foreign Office, Mr Owen O'Malley, later British Minister in Budapest and ambassador to the Polish government in exile, had guessed the truth:

> From all I hear it seems most probable that the Italians have for some considerable time been in a position to read all our correspondence with the Embassy in Rome. If this is indeed the case, we suffer under a fatal disadvantage in the conduct of relations with Italy . . . I should like to reiterate misgivings which I have expressed over and over again about our present system and my conviction that what is wrong cannot possibly be put right unless some high official, preferably from outside the Service, is given a completely free hand to examine from top to bottom the whole system for the safeguarding of information and documents and to make recommendations which I feel convinced will be radical.

Neither Sir Orme Sargent nor Sir Alexander Cadogan, then Deputy Under-Secretary of State, had previously been told of suspected leakages in the Rome embassy.[24] However, Clifford Norton, Private Secretary to the Permanent Under-Secretary, believed that it would not be worthwhile to commission a thorough-going investigation. He had no inkling of the facts, despite the report on the Rome embassy written only a week or two before, for he minuted that the result of the 'scare about Rome' (no doubt the theft of the necklace) had been to make the embassy there 'very much alive to dangers, and consequently since the end of Jan. '37 to minimise the possibility of leakage there'. O'Malley remained entirely unconvinced, observing with force that 'a report of the kind I suggest would make us all feel very uncomfortable'. Security, Norton rejoined, was under constant and anxious review inside the office, and

> naturally the subject of many discussions per annum with the heads of the Secret Service and of M.I.5. If we have any suspicion of insecurity we take steps *ad hoc*.
>
> As regards missions abroad, we believe that our cyphers are safe, and we resist attempts to simplify and thereby weaken the system. We have recently circularised missions abroad on the whole subject of safe custody.
>
> As regards the F.O. and other Govt. offices, there are clearly many risks. We have been defeated by problems of accommodation and finance in attempting to make the F.O. safer. M.I.5 conducted an investigation some years ago and are prepared to set another on foot. But I repeat that it is not the F.O. only, but the range of Govt. buildings, the wide distribution of secret papers, the system of boxes, pouches etc. that is in question. All reasonable precautions are taken: absolute security is impossible.[25]

He noted separately on this file:

> After a thorough consideration of the question whether telegrams in cipher to Rome are 'safe', I can say that all the evidence points to this being the case. I do not think that the Italians can read our ciphers. Moreover I think that the Embassy in Rome are now perhaps more fully aware of the necessity of preventing unauthorised persons from having any opportunity of access to secret papers than any other Mission.[26]

Apart from unspecified action to which another minute refers, that was apparently the end of the matter. Sir Ronald Campbell was asked to reassure Prince Paul. 'Count Ciano's reported remark' the Foreign Office told him,

> need not necessarily be founded on confidential information

> improperly obtained; it would equally well be explained as an
> intelligent guess on the part of Count Ciano in view of the well
> known friendly relations between our two Governments and of the
> close co-operation established between them. . . . In any case we
> have no information here to indicate a leakage anywhere.[27]

Thus the lamentable process continued unchecked. In the autumn of
1937, the Italians through the intercepts found materials which
displeased them about the Under-Secretary for Foreign Affairs in
Austria and complained to the Chancellor, Schuschnigg; on his
insistence, the Under-Secretary was told. He immediately informed
the British, as he thought in secrecy, of what had happened; but this
fact, of course, Ciano quickly picked up from yet another British
document.[28] The King of Greece was later compromised in the same
way; we know that Ciano obtained material, either by theft or use of
British cyphers, from Hong Kong, and exploited it in his relations
with the Japanese;[29] and the unfortunate Prince Paul, whose acuity in
these matters compares most favourably with that of the British in
whom he confided so freely, provided yet further evidence of the
insecurity of British communications, because Ciano early in 1939
had been bold enough to show the Yugoslav Prime Minister photostat
copies of two despatches sent by Campbell to the Foreign Office.
Prince Paul rightly insisted that the most secret messages should
wherever possible go from the British legation by letter, not by
telegram. He beseeched Campbell to observe the utmost discretion.

   'If it got round to the Italians that he was keeping you informed of
everything they are doing here,' Campbell told Halifax, 'his position
. . . would become untenable and (I have no hesitation in saying) his
life would be in danger.'

   Prince Paul even read out to his trusted confidant the British
Minister the secret letter in which the Yugoslav Prime Minister
(whom Prince Paul was at that moment planning to dismiss)
recounted his private conversations with Ciano; who had said, for
example, that Italy would remain true to the Rome–Berlin axis and
do everything to strengthen the triangle with Japan, which before
long should be in a position to rule the world. Ciano had also
remarked that a revolution against King Zog of Albania was brewing,
so that Italy and Yugoslavia should concert together and replace him
by joint nominee, or partition the country between them. '*Please* try to
ensure' Campbell begged the Permanent Under-Secretary in Lon-

don, 'that P. Paul's name is not mentioned in the Cabinet. It would only be a matter of hours before it got round to Grandi.'[30] In short, Campbell feared that security had been compromised in London; and some time later, Campbell himself apparently told the Prince Regent that an agent had at last been unmasked in the 'archives section' of the Foreign Office, who had a Russian mistress. She had delivered the documents to the Russian embassy, and the ambassador there had handed them to Grandi to make political mischief as he thought fit.[31] At first blush, the story seems to come from the realms of fantasy; but not necessarily so in every particular. The Maffey Report may have been obtained in London and the Cabinet memorandum about Germany which Ciano showed to Hitler with such effect is explicitly stated in *Ciano's Diplomatic Papers* to have been secured in London; since it is more than likely that the materials for that volume, published shortly after the war, were secretly furnished by the Italian Ministry of Foreign Affairs, this observation cannot be ignored.[32] When the Italians presented to the Austrian Chancellor, Schuschnigg, their complaint about the Under-Secretary, whose resignation they demanded, they not only showed the Chancellor boldly what purported to be a photostat copy of a letter from Vansittart to Eden, but said that the 'confidential agent' who had provided it was 'a member of the immediate entourage of the British Foreign Minister'. Ciano soon afterwards requested the absolute discretion of Schuschnigg, 'since it was, after all, an affair of several millions of gold lire. The Italian Government was vitally interested in maintaining this source of information, which gave a running account of the secret files in the Foreign Office in London.'[33]

Though we may rule out the idea that a member of Eden's immediate entourage was supplying the Italians with documents, we need not dismiss the notion of an agent in London; and while we may readily concede that Count Ciano did not solace his limited leisure with the study of Congreve, a clever man might have surmised that to speak about a source in London would make it more rather than less secure, because an investigator would conclude that the real source was being concealed. This is exactly what the British did think, as the Minister of State at the Foreign Office announced in 1947; the breach of security at Rome, which Hector McNeil did not exaggerate in terming 'unfortunate and inexcusable', had been investigated in 1944, with the entry of the allied armies into Rome. The Italian servant had been apprehended after the war and admitted his guilt;

he had been paid considerable sums of money by the Italian authorities. Since Signor Constantini (whom Hector McNeil did not name) was an Italian national, the British had no power to proceed against him; but 'I have no doubt that our language was not too tender'.[34]

As for the suggestion of collaboration between the intelligence services of Italy and Soviet Russia, we cannot scorn that either; it seems scarcely likely that in a matter of such seriousness the Russian intelligence services would act in such a way without the clearest authority, and we know that whatever may have transpired in London, the material purloined from the embassy in Rome was being shown simultaneously to the Italian authorities and to the Soviet embassy there through the Counsellor of the embassy, Helfand. There, for the moment at least, this tangled web must be left. The comparisons with later events in the British embassy at Ankara, and the celebrated Cicero, hardly need to be pointed up here. Mischievous rumour has it that the material for McNeil's parliamentary answer of 1947, scouting the possibility of an Italian agent in the Foreign Office, was collated by Guy Burgess.

III

Let us now consider a document, rare among those released, in which SIS tendered advice about high policy. We must suppose that this paper, pointedly headed 'What should we do?'[36] and dated 18 September 1938, was either written or approved by 'C' himself, then Admiral Sinclair. It described German aims, 'so far as they appear to have been formulated up to now' as the establishment of a general paramountcy or supremacy in Europe; the obtaining of a free hand in central and south-eastern Europe and the acknowledgement by the British of German supremacy in this area at least; a bargain with the British on these lines, in return for which 'at any rate to start with' Germany would recognise Britain's supremacy overseas; the recovery of colonies or equivalent territory abroad. Germany's objectives in Europe were said by SIS to include the absorption of at least the Sudeten areas of Czechoslovakia and, sooner or later, 'probably, the acquisition of the whole of Bohemia, it being regarded as an economic entity,' the remainder of Czechoslovakia being 'disintegrated' or converted into a state on the Swiss model, ostensibly neutral but actually under German influence; the establishment of Germany's political and economic hegemony over vassal states in the whole of central and south-eastern Europe; and extension of this principle to Belgium, Holland, the Baltic and other northern states. Further, Germany would aim to recover eventually the lost territory on the eastern or northern frontiers, and to bring about the downfall of the Soviet regime. German aims in respect of Russia fluctuated; it had latterly been maintained that a German empire could not be built up in Russia and that after the disintegration of the Soviet system, autonomous states would emerge, some or most of which Germany would exploit. However, a solution of the Czech issue might bring more concrete ideas. Germany was also said to seek economic advantages in Spain, penetration of the Middle East and the increase of British difficulties there, and the fomenting of trouble within the British Empire.

As for German methods, SIS distinguished

First and foremost, *force* or the capacity to use it. Great reliance is placed in the ability to obtain objectives by the mere threat of overwhelming force. There is determination to achieve various aims sooner or later by threat or, if necessary, use of force. Force [is] always behind German diplomacy.

Germany was therefore said to be creating the strongest possible armed services, sufficient to overcome any combination of powers; but the leaders of the German armed forces did not consider that this stage was yet reached. Germany also regarded the axis between Berlin, Rome and Tokyo as the foundation of an impregnable international position. 'The axis partners do not at present come up to expectations.'

For the immediate or near future, SIS recommended peaceful separation from Czechoslovakia, and the joining to Germany of the Sudeten German areas. The Czechs should be made to realise unequivocally that they would stand alone if they refused such a solution, which would merely forestall the inevitable; Czechoslovak security would be in far greater, and permanent, jeopardy from any solution leaving the Sudetens within the state. The process might even be extended so as to leave intact a state which would be literally Czechoslovak, compact, homogeneous and neutralised under international guarantee. The Anglo-Italian agreement of April 1938 should be brought into force as soon as a valid reason could 'even at a stretch' be found, and without giving the impression of any suspicious swallowing of principle on the British part. The Rome–Berlin axis rested on an artificial basis and while the British could and should not openly seek to break it, they could by this step and by recognition of the Italian Empire in Abyssinia make the axis much more artificial. The anonymous author of the paper also recommended a quick decision over Palestine on lines which would go an appreciable way towards satisfying the Arab world.

For the longer future, Britain should unremittingly build up her armaments and maintain them at the highest possible level:

> If we emerge from the crisis without war, we should take the lesson to heart. In all the potential enemy countries, the 'axis' ones, force is the keynote of policy, and our own policy should rest on the capacity to retaliate with adequate force. Platitudinous though it may be, our only chance of preserving peace is to be ready for war on any scale, without relying too much on outside support. In respect of allies, we cannot really trust any foreign country, but at least France is bound to us (as are we to her) by ties of necessity and we should maintain these ties on the firmest possible basis – a permanent defensive alliance. We should also do what we can to ensure that France pursues a policy as regards armaments and military and air efficiency,

on the same principles as Britain herself. It seemed doubtful to SIS whether the British could with confidence be allied with any other European country on terms even approximating to those with France. Though the 'fickle and unscrupulous' Italians would never be a stable factor in any defensive front, 'if such were desirable', Britain could at least work to keep them on the right side, treating them as equals and playing up to their pride. Moreover, she should act as honest broker between France and Italy. Japan was thought a more difficult proposition, but Britain might go some way 'even at the sacrifice of some principle, in recognising – for it has to be recognised – Japan's special position in East Asia'.

In south-eastern Europe, Britain should help Germany's 'ear-marked vassals' to become less dependent upon Germany, and encourage them to look to a strong and united Britain and France, 'short of committing ourselves to supporting them actively'. In Spain, the policy of non-intervention should be sustained, for the outcome remained uncertain. Britain should therefore try not to antagonise either side, and 'keep the way open for good relations with whatever Spain emerges. We cannot spot the winner yet'; she should draw as near as possible to alliance with Turkey; maintain the closest relations with the USA, using the crisis over Germany, and the feelings it had aroused in America, to strengthen those ties. More generally, there should be no attempt at encirclement or a defensive front, which would give Hitler a pretext for saying that hostile combinations were being built up against Germany; 'if he has that pretext it is a rallying cry and, in his eyes, justification for various dynamic and dangerous measures. In sum, Britain should try to ensure that Germany's style is cramped, but with the minimum of provocation.' Even friendship with Germany should be cultivated, though 'without sacrifice of our principles and vital interests'. There should be some adjustment in Germany's favour in respect of colonies, not made dependent on Germany's good behaviour else-where; but the British government should realise that German promises would be worth nothing when she was ready to break them. Britain should not wait until German grievances and claims became, in a regular sequence, critical. International steps should be taken to see what really legitimate grievances Germany had and what surgical operations were necessary to rectify them. If there were genuine cases for self-determination, they should be established and remedied:

It may be argued that this would be giving in to Germany, strengthening Hitler's position and encouraging him to go to extremes. Better, however, that realities be faced and that wrongs, if they do exist, be righted, than leave it to Hitler to do the righting in his own way and time – particularly if, concurrently, we and the French unremittingly build up our strength and lessen Germany's potentialities for making trouble.

The paper adds in a footnote: '*Russia*: We can never bank on this country but, to keep on the right side of this devil, we must sup with him to some extent, adapting the length of our spoon to circumstances at any given moment.'

At this distance of time, there is little need to argue the difficulties which ministers and officials faced in framing a policy towards Germany. They received during 1938 a mass of reports, some from such good sources that they could not be ignored, about German intentions. The head of SIS himself had admitted earlier that summer the particular difficulty of interpreting the German situation.[37] At his second meeting with Chamberlain, a day or two after SIS's paper was written, Hitler raised his terms. However, SIS's analysis and recommendations were not regarded as having a merely ephemeral significance; when the Permanent Under-Secretary made a broad review of British policy after the Munich agreement, he referred to the paper and we cannot fail to notice how much of the policy recommended by SIS for the immediate crisis and the longer term was followed. To take only a few examples, Czechoslovakia was intended by the Munich agreement to become a more compact state under international guarantee; the Anglo-Italian treaty was brought into force promptly; the British did try to satisfy at least some of the Arab aspirations over Palestine; they did increase their rearmament and make what amounted to a defensive alliance with France; they did try to give some economic help to the states of south-eastern Europe, and drew closer to Turkey. This does not mean that the policy was followed simply or chiefly because SIS recommended it; there is much in the paper which accords with the known thinking of the Permanent Under-Secretary and leading ministers, including Halifax and Chamberlain. The document does, however, show beyond dispute that the policy of 1938–9 was not followed because ministers preferred their own intuition, or soothing and convenient advice, to that of a well-informed intelligence service.

IV

The last of our flashes of intelligence comes from a file about the recasting of Great Britain's machinery for its assessment and collation. Within a few months of Munich, secret reports suggested strongly that the German government, and especially Hitler, were growing more hostile to Britain. The Mayor of Leipzig, Dr Goerdeler, continued to send messages which spoke of a possible revolution by the German army; but on his own showing, a considerable expansion of German power and territory would take place even if Hitler were got rid of. Mr Ivone Kirkpatrick of the British embassy in Berlin was warned that Hitler had ordered preparations for an air attack on London without declaration of war. Most of the secret reports indicated a drive to the East, rather than the West, by Germany. A summary of them drawn up by Cadogan's Private Secretary, Gladwyn Jebb, described Hitler as supreme in Germany and 'a blend of fanatic, madman and clear-visioned realist', embittered, exasperated over the British and incalculable even to his intimates, capable of throwing the machine he had created in any direction at short notice.[38]

It does not appear that the British had access at this period, through decyphering of the most secret communications or an agent, to any substantial number of German documents. A highly valued informant, to whom reference is occasionally made in published sources as 'Kn.', or 'Knight', and who may now be identified as Herr Hans Ritter,[39] sent a stream of reports through Group-Captain M. G. Christie, Vansittart's most important supplier of intelligence though not employed by SIS.[40] We learn without surprise from the official historians that Vansittart's information was being criticised in Whitehall early in 1939, and can readily sympathise with his difficulties. Giving the names of some particularly precious sources, Christie wrote to him from Switzerland on 20 January, 'Of course . . . *you will use the utmost discretion and see that they are not revealed to the F.O. or Private Secretaries or other possible leakage points.*' Christie himself was aware of the contradiction between the general tenor of his previous reports, predicting a German movement eastwards, and the theme of the information which he was sending a little later.[41]

Without doubt, secret information in December and January did play a substantial part in the acceleration of British rearmament and the decision to plan at last for a continental army and regard a German invasion of Holland as a *casus belli*. All the same, it could hardly be pretended that a Foreign Office without a machinery for the handling of intelligence, or its coordination with the information reaching the service departments, could cope with circumstances so perilous. It appears that the ambassador in Berlin, returning to his post in February 1939 after a long absence, complained of the SIS; and the Permanent Under-Secretary's reply gives an interesting and rare insight into the Foreign Office's expectations and practices:

> Our agents are, of course, bound to report rumours or items of information which come into their possession; they exercise a certain amount of discrimination themselves, but naturally do not take the responsibility of too much selection and it is our job here to

weigh up the information which we receive and to try to draw more or less reasonable conclusions from it. In that we may fail and if so it is our fault, but I do not think it is fair to blame the S.I.S. Moreover, it is true to say that the recent scares have not originated principally with the S.I.S. agents in Germany, but have come to us from other sources.[42]

In the same month, officials within the Foreign Office had been considering a proposal emanating from Brigadier-General Beaumont-Nesbitt of the War Office for the creation of a Central Intelligence Bureau in London. The Permanent Under-Secretary minuted that the scheme in its original form horrified him, for it could institute a committee outside the Office's control, which would sift all the information received from various sources and pronounce upon it. Nevertheless, he recognised that the situation must be remedied, for Foreign Office telegrams and despatches, and SIS reports, were distributed without comment to departments which had a varying ability to appraise them.

The result is that they all exercise their ingenuity upon them with, no doubt, conflicting conclusions. On *political* reports, the F.O. shd. have the responsibility of collating the mass of material and producing an appreciation. And I believe this wd. be very valuable . . . I am sure that something of this kind is badly wanted, and wd. help to keep other Govt. Depts. from hunting a lot of false trails. Is it possible?[43]

Appended to the papers is a minute by Colonel S. G. Menzies, which, as a covering note remarked, no doubt represented the views of his master: Admiral Sinclair, whom Menzies soon succeeded as head of SIS. Menzies expressed his confidence that the idea underlying the proposal was sound and necessary; but if the bureau were composed of individuals snatched from desks in their own ministries for time they could ill spare, it would fail. At least part of the staff should be permanent; and

Our own constantly recurring experience of being called upon for *ad hoc* notes on various aspects – which can only be one sided – is our strongest proof that such a machinery is badly needed.
Should later on it be decided to have inter-departmental

discussions on the subject, I have been instructed to ask that the
S.I.S. may be represented, and if eventually the scheme is
proceeded with . . ., I am to press for a nominee of the S.I.S. to be a
member of the J.I.C. Committee, bearing in mind that a considerable proportion of the information which will be dealt with will
emanate from that body.[44]

The Foreign Office's response in February expressed substantial
agreement with the view that the arrangements for the distribution
and collation of political intelligence did not yield satisfactory results,
and admitted a considerable amount of avoidable overlapping.
However, in the view of that Office, the fault lay less in the system
than in the use to which it was put;

In our opinion political intelligence is just as much the concern of
the Foreign Office as, say, naval intelligence is the concern of the
Admiralty, and insufficient use is made of the Foreign Office in its
capacity as a repository of foreign political intelligence. To take an
example, let me mention that it is only recently that we have been
asked to interest ourselves in the early stages in the preparation of
the political appreciations which form the basis of the wider
reviews of imperial strategy prepared by the Chiefs of Staff.

Before these discussions were concluded, Hitler had seized Prague
and Memel, and, acting on plausible but wrong information about a
German intention to invade Poland, Britain had given a guarantee to
that country. Within a short time, the Joint Intelligence Committee,
established earlier but essentially a peripheral body until 1939, had
taken on a new vitality and significance. It acquired a chairman from
the Foreign Office, and by all accounts rendered most notable service
in the war and afterwards. No piece of machinery could quickly make
good the lack of resources which had afflicted the intelligence services
for so long, or alter some of the attitudes and practices touched upon
in this essay. If the JIC did not provide hard and timely intelligence
about the negotiations between Germany and Russia which led to the
non-aggression pact of August 1939, it did enable Britain at last to
draw together and weigh political and military information, gained
by overt as well as secret methods; a process as necessary in times of
armed truce as in war itself.

6. Enigma, the French, the Poles and the British, 1931–1940

JEAN STENGERS

ON 11 March 1940, Colonel Louis Rivet, the head of the French Intelligence Service, wrote in his private diary: 'The decrypts of the Enigma machine are becoming interesting and numerous'.[1] What he was rejoicing at was the success of British, Polish and French cryptologists who had begun to decypher regularly the radio messages for which the Germans used their extremely sophisticated cypher machine called the Enigma. The Germans had full confidence in the Enigma: the scrambler of the machine was such an elaborate one, with three rotors and a plugboard, and the number of possible encoding positions for each letter was such an immensely huge one (it was around 5000 billion trillion trillion trillion trillion, or 5 followed by 87 zeros)[2] that they believed their cypher to be absolutely unbreakable. Their opponents nevertheless had succeeded in breaking it since January 1940. This was the result of the joint effort of two teams of cryptologists, one in Britain and the other in France. The British team was working at Bletchley, in Buckinghamshire (a now very famous name, but which remained top secret up to 1974), where the Government Code and Cypher School had moved in August 1939. The Polish cryptologists, who had escaped from their country in September 1939, were at work together with the French in a centre code-named *Bruno*, which was situated at Gretz-Armainvilliers, fifteen miles east of Paris. Both teams were simultaneously working, from day to day, on the discovery of the keys used by the Germans for the Enigma. Once discovered in one place, the key was immediately communicated to the other by special wire, and the messages of the day could then be read. 11 March was a particularly blessed day. On that date, no less than three daily keys were discovered, those of 4 March, 7 March and 9 March.[3]

What happened in January–April 1940 could not have happened without the work done in the previous years. Basic contributions to the 1940 success came from the three countries to which the 1940 cryptologists belonged: France, Poland and Britain. Our aim is to show that the French contribution was purely intelligence work; the Polish contribution consisted of science and technology; whereas the British contribution, until the spring of 1940, seems to have been only of a technological nature. These are the three main lines which we will follow.

I   FRENCH INTELLIGENCE WORK

Our main source for this part of the story is the book by General Gustave Bertrand, *Enigma ou la plus grande énigme de la guerre 1939—1945*.[4] Bertrand told what he had witnessed – and he had been the principal actor – but he also made use of excellent documents which had remained in his possession. After writing his book he handed over most of these documents to his former service, and they are now inaccessible. However, he kept some private papers which we were allowed to inspect and which are very useful.[5]

Bertrand's book, as it told for the first time a rather extraordinary story,[6] could have had the kind of success Frederick Winterbotham's celebrated *Ultra Secret* registered a year later. Actually it passed almost unnoticed.[7] It was not an easy book. It lacked any charm in either composition or style. The use of pseudonyms even made some pages difficult to understand.[8]

But it is a sound book. Whenever Bertrand's statements can be checked by other sources, they prove to be absolutely trustworthy. His testimony is confirmed and completed on some points by those of his former colleagues of the French Intelligence Service, Colonel Paillole and General Navarre.[9]

Captain Bertrand (as he then was) in 1931 was in charge of the section of that service which dealt with foreign codes and cyphers. He was not himself a professional cryptologist, but his task was to provide his colleagues in the French cryptological service with as much foreign material as possible. He was one of the first to be warned when a German offered his services to France in October 1931,[10] and when it appeared that the man was attached to the Cypher Bureau of the *Reichswehr*. That German traitor did not betray his country for any kind of ideological reason: he just wanted money. 'He liked money; he needed money for he liked still more women', Bertrand related.[11] His name was Hans-Thilo Schmidt and he was the brother of a German general. In Bertrand's section he was code-named *Asché* ('ashes'), whereas the German section of the French Intelligence Service, which was also in contact with him for the information he provided outside the field of cryptology, called him HE (which in French has the same pronunciation as the word *Asché*).[12]

Bertrand met *Asché* for the first time in Verviers, a Belgian town near the German frontier, on 8 November 1931.[13] In the next six months he met him twice, again in Verviers, on 20 December 1931 and on 8 May 1932.[14] Each time, *Asché* brought with him documents on the German codes and cyphers, especially on the Enigma, and Bertrand hastily took photographs of them.

Here is a key-point which Bertrand did not relate fully in his book, but which he confided to me in a private conversation in 1975, a few months before his death. He naturally sent the *Asché* documents to the French cryptological service, where they could be of basic use. The reception was very cool: it is, they answered, a kind of machine against which we cannot do anything, even with your documents. These people were 'zero', at least in that field, Bertrand commented. This French impotence lasted until 1939.[15] Apparently the French cryptologists did not even try to 'break' the Enigma.

But Bertrand was not discouraged. He knew how valuable his documents were, and he tried to find someone who could exploit them. He had excellent contacts with the Polish Intelligence Service and he offered them to the Poles. There the welcome was enthusiastic. Bertrand brought a first batch of documents to Warsaw in December 1931,[16] and new documents in May and September 1932.[17] He made an agreement with the Poles which he summarises in this way: 'Désormais, à *Luc* les études, à moi les recherches'[18] – 'From now on, the studies which are necessary for breaking the Enigma will be made by *Luc* [that is Colonel Gwido Langer, the head of the Polish Cypher Bureau], and I shall go on searching for documents.' But the Poles cheated. Bertrand went on seeing *Asché*, taking photographs and bringing them to Warsaw (he made six trips to Warsaw in the years 1933–7), but the Poles did not tell him that as early as January 1933 they had reached their goal in their 'studies'. We shall see that in a moment. Bertrand was told of the Polish success only in July 1939, and he was led to believe at that time that it was only a quite recent success.

Some *Asché* documents were certainly communicated to London, and as early as 1931.[19] But Bertrand never knew anything about the use the British Cypher Service made of them. So far, we do not know either.

II POLISH SCIENCE AND TECHNOLOGY

The Poles were the first victors in the struggle against Enigma. As far as we know, they were not helped by any intelligence work of their own. There are two legends in that respect which must be dispelled. The first is about a German Enigma which the Warsaw Customs Office is said to have intercepted, a bounty in that case for the Polish cryptologists. Actually the machine which the Poles seized was not an army Enigma, but a commercial Enigma, that is, a machine which could be bought on the commercial market.[20] The second story, which is told by Winterbotham, is about a Polish mechanic employed in a German factory who succeeded, after going back to Poland, in reconstructing a German machine which was of great help for both the British and the Poles.[21] This has no foundation at all. It seems to be only one of the stories which were going round at Bletchley. It was whispered there during the war that the Poles had had something to do with the British successes. [22] What exactly their part had been, nobody – except a few people who kept silent – knew for certain. Out of ignorance, legends were born.[23]

What the Poles contributed was exclusively science and technology. Our knowledge of their contribution derives mainly from the writings and testimony of one man, who by good fortune was the main man of science involved in the Polish venture: the mathematician Marian Rejewski.[24] Rejewski (1905–80), a graduate of the University of Poznan, worked on the German cypher in Poland from 1932 to 1939. After the German invasion, he fled to France and was active first at *Bruno* and later in the south of France where the French and Polish cryptologists ran a clandestine centre in 1940–2. In 1943 he escaped to Britain and served in the Polish army there, always as a cryptologist (but, the fact must be stressed, without any link with

Bletchley; the British authorities left him, as well as all other Polish cryptologists, in complete ignorance of what they were doing). As he had left his family behind in Poland, he returned in 1946 to his native country; there for years he held only second-rate and obscure positions, his former life in the West making him a rather suspect person. After 1974, however, the part he had played before the war was revealed,[25] and for the last five years of his life he enjoyed some degree of popularity. He died in Warsaw on 13 February 1980.

In 1941–2, in the south of France, Rejewski wrote a full report, in Polish, about his pre-war activities; this is a basic document.[26] In the years 1974–80, he wrote three articles,[27] gave a number of interviews,[28] and was very informative when consulted by various authors.[29]

Like Bertrand, Marian Rejewski is a very sound and honest witness. At the end of his life he had fewer documents at his disposal than Bertrand, but his memory, except on some minor points, was of an exceptional vividness. There are not many ways to check the accuracy of his testimony but when the process is possible it gives quite positive results.

The great loss on the Polish side is that of the elaborate machinery built by the Poles from 1932 to 1939 in order to break the Enigma. The bulk of the material could not be evacuated in time in September 1939; it was buried in a remote place which is now in Russian territory.[30] Two machines had been sent to France and England before the war, and one or two others were evacuated, but the material that went to France was later destroyed and we do not know whether anything has survived in England.[31] Our only sources for the Polish machinery are the descriptions by Rejewski, and also the drawings of some of the machines which he either made or approved.[32]

The Germans had adopted the Enigma for military use in the late 1920s – adopted and also adapted, for they progressively improved the basic machine, which was a commercial one. There can be no doubt that the Poles, who were extremely active in the field of decypherment (their success in breaking the Russian cypher during the 1920 campaign had proved very valuable), immediately attacked the new German system. But their efforts at first were abortive. They remained so until Marian Rejewski was given a chance. A young and brilliant mathematician, Rejewski had entered the cryptographic service of the Polish General Staff in 1932.[33] In the autumn of that year he was introduced to the material on which he was asked to work: a commercial Enigma, and a vast number of unsolved German cyphered messages. He had to work alone, in complete secrecy. In a few weeks of intense creative mood, Rejewski succeeded – and this is the great feat of his life – in elaborating the mathematical method which could solve the problem; it was an application of the theory of permutations. The theoretical tool was now in his hands. But getting to the practical solution by using that tool could take years and years. Then some day in December 1932,[34] his superior put on his table two documents. The first one was an operational instruction for the German Enigma, which contained four drawings of the machine. The second one consisted of two tables of keys for the months of October and December 1931.[35] These documents came from *Asché* and Bertrand, but Rejewski was not told anything about their origin. It was only much later, when he was working with Bertrand at *Bruno* and in the South of France, that he would learn where they came from.

With his mathematical method, with the description of the machine, with the keys for two months, Marian Rejewski could rapidly jump to triumph: in January 1933, with the help of a replica of the German machine, the Enigma messages were decyphered.

This was made possible only by the combination of Rejewski's mathematical genius[36] and the wonderful contribution of the *Asché* documents. The latter had been indispensable. Rejewski always was very positive about it: without them, he wrote in 1976, the work necessary to reach the practical solution of the problem could have lasted for a very long time – and 'who knows', he added, 'perhaps for ever'.[37]

After the first and decisive success, Marian Rejewski did not remain alone. He was joined for the work on Enigma by two other remarkable cryptologists, Jerzy Rozycki and Henryk Zygalski,[38] and the Rejewski–Rozycki–Zygalski team made headway in the next years with new mathematical methods and a number of new machines. For the building of this machinery, the first-class talents of Polish engineers, and especially of those of the AVA factory in Warsaw, were most precious.[39] No help, it must be remarked, was provided by new *Asché* documents.[40]

Progress and improvements were required mainly for two reasons: to make the finding of the Enigma keys faster and easier, and also to counteract the improvements the Germans themselves were bringing to their Enigma as well as to their methods of encypherment. The

Polish equipment was enriched successively by the *cyclometer* (combining the elements of two Enigmas), the *bomba*, devised by Rejewski (a combination of the rotors of six Enigmas), and by a system of *perforated sheets* devised by Zygalski. Mathematics and technology were going forward hand in hand.

In his 1941–2 report, Rejewski writes that the first half of 1938 marked the height of the Poles' achievements. 'We were deciphering practically every day, and often at a record speed.'[41] The discovery of a daily key had become at that time, in most cases, a matter of less than twenty minutes.[42]

In the second part of the year, however, two severe blows were to fall. On 15 September 1938, the Germans made a major change, not to their machine, but to their encyphering procedure. This disoriented the Poles for only a short time: the *bomba* offered a rapid and efficient answer. But on 15 December, the machine itself was changed in a major way: in supplement to the three former rotors, which the Poles had been able to reconstruct, the Germans introduced two additional rotors. The Enigma remained a three-rotor machine, but the operators would from now on choose three rotors out of the five which were at their disposal.

All the theoretical solutions of the Poles, after December 1938, remained valid. But from a practical point of view, their machinery became quite insufficient: they could discover only a small proportion of the German keys. It was for them a real catastrophe.

Was it because they felt relatively helpless that they resolved to let the French and the British into their secrets, as they did in July 1939? Rejewski always strongly repudiated this interpretation. The decision to put the Polish achievements at the disposal of the Western Allies, he said, was a gesture of solidarity and friendship, a contribution to the common cause. But the question remains doubtful as Rejewski himself had no part in the decision-making process. Colonel Stefan Mayer, who was much further up in the hierarchy – he was the chief of military intelligence – writes: 'As the danger of war became tangibly near we decided to share our achievements regarding Enigma, even not yet complete, with the French and British sides, in the hope that working in three groups would facilitate and accelerate the final conquest of Enigma'.[43] This sounds more realistic.

At any rate, what took place near Warsaw, on 25 July 1939, was an historic event. Two Frenchmen, Bertrand and the French cryptologist Captain Braquenié (an insignificant figure in this story)[44] had come from Paris. The British delegation was headed by Commander Alistair Denniston, the head of the Government Code and Cypher School (GC&CS). With him were the veteran of British cryptology Dillwyn Knox, who had been 'attacking' Enigma for years, and who was certainly the most eager guest of all,[45] and the head of the Interception Service of the Admiralty, Commander Sandwith.[46] To these five men, the Poles told everything – about their methods, their reconstruction of the Enigma, their own machines.

In August, two Polish replicas of the Enigma were sent to Paris by diplomatic bag, and Bertrand went in person to London to deliver one of them into the hands of Colonel Stewart Menzies, the deputy chief of the Secret Intelligence Service.[47]

The war broke out before the new intelligence axis Warsaw–London–Paris could operate. Rejewski, Rozycki, Zygalski, as well as other Polish cryptologists, fled to Roumania and from there they went to *Bruno*. In Bucharest, actually, the first Allied mission which Rejewski visited was the British legation. But the staff of the embassy was too busy to bother. If anyone at the embassy had shown some interest in his case, he might have become one of the glories of Bletchley.

III BRITISH TECHNOLOGY

As everyone knows, British activities during the Second World War in the field of cryptology remained for a long time the best guarded secret of the century. The leaks – beginning with one by Malcolm Muggeridge in 1967 – were negligible.[48] As Peter Calvocoressi has pointed out, such a degree of secrecy was 'a phenomenon that may well be unparalleled in history'.[49]

A complete change occurred with the publication in 1974 of Frederick Winterbotham's *Ultra Secret*, a publication which was endorsed by the authorities.[50] From then on, there would be a wealth of books and articles. *Enigma*, *Ultra* and *Bletchley* became magic words for success in the world of publishing.

In a first phase, always with the official approval of the authorities, a few things were published by eye-witnesses about the scientific and technical aspects of war cryptology. A paper by Professor I. J. Good, for instance, *Pioneering Work on Computers at Bletchley*, was cleared by the British Cabinet Office in 1976.[51] Then, for reasons which can only be guessed (perhaps the fear that some revelations might bear upon developments which had persisted for some time after the war), the rules became more rigid. In a written answer in the House of Commons, on 12 January 1978, the Secretary of State for Foreign Affairs, while confirming the liberality with which the war decrypts would be released to the Public Record Office, and could be used by historians, stressed the fact that 'other information, *including details of the methods by which this material was obtained*, has not been made available to the Public Record Office'. And he added, regarding those who were in the know, that such information 'remains subject to the undertakings and to the Official Secrets Act *and may not be disclosed*'.[52] That rule has since been strictly adhered to, and one man at least who asked permission to publish what are certainly now innocent things about the years 1938–40, has been forbidden to do so. Only one Bletchley cryptologist of the early times, Dr Welchman, who entered the GC&CS in September 1939, has broken the rule, in his case without risk as he lives in America and has become an American citizen.[53]

For these reasons, there is still a mist around British cryptology in the 1930s and during the war. What we know for certain is that:

(a) the British got at least some *Asché* documents from the French;[54]

(b) unlike the French, they attacked the Enigma cypher with great vigour, the operation being led by Dillwyn Knox;

(c) during the Spanish civil war, Knox succeeded in breaking a type of Enigma (less complicated than the German type) used by the Spanish nationalists.[55] After his July 1939 meeting with the Polish cryptologists, Knox sent to Rejewski a set of the small paper batons inscribed with the letters of the alphabet which he had used for his work on the Spanish Enigma. This was a salute from one great cryptologist to another;[56]

(d) great progress had been made, up to July 1939, on the work on the German Enigma, but it was not sufficient, in the eyes of the British cryptologists themselves, to have real hopes of success.

This last point is of vital importance. Professor Harry Hinsley, who as the author of the official history of British intelligence has the benefit of inside information, writes that 'as late as July 1939, GC and CS could hold out little hope of mastering' the Enigma problem.[57]

This view is fully endorsed by one of the cryptologists involved in the study of Enigma at that time.[58] This is why, to quote Professor Hinsley again, the information provided by the Poles in July 1939 proved 'invaluable'.[59]

The GC&CS immediately built on the new basis they had acquired from Warsaw. There is no indication that between August 1939 and May 1940 the British cryptologists brought any scientific addition of importance to the Polish methods. But what the GC&CS did was to exploit these methods with extraordinary energy, and above all with an abundance of means – as regards both manpower and machines – of which the Poles, in Warsaw, could not have dreamt. The most promising method, once the Germans had introduced their three-rotors-out-of-five system, was the use of the perforated sheets of Zygalski. But to master the new German combination, the number of sheets required was enormous (it amounted to 60 sets of 26 sheets each) and the number of tests required for the punching of each sheet was also enormous. It was, as Gordon Welchman says, a 'monumental task'.[60] The Poles had balked at it: they had not enough men or machines. At the meeting in July 1939, the British promised to embark on the work.[61] A team under the direction of the Cambridge mathematician John Jeffreys achieved it at Bletchley in a little more than three months.[62] By the end of 1939, Bletchley had at its disposal a whole series of perforated sheets, and another series was sent to *Bruno*.

This enabled the two teams of cryptologists at Bletchley and *Bruno* to resume the search for the Enigma keys. The first victory was that of the Poles at *Bruno* on 17 January 1940: they discovered the first German key.[63] Thus they had resumed their triumphs with the help of British technology. What followed in Britain some months later was to be of a quite different nature: science, at Bletchley, took precedence over technology.

On 15 May, just after the beginning of the offensive in the West, the Germans once again changed and improved their system of encypherment.[64] The British answer, at Bletchley, was a piece of truly inspired ingenuity devised mainly by the Cambridge mathematician John Herivel.[65] With their new cryptanalytical methods the British cryptologists were able to resume the discovery of the Enigma keys within less than a week.[66]

Shortly afterwards a major advance occurred with the introduction of the newly conceived British *bombe*. This machine was called after the Polish *bomba* and it was based upon the fundamental principles of the Polish machine. But most important improvements made the *bombe*, in some respects, a quite new thing. They were the result of the scientific achievements of principally two men: Alan Turing, the illustrious father of the computer, and Gordon Welchman, who had recently left his teaching of mathematics at Cambridge (the Cambridge school of mathematics, with Turing, Herivel, Welchman, Jeffreys and many others, is all-present in the history of Bletchley). Welchman has explained at length what these improvements were.[67] The British *bombe* was the first of a long series of other scientific and technological achievements which finally led to the construction of the first computer in the world, the *Colossus*.[68]

And now a look at the results. Speaking of the intelligence provided by Bletchley during the war, Professor Hinsley, who is the greatest expert, said in a BBC talk: 'My calculation is that supposing we had none or little as compared with the vast amount we did have, the war would have lasted about three years longer than it actually did'.[69] Menzies repeated to Bertrand the words of Churchill, who said that with that 'secret weapon', we 'won the war'.[70]

IV CONCLUSION

This is naturally another chapter of history, but our aim was to examine why basically that chapter could be written. The basis was the Polish contribution, the Polish grand gift of July 1939. In the 'might have been' of history, there is naturally the hypothesis that the British cryptologists could have succeeded by themselves during the war in getting some important results. The war period actually showed how extraordinarily talented they were. Dr Peter Twinn, who is the sole survivor among the cryptologists of the pre-Bletchley period, writes: 'In July 1939 (i.e. before the meeting with the Poles), we did have the information in our possession – in fact in our office – that was sufficient to have begun to read Enigma messages, if only we had made what in retrospect seemed a very obvious guess'.[71] The guess could have been made later – or not. But the fundamental remark seems to me to be that of Gordon Welchman who stresses the fact that a real and continuous success in the struggle against the Enigma required a very strong organisation.[72] If the GC&CS could develop on a very large scale, it was because, once they came to use the Poles' methods, they could nourish real hopes. And once these hopes were fulfilled, Bletchley could develop still more. The Poles were at the basis.

What the Poles themselves did was the result, primarily, of Rejewski's creative spirit. But Rejewski himself could have remained impotent without the *Asché* documents, and the *Asché* documents were just a bit of luck. A bit of luck, and history is changed.[73]

7. Codebreaking in World Wars I and II: The Major Successes and Failures, Their Causes and Their Effects

DAVID KAHN

CODEBREAKING'S most important historical role has been in the two World Wars. Its beginnings, however, may be traced back to the days of the Pharaohs. A letter records the intention of a foreigner to determine the meaning of fires raised by the Egyptians.[1] (No one knows if he succeeded.) Several centuries later, in 207 BC, the Romans intercepted a letter from Hasdrubal to his brother Hannibal, further south in Italy. It enabled the Romans to concentrate their forces at the Metaurus River to defeat the Carthaginians.[2] This was the only battle in Edward S. Creasy's *The fifteen decisive battles of the world: from Marathon to Waterloo*[3] that depended upon intelligence for its victory.

For between the Metaurus and the twentieth century, signal intelligence did not help armies win any more major battles.[4] The reason was mainly lack of opportunity. Messengers were hard to capture; telegraph wires were hard to tap. All that was changed by radio.[5] The public nature of electromagnetic radiation, which makes wireless communication so easy to establish, also makes it easy to intercept. Radio turns over a copy of every message to the enemy.

Before World War I, only two nations foresaw the opportunities this would create. France, which had a successful diplomatic codebreaking unit,[6] set up army intercept posts in the northeast.[7] Austria–Hungary had picked up intercepts during the Italo-Turkish

War of 1911 and had created its *Dechiffrierdienst*.[8] None of the other great powers seemed to expect to intercept military radio messages – although one of them, Russia, had highly effective diplomatic and police codebreaking agencies.[9] Despite this lack of foresight, however, every nation rapidly learned the value of interception soon after World War I broke out. One of the first was Germany.

II

In the east, Germany had but one army to defend against two Russian. She had foreseen this problem and had planned to stop the northern army first, then block the southern. But at Gumbinnen, in the north, the German troops broke and ran. Russian failure to pursue saved them. Meanwhile, to the south, the other Russian army, advancing, threatened to cut off the Germans. The German operations officer, Colonel Max Hoffmann, began moving his forces to meet this more imminent threat, even though the move left the north unprotected. When the new German commander, General Paul von Hindenburg, and his chief of staff, General Erich Ludendorff, arrived to take over from the previous commander, they confirmed Hoffmann's order. But they worried. The northern Russian army, Ludendorff said, 'hung like a threatening thundercloud to the northeast. [Its commander] need only have closed with us and we should have been beaten.'[10]

But the Germans had, largely by chance, been forging a new and important instrument of war in the radio station of German Eighth Army headquarters at Königsberg. The radio operators, having little traffic of their own to send, began listening out of curiosity to the Russian traffic.[11] Owing to Russian inefficiencies, these messages were in the clear.[12] They required only translation. And one of them early one morning lifted the burden of worry from the commanders' minds and helped them prepare one of the great military triumphs of the war. It came from the Russian northern army, and it told the Germans that that army was continuing to move at a snail's pace. Hindenburg and Ludendorff turned with easier minds to engineer the destruction of the southern army.

As they drove back, later that morning, from a conference at a corps headquarters, Hoffmann received another intercept from a signal-man at a railway station. He raced after his chiefs and handed it over as his car and theirs bumped along side by side on the rutted Polish road. Everyone stopped and studied it. It proved to be nothing less than a full roundup of the situation as the southern Russian army saw it, together with the detailed objectives of each of its subordinate corps.[13] Helped by this, and by other cleartext intercepts, the Germans encircled and destroyed the Russians almost as if in a war game. The battle, called Tannenberg by the Germans, proved one of the few decisive victories of the war. Hoffmann, its architect, acknowledged the main cause: 'We knew all the enemy's plans. The Russians sent out their wireless in clear.'[14] Tannenberg, which gave Russia its first push into ruin and revolution, was the first victory in the modern world to be made possible by signal intelligence.

But it was not the last, even for World War I's eastern front. When the Russians began enciphering their cryptograms, the Germans and the Austrians began solving them. These solutions helped the two powers win one victory after another.[15] As Hoffmann said: 'We were always warned by the wireless messages of the Russian staff of the position where troops were being concentrated for any new under-taking. Only once during the whole war were we taken by surprise on the Eastern Front by a Russian attack – it was on the Aa in the winter of 1916–17.'[16] This dramatically underlines the importance of signal intelligence in the German victory in the east and all that that entailed. Indeed, it may not be too much to claim that the establishment of Communist power, perhaps the supreme fact of contemporary history, was assisted to a certain degree by the cryptanalysis of Tsarist secret communications.

III

Signal intelligence often played a crucial role on other fronts, as well. After the Austrians had bloodily defeated the Italians at Caporetto, an Italian commission of inquiry reported with anguish that 'The enemy had known and deciphered all our codes, even the most difficult and most secret.'[17] French solution of the German military attaché code revealed that Mata Hari was a German spy[18] – and led to her execution at Vincennes one October dawn. Another French solution helped the Allies stop Germany's supreme offensives in 1918.[19] Both sides excelled at intercepting enemy field telephone conversations.[20] In 1916 the English sustained casualties in the thousands in a fierce battle to take Ovillers-la-Boiselle on the Somme. Battalions were decimated as they went over the top. When the British finally captured their objective, they found in one enemy dugout a complete transcript of one of their operations orders. A brigade major had read it in full over a field telephone despite the protest of his subordinate that the procedure was dangerous. 'Hundreds of brave men perished,' wrote the British signal historian, 'hundreds more were maimed for life as the result of this one act of incredible foolishness.'[21]

But it was the British who achieved a solution in World War I that deserves to be called the most important in history. From Sir Alfred Ewing's early struggles with German naval intercepts in August 1914 emerged a large and successful organisation of cryptanalysts, called Room 40 O.B. from its location in the Admiralty building.[22] Early in 1917 it read a coded message from the German Foreign Minister, Arthur Zimmermann, to the President of Mexico. Germany was about to begin unrestricted submarine warfare, which would almost certainly bring America into the war on the side of the Allies. To distract America, Zimmermann proposed that Mexico declare war upon the United States, and that, upon victory, she regain the territories of Texas, New Mexico and Arizona that she had lost in the Mexican–American War of 1846. The British gave their solution of this sensational note to the Americans. When it was published on 1 March 1917 it caused a 'profound sensation', and did what even the torpedoing of the *Lusitania* had not done: unified the Midwest and West with the East Coast against Germany.[23] One month later, Congress declared war. The American entry helped the Allies defeat Germany and helped bring America on to the stage of world power. No other cryptanalysis has ever had greater consequences. Neither before nor since has so much turned upon the solution of a secret message. For those few moments in time, the codebreakers held history in the palm of their hands.

IV

Up to 1914, codebreaking had been a negligible source of intelligence. World War I demonstrated its value beyond any question. Before the war only three great powers had cryptanalytic agencies. Afterward, all did. The four major nations that had not been breaking codes before 1914 – Germany, Britain, the United States and Italy – all retained their wartime agencies when peace returned.[24] Cryptology thus won widespread recognition of its importance, and so gained governmental support and a permanent organisational existence. At about the same time a technical development began that was to culminate during World War II.

This was the automation of cryptology. It took place both in codemaking and in codebreaking. The manual code and cypher systems of World War I had sagged under the heavy volume of signal traffic. Not a few cypher clerks dreamed of lightening their burden with a machine, and not a few inventors hoped to get rich by devising one. Beginning near the end of the war, a number of amateurs did devise such mechanisms.[25] Typical of these was the German Enigma machine. Devised by a Berlin engineer, Arthur Scherbius, it had a typewriter keyboard for the input and a letter plate with lights under each letter for the output. The heart of the machine consisted of three rotors. A rotor was a wired codewheel of hard rubber or bakelite about the size and shape of a hockey puck. Twenty-six electrical contacts studded the circumference of one face, twenty-six the circumference of the other. They were connected at random by wires. A letter would be represented by an electrical impulse. It would enter at a contact at one position and emerge at a contact at another position, thus encyphering the letter. The three rotors, side by side, created an electrical maze. As they turned, they changed the maze – and thereby the encypherment. The result was a rather secure cypher. The Enigma failed to sell when it was offered on the commercial market.[26] But in 1926 the German navy adopted it, becoming probably the first armed force to mechanise its cryptography. The German army followed two years later,[27] and in the 1930s the French, the British, the Italians and the Americans all adopted cypher machines. These then served in World War II.[28]

At the same time the codebreakers were automating their work. They transferred many of the repetitive processes of cryptanalysis to IBM tabulators using punched Hollerith cards. This development began taking place in the 1930s in the United States and Germany at least,[29] and probably in other countries as well. It had the effect of greatly increasing the manpower of the codebreaking agencies. In addition, other, more specialised mechanisms for codebreaking were coming into being, and during the war others emerged.[30]

These developments were still getting under way during the

interwar years. That period saw many nations solving other nations' codes. But they seemed to affect the course of world events but little.[31]

V

All that changed with the start of World War II. In discussing the cryptologic successes and failures of that conflict, three major belligerents may be eliminated. One is the Soviet Union. The public literature contains almost nothing about her codebreaking successes, and so scholars can say nothing of value about them.[32] The second is Italy. She changed sides during the war, and her codebreaking, though successful, seems to have played but a minor role in her campaigns. The third is Japan. She failed almost entirely to break American cryptosystems.[33] So, in her case, there is nothing to tell.

On the Axis side, this leaves Germany. She achieved a fair number of successes in communications intelligence. Some were even spectacular. She intercepted and unscrambled one of the transatlantic radio-telephone circuits between England and America, sometimes hearing Roosevelt and Churchill. But in general the conversations were too guarded to yield much intelligence.[34]

On the Russian front, German army communications intelligence produced much of value. Codebreaking was only one part of this. Radio direction-finding located transmitters – and thus discovered the positions of headquarters. Interception of non-encoded messages often yielded valuable information.[35] Eavesdropping on Russian field telephone conversations at Sevastopol on 21 January 1942 enabled the German 24th Infantry Division to repulse with ease some Russian counter-attacks against the encircling Germans. At 10.30 a.m. on 17 February 1944 the 17th Panzer Division overheard a conversation between two posts that gave a shocking insight into Russian command procedures:[36]

ROKOT. Thirty minutes ago my patrol came out of Oktyabr and reported that no one is there. It found only our own wounded.
TOCHKA. Why was it shot into? You're dogs, bastards, traitors.
ROKOT. The battery commander fired without an order.
TOCHKA. Arrest him and shoot him with his own pistol.
ROKOT. Acknowledged.

Russian codes were broken as well. These solutions, said Army Group North in 1944, 'contain operational combat reports, statements about assembly areas, command posts, loss and replacement reports, reports about chain of command and positions prepared for the attack'.[37]

Success was not as great against the western Allies. But German troop units in Normandy were glad to have the warning of Allied bombings that communications intelligence was able to provide in France in 1944 and that enabled them to take cover and shift equipment.[38] And one fine piece of work did yield extraordinary results. This was the German solution of the American military attaché code.[39] Among the attachés who used it was the man in Cairo, Colonel Bonner Fellers, a perceptive and hardworking officer. In late 1941 and early 1942 he reported on the events, the nature, and the course of this new desert warfare. Sometimes he named new British forces and told of British plans – probably to show what a good job he was doing. All this he encoded and radioed to Washington.

To make sure they did not lose a word of these invaluable messages, the Germans assigned two radio posts to intercept them – one at Lauf-an-der-Pegnitz, the other often Treuenbrietzen. They forwarded the intercepts to the *Chiffrierabteilung* of the armed forces high command. Here the messages were rapidly broken down, evaluated, translated, encoded in a German system, and radioed to General Erwin Rommel.[40] He was eager to see them as soon as they arrived and in January 1942 used them as he chased the British back 300 miles across the desert and approached the gates of Alexandria.[41] Hitler himself expressed the hope that the attaché 'continue to inform us so well over the English military planning through his badly enciphered cables'.[42] But just at this time the Americans changed the cryptosystem. The Germans could not read the new one.[43] And this blindness of communications intelligence was one of the factors in Montgomery's surprise at El Alamein, which Churchill called the turning of the hinge of fate.

Still, the original success and the great contributions of signal intelligence won extravagant praise from general staff officers. Colonel Ulrich Liss, a head of Foreign Armies West, one of the army general staff's two intelligence-evaluation sections, called signal intelligence 'the darling of all intelligence chiefs'. General Reinhard Gehlen, at Foreign Armies East, listed it as the most important of his sources.[44]

This was echoed by Grand Admiral Karl Dönitz. His radio interception and codebreaking service, the *B-Dienst* (short for

Beobachtungs-Dienst, observation service), provided him, he said, with half his operational intelligence.[45] The *B-Dienst* cracked one British naval code after another at the start of the war. Time after time, this told his submarines where British vessels were sailing and so enabled them to lie in wait and torpedo them. On 30 August 1940, for example, the *B-Dienst* intercepted and solved a report that convoy SC2, coming out of Sydney, Canada, would be at 50° 00′ north latitude, 19° 50′ west longitude, at noon on 6 September. U-boats sank five of the ships and Dönitz praised the *B-Dienst* as a 'major help' in the operation.[46] In 1943 the *B-Dienst* intercepted 3,101,831 messages and processed many of them on its 6 Hollerith tabulators.[47] These helped the *B-Dienst* to solve intercepts in time for the command to use them.[48]

But *B-Dienst* codebreaking was largely limited to the first two-thirds of the war. As the British improved their cypher security, and as the Americans, whose cypher machine the *B-Dienst* never cracked, flooded into the war, the *B-Dienst* lost its grip on one Allied system after another. When, in May 1944, Hitler asked the *B-Dienst* which British codes it was solving, it had to acknowledge that 'The two main English systems cannot be read.'[49] In the same way, the praise of general staff officers referred only to tactical and operational results. For German communications intelligence failed utterly to read Allied strategic communications.[50] Statistical probes showed that these cyphers could not be broken analytically. So the Germans concentrated their manpower on the lower-echelon messages that they could read. Eventually they gave up even intercepting the top-level messages.[51] This acknowledgement of defeat in the cryptologic war stood in stark contrast to the successes of the Allies.

VI

The most important of those successes took place against Japan. Japan won the first battles of the war in the Pacific. She destroyed much of the US fleet at Pearl Harbor, and sank the *Prince of Wales* and the *Repulse* soon thereafter. She conquered Guam, Wake, Hong Kong. She took Singapore and Malaya, the Dutch East Indies and the Solomons, the Philippines and Siam. Within six months, the Rising Sun shone on a tenth of the globe.

During this enormous expansion, Japan's navy used its main fleet code for about half of its messages. This was a superencyphered two-part code of about 45,000 groups. The US Navy codebreakers who were attacking it called it 'JN25b' – 'JN' for Japanese Navy, '25' for the 25th code they had worked on, 'b' for its second edition. It had come into use near the end of 1940, and by early 1942 the Americans had recovered enough codegroups to read bits and pieces of Japanese messages.[52]

By then, however, the Japanese were growing uneasy at the code's long service. They wanted to replace it. But the enormous size of their new empire, together with some administrative confusion, prevented that. They could not distribute by 1 April, nor even 1 May.[53] And so the American codebreakers continued to solve and to read Japanese naval messages.

They were reading them as Admiral Isoroku Yamamoto, commander in chief of Japan's combined fleet and her most brilliant strategist, was readying a plan to clinch Japan's victories. He would capture Midway Island. This would give him a base that would control the central Pacific and block any American approach to Japan. At the same time, his advance would lure out the remainder of the American fleet. He would fall upon it with his vastly larger force and annihilate it. This would complete the work of Pearl Harbor and would convince the enfeebled Americans to quit the war and leave Japan master of the western Pacific.

Yamamoto did not know that many of the orders he issued to his ship captains were also being read by the Americans. By the end of May, US naval intelligence had been able to piece together Yamamoto's plan. And just in time. For on 1 June, as their force was advancing, the Japanese finally changed their code. But it was too late. Admiral Chester Nimitz had already summoned his aircraft carriers from the southwest Pacific and stationed them off the flank of the Japanese, where he hoped they would not be seen. And they were not – in part because the Japanese expected no major American forces in the vicinity and were not looking for them. So after the first bombing of Midway, one Japanese admiral sent below the 93 airplanes he had held on his aircraft carrier decks armed to attack ships. He ordered them armed for land bombardment. Thirteen minutes later he was dumbfounded to receive a report of enemy ships to the northwest. He cancelled his original order and had the planes rearmed with torpedoes and armour-piercing bombs. Then his Midway bombers began returning. At this most vulnerable moment, with all planes aboard and ammunition stacked in the open, the Americans attacked. The Japanese fought off the first wave, but in the next few minutes the Americans destroyed that carrier, and later the force's three others. The work of Pearl Harbor had not been completed, but avenged.

The battle of Midway marked a turning point in the Pacific War. It put the Japanese on the defensive, from which they would never recover. It knocked the keystone from the Japanese strategy, sank four irreplaceable carriers, and doomed Japan to defeat. Midway, Nimitz said later, 'was essentially a victory of intelligence. In attempting surprise, the Japanese were themselves surprised.'[54] The army chief of staff, General George Marshall, said that because of codebreaking 'We were able to concentrate our limited forces to meet their naval advance on Midway when otherwise we would almost certainly have been some 3000 miles out of place.'[55] The solution of JN25b forged effects more crucial to the course of history than any other cryptanalysis except that of the Zimmermann telegram. For it had turned the tide of a war. It had caused a Rising Sun to start to set.

Communications intelligence contributed in two other major ways to the Allies' Pacific victory. It stepped up American submarine sinkings of the Japanese merchant fleet by one third.[56] This cutting of Japan's lifelines was, Premier Hideki Tojo said after the war, one of the major factors that defeated Japan.[57] And, secondly, it made possible in 1943 the dramatic mid-air assassination of Admiral Yamamoto.[58] This was the equivalent of a major victory, for it was as if Rommel or Eisenhower had been slain in full career during the war.

American cryptanalysts succeeded not only with Japanese naval but also with Japanese diplomatic cryptosystems. The most important of these was called by the Japanese the 'Alphabetical Typewriter '97' (for their year of 2597) and by the Americans the Purple machine. It used telephone stepping switches in its encyphering mechanism – a principle entirely different from the rotor – and thus, though the Japanese had bought an Enigma in 1934, the Alphabetical Typewriter was no near cryptographic relative of the German machine.[59] US army and navy codebreakers, led by William F. Friedman, one of the greatest cryptanalysts of all time, began attacking this top-level Japanese system around the beginning of 1939. In August of 1940, after 20 months of work that in other fields would be worthy of a Nobel Prize, they submitted their first completely solved Purple message.[60]

The Purple solution could not prevent the Pearl Harbor attack. Nor did it help much in the war in the Pacific, where the diplomats had little to do. It made its greatest contribution in the war in Europe.

For it enabled the Allies to read the messages of Japan's ambassador and military attaché in Germany as they reported on Hitler's capabilities and plans. The Germans were loyal allies. They kept the Japanese up to date with their views. And the Japanese dispatches, dealing with the topmost levels of policy, were being intercepted and read by the Allies.[61]

On 9 October 1943 the Allies read a message of a few days earlier in which Baron Hiroshi Oshima, the Japanese ambassador, reported that he had recently visited Hitler in his East Prussia headquarters. Among many other items of interest, Hitler told him that 'I am inclined to believe' that the Allies would land in the Balkans instead of moving north in Italy. About Russia, the Führer said that 'We are making our stand on the Sozh but, depending on whether or not the Soviet forces resume the offensive, we may fall back to the line which we have prepared on the Dnieper. In the north, in case worse comes to worst, we can retire to a second defence line which we have prepared across the narrow strip of land adjoining Lake Peipus.' He added: 'I think it the best policy first to slap at the American and British forces as soon as we get a chance, and then to turn on the Soviet.'[62] It is incredible to think of Roosevelt and Churchill reading these most secret thoughts of their chief enemy!

On a slightly lower level, the Allied high command was gaining valuable details of proposed German defences. Oshima and his military attaché toured the Atlantic Wall and reported on German fortifications in telegrams that the Allies also intercepted and read. These included both general information, such as that the Cherbourg defence zone was 7 kilometres deep, and very specific details of defence installations. For example, in describing the organisation of strong points, the Japanese pointed out that anti-tank flanking fire was delivered from two or three casements equipped with 40-millimetre Skoda guns and from two or three others with 50-millimetre 60-calibre guns. The anti-tank ditches, in the shape of a V, were 5 metres wide at the top and 3.5 metres deep.[63] One can imagine how valuable this sort of detail would be both to planners and to the troops during the actual assault.

Thus a solution of a Japanese diplomatic cypher provided the Allies with what General Marshall called 'our main basis of information regarding Hitler's intentions in Europe'.[64]

VII

Valuable as the Japanese intercepts were, however, they were intermittent. Real insight into German military operations could only come from a steady flow of German intercepts. And this the Allies had – thanks to the breaking of the German Enigma machine cypher.[65]

The British cryptanalytic agency, the Government Code and Cypher School, moved, about the time the war started, to a Victorian house on an estate called Bletchley Park in the town of Bletchley, about 70 kilometres northwest of London. Its codebreakers included some who were members of famous families – Dillwyn Knox, one of the brightest of the Bletchley contingent, had one brother who was the editor of *Punch* and another who was a famous Roman Catholic convert and translator of the Bible[66] – and many more who later became famous in their own right: chess champions, novelists, publishers, mathematicians. Bletchley also included a genius, the mathematician Alan Turing, who first expressed the fundamental concept of the electronic computer, and a mathematician, Gordon Welchman, whose stroke of genius in devising what he called the 'diagonal board' enabled Britain to read more German messages faster. The place glowed white-hot with talent.[67]

The Bletchley solutions are widely known under the collective name of Ultra. Contrary to some accounts, they did not play an important role during the battle of Britain.[68] Nor, to debunk another story, did Churchill let Coventry be destroyed because he believed that defensive measures would risk the secret of Ultra. Critical analyses of the documents show that this is pure myth.[69]

At about this time Bletchley Park began reading the cyphers of the Abwehr, the German military espionage agency. These included both the hand cyphers of its spies, who naturally could not carry a cypher machine about with them, and the Enigma messages of its far-flung outposts, which forwarded the spy reports, often with comments about them.[70] The intercepts told the British two important facts: that they had captured all the German spies in their islands, and what the Abwehr thought about its spies. The British deception organisation found this information very useful in persuading the Germans, before the D-Day invasion, that the Normandy landing would be a feint. And the Germans believed it with results fatal to their defence.[71]

The naval Enigma posed a more difficult problem because it was more carefully used. Bletchley was not able to penetrate it until some

Enigmas had been seized from some weather trawlers and from the U-110 in mid-1941.[72] Then, on 1 February 1942, the Kriegsmarine began using an Enigma with four rotors (instead of the usual three) for U-boat communications.[73] This was not only inherently harder to solve, but, by dividing the U-boat cypher net, codenamed Triton, from the general naval cypher net, Hydra,[74] it reduced the volume of traffic on which the cryptanalysts could work. Bletchley was stymied. Meanwhile, the *B-Dienst* was reading Allied codes. Allied shipping losses reached catastrophic levels. But Bletchley's break back in mid-December 1942 aided the new escort carriers and very-long-range planes gradually to win preponderance.[75] Eventually, the Allies were able to pinpoint and sink the fuel-carrying submarines, as well as the attack U-boats themselves, and so with Ultra's help were able to win this most decisive of battles.[76]

Germany was finally defeated on land, and here Ultra provided outstanding intelligence. The German army had, later in the war, switched to a cryptographic teletypewriter for its communications from Führer headquarters to army groups. The device, invented and produced by Siemens und Halske and called the *Geheimschreiber*, automatically encyphered and transmitted a message typed out on the keyboard in clear by the cypher clerk.[77] To solve its cryptograms in time to help the military commanders, the British developed purely electronic codebreaking machines. These worked much faster than the score or more of electromechanical devices called 'bombes' that were used to generate possible keys for Enigma messages from which cryptanalysts chose the right one. A succession of electronic machines culminated in a mechanism about the size of three large wardrobes codenamed Colossus. Its specifications were laid down by a Bletchley group headed by Cambridge mathematician Max H. A. Newman, a fellow of the Royal Society, and it was designed and built by a British Post Office research establishment team headed by engineer Thomas H. Flowers, who seems to have been chosen because in 1934 he had designed electronics into telephone exchanges for the first time in the United Kingdom. Many historians of technology regard Colossus, of which two copies were built, as the first electronic computer.[78] The Germans never took the crucial step to electronics in cryptanalysis. At Bletchley the Colossuses, backed by the bombes, helped the Allies keep their cryptanalysed intelligence flowing copiously.

The completeness and continuity of this information was its chief contribution. In Normandy in 1944, for example, Ultra was revealing routine daily Luftwaffe reports on the condition of airfields, the number and condition of anti-aircraft guns, the number of planes that could fly, unit strengths. It disclosed the location and movements of specific divisions, the subordination and transfer of units, the boundaries between units – once enabling the US 7th Army to foresee and then to stop cold a German counterattack in Alsace. It gave insights into personnel losses and problems – the death in an air raid of the chief of staff and other officers of Panzer Gruppe West, the weak-kneed response of the commander of the Cherbourg garrison to Hitler's command to hold out like Gneisenau at Kolberg.[79] Ultra seemed to reveal every single detail of enemy activity. The thousands of bits of information that it provided eased thousands of decisions for Allied commanders and helped them optimise their resources in thousands of cases. Said the US 7th Army intelligence officer after one particularly good morsel arrived: 'You know, this just isn't cricket!'[80] Altogether, Ultra let the Allies advance into Germany with far more speed than otherwise.

But though this thoroughness of detail contributed more, in its accumulation, than any individual episode, nevertheless Ultra sometimes did make spectacular contributions to victory in battle. A case in point came in Normandy. The Americans had just broken out and were pouring through Avranches. The narrow opening created a target that tempted Hitler. He directed Field Marshal Günther von Kluge, the commander in chief west, to pull at least four armoured divisions out of the front and hurl them against this bottleneck to close it. Hitler's order was, however, intercepted and solved. So were von Kluge's protests. And so, finally, was Hitler's insistence. All this came to the Allied commanders, from Churchill on down, in plenty of time for them to prepare their defences. During these preparations, the head of the US 9th Tactical Air Force met with General Omar Bradley, commander of the US 12th Army Group. They held their intercepts in their hands as they grinned at one another and said, 'We've got them.' And they had. The German attack bounced off ready American defenders.[81] Its failure ended Hitler's last hope of stopping the invasion near the beachheads. The Allies swept on through France and then Germany herself to conquer the Thousand-Year Reich.

VIII

Given these remarkable accomplishments, the question that naturally arises is: Why were the Allies so superior in cryptology? Of the many theories that offer themselves, a couple that at first seem plausible do not in fact apply.

One is that German codebreakers were chosen for their political reliability as good Nazis instead of for their brains. This did not happen with the German cryptanalytic agencies, probably because they were not regarded as very important.[82] Secondly, and somewhat paradoxically, it is not a cause of Allied superiority that the Allies were quantum steps ahead of the Germans in cryptology. They were certainly more advanced, but the Germans knew the answer to the basic question: how to solve the Enigma. Early in the 1930s the head cryptanalyst of the *Forschungsamt*, Dr Georg Schroeder, said to the head evaluator: 'Seifert, the whole Enigma is garbage!' And he proceeded to demonstrate a solution using alphabet slides[83] that was also known – at least later – to the Allies. Though a modification (the plugboard) vitiated this technique, the German cryptographers always claimed that the machine was not absolutely secure and continually suggested improvements – implying that they could see ways of breaking into the machine.[84] So the theory that the Allies knew how to solve the Enigma and the Germans did not is false and not a factor in the Allied cryptologic superiority.

What, then, *were* the factors? There are, of course, a variety of causes for so complex a phenomenon.[85] They may be divided into two kinds – external or general and internal or technical. There are four technical factors, all of which stemmed from purely cryptologic factors.

The first chronologically, and probably also the first in order of importance, is that the Allies knew the German machine. The Enigma was originally sold to the public. Even though it was modified for government use, and even though the several agencies of government had their own variations of it, the Allies knew its basic layout. To this must be added the information about its keys and operation provided by a spy. Cryptanalytically, this is of course an enormous head start. It is also a great psychological advantage. The Germans did not have these benefits. The British Typex and the American Sigaba machines were developed in secret. It should be stated that knowledge of a machine is not always essential for its solution. The British solved the later *Geheimschreiber* and the Americans reconstructed the Japanese Purple machine without any such assistance – though the Americans did have the help of knowing the texts of Japanese diplomatic messages handed to the American State Department. But familiarity with the machine cannot but help.

The second technical reason is that the Germans mainly used one machine, though they supplemented it with another during the war, while the Allies, consisting of many nations, used many. This use of one machine had several effects. First of all, it meant that the Allies could concentrate more manpower on a single problem. Secondly, the greater volume of messages encyphered in that single system facilitated its solution. Thirdly, a single system increased Allied incentive, because its solution would yield a greater prize than if it were just one system among many. None of these factors operated for the Germans, and it correspondingly depressed their efforts and results.

A third cryptologic reason is that the top rotor machines of the British and Americans were far better than their German counterpart: they were never solved. The naval Enigma, the best of the German family, came with a set of eight rotors, of which four were inserted into the machine at any one time. Gears controlled their stepping. But one form of the American Sigaba (ECM, or 'electric code machine', in its navy version) used no fewer than ten rotors at a time – five to create the electrical maze, five for moving the others in a much more irregular way than gears could. A cryptologist has said that the Sigaba was 'a generation ahead' of the Enigma. It was in fact devised a decade after the Enigma, as was the Typex, and because the British did not begin equipping their army and air force, and the Americans their army and navy, with cypher machines until the late 1930s, they could utilise this more advanced mechanism without losing capital investment. The Germans, who had mechanised a decade earlier, were stuck with an older, weaker machine.[86]

Fourthly, just as the German hardware was poorer, so was their software. Two of their operating procedures proved fatal to many an Enigma cryptogram. One was the flawed keying method used by the Germans in two forms before and early in the war. It required that a three-letter keying group, such as BVI, be repeated: BVIBVI. The Germans probably did this to enable their clerks to decypher a message even if a garble affected one of the six key letters. But the repetition also created a point of entry for cryptanalysts, which the Poles and then the British quickly exploited.[87] This keying method was later changed, but by then Enigma had been cracked. The Allies, on the other hand, used far more secure keying systems which obviated this sort of attack. The other dangerous operating procedure was the repeated sending of stereotyped messages. Regulations probably prohibited that, but day after day radiomen nevertheless composed, encyphered, and transmitted identically worded messages. Often the Allies could break into a new Enigma key because an isolated outpost continued to transmit 'Nothing to report' in the new key just as it had in the old. Similar cases took place on the Allied side, especially in the routine messages to and from convoys. But often the Allies padded their messages – put meaningless words or phrases at the beginning and the end to disguise routine beginnings and endings. Often, too, the Allies bisected messages – divided them in half and put the second half at the front, again to disguise stereotyped phraseology. The Germans seem not to have done this regularly.

To recapitulate these four technical reasons: Allied knowledge of the Enigma, the German use of one main machine versus the Allied use of many; a poorer German machine; and inadequate operating procedures. In addition, there were five general reasons, which flowed from external circumstances.[88]

Perhaps the most important was the fragmentation of German cryptanalysis. The Germans had a great many codebreaking agencies.[89] The *Chiffrierabteilung* of the armed forces high command, Pers Z of the Foreign Office, and Göring's *Forschungsamt* competed on the highest level. For a time the SD, the *Sicherheitsdienst*, the SS's intelligence arm, had its own agency. The army, the navy, and the air force each had its own unit, though there was rather more justification for that. But this multiplicity spread the available manpower, which was scarce to begin with, very thin. And it diffused the codebreaking effort. Contrast this with the concentration of effort at Bletchley Park, Britain's sole codebreaking agency, and with that in America, where the army and navy codebreaking units worked in the closest cooperation. There was some cooperation in Germany, of course. But it did not overcome the lethal effects of dispersion, which stemmed ultimately from Hitler's assigning duplicate responsibilities to his underlings so that he could retain ultimate control. The charismatic nature of his leadership enabled him to do this in many areas of government. It facilitated his rule – but it devastated his war effort, including codebreaking.[90]

Also fundamental as a reason for Allied cryptologic superiority was

Germany's aggression and the Allies' defensive posture. For intelligence is necessary to the defence, but it is only contingent to the offence.[91] Clausewitz defined the characteristic feature of the defence as 'awaiting the blow'.[92] An army can await a blow only if it believes that a blow is planned, and such a belief can be created only by information about the enemy. Thus intelligence is essential to the defence, and Poland, France, and England, basically in a defensive stance, cultivated it more. The offence, on the other hand, is 'complete in itself', Clausewitz said.[93] An attacking army does not even have to know where the enemy force is: it can march about, imposing its will, until it meets its foe. Such an army will put more of its energy into men, tanks, planes, and guns and less into intelligence, one form of which is codebreaking. This Germany did. A number of incidents and conditions demonstrate her relative neglect of intelligence – exacerbated by her early victories – and the corresponding greater attention that the Allies paid to it.

France gained the spy who provided the Allies with vital cryptologic information in large measure because she made a great – and generally successful – effort to learn about German rearmament. The Germans, though their spies sometimes delivered useful cryptologic information, never scored a coup like France's – mainly because they never tried as hard.[94] Before the outbreak of war, Great Britain had established an Operational Intelligence Centre in the Admiralty and a Joint Intelligence Committee under the chiefs of staff. Germany never took such steps.[95]

The Allies put better men into cryptology than the Germans. Bletchley Park was an unbelievable galaxy of talent. All American recruits were given an IQ test; those who scored the highest were proposed for cryptologic work. This resulted in extraordinarily high brainpower in codebreaking units. The American army agency could have staffed a first-class university in all departments, one of its leaders said.[96] No such recruiting seems to have taken place for German codebreaking. And their agencies, despite individually bright men, did not dazzle as did the Allied units.

German training for cryptanalysis, too, was poorer than the Allies'. The only textbook the *B-Dienst* had was a translation of an elementary French text.[97] Cryptanalysts learned on the job. The United States, on the other hand, had developed its own textbooks and established schools and extension courses to train cryptanalysts.[98] In the same way, the Allied instructions for cypher clerks on how to set up their machines and how to encypher sometimes explained that certain procedures should not be used because they would help the enemy solve the messages.[99] The German instructions never motivated like that.[100]

Furthermore, while the Germans remained using only electro-mechanical devices for solving cyphers, the Allies added electronic devices. The cause of this Allied advance seems to have lain in Britain's urgent need for intelligence.[101] In 1940, with invasion still a possibility, 'Bletchley foresaw that the enemy could introduce new practices which would require the [existing electro-mechanical] breaking machinery to be speeded up by one or two orders of magnitude at least.'[102] Such high speeds had been attained in the 1930s by a Cambridge physicist, C. E. Wynn-Williams. He had devised an electronic counter to tally electron-particle events that occurred too rapidly for electro-mechanical counters. Many of Bletchley's staff had come from Cambridge. They thought of his electronic device when they themselves had to accelerate machinery doing similar work, and he eventually largely designed one of the precursors of Colossus.[103] These electronic devices in effect multiplied the Allies' manpower and enabled them to do far more in a given amount of time. In Germany, despite a computer pioneer's 1940 proposal for an electronic cypher device, which might have suggested the use of electronics in codebreaking to the army's cryptologic authorities,[104] and despite a later *B-Dienst* proposal for an electronic codebreaking mechanism,[105] no agency apparently ever felt the need to build one.

All these factors suggest a widespread German disregard for codebreaking relative to the Allies, which may be attributed to German aggression and Allied emphasis on the defensive.

A third general factor was the expulsion of the Jews. The exodus or extermination of a whole people, many of them highly intelligent, cost German codebreaking – as it cost German mathematics and German physics – many useful brains.[106]

A fourth general reason was luck. Luck helped the Allies more than the Germans. It certainly played a role in the French recruiting of tiieir important spy, and it was luck that Turing and Welchman, who had ideas that greatly helped Enigma solutions and that the Germans did not have, were Britons. But it was not as important a factor as the others.

The fifth and last reason for German inferiority is the broadest: a greater reluctance to face reality. This reluctance, combined with the lack of irrefutable evidence for enemy cryptanalysis, largely kept the naval high command from conceding during several investigations that its cypher might have been broken. The officers found it difficult to admit to themselves, to their chiefs, and to Hitler that everything they had said and done was worthless and would have to be redone. The result was disaster. Of course, the Allies, too, sometimes engaged in wishful thinking. Conferences on possible compromises of systems sometimes decided, as the Germans did, that none had occurred, largely because the cryptologists did not want to go through all the work of instituting new systems – devising, manufacturing and distributing the new machines, training the personnel, and phasing the system into operation with the inevitable blunders that would call down the wrath of fighting admirals and generals. But conditions differed for the Allies. They were less crippled by arrogance than the Germans[107] and so more open to improvement. Sigaba's greater strength enabled the Americans to restore security in case of a compromise by simply replacing rotors; the Germans would have had to substitute a whole new system for the Enigma. Competition between Americans and Britons in a joint endeavour helped keep failure from being hidden for very long. Civilians headed important sections of codebreaking and intelligence agencies more frequently in Allied forces than in German;[108] because they were less concerned about their military careers than the officers and officials who headed the corresponding German sections, these civilians admitted unpleasant facts to their superiors more readily. For all these reasons, the Allies seem to have faced reality more. When an American cypher machine went astray in France in 1944, the American army code agency worked day and night to rewire the rotors of other machines, thus making the missing machine useless to cryptanalysts. And when the Americans got wind of the German solution to the military attaché code, they distributed a new system. So, as one American cryptologist has said, 'We never kidded ourselves. The Germans and Japanese did kid themselves.'[109]

These, then, are the five external conditions that helped reduce German cryptanalysis to a level inferior to Allied: the fragmentation of the German organisation compared to the unity of the Allied; Germany's aggression, which led to a neglect of cryptology, contrasted with the Allied defensive posture, which emphasised intelligence; the expulsion and killing of the Jews; better Allied luck, and greater German reluctance to face reality. When these are joined to

the four technical reasons, they help answer why German cryptanalysis was inferior to Allied.

IX

In discussing the effect of codebreaking on the war, historians must
never forget that it merely helped. Codebreaking and intelligence
alone do not win wars. Wars are won by men and guns and will; they
are won on battlefields. This helps to answer a question often asked: If
the Allies had Ultra, why didn't they win more quickly? One answer
is, of course, that they did.[110] Another is that a general has to get a lot
of his own men into place, supply them with guns, food, ammunition,
and then inspire them if he wants to win wars – and information about
the enemy does not solve those problems.

Within the framework of intelligence, however, codebreaking
became, in the course of the war, the most important form of
intelligence. Its powers exceeded those of other kinds. It could
provide higher-level information than prisoners of war. It could see
beyond the horizons of aerial reconnaissance. It could be trusted far
more than spies. In operational and tactical areas, it provided the
most valuable intelligence of all. Strategically, however, it did not
play a major role. The Germans never achieved solutions that would
have given them those insights. And by the time Ultra really took
hold, the initiative had passed to the Allies, and there were no longer
any German strategic decisions about the Allies to learn.[111]

Nevertheless, in statement after statement, high commanders on
both sides testified to the value of signal intelligence in World War
II. Chief of the German general staff Franz Halder called it 'the most
copious and the best source of intelligence'.[112] Eisenhower told the
administrative chief of Bletchley: 'The intelligence which has ema-
nated from you . . . has been of priceless value to me.'[113] General
Marshall declared that the solutions 'contribute greatly to the victory
and tremendously to the saving in American lives.'[114]

And indeed, that was the ultimate contribution of a signal intelligence. It saved lives. Not only Allied and Russian lives but, by
shortening the war, German, Italian, and Japanese lives as well.
Some people alive after World Wars I and II might not have been but
for these solutions. That is the debt that the world owes to the
codebreakers; that is the crowning human value of their triumphs.

8. Radio Intelligence and its Role in the Battle of the Atlantic

JÜRGEN ROHWER

To form a real understanding of the role which radio intelligence played in the decision-making processes at the various levels of command, and in the conduct of their operations during the Second World War, we need to have a clear picture of three aspects: firstly, the organisation and the operational methods used by the fighting services and their leaders; secondly, the different methods used by the different services of different belligerents for their respective communications, and the cryptographic systems used to make those communications secure against enemy intelligence; and thirdly, the technological methods used by the cryptanalysts on the other side and their relationship to the intelligence staffs and the decision-making bodies at the various levels of command.

Because of the relative completeness of the operational and intelligence documents available on both sides, the best example for the study of these problems seems to be the Battle of the Atlantic, in which radio intelligence was of the first importance on both sides.[1] That battle was fought from the first to the last day of the war. For the Allies, the objective was to secure the flow of shipping transporting the vital civilian and military supplies from all over the world and especially from the United States to Great Britain. The method used to defend merchant ships against attacks was a convoy system; while the aim of the Axis powers was to sever these lines of communication by using aircraft and especially U-boats to attack ships in the convoys and thus to sink more vessels than the Allied yards could replace. Their method was to attack the convoys by groups – or 'wolf-packs' –

of U-boats. Let us therefore start our survey by giving a general introduction to the Allied convoy routing system and the German 'wolf-pack' tactics, with their respective communication methods, the crypto-systems they used and the problems they presented to the intelligence staffs on the other side.

I THE ALLIED CONVOY SYSTEM[2]

As the first basis for planning, the Admiralty in London would transmit a route-recommendation to all commands concerned, about 8 days before the convoy was to go out from Halifax or from Sydney (in Canada) on the western, or from Liverpool on the eastern, side. It was based on an assessment of the enemy's situation and took into consideration the availability of the sea- and air-escort forces. This signal contained the following data:

   (i)   the ocean route positions, designated by letters;
  (ii)   the position and the date of the ocean meeting point, where the ocean escort groups relieved each other, at first in the area south of Iceland and later on off Newfoundland and the North Channel;
 (iii)   the standard route for the stragglers;
  (iv)   some secret reference points designated by code words.

Two or three days later, after coordination with the other commands concerned, the route would be agreed and the routing signal sent to the commands concerned. While these instructions could be transmitted by cable or other wire-communication networks, the port director's 'sailing telegram' was sent by radio at the time of the departure of the convoy, because by then some of the forces concerned were already at sea and had to be informed. This signal contained the points (i) and (ii) mentioned above, some information about the composition of the convoy, and details about the communications. The second part of this telegram would contain a complete list of all ships and convoys, their nationality, their position numbers, their speed, their cargo and their destinations.

Further radio communication was indispensable for effecting the filtering-in of feeder convoys and for relieving the local escort groups by the ocean escort group, but especially when orders for a change of route had to be given; for example, because U-boats had been located near the route. This unavoidable radio traffic opened up some possibilities for the German radio intelligence (*Funkbeobachtungsdienst* or *B-Dienst*). Signal traffic analysis offered clues from which, for example, convoy schedules could be deduced by studying such external characteristics of the intercepted messages as the chosen frequency and the addressees. Direction-finding offered fewer possibilities to the German side, because the bases for the cross-bearings were too narrow and convoys only rarely sent messages themselves. The Luftwaffe tracking stations, however, could often give an indication of convoy positions by locating the signals of escorting planes.

For cryptanalysis (the *xB-Dienst*) the many signals necessary for simultaneous direction of a great number of convoys at sea offered a promising source of information; and the German navy's *xB-Dienst* had been built up to a very efficient organisation after they got knowledge of the successful cryptanalytic work of the Admiralty's Room 40 during the First World War. Before the war, the Royal Navy used two main cryptosystems. There was a 'naval cypher', operated by officers only, for operational signals mainly concerning ships down to destroyers. And there was the 'naval code' operated by ratings, used first for administrative signals and messages concerning small ships and later also for signals about ship-movements. The first was based on the four-figure, the second on a five-figure, code book and both were super-encyphered by long subtractor tables of 5000 groups each, changing every month or two months.[3]

The *xB-Dienst* had achieved the first breaks into the naval code in peacetime, when it was used partly without super-encyphering. By the end of 1939 a great part of the code book had been reconstructed, as had more and more parts of the long subtractor tables. In April 1940 during the Norwegian operation, for instance, the *xB-Dienst* was able to decrypt some 30–50 per cent of the signals in the naval cypher and could deliver to the operational command good estimates about the locations and the movements of the main units of the 'Home Fleet'. But it was never possible to penetrate the separate long subtractor tables of the commanders-in-chief or the flag officers; there was not enough signal material to work on, and later these signals of the highest grade were encyphered in real 'one-time pad' cyphers. Because it was always a big logistical problem to change the code books, such changes could only be made at long intervals. Thus the

German *xB-Dienst* could solve more and more code groups, when they were in use for extended periods. In this first part of the war the German *xB-Dienst* seems to have been more successful than its British counterpart.[4]

Even after the British Admiralty, on 20 August 1940, distributed new code books based on four-figure groups for both systems to make the distinction more difficult, and started to break down the cypher circuits into smaller ones and to change the long subtractor tables partly two or three times a month, the German *xB-Dienst* had by 1 January 1941 reconstructed 19 per cent of the new code book 'Köln', as the 'naval cypher no 2' was called, and 26 per cent of 'München' or the 'naval code', as well as great parts of the tables. Because of a cryptological mistake the introduction of new indicator procedures for the long subtractor tables on 1 September 1941 made the work of the *xB-Dienst* easier than before. After 1 January 1942, when new code books and tables again came into use and the number of circuits with 'Köln' and 'München' was going up to 16 and 26, the results dropped off a little until on 6 October some code books and a few tables were captured.

But the *xB-Dienst* step by step transferred its main effort to 'naval cypher no 3', which was introduced in June 1941 to carry the growing amount of radio traffic necessary for routing and rerouting the Allied convoy system in the Atlantic, especially after the US Navy started to participate in the escort operations and took over operational control in the western part of the North Atlantic on 15 September 1941, about 12 weeks before Pearl Harbor. From the end of 1942, the German *xB-Dienst* could decrypt up to 80 per cent of the intercepted signals, but the extent of decrypting was variable and, most important, the time needed for decryption was much longer than at Bletchley Park, as we shall shortly see. Only about 10 per cent of the intercepted and decrypted signals came in time to be used in actual operations. The other signals could be used only for background information like the reconstruction of convoy timetables.

II THE GERMAN 'WOLF-PACK' TACTICS

The German 'group' – or 'wolf-pack' – tactics had been developed by the Commander U-boats even before the Second World War.[5] The first test operations started in the autumn of 1939, and the first real 'wolf-pack' operations began in the summer of 1940. These group operations of U-boats against North Atlantic convoys took place along the following pattern: approximately 10 or 15 U-boats which had sailed from Norwegian or French bases at intervals of several days, after reporting that they had passed the Iceland–Faroes gap or the area west of the Bay of Biscay, would receive orders to go for a 'heading-point', a square of the German grid map in an area in which the Commander U-boats intended to form a patrol line. When most of the boats had reached that area after five or seven days, the order for the formation of the patrol line was given. The line was so positioned that the expected convoy would have to pass it in daylight. If no convoy was picked up, the patrol line was given a direction of advance and the day's run was fixed in such a way that the group could raid the convoy on its assumed course. Upon sighting a convoy, the U-boat making the first contact transmitted a signal, and the Commander U-boats then ordered the submarines to concentrate on the convoy and attack. During the convoy operation one of the U-boats had to operate as a contact holder, send off contact signals every hour and give bearing signals for the other U-boats of the group. If this U-boat had to dive, because the convoy's escorts drove it off, another U-boat had to take over the task of contact keeping. After the convoy operation the Commander U-boats would signal a new heading point for those U-boats with fuel and torpedoes left, and order the other boats to return to the bases or to a U-boat tanker. The extensive radio traffic produced by this kind of operational and tactical guidance of the U-boat groups from the shore in its turn opened up many possibilities for the Allies' radio intelligence.

Bletchley Park at first had great difficulties with the German naval Enigma cyphers. The main problem was that the German naval 'Schlüssel M' used three rotors out of a stock of eight, instead of the stock of five used by the air force or the army Enigma. The three additional cypher rotors and their inner wirings could not be solved with the available analytical means. Even the capture of one or more rotors from survivors of the U-33, sunk on 12 February 1940, in shallow water on the Clyde did not change this situation. So in the spring of 1941, the British forces at sea were ordered to spare no effort to get on board sinking German ships or U-boats and to capture cypher machines or the materials. On 3 March 1941, this was first successfully accomplished during the Lofoten raid, and Bletchley Park could at last start real work on the naval Enigma. At the outset, this proved a very time-consuming task, and the results were coming too late to be of operational use. Only when on 7 and 8 May 1941, the British captured from the weather-reporting ship *München* an intact cypher machine, the short-signal code book, the naval grid-chart and other secret materials from U-110, was it possible to prepare a decrypting machine or 'bombe' for the possible 336 rotor sequences, instead of the 60 used up to this time by the air force Enigma. From the beginning of June 1941 the British could read the German naval signals of the circuit most commonly used, Hydra (called Dolphin by Bletchley Park) by using the captured monthly programme of cypher settings. A second operation against the weather-reporting ship *Lauenburg*, located by direction-finding at the end of June 1941, brought the cypher settings for the month of July. This breakthrough came too late to be of influence in the operations against the German surface-raiding operations, especially against the battleship *Bismarck* in May, but the captured materials gave the background to smash the German system of supply by surface oilers in the Atlantic in June 1941.[6]

However, a still more important consequence was the possibility of reading the German U-boat operational signals, at first currently in June and July, and then with some delay because it became necessary to decrypt. This third and most significant way of exploiting radio intelligence had disastrous consequences for the German 'wolf-pack' tactics. After the expansion of the network of listening stations all around the Atlantic during the autumn of 1940 and early in 1941, traffic analysis and direction-finding from the shore gave the Submarine Tracking Room of the Admiralty precise and immediate information about the positions of individual U-boats every time they sent a signal, and even indicated when U-boats had established contact with the convoy. Because on the German side there was some fear about the dangers of shore-based direction-finding,[7] the U-boats used short signals based on a code book, reducing all important terms, positions and other necessary information to a few four-letter groups. These groups were super-encyphered by the daily key of the cypher machine 'Schlüssel M', and the encyphered short signals could then be sent off in a few seconds. The German expectation that this time was too short for the enemy to get a good fix had at first been confirmed by experience in the summer of 1940; but this changed when the British became able to use a cathode-ray direction-finder. Because it was easy to pick out the contact signals, which were marked by two Greek letters at the beginning to silence all other radio stations on the frequency used, the Submarine Tracking Room could identify the threatened convoy and send a warning without knowing the contents of the signals itself. By this combined method of direction-finding and traffic analysis it was possible, especially after the introduction of shipboard HF/DF equipment, to turn convoys away at the last minute, and avoid convoy battles and losses of ships.

Moreover, these methods also gave the British great help in cracking the daily settings of the German cypher machine. Because those concerned with traffic analysis knew the normal set-up of a contact signal, and could estimate from their own situation map the contents of this signal, they could feed the 'bombes' with a possible clear text and the actual encyphered text. Only a few changes in data and terms of this possible clear text were now necessary to feed the 'bombes' with the correct 'menu' to find out the coincidence between the encyphered and the clear text. So Hut 8 at Bletchley Park got the daily key, and it was then possible to decypher all intercepted messages of the day, as quickly as the German operator, in a few minutes. All depended on the time needed by the 'bombes' to crack the daily setting. But even when, as in 1941, the time needed was between two or four days on average, it was often possible for the Submarine Tracking Room to reroute the convoy threatened by the German U-boat patrol lines in time to get clear and to avoid any losses.[8]

From July to December 1941, the Allied convoy routing and rerouting worked so perfectly that not one convoy was intercepted as planned on the North Atlantic convoy route. Only some chance meetings led to battles which could never have been avoided by this technique. The same was the case with the convoys on the UK–Gibraltar route, when German agents in Spain reported the convoys and German air reconnaissance was available to locate the convoys. On a very cautious estimate, then, about 1,600,000 gross tons of shipping losses were avoided, one of the decisive successes of Ultra.[9]

Ultra had one other very important consequence during the second half of the year 1941 in the Atlantic. Because Hitler wanted to avoid war with the USA as long as he was fighting his war to conquer the European part of the Soviet Union, he ordered the navy several times to avoid any incident with the US Navy, notwithstanding the fact that the US Navy was supporting the British and the Canadians more and more openly. The decrypted radio signals to the U-boats containing such orders gave Churchill and Roosevelt clear evidence of Hitler's intentions and the President knew that he did not have to fear a German declaration of war when he ordered the US Navy secretly to start escort and war operations in the middle of September 1941, well before Pearl Harbor.[10]

In the public memory the big set-back to the German U-boat campaign in the second part of 1941 is almost forgotten, because the U-boats during the first six months of 1942 sank more shipping than in any other period during the 'happy days' off the US east coast. But this was not – as some people think – the consequence of the big 'black-out' at Bletchley Park, brought about by the introduction of the new four-rotor cypher machine 'Schlüssel M 4' and the separation of the U-boat signals from the general naval cypher Hydra in the new Triton cypher circuit, starting on 1 February 1942. Off the American east coast and in the Caribbean, the merchant ships were running individually and unescorted and only in May did the Americans begin slowly to start a convoy system. The German U-boats had no reason to operate in groups, because they could find their targets more easily by operating singly. Therefore the need to send radio signals dropped off sharply, and even with decrypting Bletchley could have done little to prevent the heavy shipping losses. The situation changed again when Dönitz found the single operations in so distant an area uneconomic, and switched back to the North Atlantic convoy route in July 1942. Now the U-boat patrol lines without the decrypting Ultra signals were much more difficult to locate or to evade by rerouting.[11]

Bletchley Park had already learned that the U-boats used in their Triton circuit a new four-rotor cypher machine; but because there were no preparations against such an eventuality the three-rotor 'bombes' in use worked too slowly to check out the now raised cycle-length of the machine, increased from 16,900 digits to 440,000 digits. It took the three-rotor bombes 26 times longer to go through a four-rotor signal than through a three-rotor signal. And because the Germans had changed their short-signal code books too, there was no possibility of finding the cypher-clear text compromise as easily as before. On very few days could the signals be broken, when they could be identified as sent in a three-rotor cypher and the four-rotor cypher as well; only three such instances occurred in 1942. Only after 30 October 1942, when a boarding party captured from U-559 in the Mediterranean, before it sank, the new weather code and some other cypher materials did it become possible to crack the Triton cypher again, starting in mid-December 1942. At first there were some gaps and time lags, but in mid-January and during February 1943 it was again possible to break the daily settings so fast that the convoys could be rerouted around the German U-boat lines.[12]

By the end of February 1943 the number of German U-boats had risen to more than 40 in the North Atlantic operational area, and the Commander U-boats could build up three or more long patrol lines which were difficult to circumvent. He was assisted in his movements of those groups by his own *xB-Dienst* – which was able at this time to decrypt more and more routing and rerouting signals – and the daily U-boat situation reports, encyphered by 'naval cypher no. 3', which was called 'Frankfurt' by the *xB-Dienst*.[13] Then the Commander U-boats introduced a new weather code book on 10 March by giving a pre-arranged codeword.[14] This weather code had become very important for the finding of the daily key and when the codeword was decrypted at Bletchley Park, there was a great fear of a new big black-out for Triton, or Shark, as this cypher was called there. Without this vital source of information on the enemy's dispositions, it seemed almost impossible to route a convoy clear of the German 'wolf-packs', whose numbers were rising swiftly. The whole convoy system seemed to be in danger, if convoy after convoy were to be intercepted and lose to up to 20 per cent of its ships, as was the case with the four eastbound convoys SC.121, HX.228, SC122 and HX.229 in the first 20 days of March. All depended now on the speed with which Bletchley Park could solve the new cryptological problem. By concentrating all available means, including the use of 'bombes' from the air force and the army, and aided by some luck, the experts solved the problem in only ten days.[15]

Perhaps this was the greatest achievement of Bletchley Park in the whole war. Now the few additional ships and very-long-range aircraft, as well as the first support groups with escort carriers made available after the Casablanca conference in January 1943 (when Roosevelt and Churchill put victory in the Battle of the Atlantic at the top of their list of priorities), could be used in such a way that convoys in danger could be fought through by a concentration of forces. In only eight weeks the tide of this battle turned entirely, so that on 24 May Dönitz had to admit defeat. There can be no doubt about it; without the use of Ultra in this way many more ships, support groups and aircraft would have been necessary to achieve such a result, and they became available only from the late summer of 1943.

A delay of three months or more in the turn of the tide in the Battle of the Atlantic would have entailed great additional shipping losses in the Atlantic, and losses to the tune of (say) more than half a million gross tons would have upset the whole timetable of Allied strategy. In all probability, no invasion of Normandy would have been possible in May or June 1944, or even in the late summer of 1944; in general the war would have taken a quite different shape from that which it actually assumed; and among the many factors which determined the outcome of the Battle of Atlantic, with its swaying fortunes over a period of four years, we shall not exaggerate by placing Ultra first.

9. The Cambridge Comintern

ROBERT CECIL

FIRST JOURNALIST: 'What do you make of him?'
SECOND JOURNALIST: 'Secret Service, maybe.'
FJ: 'With that tie? Not on your life!'
SJ: 'There's something phoney about him, anyhow. . . . There'll be
a story in it, you bet.'
The Dog Beneath the Skin, Act I, Scene 2,
W. H. Auden and C. Isherwood (Faber, 1935)

I

MY purpose in this chapter is to examine a particular group of spies, whose activities interlocked during the Second World War and the early phase of the Cold War: Blunt, Burgess, Maclean and Philby. It is not my contention, and without access to Soviet archives it could not be proved, that this group did more damage to the national interests of Britain and her principal ally, the USA, than any other contemporary group. It might be argued, for example, that the damage done by the nuclear scientists, such as Nunn May and Klaus Fuchs, was more serious. There are, however, solid reasons for giving this particular group of Cambridge men special and collective treatment, quite apart from the secondary factor that the present writer knew all of them personally and professionally. The obvious link between these four men is that they were together at the same university and became communists at roughly the same period under the influence of similar arguments and emotions, generated by national and international developments of the day. In addition, all shared a common social and educational background, as well as talents that would have enabled them to excel (and Blunt did indeed excel) in a more honourable way of life than that of espionage. In short, there is about this group a marked homogeneity, though this does not in each and every case include homosexuality. In examining their careers, as well as assessing the havoc they caused, we may be able to draw some general conclusions about men such as these, who aim covertly to subvert from within the social and political system which has conferred on them every legitimate privilege.

One other common factor must be stressed at the outset, although it is one that has lost its force since the Second World War, when the emergence of the USSR as a superpower has finally unmasked the role that the Russian nation-state has long aimed to play in relation to the worldwide spread of communism. In the 1930s, when these men and many others went over to the communist camp, it was more plausible than it is today to believe that the promotion of communist ideology under Moscow's direction was an accident of history in the sense that it was only in the Kremlin that the revolutionary proletariat held power. It was still possible to hope that, as revolution spread to other countries, where political life had never had the secretive and autocratic character typical of Russia, it would shed some of the more repellent aspects of Soviet communism. In other words, Moscow's sponsorship of world communism had not at that date clearly emerged, as it has done today, as no more than the vehicle of Russian power. In the 1930s, when the Cambridge spies enrolled in the ranks of Soviet intelligence (which, for convenience, and despite changing nomenclature, we shall refer to as the KGB), it was still possible for them to conceive that they were working for the Comintern, the international link between national communist parties, rather than directly serving the interests of the Kremlin. Indeed, Blunt and Burgess, in conversation with one another and with friends, such as Goronwy Rees, often referred to the Comintern. Stalin, whose xenophobia extended even to foreign communists, dissolved the Comintern in 1943; but by then the men of the Cambridge Comintern were well launched on their respective careers, overt and covert.

In a brief narrative like this, one cannot depict family backgrounds in any detail. Sufficient to say that, of our four leading characters, three were raised within the conventions governing middle-class lives in the period between the two world wars. Blunt's father was Vicar of

St John's, Paddington, and sent his son Anthony to Marlborough. Burgess' father was in the Royal Navy and intended that his son Guy should follow in his footsteps; but poor eyesight caused him to be diverted to Eton. Maclean's father came of Scottish covenanting stock, but had settled in South Wales and embarked on a political career. He became President of the Board of Education in Ramsay MacDonald's government, and sent his son Donald to Gresham's School, which was noted for its high moral tone. Only Kim (as Philby was known to his friends) failed to conform by being the son of H. St J. Philby, a notable eccentric and anti-establishment figure; but the latter, by sending his son to Westminster and Cambridge, at least offered him the option of settling into the conventional bourgeois mould. At its fullest extent, the association of our group with Cambridge runs from 1926, when Blunt became an undergraduate at Trinity, to 1937, when he finally went down. Within that decade fall the Cambridge careers of Philby (1929–33) and Burgess (1930–5), who were also at Trinity, and Maclean (1931–4), who was at Trinity Hall.

Oxbridge in that decade had little in common with the 'gilded youth' of the 'jazz age', who are supposed to characterise the immediate post-First World War period. As at all periods, the majority was preoccupied with its individual interests, its examination results and its career prospects; but in the 1930s there was a highly politicised minority, who were looking at the world beyond the university with growing anxiety. The Wall Street crash seemed to herald the end of capitalism; in Germany and Italy fascism was in power and by 1936 was threatening to take control also in Spain. The USA remained aloof, and in Britain and France the democratic trumpet gave a very uncertain and wavering sound. Many serious-minded undergraduates and junior Fellows and Tutors, like Anthony Blunt and Maurice Dobb, had rejected the liberal and christian inheritance of their fathers. To this hard core of young intellectuals the schematic and revolutionary message of Marxism seemed to hold all the answers; it was a cause to which they could devote their idealism, a cause that would assuage their despair. Reinforcing their ideological commitment was the belief that the Russian Revolution had created in that country a *tabula rasa*, where the centennial privilege and authority of class had been eliminated. Among the privileged of Oxbridge the urge to purge oneself, through political extremism, of this taint of class superiority was especially strong.

Up to this point one can follow the argument without much difficulty; but it takes a leap of faith to cross the gulf between being a communist and becoming a KGB agent; it means burning one's boats. One reason why the Cambridge Comintern found it possible to take this leap is that, alongside their social conscience, ran a powerful strain of elitism. Many years later, when Philby wrote *My Silent War*, he observed, 'One does not look twice at an offer of enrolment in an elite force'.[1] All four men were fully conscious of their abilities and potentialities; not for them the long mornings on the street corner, selling the *Daily Worker*, nor the dreary meetings with the comrades, adopting resolutions. It is true that Burgess helped to promote a bus strike in Cambridge, and he and Maclean walked a short distance beside the hunger-marchers, when they neared Royston; but these were gestures far removed from identification with the working class. What impressed me more about Maclean, when I met him, was his Mandarin manner, the Balkan cigarettes and the leather armchair in his 'digs'; his communism, I thought, was just another mask. Much the same view seems to have been taken by the Board of the Civil Service Commission, which interviewed him in the summer of 1935 and saw no objection to his admission to the Diplomatic Service. Only Philby came by his solidarity with the workers the hard way; in the summer of 1933, when he went down from Cambridge, he went to Vienna, where the struggle of the Left against the forces of Chancellor Dollfuss and Prince Starhemberg was reaching its climax. For Philby, the struggle against reaction was embodied in 'Litzi' Friedmann, dark, dynamic, Jewish and communist, whom he married in February 1934. 'Red' Vienna was vanquished, but Litzi, now provided with a British passport, was able to leave with her husband to continue the fight elsewhere. It is probable that Philby was recruited around this time into the KGB.

Another characteristic, predisposing all four men to go underground, was a certain duality in their lives. It was particularly noticeable in the sex tastes of Blunt and Burgess; in pre-Wolfenden days homosexuality was necessarily something of a conspiracy. Maclean had not had a school reputation as a homosexual, but he undoubtedly had a tendency in that direction, which was released by alcohol. He was in any case aware, even as an undergraduate, of more than one split in his personality; in a light-hearted *Granta* interview of November 1933 he admitted to three conflicting egos.[2] At the peak of his work for the Kremlin he had not abandoned his hopes of becoming

'Sir Donald'. Philby's dual nature, which was less pronounced, was derived from his erratic father, who had abandoned a promising career under the British *Raj* in India and opted for Saudi Arabia and Islam. Kim admired his father, but not the flamboyant way in which he asserted his beliefs. When at the beginning of the Second World War the elder Philby was interned under Regulation 18b, on account of his fascist statements, Kim had already passed through his ostensibly fascist phase, which had been no more than a subterfuge to blur the memory of his earlier communist activity. Kim, with his stammer, diffident manner and shabby clothes, was excellently fitted, like one of Graham Greene's seedy anti-heroes, to work under cover. Burgess' pseudo-fascist phase was, like everything he undertook, unduly extravagant and his pathway into the corridors of power was devious. He failed in an attempt to enter the Conservative Central Office, but made a useful contact with its Director, Sir Joseph Ball, who had been a pillar of MI5 and appreciated the tit-bits of political gossip in which Burgess specialised. In 1936 he found a niche in the BBC's Talks Department, which offered good openings for cultivating Members of Parliament and other influential people.

Until 1937, when Blunt went to the Warburg Institute, he remained in Cambridge as a 'talent spotter', recommending able and politically malleable young men to his Soviet 'control', Otto. One of those recruited through this channel, who came from a privileged Anglo-American background, was Michael Straight, who had dual nationality. He went with Blunt to the USSR in the summer of 1935 and early in 1937 agreed to return to the USA to work for the KGB. He continued to meet his Soviet 'control' until 1941, though he insists that he conveyed no secret information and was not a spy. Readers of his book must form their own conclusions about this strange story.[3] Two recruits from less privileged families were Trinity scholars John Cairncross and Leo Long. The former passed first into the Diplomatic Service in 1936, but he was something of a misfit there and two years later was transferred to the Treasury, gravitating after war broke out to the Government Code and Cypher School (GC&CS) at Bletchley Park. Leo Long was also of above average intelligence and, on the outbreak of war, was taken on by MI14, which analysed incoming intelligence on German troop movements.

At this point it will be convenient to deal briefly with two forms of motivation, which commonly play a part in turning men to espionage, but which had little or no relevance to the Cambridge Comintern. I shall have nothing to say about either blackmail or financial gain. If the KGB had wished to apply blackmail, the obvious moment to have done so was when Blunt decided in 1945 to quit MI5; no pressure was exerted on him then or in 1951, when his 'control', Peter, advised him to leave England in the wake of Maclean and Burgess. The fact that cash hand-outs were on a minimal scale was one of the factors that made it hard to track down these agents. Maclean was probably the one indentified in 1938 by the Soviet defector, Walter Krivitsky, as 'an idealist who worked without payment'. Unlike most of his Foreign Office colleagues, he had no private means and, despite the allowances received when serving overseas, never had money to spare. When he fled in 1951 and the FO stopped his salary, his wife, Melinda, became financially dependent on her mother, Mrs Dunbar, until about two months later £2000 was remitted pseudonymously from Switzerland; this corresponded to the contribution made by Melinda to the purchase of the heavily mortgaged house in which the couple had been living since 1950. Burgess, whose fund of information about the failings of others involved him in entertainment, undoubtedly drew on a generous expense account; but when he died in Moscow his estate in this country amounted to no more than £6220. Blunt died leaving over £850,000; but this covered works of art, royalties and other gains of his legitimate career. Philby was very hard-up at certain periods, notably after his enforced retirement from SIS in 1951. He had, however, been financed by the KGB on his first trip to Spain in 1937 as a freelance war correspondent; he was closely questioned about this when, after 1951, he was interrogated by MI5. His cover as a journalist in Spain was not adequately established until *The Times* took him on to their staff. On the outbreak of the Second World War he accompanied the British Expeditionary Force to France as *The Times* correspondent. Maclean had embarked on his first spell of duty overseas in September 1936, after eleven probationary months in the Foreign Office. He was a Third Secretary at the embassy when I linked up with him again in Paris in 1938. I was struck by the change that had come over him since I had last seen him in Cambridge four years before; instead of the assured, authoritative young man I had known, I met one who seemed often nervous and ill at ease. I did not look for any sinister explanation; it was the period of the Munich crisis and the embassy was under pressure. It was also clear that Maclean had no taste for diplomatic social life; he had become something of a loner, who fitted in better with the restless student life of the *Rive Gauche*. It was there, towards the end of 1939, that he met Melinda Marling, who was ostensibly living the life of a student on an allowance from her mother, Mrs Dunbar. She was an attractive girl and intelligent enough to be a companion for her future husband; but she was uninterested in politics and would have been one of the last to suspect Maclean of leading a double life. In June 1940, when the Germans were at the gates of Paris, they got married, hurried to Bordeaux and were evacuated to England with the other embassy staff. There Maclean settled down in the General Department of the Foreign Office, which was largely concerned with the blockade and liaison with the Ministries of Shipping and of Economic Warfare.

It might be asked whether, at the Paris stage of his career, Maclean was in a position to harm British interests. The answer must be in the affirmative. Even a Third Secretary saw copies of virtually all correspondence, including the letters of the ambassador, Sir Eric Phipps. In his previous post in Berlin Phipps had shown himself a stout anti-Nazi; but in Paris he had formed the strong impression that the French would not fight and this had made him an advocate of appeasement. If, as one must assume, Maclean was reporting in this sense to his Soviet 'control', this opinion would have confirmed similar reports emanating from Burgess, who through the so-called 'Homintern' network had wormed his way into the confidence of Daladier's *Chef de Cabinet*, Edouard Pfeiffer. Such reports can scarcely have failed to influence Stalin during the critical period in the summer of 1939, when he was making up his mind to ditch the democracies and throw in his lot with his fellow dictator, Hitler, as he finally did in August. After war had broken out, it would have been possible for Maclean to report the existence of Anglo-French military plans to support Finland in her winter war against the USSR, and to attack Soviet oil wells in Baku, in order to reduce the volume of oil flowing into the Nazi war machine.

In retrospect one asks oneself why the signature in 1939 of the notorious pact between Hitler and Stalin failed to provoke any casualties among spies working for the latter. Part of the answer is that they ignored the honest effort made by the Anglo-French negotiators in Moscow to forestall Stalin's defection. Even after war had broken out Michael Straight, for example, was assuring his Soviet 'control' in Washington that 'the pact had been a military necessity, given the refusal of the British and French governments to join in a common front against Hitler'.[4] This continues, to this day, to be the explanation offered by the Left; but it is too feeble to bear the full weight of an answer to the query posed above. The probability is that some communist 'moles' were indeed so shocked by the pact that they dropped out of the conspiracy and out of sight. Goronwy Rees in his autobiography states that Burgess was one of those shaken by the news from Moscow. Blunt, however, has denied that this was the case; both he and Burgess exculpated Stalin in the same way as Straight. They were on holiday in France when the news reached them; they at once returned to England, because they knew that Stalin's decision meant war – the war in which the capitalist powers would destroy one another, as Marxists had long prophesied.

There is evidence in Rees' book pointing to himself as the conspirator who was shocked. He had had a distinguished academic career at Oxford and was a Fellow of All Souls' when he met Burgess in 1932. Soon afterwards Rees gave up his Fellowship, though he had no other means of support, and went to Vienna and Berlin, where, as he later wrote,[5] 'I played at conspiracy with the decimated and demoralised remnants' of the German Communist and Socialist Parties. The reason that Rees gave for this move, which is reminiscent of the course followed by Philby, is that he intended to write the life of the nineteenth-century German Socialist Lassalle. Since this book was never written and could in any case have been researched whilst retaining the All Souls' Fellowship, it is not a reason that bears inspection. He goes on to relate a surprising amount of information about Burgess' espionage activity,[6] including the fact that Blunt was a fellow conspirator. Burgess was never a reticent man, but even for him such indiscretions strike one as implausible, unless he had good reason to trust Rees. However that may be, it is a fact that Rees joined the Territorial Army in 1939 and served throughout the war, without arousing any suspicion of divided loyalty. This behaviour was consistent with the assertion of Blunt that Rees had indeed separated himself from Blunt and Burgess, after giving an undertaking not to betray them. Rees observed this undertaking until the flight of Burgess in 1951, when he gave information about both men to MI5; his charge remained unproved in relation to Blunt until the latter was 'shopped' by Straight in 1963.

After the fall of France, Philby found himself back in London without a job. It was Burgess, the 'fixer and mixer', who made the break-through, exploiting a contact with Colonel Lawrence Grand, the organiser of the new subversion and sabotage section of SIS, known as Section 'D'. By the time Churchill became Prime Minister it had been realised that the basic incompatibility between secret intelligence and sabotage would ensure that Section 'D' would always remain an unwanted step-child of SIS. The Section was therefore reconstituted as the Special Operations Executive (SOE), and removed not only from the control of SIS, but also from that of the Foreign Office. Partly for reasons connected with coalition politics, SOE was placed under Hugh Dalton, the Labour Minister of Economic Warfare. The reorganisation enabled the new management to rectify Grand's mistake by ridding themselves of Burgess; Philby precariously survived, until in September 1941 friends in SIS and MI5, wishing to strengthen the Iberian sub-section of the SIS counter-espionage Section V, remembered Kim's knowledge of Spain, while conveniently forgetting his former affiliation with Franco, who had awarded him a decoration. The man mainly responsible for this disastrous appointment was Colonel Valentine Vivian, who was in charge of all counter-espionage (D/CSS) and a friend of Kim's father. Before Kim was interviewed by Felix Cowgill, who had been head of Section V since January 1941, the latter was assured that Kim's security clearance had been completed. In Section V Kim was able to team up with an old friend from Westminster days, Tim Milne, who had shared some of his European journeys as an undergraduate.

Whilst Burgess was taking a step back, by reverting to work with the BBC, Blunt had succeeded in penetrating into the heart of the Security Service. He had joined up, when war broke out, and been sent to a training camp for Intelligence Officers. Recalled on the advice of MI5, who had discovered that he had visited the USSR and once sent a contribution to a Leftist magazine (it was rejected), Blunt was interviewed by the Deputy Director of Military Intelligence, who proved hostile to MI5 and sent him back to camp. After the fall of France, Blunt found himself homeless in London and was taken into the flat of Lord Victor Rothschild, who had been recruited into MI5 by one of its senior officers, Guy Liddell. It was not long before Liddell had also recruited Blunt, who thus penetrated into the heart of the very organisation that had tried to sabotage his military career. When during the 'Blitz' Rothschild moved out of London, Burgess moved into the flat with Blunt. The latter's main task was the surveillance of

neutral Missions in London, which were obvious targets for exploitation by the Intelligence Services of the Axis powers. Surveillance
extended to couriers and their diplomatic bags, and Blunt proved
adept at the delicate manoeuvres necessary to deprive couriers of
their bags for just long enough to permit scrutiny of the contents. He
once or twice attended meetings of the Joint Intelligence Committee
(JIC), but was never a regular member. When in April 1944, in
anticipation of the D-Day landings, diplomatic privileges were
suspended, Blunt was assigned to Supreme HQ Allied Expeditionary
Force (SHAEF) to work on deception plans.

By the spring of 1944 Philby had earned very high marks in
Section V, especially in connection with his adroit handling of the
intercepted signals intelligence (sigint), which nourished the whole
intelligence community. Within MI5 it was held that Philby was
more generous than his immediate superior, Cowgill, in permitting
distribution of the encyphered messages of the *Abwehr* (German
Military Intelligence), which were known as ISOS. These, like all
sigint, were controlled by the Head of SIS ('C'), in his capacity as
Head of GC&CS at Bletchley. Cowgill's operation of the 'need to
know' principle did not suit Philby, who knew that there was at least
one other member of the Cambridge Comintern in MI5, who could
make use of ISOS for purposes that had nothing to do with the British
war effort. Philby was well able to exploit both the feuds within the
intelligence community and, nearer home, the jealousy felt by Vivian
for Cowgill.

When Cowgill was recruited into SIS in 1939 as an anti-
communist expert, he was assured that, when it was possible to
develop this work, he would be placed in charge of it. The imminence of
war with Germany, however, postponed such a development; the
only harbinger of the future anti-communist section (Section IX) was
a small records unit. Philby in his book dates the struggle to reactivate
Section IX as early as 1943, presumably with the intention of
implying that SIS, with Foreign Office connivance, was embarking
on the Cold War long before the Hitler war was over. In fact, no
change was made in relations between Sections V and IX until late in
1944, though there is no doubt that Philby's ascendancy over the mind
of Vivian, as well as his insinuations against Cowgill, are of earlier
date. When in late October 1944 Cowgill returned to London, after
setting up Special Counter-Intelligence Units in liberated Europe, he
found on his desk the bald announcement that Philby would assume

charge of IX in the following month. Cowgill submitted his resignation and V was taken over by Milne, a fact that Philby curiously fails to record in his book. Philby at one stroke had got rid of a staunch anti-communist and ensured that the whole post-war effort to counter communist espionage would become known in the Kremlin. The history of espionage records few, if any, comparable masterstrokes.

A word must be added here about liaison between the FO and SIS, for which the Foreign Secretary was responsible in cabinet. Criticism of SIS organisation led in 1942 to the appointment of Patrick Reilly (now Sir Patrick), a member of the Diplomatic Service, as Personal Assistant to 'C' (PA/CSS). 'C' (Sir Stewart Menzies), unlike most regular soldiers, had scant respect for hierarchy and whoever occupied his outer office was likely to have his ear. Reilly soon had a firm grasp on the affairs of SIS, even though he was of relatively junior rank and was not promoted to First Secretary until the summer of 1943, shortly before his transfer to liberated Algiers. I then moved into his place from the FO, where I had been assistant to Peter Loxley, the Private Secretary of Sir Alexander Cadogan. The latter, as Permanent Under-Secretary, had responsibility not only for SIS, but also for the task of trying to harmonise the overlapping, and sometimes conflicting, functions of SIS, SOE and MI5. Some years elapsed before such work was institutionalised in the form of a Department of the FO. Around the time of my appointment in SIS 'C' selected from within the organisation a senior ex-naval officer, Chris Arnold-Forster, to be his Chief Personal Assistant.

Contrary to what is asserted by Philby in his book, the Foreign Office had no hand in the manoeuvre by which he ousted Cowgill. When the time came, however, to delineate the size and scope of the new anti-communist Section, consultation with the Foreign Office was doubly necessary. First, there were financial implications, carrying over into the post-war period. Secondly, a tradition had grown up that the senior counter-espionage officer at an important Mission should have 'cover', usually as Passport Control Officer. This concession required not only the approval of the Foreign Office, but also that of the Head of Mission. Right up to the outbreak of war, cases had occurred, in which a Head of Mission, who was hostile to secret intelligence, had withheld his permission and other arrangements had had to be made. Hostility arose partly because some Heads of Mission objected to transmission of intelligence to London from an unknown source, and partly because of fear that the activities of the

Passport Control Officer might land the Mission in trouble, even though in friendly countries he was supposed to cooperate with local counter-espionage authorities. The exigencies of war led to a considerable increase in diplomatic cover, but some diplomatic and most consular officers (the two Services were about to be amalgamated) hoped that, after the war, strict limitations would be reimposed.

In late February or early March 1945 there arrived on my desk the document that Philby describes in his book as 'the charter' of Section IX.[7] It included a substantial number of overseas stations to be held by officers under diplomatic cover, who would be directly responsible to the Head of IX. With hindsight, it is easy to see why Philby pitched his demands so high and why he aimed to create his own empire within SIS. Quite apart from his covert aims, it is also clear that he foresaw more plainly than I the onset of the Cold War, bringing with it more menacing surveillance and making necessary more permanent use of diplomatic cover. My vision of the future was at once more opaque and more optimistic; I sent the memorandum back to Philby, suggesting that he might scale down his demands. Within hours Vivian and Philby had descended upon me, upholding their requirements and insisting that these be transmitted to the FO. Aware of the fact that I was in any case due to be transferred in April to Washington, I gave way; but I have since reflected with a certain wry amusement on the hypocrisy of Philby who, supposedly working in the cause of 'peace' (as Soviet propaganda always insists), demanded a larger Cold War apparatus, when he could have settled for a smaller one.

For Burgess, too, 1944 was a good year; he re-entered government service by joining the FO News Department. After Labour's victory in the election of July 1945, one of his investments paid off: Hector McNeil, whom Burgess, whilst at the BBC, had brought before a wider public, became first Parliamentary Under-Secretary and then Minister of State at the FO. He appointed Burgess as one of his personal assistants and in the following year insisted, against advice from FO officials, that Burgess should go before the Civil Service Commission as an 'over age' candidate for establishment. In January 1947 he was taken into Branch B of the Foreign Service, having been rejected, much to his chagrin, for Branch A. The one failure, from the KGB's standpoint, was Blunt's decision not to accept a permanent appointment in MI5. That his Soviet 'control', Peter, should have acquiesced and allowed Blunt to become a 'sleeper' seems to suggest more finesse in handling agents than is usually associated with the KGB. It may also imply that the KGB had another well-placed agent in MI5. Blunt, on a visit to occupied Germany in his old capacity as art historian, went to see Long, who was considering his future after demobilisation, in order to persuade him to apply for a post in MI5. Long appeared to agree, though without enthusiasm; the project did not materialise.

At the end of the war in Europe, therefore, three members of the Cambridge Comintern were strategically placed within the machinery of British external relations; there they remained, fulfilling various functions, for nearly six years. This infestation obliges us to take a closer look at the security of the FO and SIS. The pre-war Diplomatic Service had seen no need for security within its ranks, which were thought to be safeguarded by the tradition of public service in the class from which it was recruited. The Service had the compactness of a family and, as in well-ordered families, there were areas into which one did not pry. The Principal Private Secretary, who fulfilled until 1945 the function of Head of Personnel, was reputed to have a file labelled 'D. and A.' These letters were held to stand for 'Drink and Adultery'; worse offences were not contemplated. It follows from this attitude that, in so far as security entered the heads of pre-war members of the Service, it was associated with box keys and safe combinations; in other words, it was an aspect of administration. This at once removed it from the purview of the 'high fliers', since it was well known that the path to advancement lay through political reporting and not through administrative detail.

Given this attitude, it is hardly surprising that until 1940 the FO had no security officer at all. This could not continue after it was revealed that the Kremlin had an agent in the Communications Department in the person of J. H. King, who was convicted in October 1939. In February 1940 William Codrington, an ex-diplomatist, was appointed unpaid adviser on security with direct access to Cadogan. He had no staff, but in 1944 he enlisted Sir John Dashwood, deputy Vice-Marshal of the Diplomatic Corps, to help with the 'Cicero' case. This was the case in which the Albanian valet of Sir H. Knatchbull-Hugessen, the ambassador at Ankara, was opening locked boxes consigned to the ambassador's residence after Chancery hours. None of 'Snatch's' contemporaries seemed surprised that he survived this episode and went on to become ambassador at Brussels.

Codrington retired in August 1945; it was not until October 1946 that a small Security Department was set up under G. A. Carey-Foster, who had had a distinguished wartime record in the RAF. Until the débâcle of May 1951, he never had the full cooperation of his superiors; for example, his recommendation that all members of the Service should be 'positively vetted' was turned down, except for new entrants, and only brought into force for existing staff after the flight of Maclean and Burgess.

An important aspect of FO security was its liaison, through Cadogan's office, with SIS and MI5, reinforced in relation to the former by the secondment of the officer holding the post of PA/CSS. As the war came to an end, this liaison was disrupted. Loxley was unhappily killed, flying out to the Yalta Conference. Victor Cavendish-Bentinck, who had been Head of Services Liaison Department and Chairman of the JIC, was briefly inserted into the hierarchy, but in August 1945 was nominated ambassador at Warsaw. I was removed from SIS without replacement. At the end of the year Cadogan was withdrawn to become the first resident representative at the UN. These drastic changes coincided with the post-war reorganisation of SIS and Philby's setting up of Section IX. It was a bad moment at which to relax FO supervision over SIS.

II

Fighters for no one's sake
Who died beyond the border.

W. H. Auden, 'Missing', *Collected Shorter Poems* (Faber and Faber, 1950)

Before Philby had been in charge of Section IX for a year, he was twice alarmed by defection from the Soviet ranks. In September 1945 Igor Gouzenko, a cypher clerk in the Soviet embassy at Ottawa, defected with information leading to the arrest of a number of nuclear spies. One of those implicated was Alan Nunn May, an atomic scientist, who had been at Trinity Hall, Cambridge, with Maclean. Philby was a helpless participant in the secret meetings at which it was decided to arrest May, who in the following year received a ten-year sentence. The second Soviet defection, that of Konstantin Volkov, touched him much more closely and, if he had not succeeded in frustrating it, would certainly have ended his double career and probably those of Maclean and Burgess. In August 1945 Volkov, who had recently been transferred from KGB HQ in Moscow to take up a post under consular cover in Istanbul, paid a call on the acting British Consul-General. It was not a routine call; instead of exchanging the usual banalities, Volkov insisted on seeing John Reed, who was acting Head of Chancery during the summer migration to the Bosphorus of the Ankara embassy. Volkov, who insisted on dispensing with the services of an interpreter, knew that Reed, who had served at the embassy in Moscow, was Russian-speaking. Volkov disclosed that he wished to defect and, in return for asylum and a substantial sum of money, would provide valuable intelligence, including the names of all Soviet agents in the Middle East. He produced a selection of his wares for transmission to London, but insisted that it should not be conveyed by telegram or despatch, because there were two Soviet agents operating in the Foreign Office and one in counter-intelligence; a handwritten communication must therefore be sent by diplomatic bag to a high official, demanding an answer within three weeks. If none were forthcoming, he would assume there was no interest in his offer.

The ambassador, Sir Maurice Peterson, to whom Reed at once reported, was one of those who nurtured a mistrust of everything connected with secret intelligence. He agreed, with some reluctance, to sign a covering letter to Sir Orme Sargent in the Foreign Office, who largely shared his prejudice; but he emphasised that the embassy could only act as a post office; SIS must handle the distasteful business themselves. As a bag was leaving next day, Reed sat up half the night translating and transcribing, until he had completed a memorandum based on Volkov's disclosures. It was inescapable that this memorandum should land on Philby's desk; it was not inescapable that he should have been allowed, on various pretexts, to procrastinate long enough to warn the KGB and give them time to take preventive measures. If Peterson had addressed his letter to Cadogan, who was responsible, as we have seen, for liaison with SIS, and if there had still been a representative of the Foreign Office in SIS, who could have insisted that Volkov's offer be handled with appropriate urgency, either Philby's delaying tactics might have been defeated, or the latter would have become an object of suspicion. As it was, the airwaves hummed with traffic between the KGB in London, Moscow and Istanbul, and when Philby finally reached Istanbul Volkov had disappeared. It was the very day on which his time limit expired.

When Reed asked about the reason for so much delay, he was astonished to be fobbed off with the reply that an earlier visit would have upset leave schedules. Reed did not suspect treachery so much as gross incompetence; but in September, when Philby had returned to London and the embassy to Ankara, Reed was shocked to get word from Istanbul that a Soviet military aircraft had made an unheralded landing there and a body, bandaged and strapped to a stretcher, had been carried on board.[8] Some enquiry into this sorry failure of counter-intelligence might yet have been mounted in London, if Peterson had been sufficiently interested to pursue the matter; but Philby was not interrogated until after the disappearance of Maclean and Burgess. It is painful to record that in 1946 Peterson was promoted to be ambassador at Moscow. Equally disturbing is the fact that within SIS Vivian accepted, and later gave currency to, the story that Volkov might have been betrayed by an unguarded telephone call from Istanbul to Ankara by a British official. This attempted exculpation of Philby carries no conviction; only three senior British officials (Knox Helm, the Minister-Counsellor was the third) knew of Volkov's proposition; all three were in Istanbul at the operative period and none had any reason to communicate on the subject with Ankara.

Early in 1947 Philby, fortified by the award in the previous year of the OBE, reappeared in Istanbul as head of the SIS station with rank of First Secretary. It was his first overseas posting and, in the light of the continuing tension between the USSR and Turkey, it was a highly appropriate one for the former head of Section IX. His main task, which was to be pursued in cooperation with Turkish counter-intelligence, was to recruit agents who would be able to establish lines into the USSR and, ostensibly with this aim in view, he undertook a survey of the rugged frontier area bordering on Transcaucasia. The outlook was not as promising as it would have been if Stalin, immediately after the war, had not deported to Central Asia and Siberia whole ethnic groups, such as the Crimean Tatars, Chechens, Kalmyks and Karachai, which were accused of having collaborated with the German invaders. Some Armenians were found, however, who could be induced to venture into the Soviet part of their homeland, and these were pitilessly sacrificed to the vengeance of the KGB.

Philby was accompanied to Istanbul by his second wife, Aileen (née Furse), by whom he had already had three children by the time he married her in September 1946. He had finally parted before the war from his first wife, Litzi, who had kept up her activities as a communist agent and by 1946 was living in East Berlin. Presumably Philby had not taken steps earlier to obtain a divorce for fear that disclosures about her would have an adverse influence on his career. By 1946, however, his standing was so high that he could take the risk, relying on Vivian's sympathetic attitude towards this youthful folly. In any case, if his further career in SIS was to prosper and posts with diplomatic 'cover' were to be open to him, he could no longer delay regularising his relationship with Aileen. In the event, his confidence in the almost avuncular indulgence of Vivian was fully justified; the tell-tale traces of Litzi in the file were duly noted – and ignored. Aileen was unhappy in Istanbul and was, no doubt, relieved when Kim was transferred in the autumn of 1949 to Washington to undertake liaison with the FBI and CIA. One unfortunate area of Anglo-American cooperation was the setting up of a 'Committee of Free Albanians', eager to rescue their land from the grip of the communist dictator, Enver Hoxha. Armed with the foreknowledge supplied by Philby via the KGB, the forces of the dictator lay confidently in wait for the landing parties.[9]

Maclean's four years at the Washington embassy were the high point of his career, both as a British diplomatist and as a Soviet agent. He had arrived in 1944, when Anglo-American plans for the post-war world were beginning to take shape; he left in 1948, having seen the Marshall Plan (ERP) launched and having taken part (I was also a participant) in the first secret meetings that in the following year were to give birth to NATO. During this period he was admirably placed to throw light on the main question which, above all others, must have been exercising the mind of Stalin: was the post-war era to be one of American hegemony, or was there to be an advance of world communism commensurate with the sacrifices of the USSR in the war against Hitler? Throughout this crucial phase of history Maclean was making regular reports to his 'control' in the Soviet Consulate-General in New York. Washington in 1944, its monuments apart, was a small town much swollen by the bureaucratic influx of wartime. Accommodation was hard to find and Maclean was at first unsuccessful; it was natural, therefore, that his first son, Fergus, was born in New York in September and it was not until Christmas that Melinda joined her husband in Washington. In the summer of 1946 she went back to New York for the birth of their second son; by this time the pattern of Maclean's movements at weekends was well established and occasioned no surprise. He was in no danger of being shadowed; the threat came from another Soviet cypher clerk – not a defector, like Gouzenko, but one capable of briefly employing an inferior cypher for intelligence of top secrecy. Through this oversight American cypher-breakers would in due course piece together the alarming discovery that in the early summer of 1945 the British embassy had housed a spy, code-named Homer, who was sufficiently well placed to have access to telegraphic messages passing between Churchill and Truman. It was as well for Maclean's peace of mind that he knew nothing of this at the time.

Meanwhile his quiet efficiency inspired confidence; in March 1946, when Michael Wright left Washington, Maclean was made acting Head of Chancery. In this capacity he showed himself a stickler for security; not even the ambassador, Lord Inverchapel, was spared. When in 1946 Inverchapel took up his appointment at Washington, he had imprudently brought with him, as his valet, Evgeni Yost, who was not only a Soviet citizen, but had been a present from Stalin. Yost had been an employee of Inverchapel's predecessors as ambassadors at Moscow until called up for military service in 1941. At the end of the war, when Inverchapel was leaving Moscow, Yost was in trouble with the Soviet authorities and managed to convey an appeal for help to the British embassy through his sister, who was still employed there. When in the euphoria of victory and departure Inverchapel was asked what present he would like from Stalin, he requested the liberation of Yost, who was duly delivered to the ambassador as he took his leave. It seems unlikely that the KGB would have had time to brief Yost as a spy, even if he had been regarded as of suitable origin (he was a Volga German); but it was impossible to reassure the American press, let alone the FBI, at a time when, unnoticed by Inverchapel, the Cold War was gathering momentum. It was Maclean who took the lead in suggesting to the ambassador that he and his valet, however guiltless, were not advancing the cause of Anglo-American relations. The admonition went unheeded, but it certainly did Maclean's reputation no harm.[10]

At the end of 1946, when Maclean was relieved of his duties as acting Head of Chancery by the arrival of Denis Allen, he was selected for an important new assignment by Sir Roger Makins (now Lord Sherfield), the Economic Minister, who was responsible for liaison with the Americans on atomic development under the code name

'Tube Alloys'. Although the McMahon Act had excluded Britain from direct participation in American production of nuclear weapons, there were still areas, such as estimating availability of uranium, where information was shared with the USA's original partners, Britain and Canada. Maclean became one of the joint secretaries of the Anglo-American Combined Policy Committee and held a pass admitting him to the premises of the US Atomic Energy Commission. In November 1947 he and Klaus Fuchs were among the delegates to a conference in Washington to decide which of the wartime secrets of nuclear fission could now be declassified. It is unlikely that Maclean and Fuchs knew of one another's clandestine activities. When in February 1950 Fuchs was arrested, it must have come as a sharp reminder to Maclean of the risks he was running.

Working with him at this period, I was less conscious of strain and tension than I had been in Paris ten years before. He was uncommunicative, but this was nothing new. He consumed a good deal of whisky, but he was never the worse for drink when it mattered. He played a vigorous game of tennis. There was no whisper of homosexuality. These impressions were shared by seniors in the Service; when Maclean left Washington on promotion to Cairo, he was the youngest Counsellor in the Service. Only to Melinda, as she confessed to my wife, was Donald becoming something of an enigma. Now that the war was over, why did he still work such long hours? Now that his career had prospered, why could he not relax and enjoy life? Why did he drink so much? Now that he was a father and evidently fond of his sons, why could he not find more time to spend with his family? Out of these tremulous queries, which might have been echoed in a number of diplomatic families, an imaginative writer has reconstructed a shambling, degenerate figure, and has then marvelled that it escaped detection. To solve this conundrum, other writers have then assumed a platoon of spies, each man protecting another. Yet the truth is bad enough, without the profitless embroidery. It is possible to hate treason without making a caricature of the traitor.

When we turn, however, to the eighteen months of Maclean's stay in Cairo, it is clear that whatever disintegration had already begun was greatly accelerated. A plausible explanation is that fourteen years of leading a double life was taking its toll. It is also probable that, by the end of 1949, he had learnt that the British and American Security Services were narrowing down those suspects who had been serving in the Washington embassy at the time of the 'Homer' leakages. Philby had been briefed on this delicate subject, before he went to Washington in September 1949, and he was keeping the KGB informed. Whilst Maclean was in Cairo, therefore, he may well have been faced with the agonising decision that finally confronted him in May 1951, namely whether to desert his family and take refuge in the USSR, or stay and try to brazen it out, as Philby himself was to do. Because of the homosexuality displayed by Maclean in the last two years before his flight, his role as the father of a young family has been overlooked; he certainly retained sufficiently possessive feelings about Melinda to resent the pressing attentions paid to her by a wealthy Egyptian; indeed this may well have been a contributory factor in his decline.

Whatever the proximate cause of his crack-up, there is no doubt that it took the form of excessive drinking, which he made less and less effort to conceal. Moreover drink, as Melinda told my wife later, brought out in Donald latent tendencies both to violence and homosexuality. In addition, male prostitution could be practised in Cairo with more anonymity than would have been possible in Washington. The best known episode connected with violence (though it has become somewhat inflated in the telling) was the ill-fated expedition up the Nile, when Maclean, scuffling with the First Secretary, broke the latter's leg. He did not return to Cairo next day with the rest of the party, but stayed sun-bathing on an island in the river with a colleague from another British mission, who was on local leave. According to the latter, they discussed 'everything under the sun'; Maclean was in contrite mood, but never let slip the least indication that he was harbouring guilty secrets. He was fortunate in the loyalty of his colleagues and in the fact that the ambassador, Sir Ronald Campbell, who had been Minister in Paris when Maclean served there before the war, had a high opinion of him and was reluctant to damage his career. His reports on his staff failed to prepare the Foreign Office for the disaster that occurred in May 1950. In that month a suitable drinking companion (for he was astute enough still to select them with some care) appeared in Cairo in the person of the late Philip Toynbee. This time the riot went too far even for Campbell: Maclean and Toynbee broke up the flat of a girl who worked in the US embassy library; the 'special relationship' was threatened. Maclean was sent home.

If we return to the career of Burgess, we see equally clearly the onset of disintegration. As a spy, he had reached his peak of usefulness in the outer office of the Minister of State; but by the end of 1947 even McNeil could not fail to realise that Burgess' insanitary habits, irregular hours and outrageous discourses made him unemployable in so conspicuous a situation. The minister had the shrewd idea of passing off this losing card on his parliamentary colleague, Christopher Mayhew, who was organising the Information Research Department with the aim of supplying missions abroad with factual information about communism. Evidently such a department required experts in communism, though not necessarily communist sympathisers. Burgess had been unwisely placed in the former category and was eligible for appointment, but Mayhew had his doubts. He agreed with some reluctance to take Burgess for a trial period. This lasted long enough to allow Burgess to visit a number of missions for the ostensible purpose of marketing the wares of the new Department; Istanbul was included in his itinerary and he stayed with Philby, much to the distress of Aileen. No doubt the KGB, if they were kept informed of Burgess' indiscretions and misdemeanours, were equally distressed. Enough reached Mayhew's ears for him to dispense with the services of Burgess, who fell back, like a dead-weight of stinking fish, on to the hands of Personnel Department.

In the autumn of 1948 the Far Eastern Department was persuaded to give Burgess house room. There he overlapped briefly with young George Blake, who had been taking an orientation course in the Department before assuming his first appointment with consular cover as Vice-Consul at Seoul, South Korea. Although there is reason to doubt the statement made at Blake's trial in 1961 that he was only converted to communism after falling into the hands of the invading North Koreans in June 1950, it is certain that his recruitment into SIS owed nothing either to Burgess or to Philby. Indeed the latter had already gone to Istanbul when the first interview took place in Germany between Blake and a representative of SIS. Burgess, in his new Department, drew fine distinctions between Soviet Leninism and the agrarian populism which he detected emerging in Red China. This was a congenial task, since it gave some legitimate scope for his anti-Americanism; even before the outbreak of the Korean War, the US government was moving towards the contrary view that the USSR and the People's Republic of China (PRC) constituted a Marxist-Leninist monolith. This disastrous assumption was to colour US China policy for the next twenty years. It is possible that Burgess' arguments contributed in some degree to the recommendation made by Ernest Bevin and accepted by Attlee's Cabinet in December 1948 in favour of *de facto* relations with the PRC.

By the summer of 1950, however, Burgess' days in the Foreign Office were numbered; his protector, Hector McNeil, had been replaced as Minister of State by Kenneth Younger; in any case, if he was to remain in the Foreign Service, he had to show himself capable of serving abroad. He had no wish to leave London; indeed it is conceivable that Personnel Department, by insisting, hoped to precipitate his resignation. If so, their hope was disappointed. He had no other employment in view; moreover we have the evidence of Goronwy Rees that at this period 'for the first time since I'd known him, he seemed to be short of money'.[11] With evident misgiving Burgess accepted his appointment as a Second Secretary at Washington. The embassy there was a miniature Foreign Office and it was presumably hoped that Burgess and his displeasing vagaries would be lost in the crowd. If so, this hope, too, was disappointed. Words of warning were sent on ahead of Burgess' arrival to the Head of Chancery, Security Officer and others; but such warnings had to be muffled for fear that the ambassador, Sir Oliver Franks (now Lord Franks), would refuse to have him on his staff. In any case, Burgess' reputation had preceded him and Sir Hubert Graves, who handled Far Eastern affairs, flatly rejected the original proposal that the new Secretary should demonstrate his expertise in this field. Burgess was accordingly assigned to Middle Eastern affairs under Denis Greenhill (now Lord Greenhill); it proved for both a disheartening experience.

Of all the discontents aroused by Burgess' transfer to Washington, Philby's must have been the most acute. He had offended against a basic law of espionage, by continuing his association with Burgess and confiding in him, and the KGB had unwisely indulged this imprudence. Burgess, in whose vocabulary the word 'imprudence' had no place, had proposed himself as a guest, much to the distress of Aileen. If Philby rejected this proposal, he would not only lose whatever control he might be able to exert over his guest, but he would risk falling victim himself to one of Burgess' drunken and malicious indiscretions. It was not very reassuring that Burgess, before his departure from London, had been overheard at a party telling a friend that he suffered from 'a Sir Roger Casement complex'. Philby chose what seemed to be the lesser evil and agreed to give Burgess bed and board. It proved to be a fatal decision.

During the summer of 1950, the Personnel Department was grappling with the problem of what to do with Maclean. The evidence of his letters to Melinda suggests that he genuinely believed himself to be in need of medical or psychiatric help. This view was shared by the Personnel Department; moreover all the evidence in their files depicted a man of great ability, who had suffered a nervous collapse. It was not unreasonable, therefore, to prescribe sick leave and treatment by a psychoanalyst; the mistake lay in allowing him to pick his own analyst, upon whose discretion he could count, instead of one chosen by the Treasury consultant, whose loyalty to his country might have come before his loyalty to his patient. Whatever hints he may have let slip under analysis were never picked up. The treatment was inconclusive; but two points on which everyone agreed were that Maclean needed a spell at home, and that the return of Melinda, who had been in Spain with the boys after packing up in Cairo, was essential. Melinda was willing to cooperate and subsequently became pregnant.

The Foreign Office, having decided not to demote Maclean, was still faced with the problem of where to place him; if his sick leave were prolonged beyond 1 November, he would have to go on half-pay and could not have supported his family. The only vacant departmental headship was that of the American Department, in which I was serving as Assistant for Latin-American affairs. The responsible Deputy Under-Secretary was Sir Roger Makins, who had formed a high opinion of Maclean's work in Washington and was willing to accept him. When in the summer of 1951, after Maclean's disappearance, I was appointed to replace him, the grave importance of the post was impressed upon me. I was correspondingly amused to read in *Hansard* some four years later Macmillan's somewhat derogatory reference to the post in the course of the debate in the Commons.[12] It was, indeed, no more than a debating point. While Philby, exceptionally, was in a position to influence operational decisions, it is no part of the duties of espionage to risk one's 'cover' by trying to do so. What was significant about the post was not what Maclean did, but what he saw. In April 1951, when the net was about to close, some restriction was placed on the more highly classified material reaching him; to cut off all of it would have alerted him prematurely.

Although latterly, when Maclean realised that he was being shadowed, his meetings with his 'control' must certainly have been suspended, there can be little doubt that this final period of his work for the KGB was of considerable value to them. Chinese intervention in the Korean War in mid-October 1950 had much intensified Cold War tensions, including tension between the USA and her principal allies. The wish of MacArthur to carry the war to the PRC led to fears in London that he might induce Truman to employ the A-bomb. In December 1950 Attlee went at short notice to Washington with the intention of averting this danger. Among the secret papers, which I unearthed in Maclean's steel filing cabinet after his flight, was a copy of the Prime Minister's report to Cabinet on his visit. On the other hand, neither Burgess nor Maclean would have been privy to operational decisions and it is hard to give credence to MacArthur's later complaint that they had frustrated his efforts by disclosure of his plans to the enemy. In any case, there was no premature disclosure of his most spectacular surprise operation, the seaborne landing at Inchon in mid-September 1950.

Although on evenings when Maclean stayed late in London he had begun to let himself go in haunts such as the Gargoyle Club, where he thought himself relatively safe, he remained in control of himself at the office. I recall only the odd remark, critical of MacArthur, but nothing that others of us, when off-duty, might not have echoed. That he was still choosing his drinking cronies with discretion is shown by the fact that, before he quit for good, none of them saw fit to inform the Foreign Office of the suspect remarks that surfaced later in the reminiscences of those who were wise after the event. The most singular of these late-night encounters was that related by Goronwy Rees,[13] who had not seen Maclean for fifteen years. 'You used to be one of us, but you ratted!', exclaimed Maclean in drunken rage. If there was no substance in this allegation, it seems very strange that Maclean, meeting Rees again after so many years and, for some reason, wishing to insult him, should have done so in a manner calculated to incriminate himself.

By April 1951 all other candidates for the unenviable role of 'Homer' had been eliminated and the finger was pointing unmistakably to Maclean. Philby was the spider at the centre of the web, since communication between MI5 and the FBI passed through his office in Washington. There was an understanding between the two Security Services that neither would take a decisive step without having first informed the other. The hope had been that Maclean would incriminate himself in such a way that it would be unnecessary to use the cryptanalytic evidence, which could not be produced in a court of law. Surveillance was applied in London, where he might be expected to rendezvous with his 'control' or use a 'dead-letter' box; it was not extended to Tatsfield, where he and Melinda were living. This information was known to Philby, but was not independently available to Burgess; indeed Philby claims to have consulted his 'control' on the question whether to initiate Burgess 'into the secret of the British Embassy source'.[14] The decision to do so, whoever may have been responsible, was to have unfortunate results for Philby himself.

Philby goes on to insist that Burgess, in order to play his part by warning Maclean and aiding his escape, engineered his own precipitate departure from Washington, by means of collecting tickets for speeding from the Virginia State police whilst giving a lift to a homosexual pick-up. There are two features of this story which fail to carry conviction. First, although Burgess may have collected more tickets than usual on that particular day, neither his speeding, nor his tendency to pick up stray homosexuals was in any way a novelty; it just happened to be his unlucky day. Secondly, we have Greenhill's evidence that Burgess 'was apparently boiling with rage' on leaving the ambassador's room after sentence had been passed on him.[15] It seems highly unlikely that Burgess would have thought it worth his while to put on an elaborate show for the benefit of Greenhill, who could not have been expected to feel anything but heartfelt relief at seeing the back of his unmanageable subordinate. It seems altogether more probable that it was the imminent departure of Burgess, coinciding with the accelerating pace of the FBI investigation, which gave Philby the unprofitable idea of making use of Burgess' services. Philby had his misgivings, however; his parting words to Burgess were: Don't you go too!' Shortly before Burgess left Washington he met Straight, apparently by chance, and had a confused conversation with him about the Korean War. Straight claims to have threatened to turn in his friend to the authorities; but friendship prevailed'.[16]

Meanwhile in London the Permanent Under-Secretary, Sir William Strang, had been informed of the case against Maclean; he had expressed his astonishment and dismay and asked Makins to keep an eye on the suspect. It remained to obtain the approval of the Foreign Secretary, Herbert Morrison, for Maclean to be interrogated. One writer has stated that it was Morrison who 'quashed the delaying tactics of his senior officials'.[17] This is without foundation; indeed Morrison's first knowledge of the matter was when he gave his authority during the week ending Friday, 25 May (the day of the flight) for Maclean to be taken in for interrogation on the following Monday. A more interesting question is why this step was not taken before the weekend. The answer is that, in accordance with the undertaking given to the FBI, Hoover had first to be told. The only senior official against whom some criticism might be levelled was Makins, who failed to pass on to Carey-Foster, for the information of MI5, that Maclean had asked to be excused from coming to work on the morning of Saturday, 26 May. Permission could have been refused, without exciting suspicion, on the ground that I, as Assistant, was on leave at that time. The effect of refusal would have been that either Maclean and Burgess would have had to alter their plans, or MI5 would have been alerted on Saturday morning, when Maclean failed to reach London on his usual train. As it was, MI5 were reassured to learn that Maclean's absence had been authorised, and the alarm was not sounded until Melinda telephoned to the FO early in the afternoon of Monday, 28 May, to report her husband's failure to return from his weekend trip to France. By that time both men were safely behind the 'iron curtain', though no irrefutable confirmation of their whereabouts was forthcoming until they appeared at a press conference in Moscow in February 1956.

By the date of the flight the usefulness of both men to the KGB had virtually ended; the real casualty was Philby, whose close association with Burgess could neither be denied, nor fully explained. When the latter got back to London, he was under notice to leave the Foreign Service, because of his misdemeanours, but he was not suspected of espionage. Until a late stage before his final departure, his behaviour was consistent with an awareness that this was his situation; he planned a holiday with his latest 'boy friend', and looked around for employment in London. Indeed, his dilatoriness worried Philby, who wrote him a letter warning him, in guarded terms, that 'it was getting very hot in Washington'. After Burgess' flight, this letter was rescued from his flat by Blunt, whose help had been invoked by MI5 in securing entry without the tedious preliminary of obtaining a search warrant. Since Blunt himself was shortly to be interrogated, MI5's approach to him argues, at best, a certain naïveté. Burgess, on return to London, had made contact with the KGB man, 'Peter', in order to make arrangements for Maclean's escape. Subsequently, however, he asked Blunt to act as intermediary. This suggests that some incident, real or imaginary, alarmed Burgess and gave him the erroneous idea that he, like Maclean, was under surveillance. He may have been influenced by the threat uttered by Straight in Washington, or he may have come to fear that his incautious meetings with Maclean in London had been observed. It is unlikely that Burgess, irresponsible as he was, would have decided to go without first consulting 'Peter'; if the latter gave his approval, he made a serious mistake. One indication that he may have done so is that when, shortly after, Blunt came under interrogation, 'Peter' advised him, too, to make good his escape. It must be difficult for KGB men, even when acclimatised to life in the West, to grasp that the legal system of a civilised country precludes interrogation with use of drugs and threat of torture.

Since the primary purpose of this chapter is not to provide biographies of these spies, but rather to evaluate their espionage activities, we need not follow their careers in any detail beyond this point. Only Philby continued to work for the KGB, though his services were in suspense from the time of his dismissal from SIS in the summer of 1951 until his re-employment under press cover in Beirut in 1956, after being exonerated in the House of Commons by the Foreign Secretary, Harold Macmillan, in November 1955. At that time he had received, through Blunt, a message of encouragement from the KGB. This was probably Blunt's last service to the KGB before his exposure to the FBI by Michael Straight in 1963. At the beginning of that year Philby, under pressure from SIS to make a full confession, covertly left Beirut to join his friends in Moscow. The rights and wrongs of the decision to re-employ him cannot be discussed here; all that can be said is that, during his stay in Beirut, he was not in a position to injure British interests, except in so far as the employment of such a man in any capacity was injurious. Burgess died in Moscow in 1963 not long after Philby arrived there. Philby soon made contact with Maclean, who had never been a close friend, and seduced Melinda, thus destroying such domestic harmony as she and Donald had managed to re-establish. Maclean, after a long illness, died in Moscow in March 1983 and was spared a eulogy by Philby, who did not attend the funeral. His ashes, like those of Burgess, were brought to this country for interment. About a fortnight after Maclean's death Blunt died suddenly in London. In the preceding weeks Straight had been in London, promoting the sale of his book and propagating what Blunt regarded as a misleading account of their former association. There was no final meeting between them.

Both Philby and Maclean wrote books in exile. Philby's, to which reference has already been made, was an attempt to glamorise the life of a spy, whilst viciously denigrating the Anglo-American intelligence community; it was thus a continuation of the destructive work begun by the successful flight of Maclean and Burgess. The failure of MI5 to apprehend them and the reluctance of MI6 to accept that Philby was the 'third man' made a dismal impression on the FBI and CIA. This was all the more damaging at a period when McCarthyism was still strong and the Senator was charging the US State Department with harbouring communists and being altogether too amenable to British influence. The break-down in Anglo-American cooperation in the field of intelligence was a rich harvest for the KGB.

Maclean's book,[18] which was published in this country in 1970, was written at a time when détente between the USA and the USSR had begun, but the *Ostpolitik* of the Federal German government was in its infancy. West Germany is, therefore, depicted as the main villain; the USA is regarded as unregenerate, but at least capable of seeing that its best interest lies in helping the USSR to maintain world peace. It is in promoting this endeavour that Britain, by exerting her influence in Washington, is seen by Maclean as playing a useful, if subordinate, role. If this was indeed the view he held, one must ask oneself whether he recognised what a penetrating light it shed upon the futility of his own career in espionage. There can be little doubt that he and Burgess, in their reports to the Kremlin, had given full rein to their anti-Americanism and so fuelled Soviet belief, at crucial moments of the Cold War, that the USA was at least half-way to becoming a fascist power. In short, these careers had not been a contribution to the world peace that they extolled, but had intensified and prolonged the Cold War. The real work for peace and understanding had been done by their former colleagues, who had continued to serve their country, and to foster the delicate buds of détente, which blossomed, however briefly, at Helsinki in 1975. But for Maclean's fatal decision as an undergraduate at Cambridge, he could have become an effective part of this more hopeful process and ended an honourable career as Sir Donald.

What moral should we draw from this cautionary tale? It is, surely, that ideology confers a great advantage upon the Intelligence Service that subscribes to it. Z. K. Brzezinski defines ideology as combining theory and action with a 'consciousness of purpose and of the general thrust of history. It gives its adherents a sense of consistency and certainty that is too often absent among those . . . brought up in the tradition of short-range pragmatism.[19] The dismal series of events that we have recounted illustrates this definition admirably and points the contrast between British and Russian practice. Between the wars, whilst Lenin and then Stalin built up first a massive internal security system and then a foreign intelligence network, Britain ran down and starved both MI5 and MI6. In respect of MI6, no operative anti-communist section had been set up before 1939, when the imminence of war with Germany absorbed all available resources. By way of contrast, the USSR began in the late 1920s to develop a long-term plan of marked subtlety and sophistication. It involved openly communist university teachers, such as Maurice Dobb, who – whether consciously or unconsciously – prepared young minds to receive the implantation; also talent-spotters, such as Blunt, who made a selection from among those implanted of the ones who had an aptitude for the double-life. This chosen band was then handed over to Soviet 'control', which instructed them to renounce communism and embark upon careers that would in due course place them in situations of strategic advantage.

The resultant contest between Soviet intelligence and British counter-intelligence resembles – at least until the late 1950s – a football match between Manchester United and the Corinthian Casuals in the years of the decline of amateurism. Nonetheless the outcome would not have been so onesided if it had not been for another ideological factor affecting the political education of the young and the climate of opinion in which they grew up. They had begun, even before any serious threat of fascism emerged, to give the benefit of the doubt in any crisis, demanding exercise of critical judgement, to those standing on the political Left. If Stalin was said to be killing *Kulaks*, the capitalist press had invented the stories. If he had made a pact with Hitler, it was because Chamberlain had been trying to enmesh the two dictators in war. The intellectual Left had long since captured the high ground held by those who believe that all those using slogans about 'the people' and 'the peace', however contradictory their immediate actions might seem to be, would in the long run be seen to have acted 'compassionately' and to be the true 'friends of humanity'. No one promoted this cause more effectively than the *Weimar* communist, Leonhard Frank, author of *Man Is Good* and coiner of the catch-phrase: 'Left, where the heart is'.[20] The delusion that the apparent totalitarianism of the Left could always be distinguished from the obvious totalitarianism of the Right was reinforced by a curious aberration of modern political thought which, unlike that of Aristotle, saw politics in linear terms, so that the line extending to the Left, however far it reached into extremism, could never meet the line extending in the opposite direction and ending in fascism. Even after physics had abandoned straight lines, it seemed to be hard for the political scientists of the Left to see that the two extremes must inevitably meet in a form of totalitarianism in which distinctions between Left and Right no longer had any meaning. This was the political climate in which Blunt, Burgess, Maclean and Philby were raised. If anyone believes that today this climate and these delusions no longer exist, he or she must be a person who neither reads newspapers nor watches television.

10. Secret Intelligence in the United States, 1947–1982: the CIA's Search for Legitimacy

HARRY HOWE RANSOM

I

WHY has the United States secret intelligence system been perpetually in controversy while other nations' intelligence agencies usually are isolated from public policy disputes? With that as the central question this chapter will explore the American intelligence experience in the three and a half decades since the Second World War. It will place emphasis on the political and constitutional, rather than operational, issues. During this period the Central Intelligence Agency (CIA) was constantly striving for a legitimacy that has remained elusive.

The isolationist heritage of the United States, the American suspicion of centralised government power embodied in diffused executive-legislative authority, and violent swings in perceptions of national security – all have prevented the nation from coming to terms satisfactorily with the organisation and management of the central intelligence function. Also, American idealism periodically raises its troublesome head. These factors have deprived the CIA of legitimacy and impaired the fulfilment of its missions.

The CIA's history since its founding in 1947 has been one of sharp fluctuations between the secrecy and freedom of action that nations normally grant their intelligence agencies and the strict accountability and legislative monitoring provided by the American constitution.

How to explain these swings? Why has America seemed at times embarrassed to acknowledge the possession of a secret intelligence arm of government?

A permanent secret intelligence system within the American constitutional framework created unique policy dilemmas from the beginning. Other nations barely acknowledge the existence of intelligence agencies. Although the intelligence function is as old as international relations, in the United States coordinated central intelligence was not accepted as a necessity, except in wartime, until Congress created the CIA in 1947.

Controversy enveloped questions of purpose, functions and organisation for central intelligence as the Second World War ended. A strong consensus prevailed that surprises, such as the attack on Pearl Harbor in 1941, must be avoided in the future by a permanent, centralised organisation. The wartime experience with the Office of Strategic Services gave strong impetus for post-war reform. The OSS experience also provided a personnel base, and an organisational style for American post-war intelligence.

Proposals for intelligence reform nonetheless stirred internal bureaucratic conflict over what, exactly, was to be the structure for the post-war system as well as questions of jurisdiction and of the assignment of roles and functions. Although the bureaucratic combat raged for two years over jurisdictional issues, ultimately little public debate was heard in Congress on the organisational questions. Congress was assured at the outset that the CIA would not have domestic espionage roles, and led to believe that CIA's principal role, in serving the presidency, would be as an information coordinator. Information would be gathered primarily by the State Department, the armed services and existing intelligence bureaux. It was generally assumed that the CIA would have very limited operational functions. No public discussion or even hint was heard that the CIA was to be used as an instrument for overseas covert political action. A general theme of this chapter is that the CIA's later problems were a consequence in part of the way in which the agency came to be assigned to a variety of disparate secret functions after 1947.

II THE EARLY YEARS

The CIA was born in the year that the Cold War was declared.

President Harry S. Truman told Congress in his 1947 message requesting aid for Greece and Turkey, both seen as threatened by Soviet communism, that the United States must resist communist expansion everywhere in the world. Cold War or not, the functions of the CIA were sharply circumscribed in the original legislation. No major operational functions overseas and no domestic spying or internal covert operations were explicitly assigned to the CIA. Concern for civil liberties was evident, but perhaps greater concern was felt for protecting the existing intelligence functions of established departments. Granted, the legislative charter was written in ambiguous terms, but CIA was not understood to have been assigned covert operational functions overseas. The State Department, the Federal Bureau of Investigation and the armed services had waged successful struggles to retain a high degree of intelligence autonomy.

From the start, CIA's principal bureaucratic advantage over the established agencies was that it served the Presidency, and was accountable only to the National Security Council, which the President headed.

Relations between the United States and the Soviet Union continued their trend towards hostility after 1947. In 1948 a 'war scare' occurred when some military advisers suggested the possibility or, indeed probability, of imminent war with the Soviet Union. In February 1948 the communists seized political command in Czechoslovakia; simultaneously the governments of France and Italy were threatened by communist gains at the polls; and in the United States the Army intelligence chief had received word from the Commander in Chief of the European Command, General Lucius Clay, forecasting that war with the Soviet Union might come suddenly. During this period the CIA was launched into a massive programme of covert operations to combat the perceived red offensive. Specifically, the National Security Council approved NSC 10/2, a secret paper sharply increasing the scope and range of covert actions directed at the Soviet Union. The programme included political warfare, economic warfare, psychological warfare and some paramilitary operations.

This state of heightened hostility towards Russia prompted Congress to amend the National Security Act in 1949, granting the CIA an extraordinary 'peacetime' secrecy. The Director was charged with protecting the sources and methods of the agency. Even Congress could be excluded from such information. The CIA Director was exempt from requirements that he disclose, even to

Congress, the staff size and budget of the agency; and he was authorised to expend at his personal discretion funds for secret operations. Some members of Congress had protested against this secrecy and blank cheque. There were able only to get assurances that all CIA operations were to be overseas; fears of a domestic *Gestapo* were dismissed as groundless. Prohibitions on any CIA spying within the United States appeared to be unambiguous in the statutory charter.[1] But the degree of secrecy granted the agency was likely to make future Congressional oversight difficult. The year 1949 being a time of great international tension, questions about accountability were not pressed in Congress.

The CIA was granted exemption from normal accountability in the year when most leading officials were nervous about the possibility of war and had persuaded the public and Congress of a clear and present danger. During this period the North Atlantic Treaty was signed, the Soviet Union exploded its first atomic device, and communists achieved political control of China. Top-security planners were at work shaping National Security Council paper 'No. 68', a scheme to remobilise American resources for a cold, and perhaps a hot, war with Russia. In this secret planning document, the now-famous 'NSC-68', a major operational role was assigned to the CIA for espionage, as well as psychological warfare, covert action and even paramilitary operations.

In a period dominated by a 'war-scare' the CIA received from the President a charter for conducting what was, in effect, a secret Third World War. Within a year or so after the 'war-scare' of March 1948, the CIA was secretly given its initial covert action missions against the Soviet Union. According to Harry Rositzke, a major participant, the CIA was assigned:

1. To collect secret intelligence on the Soviet Union itself . . . .
2. To place American agents within the Soviet intelligence services . . . .
3. To carry out covert actions designed to weaken Soviet control over its own population and the peoples of Eastern Europe . . . .[2]

The containment policy had been expanded to include aggressive action within the Soviet Union. The CIA set out to counter the communists in the Italian elections in 1948 and came away feeling successful. In some of its other more difficult assignments, such as arming anti-communist guerrillas and in the conduct of sabotage behind the Iron Curtain, the going was rougher and the results counter-productive. But all of this had a profound effect upon the future of the CIA; most significantly the agency came to be dominated by the covert operators. The intelligence function got second priority. The cost of this in efficient intelligence performance was to be high.

For example, the North Korean invasion of South Korea came as a surprise in June 1950. American leaders were misled by national intelligence estimates. The net estimate at the time was that a war in Korea would not happen. When North Korea invaded the South on 25 June 1950, President Truman decided to intervene with American troops and the United States began a military mobilisation. During this period the Central Intelligence Agency began a major expansion, in personnel, in funds and in roles and missions.

The CIA's formative years, 1946–52, left an indelible mark on the agency's subculture and operating priorities. Other than prohibition against domestic spying, the agency operated with minimum executive controls and with little Congressional supervision. Most striking was the growth in size of the agency. By 1953 the CIA had grown to six times its 1947 size. Its covert operations budget had increased more than twentyfold. The Deputy Directorate for 'Plans', the division responsible for espionage and covert operations, came to command the major share of the agency's budget, personnel and resources by the end of 1952. Clandestine collection (espionage) and covert action (political intervention) accounted for three-fourths of the agency's budget by 1952.[3] Almost two-thirds of CIA's employees by the end of 1952 could be accurately described as clandestine operators. While some of this activity was in pursuit of information, most was devoted to various forms of political intervention, much of it, in effect, 'aping the adversary' or reacting in kind to the real or imagined covert activities of the Soviet Union. The policy of the United States was worldwide containment of the Soviet Union; the CIA was on the front line attempting to implement this policy. The agency's leadership was asked few questions by responsible political authority, because a foreign policy consensus existed. 'Trust in honourable men' was the accepted operational code.

Caught up in the fever of Cold War after 1948, and particularly after the Korean War began, the CIA came to be mobilised on a war footing. If foreign policy was mobilised after 1950, so too were the conceptions about the organisation and functions of the CIA.

Decisions made and lack of conceptual clarity about organisation and functions during this period were to be the basis for some of the CIA's major problems later.

In steady progression over these years, the CIA became less a coordinator of information and more an independent producer of intelligence. The agency also began to develop an ever-expanding capability for secret political action overseas. The original idea of an agency independent of particular ideologies and policies, strategies or programmes was gradually diluted as the CIA began to display the features of an independent organisation, a huge bureaucracy in its own right, with its own foreign policy, its own bureaucratic turf to protect, its own secret communications channels, its own airlines and secret armies, and vast sums of unvouchered funds.

Furthermore, as the CIA evolved and grew, it became fractured into many separate compartments; intelligence, counter-intelligence, security, covert action, technical services and many other segments. Each became isolated from the other and it was increasingly difficult for the CIA Director effectively to coordinate all the separate parts of the agency, let alone provide coherent leadership as the 'Director of Central Intelligence' for the ever-expanding intelligence units outside the CIA.

The point here is that in these formative years, inadequate attention was given to a conceptual framework for central intelligence. Policy and organisational choices were made that would return to haunt the CIA in later years. In sum, the following features characterised the intelligence system in its crucial initial period, 1946–52:

(a) An ambiguous statute that was designed as an organic charter for the CIA, but in truth papered over the unwillingness of the various pre-existing departments and their intelligence units to accept the concept of a centralised intelligence system.

(b) Perceptions of a Soviet threat that quickly transformed the CIA into a dual agency preoccupied with clandestine activities and covert political action overseas, spurred on by a staff of Office of Strategic Service (OSS) veterans of the Second World War, who were more interested in clandestine capers than in intelligence analysis and reports. An *esprit de guerre* permeated the intelligence system created in 1947.

(c) The consequent development of the CIA into an additional agency for intelligence and operations, leaving the coordinating functions in the shadows. Not long after 1947 there were the beginnings, in effect, of 'two CIAs'.

(d) A failure of Presidents, and of Congresses as well, to comprehend and be attentive to the intelligence function and sensitive to the delicate and important balances that need to be maintained within an intelligence system. Instead of being a modest staff arm of the Presidency, the CIA had grown sixfold since its start, and was a vast and to some extent inherently unmanageable intelligence apparatus. Allen Dulles once said that an intelligence system is 'an ideal vehicle for conspiracy'. The American intelligence system, even by 1952, had become infected, at the very least, with a bureaucratic propensity – some might call it conspiracy – to further the importance, growth and influence of the CIA in the national security field.[4]

III THE ALLEN DULLES YEARS

Hostile relations with the Soviet Union continued throughout the 1950s. Consequently, this was a period of intelligence permissiveness, with casual direction from the Presidency and almost no meaningful monitoring by Congress. Allen W. Dulles joined the agency in 1951 as chief of covert operations (DDP) and was named Director in 1953 by President Eisenhower. He served until 1961. In what might be called the 'Dulles era', accountability procedures that were routine for most government functions were waived for the CIA. Responding to political pressures in the mid-1950s, however, significant movement occurred towards the creation of at least a semblance of mechanisms for Congressional accountability. These changes occurred, significantly, at a time when the US and the USSR were engaged in 'summit' meetings in the hope of easing tensions. Even so, the Eisenhower years were characterised by an aggressively pursued goal of worldwide containment of communism. In the 1952 Presidential campaign, Republicans were highly critical of the Democratic Administration's 'passive' containment. Eisenhower promised more aggressive foreign policies in dealing with Russia. He cited the communist takeover of China, Soviet dominance in Eastern Europe and the Korean War as consequences of US timidity. His leading foreign policy adviser, John Foster Dulles, spoke of 'rolling back' communism and 'liberation' of Eastern Europe. Containment was to be expanded from Central Europe to other areas of the globe, not only in the Middle East, Africa and Southeast Asia but also East Asia and Latin America. The CIA was seen as a tool for maintaining the *status quo* in many sections of the world threatened by revolution. Secret operations grew enormously during this period and were authorised and undertaken with few of the normal checks and balances of the American constitutional system.

During this period the Central Intelligence Agency was, if not a 'rogue elephant', at least a major instrument of foreign policy operating in semi-independence. Keep in mind that the CIA Director and the Secretary of State were brothers. Rather than being an adjunct of the State or Defense Departments, the CIA, in the words of one of its most authoritative historians, 'assumed the initiative in defining the ways covert operations could advance U.S. policy objectives and in determining what kinds of operations were suited to particular policy needs'.[5] The CIA undertook major covert operations to alter the governments in Iran and Guatemala in 1953 and 1954. The United States role in these operations was not widely known at the time. Later, information was leaked to the media, designed to create the impression that the CIA was a foreign policy instrument of cool, bloodless efficiency. The CIA, it was argued, had managed to remove, with little bloodshed, two allegedly communist-leaning leaders, Mossadegh in Iran and Arbenz in Guatemala.[6]

Word of CIA's presumed successes strengthened the 'Clandestine Service' within the CIA. In the process, the intelligence function of the agency came to be de-emphasised. Furthermore, the absence of Congressional controls and monitoring procedures risked mistakes and political bad judgement. An 'anything goes' atmosphere characterised the Clandestine Service.

Perhaps this is how the excesses and abuses came about. One example is the agency's drug-testing programme. Details of this were not publicly revealed until 1975 when the CIA's testing of exotic drugs on unsuspecting individuals was publicised. Drugs were given experimentally to individuals without the participation of medical and scientific personnel. One person is known to have died in the process. Those responsible for the drug testing were apparently exempt at the time from accountability and control procedures.

Most notable during this period of permissiveness, however, is the reality that until 1955, covert action projects were undertaken without formal approval mechanisms by responsible political authority. When the NSC initially authorised covert action in 1948, it was assumed that the State and Defense Departments would provide policy control. As covert operations expanded in volume in the early 1950s, general guidelines rather than specific review of projects became the norm. Strict accountability to responsible political authority was not applied. In 1955 the National Security Council issued two policy directives, formalising control procedures for approving proposed covert actions. The external political environment forced these changes. Even so, not until 1959 were rigorous approval procedures applied. Before then, meetings of control groups were infrequent; they became weekly in 1959. Not until after the Bay of Pigs episode in 1961, however, did a routine, formal review mechanism for covert operations exist. Congressional monitoring was equally casual through most of the 1950s.

Within a few months after the death of Stalin in March 1953, the posture of the Soviet Union was perceived to have changed. Gradually the tone in the relations between the US and the USSR became less hostile. A Soviet-American 'summit' meeting at Geneva was proposed, to discuss possible disarmament schemes and to attempt to ease East–West tensions. By mid-1955, a 'spirit of Geneva' was the popularised slogan characterising US–Soviet relations. Even with a foreign policy consensus, and a cordial relationship between the CIA and the Congressional leadership, rumblings of discontent were heard within the intelligence community about Allen Dulles' administrative leadership and concern was voiced by liberal Democrats about the 'invisible government' aspects of the intelligence system. Some felt that accountability and effective external policy control were absent, with inherent long-term dangers. Meanwhile, a Commission on the Organization of the Executive Branch of Government, with Herbert Hoover as chairman, was created in 1954. A Hoover Commission task force under General Mark Clark was assigned to study the intelligence system. The Clark Task Force found serious administrative weaknesses within the CIA, and expressed alarm about the absence of external policy controls and Congressional oversight. They recommended to the full Hoover Commission that a monitoring group be established, composed of members of Congress and distinguished citizens. This idea was rejected. Instead, the Commission proposed a joint Congressional oversight committee and a separate group of private citizens to oversee intelligence operations for the President.

In January 1955, Senator Mike Mansfield introduced a resolution proposing a Joint Congressional watchdog committee. For over a year Mansfield's proposal was under study in Congress – it was the year of the 'Spirit of Geneva' – and backed by 35 co-sponsors in the Senate.

In opposition, the CIA mounted a powerful behind-the-scenes counter-attack on proposals to widen the circle of knowledge and to strengthen policy control of covert operations. Dulles quietly persuaded the Presidency as well as Congressional leaders that a Joint Congressional Committee with full access to CIA secrets would compromise the effectiveness of the secret intelligence system.

The proposal was opposed by the 'inner club' of the Senate, particularly Senate leaders such as Russell, Hayden and Saltonstall – who were already privy to some secret CIA information. Joining them were Senator Alben Barkley, former Vice-President and NSC member, and Senator Stuart Symington, former Air Force Secretary, who strongly opposed a joint intelligence committee. The measure was voted down 59 to 27, in April 1956, more than a dozen original co-sponsors having withdrawn their support.

It was during this period, 1956–7, however, that Congress began to take significant steps towards rigorously monitoring the intelligence system. Oversight subcommittees of the Armed Services and the Appropriations Committees were formally established in the Senate. The House Armed Services Committee also authorised an intelligence subcommittee. In the Appropriations Committee, an informal group was designated by Chairman Clarence Cannon, but its membership remained secret. But this was no more than a first step, for even with these arrangements, little staff time was assigned to monitoring intelligence operations. The committees did not meet regularly and staff assistance was extremely meagre. 'Oversight windowdressing' might be the most accurate way to characterise these efforts.

As suggested at the outset, the Allen Dulles years were critical in that they established patterns of permissiveness for the CIA that would influence its later organisational life. Rather than functioning in a supporting role, as a staff arm of the presidency, the CIA in the

1950s became an independent bureaucracy – with its own policy preferences and resources for conducting a secret foreign policy.

The clandestine side of the agency came to dominate the organisation. The intelligence system became further fragmented. The CIA may be said to have failed to create a true intelligence 'community'. The leadership barely tried to do so. Executive and Congressional control mechanisms had a small beginning, but they were not taken seriously in either the executive or legislative branch. The Dulles years were an era when the slogan 'trust in honourable men' became an intelligence operational code firmly entrenched in the hearts and minds of both the executive and the legislative leadership.

Furthermore, the prevailing moods of this period are well symbolised by the words of the 'Doolittle Report', issued by a special committee of the Hoover Commission study of the Federal government's organisation in 1955.

> [W]e are facing an implacable enemy whose avowed objective is world domination by whatever means and at whatever cost. There are no rules in such a game. Hitherto accepted norms of human conduct do not apply. If the United States is to survive, long-standing concepts of 'fair play' must be reconsidered. . . . We must learn to subvert, sabotage and destroy our enemies by more clever and more sophisticated, and more effective methods than those used against us.[7]

The CIA leadership had tasted the heady wine of short-term covert-action successes in Iran and Guatemala. The belief became widespread in the higher councils of government that the nation had at its command a sharp and effective tool for fixing foreign political systems that might go wrong – in terms of American interests – in various parts of the world. Meanwhile, in the words of an authoritative history of central intelligence in the period under survey: 'Policy makers did not look to the Agency for information and analysis'.[8] Perhaps that is the most significant statement of all; the CIA had become something more, and something less, than the intelligence system that Congress had intended to create in 1947.

IV THE KENNEDY–JOHNSON YEARS

At the outset of the Kennedy–Johnson Administration no compelling incentives existed to stimulate reform of the intelligence system. Advisers who surrounded Kennedy were generally satisfied with the operational modes of the intelligence system. Kennedy may have wanted to replace Allen Dulles as CIA Director, but continuity in that job was accorded a high priority, and he was not inclined to challenge an entrenched Cold War bureaucracy. Consequently, this was not a period of agitation for substantial intelligence reform. Behind its high wall of secrecy, the intelligence system evolved into a giant bureaucracy, uninhibited by detailed executive monitoring, legislative oversight or strict accountability. Kennedy discovered the chronic weakness of the system in April 1961. After the Bay of Pigs fiasco, the leadership of the CIA was held accountable for failure. Within six months after the Bay of Pigs, Allen Dulles and his principal deputies were gone from the agency. But surprisingly few structural changes followed the Cuban disaster.

Reaction to the Bay of Pigs fiasco in the direction of basic internal reorganisation or more effective forms of external oversight was no doubt inhibited by the continuing assumption that the Soviet Union was a clear and present danger to United States security. While John F. Kennedy was disillusioned about the professionalism of the intelligence system as a result of the abortive Cuban expedition, he nonetheless saw the nation to be in imminent danger of losing out to 'world communism' in various parts of the world. The intelligence apparatus continued to be viewed as a vital tool of American foreign policy, and the 'trust in honourable men' formula was considered to be adequate. In his days as a US Senator, Kennedy had been one of the early supporters of legislation strengthening Congressional oversight of secret intelligence. As President he resisted the idea. From the White House, he was preoccupied with such crises as the Berlin Wall, the Vienna summit meeting with Khrushchev, the situation in Laos, Vietnam and the Congo, and later the Cuban Missile Crisis. In these brink-of-war crises, he was not disposed to give high priority to intelligence reform. As a consequence, the intelligence system continued to have virtual immunity from questioning. Little attention was given to the reality that the Bay of Pigs, the Berlin Wall and the Cuban missile crisis had uncovered basic flaws in the intelligence system, both in its intelligence and covert-action features. The Kennedy Administration had reaffirmed the Truman Doctrine, in effect endorsed the 'domino theory' and was moving ahead with programmes for military superiority, flexible response, counter-revolution and 'nation building'. Khrushchev's avowal of support for wars of national liberation, and the subsequent Soviet efforts to put strategic missiles in Cuba, sharply diminished constituencies for those few libertarian-minded (or neo-isolationist) members of Congress who continued to worry about the dangers of 'invisible government' associated with a huge, unaccountable intelligence apparatus.

Lyndon Johnson's first question at the time of Kennedy's assassination in Dallas was whether the communists were striking the first blow. As President, Johnson incorporated all the cold war assumptions about containment, 'dominoes' and the need for the United States to be the world policeman. In the new Johnson Administration, little concern was visible at highest levels of government about problems of intelligence policy, organisation or accountability. A rising involvement in Southeast Asia, particularly after US military intervention escalated in 1965, eliminated any concern about the 'intelligence problem' that might have been present.

Yet an underlying nucleus of concern about the dangers – and inherent inefficiencies – of the intelligence system was ever present. Striking a rough estimate from voting patterns, some 10 per cent of the House membership and perhaps 20 per cent of Senators were uneasy about the intelligence system's freedom from accountability. Certainly there was no dearth of reform proposals during this period. These often took the form of proposals for greater access by Congress to details of intelligence operations. For example, in 1963, Representative John Lindsay, then a liberal Republican from New York, proposed a detailed probe of the CIA. His effort failed to gain support. In the Senate, Eugene McCarthy tried in 1966 to persuade the Foreign Relations Committee to conduct an investigation of CIA effects on foreign policy. Although substantial debate was generated, the Senate's 'inner club' prevailed and McCarthy's proposal failed. As a consequence the anomaly persisted of the Senate Foreign Relations Committee being excluded from a role in intelligence policy-making.

Efforts at reform can be correlated with the so-called 'Spirit of Glassboro' when President Johnson met Premier Aleksei Kosygin in New Jersey in 1967. In addition, a correlation exists between opposition to the Vietnam War and disclosures by the mass media of a number of major CIA covert operations, and an increase in the number of proposals – and support for them – to make the CIA more accountable to responsible political authority.

Opposition to the Vietnam War clearly motivated *Ramparts* magazine to disclose in February 1967 CIA's programme of secretly subsidising dozens of American private, voluntary organisations. These included student associations, religious, labour, journalistic, academic research, publishing and almost any organisation with overseas programmes. The CIA secretly supplied millions of dollars to private groups, hoping to counter Soviet sponsorship of front groups overseas. Private organisations of all kinds – often unknowingly to rank and file members – were instruments of American foreign policy. A striking example of a beneficiary of this programme was the National Students Association, a student-managed organisation made up of some 300 member universities in the United States. Between 1952 and 1967, the NSA was secretly subsidised by the CIA with more than $3 million for international programmes. The purpose of the money was to ensure that the United States be represented by American students at international youth conferences where communist youth movements were strongly represented. When it became public knowledge that the CIA had covertly invaded the American private sector for cold war purposes, the reaction was the strongest negative protest in the CIA's history. This was evidenced in press and public criticism. President Lyndon Johnson reacted by ordering an end to CIA financing of the NSA. The President also appointed a three-man committee to review the entire secret subsidy programme. Under-Secretary of State Nicholas Katzenbach headed a committee that recommended the abolition of secret financial assistance by the Federal Government to any of the nation's educational or private voluntary organisations. This recommendation was accepted and the storm subsided.

North Vietnam and Vietcong military forces launched a massive offensive on 30 January 1968 during the Vietnamese *Tet* holidays against every base and urban centre in South Vietnam. Although the Vietcong penetrated the American embassy compound in Saigon, this offensive was ultimately a military defeat for the north. But in knocking over the 'essential domino' – American public opinion – North Vietnam won a major psychological victory. The discouragement of the *Tet* offensive, after American leaders had been saying the war was going well, signalled the end of the cold war consensus in the United States.

With the end of the foreign policy consensus came the beginning of fundamental changes in the intelligence system. By the later 1960s, some signs of change were visible, yet behind the scenes covert actions had continued to dominate CIA operations. Some efforts had been made to improve the intelligence estimates, taking advantage of significant technological advances that abetted collection. Furthermore, the scene of many operations shifted to Third World areas.

The quality of CIA leadership and performance came under increasingly close scrutiny, particularly in the face of questions raised after the various intelligence crises of the 1960s: the downing of the U-2 over Russia (1960); the Bay of Pigs (1961); the Cuban Missile crisis (1962); and the overthrow and assassination of President Diem of South Vietnam (1963). These events stimulated doubts about the CIA's efficacy. Even so, the internal system of the agency – its structure, its personnel and its operating codes – remained fundamentally unchanged from the previous decade. For example, John McCone, who in late 1961 succeeded Allen Dulles as CIA Director, continued to spend 90 per cent of his time on clandestine activities.

What had changed by the end of the Kennedy–Johnson era was the tolerance level – in Congress and in the mass media – of secret operations that had gone wrong, had been patently unwise, or had violated basic constitutional principles. What America will tolerate in times of a consensus foreign policy is not the same as what is tolerable when the consensus evaporates.

The 'Watergate' scandals and related disclosures involving the CIA, and the later Congressional and media exposures of intelligence misdeeds, possibly would never have happened had the foreign policy consensus held into the 1970s. But by the end of the Kennedy–Johnson era one could only see harbingers of a later flood of efforts to reform the intelligence system, and to set limits on its operations.

V THE NIXON–KISSINGER YEARS

The dissolution of foreign policy consensus that began in 1968 with the '*Tet* Offensive' in Vietnam was the beginning of the CIA's most critical period, critical because CIA lost its immunity from close public surveillance. Indeed, the legitimacy of the agency came under a cloud which remained for more than a decade.

Richard M. Nixon's first major foreign policy statement as President argued that the post-war era in international relations had ended. By this he meant that bi-polarity had ended. China had replaced the United States as the dominant foe of the Soviet Union. And Russia had achieved a rough parity in military power with the United States. Nixon also suggested that an upwards spiralling arms race endangered both superpowers. Consequently a 'Nixon Doctrine' was proclaimed, suggesting in imprecise terms a new foreign policy of negotiation, reduced American foreign interventionism, and the hope for greater burden-sharing by US allies. Containment of the Soviet Union was not abandoned as a goal; it was asserted in a less strident rhetoric. Eventually these ideas emerged in the new language of détente.

One consequence of this cold war truce was that the CIA as an instrument of cold war interventionism lost its immunity from Congressional probing and criticism. Eventual disclosures of a variety of CIA covert operations confronted the CIA with a legitimacy crisis. The release of the 'Pentagon Papers' in 1971 was the beginning of widespread distrust of the government's deceptive methods for taking decisions. In the eyes of some critics, covert operations had been a major cause for America's entrapment in a Southeast Asian quagmire. President Nixon was confronted by a Congress that was aggressively reasserting itself. First came the National Commitments Resolution in the Senate in 1969 – limiting presidential power – followed by the repeal in 1970 of the Gulf of Tonkin Resolution which in 1964 had given the President a free hand in Southeast Asia.

President Nixon's 1972 trips to China in February and to Russia in May and the first round of the SALT agreements set the stage for major shifts in the public view of the Soviet threat. The public got the impression that the Cold War was over. Détente was now the popularised slogan. The climate was right for Congress to challenge presidential power, and the secrecy and appropriateness of covert operations became major policy issues. The War Powers Act, passed by Congress over presidential veto in November 1973, is a major example of a generalised challenge to the 'imperial' presidency. Covert actions overseas began to diminish in number in the late 1960s. This decline was a consequence of détente. It also reflected the overall retrenchment in American foreign policy, attributable to dissent about the Vietnam War, accompanied by the more aggressive Congressional role in determining foreign policy.

Two major examples of CIA covert activity, when they became public knowledge, contributed to making the policy, organisation and control of the CIA a major public issue. One was the disclosure that the CIA had intervened in the electoral process in Chile, ending with crude secret efforts to undo the election of Allende as President and an ambiguous CIA complicity in his ultimate overthrow and death. The other was the disclosure that the CIA violated its Congressional charter by engaging in domestic spying on anti-Vietnam War dissidents within the United States. The manipulation of Chilean politics received widespread, bi-partisan condemnation. The CIA's domestic spying and its complicity with the Watergate scandal were even more seriously damaging. CIA defenders are quick to note that the CIA abuses were at presidential command. The main point is that the CIA's vulnerability in the face of these disclosures reflected a redefined foreign policy, the evaporation of foreign policy consensus, and most importantly, changes in some of the basic cold war assumptions. This period was characterised by summit meetings in Washington, Moscow and Peking, wide-ranging international agreements at Vladivostok and Helsinki, trade agreements and cultural exchanges. Accompanying these events were deep suspicions about the activities of the CIA and about the adequacy of arrangements for oversight, accountability and evaluation of performance. The time was propitious for intelligence reform.

VI THE CARTER YEARS

Intelligence reform began in earnest in 1974 when Congress, reacting to disclosures about US intervention in Chile, and to revelations about a secret war on Laos, circumscribed CIA's covert operations by strict legislative control measures. These took the form of an amendment to the Foreign Assistance Act of 1974 (Section 622, 75 Stat. 424) which became known as the Hughes–Ryan Amendment. After a quarter of a century of tolerance or inaction, Congress made an effort to return to its original conception of the CIA as an agency for intelligence only. Congress stipulated that in the future the CIA was to be used overseas only for intelligence purposes. Covert action was to be limited to those presumably rare cases in which the President could certify to Congress that vital national interests were involved and Congress was to be informed of the details of all covert operations in a timely fashion. Since Congress has widely diffused authority in foreign affairs, covert actions had to be reported to as many as eight committees including House and Senate Committees on foreign affairs, armed services, appropriations and intelligence. Congress intended to inhibit covert action and the Hughes–Ryan amendment certainly would have that effect.

Meanwhile the CIA became the target for study by other groups. A Commission on the Organization of the Government for the Conduct of Foreign Policy, known as the Murphy Commission, undertook detailed studies and concluded in its 1975 *Report* that 'firmer direction and oversight of the intelligence community are essential'. Disclosures of domestic spying by CIA raised such a furore that President Ford felt it necessary to appoint a commission under Vice-President Rockefeller. Ronald Reagan and other well-known conservative leaders were members. The Rockefeller Commission reported that the CIA had violated its charter in its domestic spying activities. Its report called for new congressional and executive mechanisms to oversee the intelligence system more carefully. Specific organisational reforms were recommended, including a Joint Congressional Oversight Committee.

But the Congressional investigations in 1975 and 1976 attracted the greatest attention. A Senate select committee, under Senator Frank Church, produced a great volume of hearings and reports, its final report suggesting 87 recommendations for reform. The recommendations stressed the need for more effective Congressional oversight and clarified systems for internal accountability. Perhaps the most important recommendation was that Congress enact a new statutory intelligence charter, specifying the functions, and the restrictions, for each of the national intelligence agencies.

The investigation in the House of Representatives, under Representative Otis Pike, was a tempestuous affair, bringing the committee in frequent confrontation with the President, Secretary of State Kissinger and the CIA. In the process, the House committee, like its Senate counterpart, created a substantial volume of illustrative materials, published in its hearings and reports. It became so enmeshed in controversy that its final report was suppressed by the full House; nonetheless its contents leaked to the press, and its findings reflected badly on intelligence performance. Its reform recommendations were published, and like the Senate, the Pike Committee recommended major changes, including a new legislative charter for the intelligence agencies and the creation of a permanent House Select Committee for intelligence oversight.

In campaigning for the presidency in 1975–6, Jimmy Carter ran against the CIA. His campaign rhetoric frequently mentioned 'CIA abuses' which he promised to curb as President; he ran on a 'reform CIA' platform. His campaign speeches made frequent references to 'Watergate, Vietnam, CIA'. Senator Walter F. Mondale, Carter's choice as the Vice-Presidential nominee, had been an active member of Frank Church's select intelligence committee. Carter and Mondale promised the American people a remodelled intelligence community that would provide more timely and accurate information, and be subject to more effective oversight. Such objectives would be achieved by more careful executive monitoring and by a revised legislative charter that would stipulate intelligence agency duties and specify prohibited activities. Congress would be made a full member of the decision-making team, with access to information about secret operations, as well as authority over intelligence legislation and appropriations.

Earlier, President Ford had endeavoured to neutralise intelligence as a partisan issue by an Executive Order, issued on 18 February 1976 (Executive Order No. 11905) responding to the major disclosures consequent to the various Congressional investigations. Ford's order dealt mainly with internal organisation, particularly the authority of the Director of Central Intelligence, which was greatly strengthened. Accountability was clarified and the presidential office was placed in the line of command for covert operations. 'Plausible deniability' in which previous Presidents could disclaim knowledge of covert operations that became exposed was prohibited. Some critics believed that Ford's reforms did not place adequate limits on intelligence agency actions. Critics felt that standards for accountability and limits on covert operators were too loose.

By the end of 1975 the CIA issue had become a partisan political issue. Sentiments for counter-reform were already visible. In late December Richard Welch, the Chief of Station for CIA in Athens, Greece, was murdered by unknown assailants. His name had been publicised in an Athens newspaper, although his identity and residence were well known. Earlier, Philip Agee, an ex-CIA officer, published a book, *Inside the Company: CIA Diary*,[9] one feature of which was to reveal a substantial list of CIA secret agents. This began the practice by some radical groups of disclosing the names of many CIA agents in sensitive posts overseas. Public reaction to this tactic was generally negative and it strengthened counter-reform activity.

CIA Director William Colby was replaced in January 1976 by George Bush, an active politician, former chairman of the Republican National Committee and a man with presidential ambitions. In dismissing Colby, President Ford implied that Colby had been too cooperative with the media and Congressional investigations. Bush's assignments were to improve CIA morale, to repair the agency's public image and to strengthen Congressional support for the agency. The President hoped that an effective politician like Bush could 'turn around' the CIA issue, limit the damage from some reforms supported in Congress, and take advantage of the growing sentiment that the CIA had been too much exposed and was threatened by reform proposals and the antics of disaffected CIA personnel.

VII EFFORTS AT CHARTER REFORM

Jimmy Carter had made a commitment in his campaign for the presidency to reform the intelligence system. Accordingly, the Carter Administration attempted to guide Congress in shaping an omnibus charter for all of the major intelligence organisations, particularly the CIA and FBI. The idea was that existing statutes and executive orders would be codified, the intelligence organisation rationalised, and, most importantly, limits would be set on the permissible behaviour of secret agencies.

In organising his new administration, President Carter made the landmark decision of replacing the Director of Central Intelligence. Up to this point directors had not changed with an incoming administration. In all previous changes of administration, the incumbent CIA chief had continued in office, which has no fixed term. President Carter nominated Theodore Sorensen, who had served as a principal White House aide to President Kennedy. He was later active in New York politics. The nomination was opposed by powerful forces in the Senate, as well as elements of the intelligence establishment. The nomination eventually was withdrawn and the President turned to a more acceptable nominee, Admiral Stansfield

Turner. Now the office had been symbolically politicised, with Carter being the first President to see his initial choice of CIA Director denied, as well as the first President to change the CIA directorship with a new administration.

Not content simply to work with Congress to shape a new intelligence charter, the President's staff also drew up an intelligence executive order. Issued on 24 January 1978, the President's order implemented many of the recommendations of the Church Committee (Executive Order No. 12036). Of its twenty-six pages, eight dealt with prohibited activities. Accountability was focused and provisions for presidential and Congressional oversight were detailed. The Executive order was to serve as a stop-gap mechanism until such time as Congress could complete work on a new statutory charter. But it was during this period that public and Congressional opinion began to change regarding the growth of Soviet military power. The opinion became widespread that the intelligence agencies had underestimated Soviet intentions and capabilities. Soviet military power, particularly in long-range missiles and bombers, now appeared to be greater than had been predicted. Furthermore, developments in the Third World – especially Angola, Yemen and Ethiopia – carried the image of Russia on the move, aided by Cuban soldiers, against an increasingly defenceless United States. Events in Iran, which found the United States both misinformed and powerless, capped by the Soviet invasion of Afghanistan, created at least the beginnings of a new cold war consensus.

Intelligence reformers by the late 1970s were again on the defensive. The intelligence establishment had been successful in persuading many of the interests of the pluralistic decision-making system that radical reform of the intelligence system was unwise. The balance shifted and the weight was now on the side of security for the state rather than liberty for the individual. Fewer voices were heard supporting CIA reform and more were advocating the strengthening of both the intelligence and covert-action capabilities of the CIA.

In early 1978 a 263-page bi-partisan bill incorporating an omnibus intelligence charter was introduced in the Senate. The bill was the product of several years of executive-legislative negotiations and attempted to deal with the major problems of the various intelligence agencies. By 1978, however, the apparent consensus favouring a reform charter had dissipated. The bill died with the 95th Congress. In the next Congress, a less complex bill was introduced, but this effort to write a charter with fewer detailed restrictions was unsuccessful.

While charter reform maintained substantial support among the leadership of the House and Senate intelligence committees, the Presidency and the intelligence community no longer had a unified purpose. As Senator Patrick Moynihan quipped: 'Carter has now discovered that it is *his* CIA!' And while CIA Director Stansfield Turner continued to express support for a broad-gauged intelligence charter, he was unyielding – presumably with Administration support – on a number of points: opposing prior notification of Congress regarding covert operations, objecting to prohibited use of the media, academics and the clergy for intelligence 'cover', stressing need for strong sanctions for those disclosing the names of agents, and favouring exemptions for the CIA in the Freedom of Information Act. Meanwhile, relations with the Soviet Union had turned decidedly hostile and prospects for Senate ratification of the SALT II arms limitation treaty were rapidly fading. In this context, intelligence agency reform was losing political popularity. An example of the new mood is evident in President Carter's 1980 State of the Union address. Keep in mind that Carter had promised as a presidential candidate to curb CIA abuses. In January 1980 he continued to advocate 'quick passage' of a new charter stipulating what CIA should and should not do. But he added 'we must tighten our controls on sensitive government information and we need to remove unwarranted restraints on America's ability to collect intelligence'. The one-time advocate of intelligence reform was now stressing 'unwarranted restraints'. The intelligence reform movement became embroiled in 1980 election year partisanship. The Senate Committee worked diligently and its staff remained committed to reform, but after numerous revisions and shortenings of the bill, it was obvious that no version of the bill was acceptable to the contesting interests. Forces supporting the *status quo* gained the stronger position in the shadow of 1980 politics. But Congress was not going to set aside the matter without asserting its own independence. Within Congress, consensus was strong for a more detailed Congressional oversight. A majority of the members evidently thought that it was good electoral politics as well as good policy to assert a meaningful Congressional role in intelligence decision-making.

And so improved Congressional oversight became the goal as the Senate Intelligence Committee dropped most other details of charter reform in 1980. Legislation was passed and signed by the President, limiting the reporting of the intelligence agencies to two instead of eight committees, expanding the oversight coverage to other intelligence agencies including the CIA, and giving the House and Senate intelligence committees access to all intelligence information, including the right to be notified in advance (except in special situations) of all covert operations. Should the President decide to limit prior notice of a covert action because of 'extraordinary circumstances affecting vital interests of the United States' then he must at least inform the ranking members of the House and Senate Intelligence Committees, the Speaker and the minority leaders of the House and the majority and minority leaders in the Senate. And so Congress was by statute made an informational if not decision-making partner with the Executive on covert actions.

On the front of party politics, the Republican National Committee, in late summer 1979, issued a 12-page intelligence broadside, chastising the Democratic Administration for its intelligence policy, blaming Democrats for weakening and politicising the intelligence system, and charging that the Democratic Congress had favoured debilitating intelligence remedies. Eschewing detailed reforms, the Republican position advocated return to the National Security Act of 1947, with its comfortable ambiguities. Republican sentiment favoured amending the original act rather than adopting an omnibus charter filled with do's and don'ts. Patently the Republicans had determined that intelligence policy and organisation would be a major 1980 campaign issue. The Democratic Party platform in 1980 played down the intelligence issue. In a general plank on defence it meekly stated 'we will act to further improve intelligence gathering and analysis'.

The Republican platform for 1980 had a detailed intelligence plank. It decried the Democrats' weakening of the intelligence system; cited a 'strong national consensus' to strengthen it; and set forth a number of specific recommendations that carried the flavour of 'unleashing' the CIA by amending some of the restrictions the Democrats had placed on secret operations. In effect little choice on intelligence policy was offered in 1980 by the two major parties. The 1980 election, however, saw one outspoken intelligence reform candidate. He was John Anderson, the Third Party candidate. Anderson's approach to intelligence policy was clearly one that would place severe limitations on secret intelligence. He supported Congressional oversight; advocated consultation with Congress on covert operations; would forbid covert CIA use of journalists, academics and clergy; and he opposed any equivalent of an official secrets act, for example, legislation that would punish writers who have not been intelligence employees.

VIII REAGAN'S COUNTER-REFORMS

As President, Ronald Reagan in his first two years fulfilled few of the campaign promises on intelligence that required legislation. The Reagan Administration pressed for amendments to the Freedom of Information Act, legislation to protect the identities of secret agents, and did increase the intelligence budget by more than 15 per cent. But excepting increased budgets, Congress had not resolved most of the major intelligence issues by mid-term in Reagan's Administration.

On 23 June 1982 President Reagan signed a bill making it a crime to disclose the name of a government covert intelligence agent even if the information were obtained from public sources. The Administration had returned to essentially a cold war stance in relations with the Soviet Union. The situation in Poland was added by Administration spokesmen to the earlier events in Afghanistan as proof of Soviet imperialism. There was much cold war talk of growing Soviet military power and the menace of Russia's secret service (KGB) within the United States. This created an atmosphere in which the secret intelligence agencies could operate in a much wider circle of permissibility.

This new tone in approach to secret operations by the Reagan Administration was signalled by William J. Casey's nomination to be Director of Central Intelligence. Casey had been Reagan's political campaign manager, had served with high rank in the Office of Strategic Services (OSS) in the Second World War, and had pursued a varied and controversial business and government career. Barely a few months into Reagan's Administration the CIA was again involved in controversy stemming not only from Casey's freewheeling style, but because he appointed Max Hugel to head CIA's covert operations branch. Allegations of irregular business dealing led to Hugel's quick resignation, and for many months Casey's own business background was under detailed Senate scrutiny. These events were a worthy plot for a Gilbert and Sullivan operetta. Casey was finally cleared by the Senate committee, which declared unenthusiastically that he was 'not unfit' to continue as CIA Director. The Reagan Administration's first year was unsuccessful in efforts to build a favourable new image for the CIA.

Reagan's intelligence advisers meanwhile spent much of the first year drafting an executive order delineating organisation, rules, functions and limits for the intelligence system. In the process, several drafts were circulated, the initial versions of which removed many of the restraints on CIA actions that Presidents Ford and Carter had imposed. Although earlier drafts of the proposed new executive order were never released, leaks indicated that they authorised the use of 'intrusive techniques' including searches, physical surveillance and infiltration of domestic organisations. It seemed that security was given higher priority in some cases than civil liberty. Cold war assumptions resembling those of the 1950s seemed to inform these proposals. Admittedly, major emphasis was placed on controlling terrorist activity and the international flow of narcotics, as well as espionage efforts within the United States by foreign intelligence services.

On 4 December 1981, President Reagan's intelligence executive order in its final form was published (Executive Order No. 12333). Its principal difference from the orders of Ford and Carter was that the authority of intelligence agencies to collect information from Americans at home and abroad was broadened. Civil libertarians viewed the order as unwise, but many acknowledged that it was not as bad as earlier drafts had indicated. Conservatives hailed the new order, but some thought that it did not go far enough in 'unleashing' the CIA. Clearly consultations with the intelligence committees of Congress had forced the Reagan Administration to less radical changes in the rules. In issuing the order, President Reagan noted that the new order was 'consistent with my promise in the [political] campaign to revitalize our nation's intelligence system'.[10]

The change from détente to confrontation with the USSR produced in 1981 a political climate within the United States favouring the intelligence agencies, just as it favoured the allocation of more resources for national defence. Those civil libertarians wishing to limit secret intelligence operations strictly were able to gain by vigorous debate a redressing of the executive-legislative balance. Five years of effort at reform resulted in a statutory as well as a political expectation that legislators would have a consultative voice in the intelligence rules of the game. A relatively small number of bi-partisan watchdogs in Congress managed to force a right-wing administration on to a middle ground in intelligence policy. Congress performed its classical function: it set limits. Yet civil libertarians lost some ground, for what were seen by reformers in 1975–6 as unacceptable 'abuses' had been legitimised by Reagan's executive order. These activities included CIA investigations of foreign-sponsored activities within the United States, physical surveillance of Americans abroad, covert operations within the United States, opening of mail in the United States, and cooperation by the CIA with local law-enforcement agencies. Perhaps worse things have been prevented: unrestrained infiltration into American organisations, Presidential authority to order wiretaps, loose authority to investigate 'leaks', and waiving of the duty of intelligence agency heads to report wrongdoing by their employees. Once again, by 1982 the intelligence rules had been shaped to reflect the external threat perception. Once again 'The Russians are coming' theme was voiced by national leaders and powerful media elements were suggesting that KGB agents were hiding behind every bush. The pendulum had swung again, but not as far to the right as in the past. 'Trust in honourable men' was again the operational code, but the 'honourable men' were now required to share some of their deepest secrets with a select few Congressional members.

The question posed at the outset of this chapter was why the United States intelligence system has been constantly involved in controversy while other nations successfully isolate intelligence services from public controversy. What explains the wild swings between permissiveness and public accountability? This question is not easily answered by reference to such variables as partisan politics, changes in White House control, or by domestic ideology. What stands out specifically as a pivotal or dominating variable is the state of relations between the United States and the Soviet Union. Other variables include the political climate and personalities nourished by the degree of hostility or cooperation in US–USSR relations. More generally, the degree of foreign policy consensus is a factor of great influence.

Figure 1 illustrates this conclusion. Stated simply, in times when a cooperative spirit characterises US–USSR relations, intelligence agencies are subjected to greater public accountability than in time of hostility. When relations are hostile, intelligence agencies are

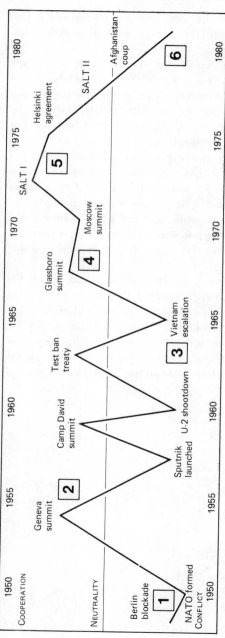

FIGURE 1 US–USSR relations, 1948–80

From data assembled by Edward Azar and Thomas Sloan as adapted by Charles W. Kegley, Jr. and Eugene Wittkopf in *American Foreign Policy, Pattern and Process*, 2nd ed., (New York: St. Martin's Press, 1982), p. 58

1 The CIA created by Congress in 1947, granted extraordinary secrecy in 1949

2 Efforts in 1955 in imposing tighter CIA controls, partly successful; Presidential advisory board established; Congressional oversight stronger

3 A period of great tolerance of CIA secrecy and covert action, 1960–5

4 Some CIA covert activity sharply questioned in Congress and the media, 1966–8; CIA cover 'blown' on secret subsidy of US private organizations

5 Congressional investigations of CIA, 1974–6, domestic spying and some foreign actions exposed. Radical reforms proposed; Carter runs on 'leashing CIA' platform

6 Cold War resumes, 1979–82; Reagan runs on 'unleash CIA' platform; some intelligence counter-reforms succeed

'unleashed' and counter-reforms dominate intelligence policy. Foreign policy tensions enable the 'Trust in honourable men' operational code to be reasserted.

Here we have a key to understanding American intelligence policy in the past, and perhaps the basis for predictions. The difficult analytical problem derives from the reality that central intelligence contributes substantially to the perception of the threat of the Soviet Union. That is one of its major tasks. The dangers of self-fulfilling prophecy, therefore, are ever present. In simplest terms, the Central Intelligence Agency has a bureaucratic self-interest in the continuation of cold war. Only a sophisticated Presidency; an alert, watchdogging Congress; and aggressive inquiries by the press and by scholars can offer some hope of maintaining a proper balance in the future between intelligence secrecy and public accountability; between self-serving, distorted views of foreign events and reality; and between self-defeating covert actions and the application of beneficial influence in foreign areas.

Meanwhile America remains ambivalent about its secret intelligence apparatus. This ambivalence has many roots in the political culture.[11] But perhaps its main cause is the conceptual and definitional confusion in which the United States intelligence system has evolved. A tendency to place war and peace in tight, separate compartments has produced wild swings between permissiveness and national guilt. Intelligence professionals all the while wearily pursue the Holy Grail of legitimacy.

11. The History of the D-Notice Committee

ALASDAIR PALMER

THE traditional attitude of the British governing class to the dissemination of information has had a lot in common with the ancient public school attitude to sex. Ideally, it does not happen. If it turns out to be unavoidable, it should be carefully controlled and regulated, like some form of disease. How it is in fact done should never be mentioned in public; and if anyone goes too far and breaks the gentleman's code of practice, he should be expelled immediately.

The rise and decline of the 74-year-old D-notice system, like the history of the Parliamentary lobby, illustrates this code with remarkable accuracy – especially as it has been administered by a tried and trusted method of the public school, the prefect system: a technique of divide and rule in which the guilty conscience of some is transformed into the absolving role of captor of others. Like the old school attitude to sex, it has relied heavily on the guilt complexes of the controlled for its effectiveness. Both have suffered serious – and probably irreparable – damage over the past fifteen years. Discussion of defence and intelligence matters, has, like sex, come to be seen as too important and enjoyable to be left to the professionals alone. Too many serious mistakes – and too much operational ineffectiveness – have come to be traced to the period of repression for the full canopy ever to be quiescently accepted again.

The love affair of the British administrative and intelligence establishment with secrecy first started to have consequences for the press in 1898. During the worse than usual annual crisis of Anglo-French relations, the Director of Military Intelligence picked up the newspapers and, to his horror, read article after article giving away 'the composition of the garrisons of all home defended ports . . .

227

the existence of submarine defences at Portsmouth, Falmouth and other ports . . .'.[1] Thunderstruck, he instructed the Adjutant General, Sir Evelyn Wood, to work out some way of preventing a recurrence. Wood's first reaction, in spite of registering that 'we are all proud of the freedom of the press and recognise that freedom is essential to our national vitality' was to propose a total ban on all defence matters, the 'simple and effective remedy of prohibiting the publication altogether of any military or naval news, except that supplied by the War Office and Admiralty'[2] – the method adopted in Prussia by the Imperial Decree of 7 May 1874. Wood recommended drafting a bill to give the British government the power, whenever it felt an emergency arose, to declare the prohibition in force. Trusting to the decency of the old boy network, he ended his memo with the claim that such a blanket prohibition would find favour with those who controlled the press.

It took some time for the War Office to realise that the invisible strings of 'old school' type loyalty were the ones that needed pulling. On being alerted to the danger, Whitehall's initial reflex was to reach for the unsubtle and obvious method of parliamentary legislation. First the search for a scapegoat for burnt fingers in the Boer War, then the experience of watching the Russians lose hopelessly to the Japanese in 1905 (where the obsessive secrecy of the victors was contrasted with the almost open-door policy of the losers), convinced officialdom that some degree of press control – enforced by law – was essential.[3] The Russians were seen as the latest addition to the list of countries whose war effort was wrecked by misplaced confidence in the press, a scrapheap deemed to include France (during the war against Prussia in 1870 a German major had ascertained 'the composition of all the French corps and their strategic disposition' from the French newspapers); and America (by default: had she not been overwhelmingly powerful, she would have lost in 1898 against Spain because 'every military movement was chronicled in the American papers').[4] It all added up to a single lesson: the essential weapon of modern warfare was secrecy, and that, as far as the administrators were concerned, meant shutting up the press. The message had been rammed home by press disclosures of British defences during the Russo-Japanese War itself – the Russian fleet had fired on some fishing boats off Dogger Bank, a state of emergency was declared, and 'the newspaper industry's contribution was a telegram notifying that 4 ships were steaming up from Gibraltar'.[5]

Despite some support from *The Times* – whose managing editor was a close associate of Adjutant-General Wood, and seems to have initially suggested some form of control to him – the War Office was convinced that the press would be hostile to any form of control enshrined in statute. Nevertheless, at this stage, they could see no alternative to legislation enforcing total prohibition, and a parliamentary draughtsman was set to work. Fearing that a comprehensive anti-censorship press campaign could kill the bill, the Committee of Imperial Defence decided to conduct a comprehensive survey of editors' attitudes to the proposed legislation. Uncertain of how to approach such wild and uncivilised creatures as newspaper men, it was decided to set a thief to catch a thief. Sydney Brooks, a sympathetic freelance journalist and would-be 'capital fellow' eager to become part of the Club, was used as cover. He wrote to the 200 or so editors of national and provincial newspapers, claiming that, as a patriot first and a journalist second, he believed the bill enforcing censorship was the only decent thing. Did the editor not agree?

Even when the suggestion came from a fellow journalist, most did not – at least, not in detail.[6] Brooks was so full of enthusiasm himself that he seems hardly to have noticed. Consequently, he received an unpleasant shock in 1906 when his proposal for a bill failed to gain acceptance from the AGM of the Newspaper Society. The assembled hacks seem to have been persuaded by a letter from Sir John Leng, editor of the *Dundee Advertiser*, and veteran of over 60 years experience – knighted for services to journalism. He argued that the proposals would 'produce a state press, directed and controlled by not improbably incompetent and injudicious underlings of government departments, altogether alien to my idea of what an enlightened and influential press should be'. What seems to have upset him was the suggestion, implied by the proposed legislation, that pressmen could not be trusted: 'It will be a bad day for the press of this country', he wrote, 'when their patriotism and intelligence cannot be relied on without their being placed in bonds their predecessors have never borne. . . .' A similar sentiment seems to have alienated others who were otherwise far more sympathetic to Brooks than Leng. The concern with which the government viewed Leng's protest may be gauged from the fact that Sir George Clarke, Secretary to the CID, sent a personal letter to him at the request of the Prime Minister, trying to soothe his worries and impress upon him the urgency of making the (of course unintentional) disclosure of secret information by the press impossible.[7] Leng was not convinced, but *The Times* was, publishing an article on 'The Press as Intelligence Agent in Wartime' and a leader recommending some legislation. Nevertheless, when the Institute of Journalists considered the proposals in May of that year, the 'Leng effect' was obvious. A. S. Robbins, the President-elect, attacked censorship in general and that of the British press during the Boer War in particular, and, to cheers, stated that

> the policy of secrecy in regard to war led as an inevitable consequence to the concealment of jobbery, corruption and sometimes crime . . . with every desire to assist the government and prevent publication of news of value to the enemy, I hope Parliament will never sanction any measure preventing the publication of news of value to the country in time of war or preparation for it.

These men felt as deeply suspicious of the alien official network that distrusted them as that network did of the interests and values they represented.

Back in Whitehall, the Adjutant-General preferred not to press ahead with a bill for the moment, so that it would be possible to 'pass a drastic one when the iron was hot': a piece of deviousness which was to pay impressive dividends in 1911, when the Official Secrets Act was pushed through on a wave of spy hysteria. In 1901, it simply meant adding a clause to the existing Press Bill to empower

> any justice or chief officer of police, if he has reasonable cause to believe . . . an offence is *about* to be or has been committed . . . may by written order authorize any constable to enter, if need be by force, any place in which he has reason to believe the newspaper, magazine or pamphlet is being prepared and search for and seize any copies of the publication and any materials used in the preparation thereof.

The Director of Public Prosecutions, Lord Desart, had recommended that on the grounds that in other cases where prevention was important – 'such as diseased animals, obscene books, dangerous drugs, etc.' – it was granted. Sir George Clarke, who had just written to the Newspaper Society trying to persuade them away from Leng's line, had the sense to veto that clause, on the grounds that 'domiciliary visits have a rather Russian flavour about them which is bound to cause bitter resentment'.[8]

But confrontation remained the order of the day, and the War Office continued to pursue a tough and uncompromising attitude towards the draconian bill. The result was that press and government relations went into a downward spiral, and a kind of intermittent trench warfare based on mutual distrust and suspicion began. Brooks – the War Office cover – would write an article emphasising the seriousness of the situation, begging the politicians to get on with it and pass the bill, present the press as desperate for protection 'against a liberty it cannot in the nature of things help abusing' and make the risible claim that 'the mere fact of [legislation's] existence would necessarily entail as a corollary a fuller, quicker, and more adequate supply of news'.[9] A genuine journalist would then write an article on some aspect of the armed forces which would upset the Admiralty or War Office. An example of this sort of thing appeared in the *Daily Express* on 2 December 1907 – a report noting the below expectation performance of some new guns and fire-fighting equipment, despite the fact that the trials were, according to the Admiralty, 'secret . . . and steps had been taken to prevent unauthorised persons from being present'.

The reason for the hostility of the press sprang mostly from what it perceived as the patronising and at times almost accusatory style of those behind the proposed legislation. The administrators were treating newspapermen not as the patriots they actually were, but as potential traitors. The bill 'casts a slur on the honour and discretion of the newspaper proprietors and editors' claimed the *Sunday Times* on 2 March 1906, obviously upset at being cast in a net meant to catch those most despicable and lowly of beings, foreign spies. The Institute of Journalists also protested that the bill was 'calculated to limit the freedom of the press to an extent not conducive to the public interest', while even *The Times* came out of the closet and opposed the bill. 'The Lord Chancellor has produced a bill which is frankly absurd', it claimed in unusually unequivocal language, since it would 'place in the hands of every official, no matter how humble, a general purpose *lettre de cachet* to be used at his own sweet will against . . . the general public, and particularly the press'. The Newspaper Society's condemnation effectively cremated Brooks and the War Office's hopes of press acceptance of the bill. Outraged at being treated as a potential traitor, Ernest Parke, Secretary of the fledgling Newspaper Proprietors' Association, read a paper attacking the proposals at a special conference. The Newspaper Society decided that 'no good cause has been shown for suspecting the patriotism and discretion of those who conduct the newspapers of this country . . . there is no need for legislation'.[10] Furthermore, Parke was furious that their associations were put on the same level as organisations that consisted of mere journalists. These were to have an equal power on the Press Advisory Council which the Admiralty and War Office proposed to help smooth censorship, when in fact they had 'no claim to an equal voice with the newspaper proprietors in regard to important questions affecting the control of their business and also in regard to prosecuting them for alleged offences under the act'.[11]

Careful exploitation of patriotic sentiment mixed with social snobbery was eventually to enable officialdom to get the press first to forge, then step into, manacles of its own accord. The Director of Naval Intelligence was the first to suggest introducing the public school ethic:

> a simple method, worthy of trial, is to put the press on their honour in the schoolboy sense of the term, prior to any experiments which the Board may wish to keep secret, by issuing a communique to the press association stating what is going to be carried out and asking them to cooperate in the publication of information likely to be of value to foreign countries.[12]

It took time, however, for the War Office to realise that this method was more effective than trials of strength, largely because general staff still thought of the press as a bunch of rapacious capitalists, incapable, like all tradesmen, of thinking further than a balance-sheet, or of any motive higher than profit. 'No appeal to the patriotism of the proprietors would have much effect in this age of competition', intoned a solemn memorandum of 1909, which went on to assert that if general staff simply pleaded with the press, it would be 1870 all over again, with Great Britain playing the role of France to a Prussia which swept all before it.[13]

Throughout 1909, the pressure for restrictive legislation – against all sources of espionage, including the press – increased in proportion to the intensification of the arms race with Imperial Germany. The spectre of spies started to obsess the nation. The Secret Service Bureau, ancestor of today's MI5 and MI6, was founded to improve both the supply of other nations' secrets and the protection of Britain's own.[14] A subcommittee of the CID was delegated to reform the Official Secrets Act as a necessary condition of control of the espionage menace; and when inevitably the question of the press came up again, it was lamented that 'a case had recently occurred of secret information being published by a daily newspaper regarding the construction of a battleship. In the present state of the law we are unable to prosecute the editor of this paper for publishing this information'.[15] As a result Asquith delegated a separate special CID subcommittee to see how the press could be persuaded, or made, to consent to a bill to keep itself quiet. But the future did not lie in legislation, and general staff's cynicism was misplaced. Northcliffe had already been in touch with War Minister Haldane, urging him to start training press censors in anticipation of the inevitable war immediately, as 'one knows how Moltke and Bismarck watched the Press and in those days it was only in its infancy'.[16]

Asquith's CID subcommittee convened under the chairmanship of Winston Churchill in 1910. Brooks had meanwhile been at it again, enthusiastically sounding out editors for their support of a new bill, but had again received a dusty set of replies – even he had to admit that 'the reception which the Press might be expected to accord to a measure . . . was not favourable'.[17] Undefeated, he suggested pushing the bill through anyway. The CID demurred, at Churchill's request: having had some experience of the newspaper world, he understood its insecurities, and opined that it would respond better to an apparent caress than to the overt wielding of a clumsy club. Pretend to take them into confidence, establish 'some organisation for the dissemination of military and naval news of a harmless kind and it might be considered by the Press as some compensation for being muzzled'.[18] Convinced it had nothing to lose, the subcommittee was converted, believing on 16 June 1910 that

> if legislation is not proceeded with, the Press Bureau might by indirect means secure in large measure that control which we so greatly desire . . . if skilfully handled, the Press would in all probability come to regard the Bureau not only as a source of information, but as a friendly advisory [and] a considerable measure of the control desired might be obtained.[19]

Revelations by the *Morning Post* in an article on 'The Guardianship of British Ports' during the Agadir crisis of 1911 provided an additional spur to action. The CID subcommittee, along with general staff, was furious. 'The total lack of discretion on the part of the superior staff of the most respectable and "patriotic" newspapers could hardly be better illustrated', thundered its report.[20] The CID commissioned Reginald Brade, an assistant secretary at the War Office, to reopen negotiations with the press in the hope that he might succeed where Brooks had failed. Brade turned out to be the ideal Machiavellian civil servant who operated on the principle that one should 'never take by force what one can get by fraud' – the perfect maxim, as it turned out, for the job. Brade made contact with Nicholson, *The Times'* managing editor who had put Wood in mind of the principle of total prohibition in 1898. After initially repeating that suggestion, Nicholson came up with what turned out to be a good idea: he instructed Brade to contact in confidence the proprietors, who were better organised than editors, had no particular professional interest in disclosure, and 'what's more important had . . . complete control over the Press'.[21] While Brooks was emblazoning the old pleas for legislation all over the July issue of the *Pall Mall Gazette*, Brade was quietly arranging confidential meetings with proprietorial organisations. Whereas the Newspaper Society had no authority over the editorial content of member companies, such corporate bodies as the Joint Committee of Federations of Newspaper Owners, with whom Brade met in July 1911, did. He suggested they form a joint committee to arrange 'a permanent order of procedure' for keeping material out of the papers. Ernest Parke, the Secretary of the NPA who had opposed controls in 1908, was so thoroughly flattered to be treated respectfully by the War Office that he drew up the formal constitution of the proposed committee. He it was who succeeded in empowering its members 'to withhold from publication in the Press information which at times of emergency it might be against the public interest to make known'.[22] Although a mere manager of the Press Association was on the committee, he was delegated to be Secretary and was landed with the donkey-work – minute-taking, conveyance of decisions and operation of the machinery. Parke and he were to be called up if ever the Admiralty or War Office were confronted with an emergency that 'did not admit of even a moment's delay'. From then on Prefect Parke, having been accepted into the seniors' common room, did everything he could to aid their power.

With that the committee was set up. It was to work extremely effectively in the eighteen months or so it had to operate before the outbreak of war.[23] The proprietors were happy, feeling that the committee's consultation marked recognition of their worth and patriotism, proof at last of ministerial faith in their trustworthiness. This, as it turned out, was a delusion. Brade's façade of trust and abandonment of legislation was a fraud. The Official Secrets Act had been passed earlier that year, and in his memo on the formation of the committee, which is worth extensive quotation, Brade slyly enscribed that

> it may be noted that in the record of the negotiations above, there is no closely drawn definition of the scope of the new committee's powers and functions. This is not unintentional . . . I have confined myself, when explaining our objects, to pointing out the need for organisation in the cases of a resort to the precautionary measures of defence. . . . The great point seemed to be to induce the Press to work together and in conjunction with us. This has been secured, and it is left to the future to develop occasions of usefulness outside the cases named. So far nothing has been done or said which will limit the functions of the committee. Legal advice as to the scope of the new Official Secrets Act [suggests] the power of the department is not so meagre as it would appear . . . we have inferred [from advice given by the Director of Public Prosecutions] that in certain circumstances the Act could be used against a newspaper. We have a note on our official papers to the effect that the speedy passage of the Act was due to a general understanding that the new measure was not directed against any new class, but against that which the former Act was aimed, viz the spy class, and that to use it against a newspaper merely for publishing news useful to an enemy would amount to a breach of faith with Parliament. But there is no record to this effect in the official versions of the debates.[24]

The War Office had got everything it wanted: press consent to censorship, and, in effect, a bill to enforce it. The arrangements leading to the committee augured well for its future: they had been conducted without any publicity, so ignorance ensured there was no opposition. The Committee's documents were classified as secret, and prefaced by the rider that 'it is important that the function and existence of this committee not be known more widely than is necessary for the framing of similar schemes'. Parliament was never informed of the committee, and the closest Churchill got to disclosing it was an opaque answer to a Parliamentary question in January 1913 about a paragraph in the *Scotsman* on Admiralty oil tanks: 'it is believed in cases where information is recognised as secret and directly affecting the defence of the country, the government may rely on the cordial cooperation of the newspaper Press in preventing its publication'.[25] The Admiralty and War Office had by quiet manoeuvre and deception managed to obtain a virtual *carte blanche* for the suppression of defence information (since they decided when the national interest was threatened), with statutory backing – something that had proved quite impossible to achieve by open procedure. Brade was the only one really accorded establishment acceptance. He ended up with a knighthood.

This apparatus collapsed, however, on the outbreak of the First World War, when it became obvious that the war required full censorship, not merely the piecemeal suppression of defence data. The Press Bureau was formed on 13 August 1914. It supplanted the committee, and was initially run on suitably Japanese lines – Kitchener's ban on correspondents at the front lasted for almost two years, delivering a blow to government-press relations from which they did not ever fully recover, and the Defence of the Realm Act left newspapers in no doubt as to the penalties of indiscretion. The government had openly proclaimed its intention to punish, and punish severely (conviction by court martial meant, in theory, life imprisonment). But, in the event, newspapers were as willing as general staff to distort truth to promote victory for the patria. The legacy of the Admiralty, War Office and Press Committee was a system of 'private and confidential notices', sent out to editors containing requests for the suppression of certain bits of information. Several hundred of these 'D-notices' were issued during the war, all of which were complied with, including those which banned reference to the industrial disputes and strikes of 1917.

This method of censorship, plus the fact that the War Office did not give in to an urge to take over newspapers and run them from the inside, convinced officialdom that censorship throughout the war was voluntary. They were unable to understand why the press was so ungrateful for the freedom it was granted. Major General Thwaites, Director of Military Intelligence, wrote in a memo after the war, that 'the Press, which never failed to criticize and abuse censorship, was hardly less ignorant than the general public, and gloried in publishing articles on the subject of quite unimportant blunders by the censors . . . in fact submission to censorship of matter was voluntary'.[26]

What caused resentment from pressmen was, as before the war, less censorship than hurt pride at being treated by the War Office as detrimental to the war effort, as unpatriotic and potentially traitorous instead of decent, responsible and upright. The D-notices worked effectively because they treated editors as worthy of official confidence. The press was, from the outset of the war, overwhelmingly ready to print rousing, morale-inspiring stories, regardless of factual foundation, and exercised a self-censorship of which general staff could have been proud. *The Times'* correspondent with the French armies in Lorraine made no mention of the massive losses sustained by the French in the first weeks of the war. Despite his hostility to the Dardenelles campaign, Northcliffe and his papers remained silent on the extent of the losses it was causing. What the public got instead were stories bearing such titles as 'German Army Demoralized – Troops Starving' or 'Despairing Officers and Men Commit Suicide'.[27]

The War Office recognised the contribution made by the press in the course of a confidential comparison between the German and British methods of war censorship made in 1919. The German war effort, claimed the comparison, was done real harm by the military takeover of the press that took place there. The public were alienated, not won round, by a diet of stories as prepared for them by military men, and the inevitable cracks in the unworkably rigid and precise censorship code were exploited to the full by embittered journalists. The German High Command had 'failed to understand the radical differences in thought that existed between the Prussian Staff Officer, the newspaper world, and the general public',[28] and the result was the opposite of what was intended – the crumbling of confidence in the military establishment instead of its reinforcement.

The British system was much more effective, and its strength lay precisely in its originators' shrewd understanding of social tensions, hierarchical sentiment, and feelings of inferiority. It avoided the impression of vice-like control of civilian institutions, and left the press to make up its own stories of non-existent British successes, which were, as a result, much more convincing. The outwardly gentle approach, forced on the War Office by press opposition to its legislative ambitions, now became official policy.

After the war ended, the temptation to retain the arrangement for control was too much to resist. The Foreign Office kept its News Department, employing a full-time salaried staff to try and convert the press to the FO world view,[29] and the War Office revived the press committee. The excessive caution that this represented – after all, no-one believed then that another major conflict was possible – was the War Office's attempt to keep the press sensitive to its need for deference and restraint.

The committee had been set up to deal with the censorship of technical information during war or emergency. It proved extremely hard to adapt it to a fruitful role in a time of peace which lacked international tension of the sort which had mesmerised the nation before the war. This was not a boom era for weapons development and military intelligence. Declining interest in defence news served to eliminate the kind of disclosures the pre-war committee had striven to prevent far more effectively than the War Office directives. Consequently the committee had almost nothing to do. It gradually disintegrated of its own accord as a medium for press control. But not without some struggle from Whitehall, which refused to accept that the committee no longer had a role to play. By 1922, when the Chanak crisis threatened to precipitate a war with Turkey, Lloyd George had notified the press of what he wanted kept out, independently of the committee. The CID response was an enquiry into departmental coordination. It was to find ways to ensure the committee's resources were not forgotten. As a panacea, its report recommended the committee extend its activities: it should consider whether 'some method of preventing the publication of information of a political nature might be devised'.[30]

Brade's carefully ambivalent statement of the committee's scope now started to look as if it might pay further dividends. Whitehall had already begun to extend the tentacles of the committee beyond purely national security concerns, since it had issued a D-notice to suppress a trivial scandal relating to Queen Alexandra's sister.[31] A representative from the Foreign Office, whose work was to keep sensitive items of foreign news 'in its political aspect' out of the papers, now looked set to join the committee.

Astonishingly, this proposal got the consent of the press representatives. The War Office pushed it through by a trick: they raised the matter at the end of an ill-attended meeting – only about half the press members were present – and then kept it out of the official minutes. The proprietors who were there outdid all War Office expectations: they even agreed to using the committee for the censorship of subversive home news. The Bolshevik threat worked on these men of property in a way that surprised even the committee's Secretary, Oswyn Murray, who was a worthy successor to Brade. He was quite prepared to exploit the fiction that proprietors were empowered by the press as a whole to bind it to agreements made in the committee. (In fact, the committee's existence continued to be kept as quiet as possible by all concerned, and the proprietors did not seek – or get – mandates from the organisations they nominally represented for decisions they made.) Murray was particularly concerned to preserve the façade of voluntariness about the process, so that the press was represented as agreeing that it would be 'necessary to convey to such papers as the *Daily Herald* and extreme communist journals requests for the suppression of objectional matter connected with industrial questions'.[32]

In the event, the CID vetoed this extension. Lord Salisbury, its chairman, had the political acumen to realise that if newspaper men who did not sit on the committee got to hear about it, there would be uproar. Its transformation into a political tribunal, passing judgement on what items and opinions were fit for front pages, would wreck Whitehall's currently cosy relations with the press – whatever the proprietors present had said. If the Prime Minister or anyone else wanted to make requests for political censorship, these should emanate from him, not from the committee.

The committee then reverted to a state of suspended animation, which seems to have been its lot for the next 25 years. Its existence seems to have been forgotten by everyone not actually on it. When, in 1931, the *Daily Telegraph* published a report by its defence correspondent on the trials of a new aiming device, and the Admiralty wanted to prevent a repetition, Admiral Usborne had the brilliant idea of creating a committee which would inform the press beforehand of the information the Admiralty would rather not have published, since he felt 'sure that if the British press is taken to confidence in this way before the event, the result will be much happier'. A curt letter then arrived from Sir Oswyn Murray informing him that 'the A.W.O. & P. committee was brought into existence to deal with just this matter many years ago . . . the Admiralty have only themselves to blame for cases in which they have not taken steps through the committee to prevent publication of the details. The War Office and Air Ministry habitually use the committee in such cases.' Murray here exaggerated a little, as he must have known, for he sent a confidential circular to all service departments 'reminding them of the committee's existence'. Quite right: neither Air Vice-Marshal Burnett, nor anyone else at the Air Ministry had ever heard of it – although it officially had joined the scheme just after the war. The only record of the War Office's recognition of it is a letter Murray received in July 1932 from Sir Herbert Creedy asking whether, since the network used for communicating D-notice committee decisions had not been used for the last ten years, it was worth keeping. Caution won the day and it was decided to preserve it – even though the committee had not met since 1923.[33]

Meanwhile, Sir Vernon Kell, head of MI5 and veteran communist hunter, was getting anxious lest D-notices (which were still sent to newspapers despite their age) should fall into the hands of Soviet sympathisers. His plan was to restrict their circulation to certified patriots only, and keep them away from the 'many persons connected with the press who are members of the Communist party'. Murray conferred with Robbins of the Press Association (but not with the committee, which seems to have disintegrated) and decided there was no threat. Considering the uninformative nature of D-notices of the time, it is a mystery why Kell should have thought there was.[34] His exaggerated anxieties appear even more remarkable when viewed against the background of monumental indiscretions during the 1920s by the government itself – in particular its repeated revelations that Britain had broken Soviet codes.[35]

After 1923, the D-notice committee did not meet again for 23 years. No mention of it was made when, at the end of 1938, the booklet of Defence Notices was entirely revised to pave the way for full censorship in the event of war, and it played no part in the establishment of the Ministry of Information press bureau. The committee as reconvened after the end of the Second World War had really very little in common with its predecessor. It was, in effect, simply a continuation of wartime censorship with the sop of a channel for the press to air grievances thrown in as a concession to the formal cessation of hostilities. Since hot war with Germany was replaced by cold war with Russia, there was an easy justification for continued secretiveness. The total, Japanese-style opacity with which the government wished to cloud the construction of the British Bomb provided a further impetus for the committee, since no detail connected with atomic power was too trivial to hide from the public.[36] D-notice 256 prevented the press from mentioning the purpose of Aldermaston until 1953. And even press members of the committee were not allowed to know of its existence until 1951, when it was decided to trust them with that knowledge in order to ensure they were stopped from spreading it further.

The changes in the nature of the committee stemmed from its continuity with wartime censorship. Its secretary was no longer a man from the Press Association, but a serviceman: Admiral Thomson, who had directed war censorship as Chief Press Censor. He had been very successful in that post, principally because he had acknowledged that the press had a legitimate right to a maximum of information consistent with genuine security requirements. His approach was homely and avuncular:

> I was never happy unless and until every newspaper man with whom I had dealings regarded me as a friend. I felt when I was talking to any of them: 'This fellow and I are both earning our living. At the moment we have also another object which is common to both of us – to ensure that our people at home and the world at large have all the news there is about the war, provided the enemy doesn't gain by it'.[37]

He gained the press's trust and respect by passing much matter that government departments wanted censored. 'Is there a genuine security objection? I would ask . . . hundreds of deleted passages I have marked "stet" because I could not see that there were proper grounds for secrecy'.[38] Added to an unprecedented degree of national cohesion, Thomson's approach produced remarkably good-humoured acceptance of censorship.

His appointment as its secretary thus gave the D-notice system a certain credibility with the press. Representatives on it were men with whom Thomson had worked for the last five years. They were active journalists – editors, not proprietors. The latter were not considered for seats on the committee, Thomson having not dealt with them during the war. Their relative influence over editorial content was also declining, as was unquestioned acceptance of their superiority over editors in the pecking order. But one relic of Brade's old system did survive: press representatives were appointed through the medium of proprietors' organisations – the Newspaper Proprietors' Association, the Periodical Publishers' Association, and the Newspaper Society.

Thomson advised journalists not to bother with committee, but simply to ring him up whenever a story that looked potentially troublesome appeared. He managed to persuade the Admiralty to abandon a catch-all D-notice, which had been drafted in the spirit of *début-de-siècle* Portsmouth, and got *ad hoc* restrictions to replace general statements of principle, with quiescent results.[39] There was not, of course, much consultation on the procedures dictating the type of material to be excluded. The directives were one way – from Admiral Thomson to the press. Thomson's genial personality, his apparent independence from Whitehall (his office was in Belgrave Square, not in the MOD – by whom he was not paid either) and his sympathetic understanding of press requirements helped sustain the system. But gradual changes in the nature of British society, accelerated by the 'People's War' against Germany, were in the long run fatal to the efficient functioning of the D-notice committee. The Influential Britons' Club was losing its hold, and entrance ceased to be looked upon as an essential prerequisite of genuine success. Class sentiments were starting to take a different form to the old blanket deference to existing club members. The profession of journalism was beginning to have an independent, and significant, status of its own. With the waning of proprietorial influence, that status was bound up with the successful exposure of the incompetence, failure, or malice of the administrative class – and thus club members. As a result, the oil of social deference that had greased the smooth running of the D-notice system began to dry up. The system had to appeal to different feelings if it was to work in the new climate.

This it did. With the coming of the Cold War press censorship on defence and intelligence was presented as essential if the nation's interests were to be upheld. It was precisely because the nation had naïvely turned its back on everything to do with defence after the First World War that it had been stabbed there – nearly fatally – by the next one. Editors and journalists believed that the rationing of information, like the rationing of food, was a deprivation which had to be endured in the national interest.[40] Where that belief failed to be sufficiently powerful, the D-notice committee utilised fear. The continuity with wartime censorship meant the system was now widely identified with the Official Secrets Act, and the Whitehall members of the committee did nothing to discourage that belief, once itself a closely guarded secret. The alternative to compliance was believed by everyone to be imprisonment. The connection with a voluntary gentleman's agreement was thus severed – the only remnant of that was Thomson's assurance of protection: if he passed a piece that nevertheless ended in the prosecution of the editor, he would stand up in court and make it clear that he had been responsible for publication.

Thus the gradual erosion of the original coping-stone of the voluntary system – a sort of patriotic snobbery – meant that the post-war committee required two beliefs from journalists in order to work effectively. The first was that the system genuinely served the interest of national security, and national security only. The second, that failure to comply with the system ensured conviction under the Official Secrets Act – and symmetrically, that compliance provided protection from it.[41]

The effectiveness of the D-notice committee as an organ of censorship has been eroded in proportion to the decline of those two beliefs. Responsible for the eradication of the second has been the prosecution or putative prosecution of journalists for articles published after clearance of the D-notice committee. The worst and most damaging incident happened in 1971, when Jonathan Aitken, then a freelance journalist, and Brian Roberts, editor of the *Sunday Telegraph*, were acquitted (and awarded costs) after being prosecuted for writing and publishing an article based on a confidential assessment of the Biafran War which the secretary of the D-notice committee, then Sir Norman Denning, had cleared.[42] Since then, Whitehall has adopted the policy of denying that the committee's proclamations have any protective connection with the Official Secrets Act (OSA). This has caused some confusion with the press, and the Press Chairman on the committee – J. M. Ramsden, editor of *Flight* – still claims the committee's function is to act essentially as a buffer between press and OSA,[43] as do most of the newspapermen who are in favour of it.[44] It seems inevitable that since D-notices are, on any interpretation, reminders that the publication of certain items is potentially dangerous to the security of the realm, their connection with the OSA, which deals with precisely the same subject, cannot be broken. What Whitehall is keen to deny is that, as a matter of law, violation or compliance with a D-notice entails prosecution under the OSA or protection from it.[45] The denial does not stretch to claiming the converse: that breach of a D-notice would certainly not end in prosecution.

That, however, is what would seem to be required if the system were to be truly voluntary, and it is what the proprietors back in 1911 thought they were agreeing to. On the other hand, officialdom has all along admitted to itself, if not to anyone else, that mere trust left a gap that force had to fill. Hence that second belief, that compliance with the D-notice system renders one safe from prosecution, cannot be wholly dispensed with.

An earlier event which contributed much to the loss of that belief by many of the press was the attempt by Sir Harold Wilson to 'get' Chapman Pincher for an article he published in the *Daily Express* on cable vetting. As with the Aitken case, the piece was cleared by the D-notice secretary, then Colonel Lohan, who operated on Thomson's method of continual personal contact rather than through occasional convenings of the committee. Pincher played his information on the vetting of all cables leaving this country (and not just the diplomatic ones) for all it was worth, so Sir Harold woke up to read of the extension of 'Big Brother methods' and the Labour government's trajectory toward 1984-style snooping. Pincher's hostility to defence cuts and his ability to ferret out embarrassing information had already piqued Wilson, who lost his power of self-control in the face of this last goad. The D-notice committee was convened to look into how it had happened and what should be done to Pincher, whereupon uproar, and the resignation of the Newspaper Society's representative. Sir Harold then switched to a committee of Privy Counsellors under Lord Radcliffe, which failed to find in his favour, vindicating Pincher instead. Wilson refused to accept its findings, and published a White Paper claiming the article constituted a serious breach of national security. The press rounded on him with one voice as a result, and in the ensuing Parliamentary debate, Wilson launched an attack on Lohan, first claiming he had never been fully vetted, then firing him.

This sequence of events was evidence to the press that cooperation with the D-notice committee was not a reliable guide to a journalist's safety: Pincher, who had loyally knuckled under, only narrowly missed being trodden on. But more importantly, it shook faith in the belief that D-notices were invoked only in cases where the national interest was genuinely at stake. Wilson himself seems to have lost that belief, and it looks as if that was responsible for his bungled lunge at Pincher but successful swipe at Lohan. He appears to have believed that Lohan was in league with Pincher, bending D-notice rules and waiving security requirements so that the *Daily Express* could publish anti-government smears: the substance of his parliamentary attack against Lohan was his 'overclose association with journalists and especially with Mr Chapman Pincher', and his action was to shut Lohan's replacement inside the MOD (now the secretary's official residence). The 'personal approach' which Admiral Thomson had so carefully cultivated and Lohan had attempted to follow was now seen as the basis of bias. For Wilson it represented a kind of corrupt anti-governmental cabal, while for the press the retrospective attempt to punish the secretary for letting through an item of obvious and legitimate public concern resulted in the system being perceived as untrustworthy at best and a sinister conspiracy against press freedom at worst.[46] The club spirit that had so helped the setting up and working of the committee in the good old days now threatened to tear it apart. There were now two rival factions, warring for allegiance, each as suspicious of the treachery and trickery of the 'outsiders' as the other. In that atmosphere, a return to quiet consensus was impossible.

The affair seems to mark the point at which the concept of the national interest had become sufficiently contested to be unusable as the basis for an unanswerable case in an official demand for censorship. Universal voluntary press acceptance of D-notice directives is impossible without this, since it depends on strict separation of items which concern political opinion from items which concern national security. Without such a separation, the system simply becomes indistinguishable from political censorship, and no editor will voluntarily agree to what he perceives to be that.

The separation between the two is never absolutely clear, except perhaps during a war fought for national survival. But the mystification of the dividing line constitutes a definite, persistent process during peacetime: and its clarity has constantly been eroded since the war, as pluralism, to which all major parties are officially committed, has dissolved 'the national interest' as a single entity wieldable at will – and without opposition – by Whitehall.

The lack of such an overarching interest to which all members of the state are committed above anything else, and thus can agree upon before they part company, has meant the identification of the D-notice committee with sectarian censorship, departmental cover-up, and the putative suppression of issues of public importance. Perceptions of that type, even if they constitute a minority of press reactions, make a system of voluntary censorship incoherent in theory and unworkable in practice. Those who feel their political opinions are being smothered will simply opt out, and without being transformed into a system of outright censorship, with D-notices backed by the full force of the Official Secrets Act, the system collapses. Censorship in the name of the national interest must be universal if it is to have any point. Otherwise even sympathetic editors have no motive to comply: they simply lose out on potential scoops without the compensation of feeling that they are keeping Britain safe from Bolshevism.

That roughly is what has happened since the war. The process began in 1956 with the *Guardian* breaking a D-notice covering proposals for a new supersonic bomber force. A putative extension of the system in 1961 to prevent the publication of all but officially released information on weapons systems was universally opposed as designed to stifle criticism of policy. When in 1963, 'Spies for Peace', a group of anti-nuclear protesters, published the location of the underground headquarters intended for use by the government in the event of nuclear war, the D-notice committee was utilised to try and prevent the press from registering where these were – even though the Aldermaston March had stopped off at the one at Warren Row in Berkshire, and the police had actually marked the way to another one outside Edinburgh. The *Guardian* took no notice, and neither did most of the other papers.

The use of the system to try and cover up the publication of the names of defectors and traitors – persons whose identity would obviously be known to the Russians – did much to sever its automatic identification with the national interest. The most notorious incident concerned the treacherous George Blake in 1961, when two D-notices were sent round, the first requesting silence on details of his trial, the second demanding that the information in foreign newspapers – even when these were on sale in this country – be withheld. There were others. One in 1963 affecting the *Daily Telegraph* was symptomatic of the return to the downward spiral of mutual mistrust and suspicion that had dogged relations of the Fourth Estate with the First in the opening decade of the century, and from which the D-notice committee was initially a brilliant way out. The paper got wind that the Russian defector Golitsin was in England. It showed the story to the committee, and was advised to delete most of it. The editor was unconvinced, and informed the authorities that he was going ahead with publication. MI5, in collusion with the Chairman of the

Committee, the Permanent Under-Secretary of Defence, then got its own back by sending a D-notice over the Press Association's wire service to all newspapers which contained every detail of the *Telegraph*'s story. There was only one change: Golitsin's name was altered, allegedly accidentally, to Dolnytsin.[47] As a result, the *Telegraph* lost its scoop and was duped into publishing false information.[48] It did not say a great deal for a system that was meant to involve confidence from each side, not confidence tricks played by both. A third case concerned articles the *Sunday Times* wished to publish in 1967 on the career and defection of Philby, which had occurred five years earlier. The Foreign Office tried to prevent any names being revealed. But by then, Harold Evans, Editor of the *Sunday Times*, avowed that he was 'not prepared to take assurances from the D-notice committee, and I very much resented getting not one but two D-notices in an attempt to prevent the publication of the Philby story'.[49]

The result of such cases was an increasing tendency by editors to trust their own judgement and not the committee's. When in 1963 Lord Balfour of Inchrye claimed that no minister could honestly say that he was unaware of instances where D-notices 'have been used to cloak individual or departmental failure', the system soldiered on without an outcry, both because of the widespread press fear of consequences of violation, and because of the residual conviction that such cases were the exception not the rule. By 1980, when Duncan Campbell, the most thorough journalist on the technical side of intelligence matters, and Bruce Page, his editor at the *New Statesman*, brushed against the system's secretary over a story about corruption in the Hong Kong Secret Service, they regarded the system with contempt, convinced that manipulation and cover-up constituted the rule not the exception. The fuss they kicked up generated the 1980 Inquiry by the Defence Committee into the D-notice system, which nearly resulted in its abolition. Campbell operates outside the tentacles of Whitehall patronage which he believes can trap defence correspondents into the Whitehall world-view, building his stories from the careful examination of openly published sources, leads from disaffected government employees, and his own expertise. The fact that Campbell, despite a failed attempt to imprison him under the Official Secrets Act, is able to operate without giving the D-notice system a second thought shows how completely it has lost what hold it had. His predecessor in the role of ferret-in-chief, Chapman Pincher,

of diametrically opposed political views, used the system constantly
in the 1950s and 1960s, but ended up despairing of it, and using his
own judgement, primarily because he felt that after the 1967 D-notice
affair he could not get an impartial judgement out of it.

The conviction that the committee is not a reliable guide to the
location of the national interest has thus been responsible for its
increasing irrelevance.[50] Journalists have never felt represented on it.
This is not surprising: the proprietal organisations which appoint
committee members are not bodies with which working journalists
have much contact. They constitute loose federations which deal
primarily with labour and commercial relations. They have no right
to control over editorial content, and no authority over it: the
associations exist for a quite different purpose. Those chosen by the
trade organisations to sit on the committee have never been formally
empowered to commit member magazines to the decisions they make,
and there is, unsurprisingly, no codification of the criteria on
which those decisions will be based. Small wonder, then, that to
the *New Statesman*, for example, the decisions of J. M. Ramsden,
the representative of the Periodical Publishers' Association to
which they both belong, appear arbitrary and irrelevant. Editors, if
they are worried that a story may cause damage to the nation's
security, will make their own inquiries with contacts in the relevant
ministry, and not wait for another rival editor to take the decision for
them. The committee is by-passed by most newspapers as a result. In
some cases, it is even by-passed by its own members. When Geoffrey
Prime was convicted of espionage in 1982, both BBC and ITV
showed aerial photographs of GCHQ, despite a D-notice which
formally forbade them.[51] No meeting was called to ratify that.

So, as was the case between the wars, the system has lapsed largely
because it has become an irrelevance. Market forces have played
some role once again: the formidable increase in the technological
wizardry of nuclear warfare and intelligence makes the detail so
complex that the public cannot begin to understand it, let alone take
an interest in it. The lack of public demand for technical details
means, in the press at least, there are few suppliers of it.

What are the prospects for the D-notice committee, now that it is a
club of which no-one really wants to be an active member? Is it
doomed to be a relic of the past, a quaint little monument to the age of
deference and respect whose abolition is too painful for officialdom to
contemplate? Admiral Ash, the present secretary, does not think so,

though even he has to admit the past fifteen years have not been entirely happy ones for the committee, and that trust lost will take time to rebuild. Ash's mild and unpatronising manner certainly makes him the sort of person who could achieve the task of reconstruction. But could anyone get it working again?

Probably not. Journalists, academics and the public have become interested in security issues, and inhibitions, once broken, are very hard to reintroduce. Relations between press and government came close to collapse during the Falklands war. The undercurrent of mistrust was broken only by bouts of bitter acrimony: the government accused the press of jeopardising the success of the Task Force and undermining the war effort, the press accused the government of trying to transform the media into a propaganda machine.[52] This was exactly the kind of situation the D-notice system had been set up to deal with – and it played no significant role in it.

At present, no-one has a clear idea of how to reconcile the principles of public participation and the independence of the media with the inevitable secrecy required for the sake of the national interest, primarily because of increasing disagreement on what constitutes that national interest. Informed discussion of a whole range of previously untouchable issues – policies for nuclear war, internal security and intelligence-gathering – can no longer be wished away by the old methods. Henceforth debate can be prevented only by legal sanctions. Set against this background, Admiral Ash starts to look rather like a housemaster brought out of retirement to reintroduce the old values of deference, hierarchical consciousness and sublimation by sport into a school that, meanwhile, has replaced cold baths and fagging by girls and rock music.

Notes and References

Documents held at the Public Record Office, London, are crown copyright and are reproduced by permission of the Controller of HM Stationery Office.

INTRODUCTION   *Christopher Andrew and David Dilks*

1. David Dilks (ed.), *The Diaries of Sir Alexander Cadogan O.M. 1938–1945* (London, 1971), p. 21.

2. Interview with Professor Hinsley in Part 3 of the BBC Radio 4 documentary series 'The Profession of Intelligence', written and presented by Christopher Andrew (producer Peter Everett); first broadcast 16 Aug 1981.

3. F. H. Hinsley *et al.*, *British Intelligence in the Second World War* (London, 1979–). The first two chapters of volume I contain a useful retrospect on the pre-war development of the intelligence community. Curiously, despite the publication of Professor Hinsley's volumes, the government has decided not to release the official histories commissioned by it on wartime counter-espionage and deception. The forthcoming (non-official) collection of essays edited by Ernest R. May, *Knowing One's Enemies: Intelligence Assessment before the Two World Wars* (Princeton) promises to add significantly to our knowledge of the role of intelligence on the eve of the world wars.

4. House of Commons Education, Science and Arts Committee (Session 1982–83), *Public Records: Minutes of Evidence*, pp. 76–7.

5. Chapman Pincher, *Their Trade is Treachery* (London, 1981). Nigel West, *A Matter of Trust: MI5 1945–72* (London, 1982). Both volumes contain ample evidence of extensive 'inside information'.

6. Nigel West, *MI5: British Security Operations 1901–1945* (London, 1981), pp. 41, 49, 58. One of the most interesting studies of British peacetime intelligence which depends on a substantial amount of inside information is Antony Verrier's history of post-war British foreign policy, *Through the Looking Glass* (London, 1983). Though Mr Verrier's references are inevitably far from complete, they are generally sufficient to indicate at what points he depends on unattributable evidence. Nigel West, *MI6: British Secret Intelligence Operations 1909–1945* (London, 1983) was published after this volume went to press.

7. *German Spies in England* was first published on 17 Feb 1915; the sixth edition appeared on 6 Mar 1915. Le Queux's career is examined in chapter 2 of Christopher Andrew's forthcoming history of the British intelligence community.

8. Thames Television advertisements in most of the Sunday press, 4 Sept 1983.

9. *Sunday Times*, 4 Sept 1983. A rather different but by no means uncontroversial version of Reilly's life appears in Michael Kettle, *Sidney Reilly: The True Story* (London, 1983). The *TV Times Special* produced to accompany the Reilly series contains an 'exclusive extra episode' by the scriptwriter Troy Kennedy Martin which describes a dramatic encounter between Reilly and Sir Mansfield Cumming, head of SIS, in 1924. This episode aptly illustrates some of the limitations of Mr Martin's research. Cumming (whose name Mr Martin consistently misspells) died in 1923.

10. H. Montgomery Hyde, *Cynthia*, Ballantyne Books edition (New York, 1979): a more valuable work than the publisher's sensational presentation suggests.

11. See, for example, T 162/76, E 7483/1 on the Passport Control Officers; and FO 366/800 on the Government Code and Cypher School.

12. See, for example, House of Commons, *Public Records*, cited in note 4.

13. FO to Sir R. Campbell, 20 Feb 1939, FO 371/22944, C 2190/421/62.

14. Sir P. Loraine to Sir L. Oliphant (FO), 17 June 1932, enclosing minute by N. Mayers; and FO minutes by P. J. Dixon and W. J. Childs. FO 371/16009 E 3389/56/65.

15. We are indebted to Ian Nish for information on Japanese usage.

16. See below, p. 205.

17. Ewan Butler, *Mason-Mac* (London, 1972), p. 75. Interestingly, it was decided not to attempt Hitler's assassination during the war.

18. Christopher Andrew, 'France and the German Menace', forthcoming in Ernest May, *Knowing One's Enemies*, and 'The Mobilization of British Intelligence for the Two World Wars', in N. F. Dreisziger (ed.), *Mobilization for Total War* (Waterloo, Ontario, 1981).

19. R. C. Elwood, *Roman Malinovsky* (London, 1977).

20. W. C. Beaver, 'The Development of the Intelligence Division and Its Role in Aspects of Imperial Policymaking 1854–1901' (Oxford D. Phil dissertion, 1976).

21. Major-General Lord Edward Gleichen, *A Guardsman's Memories* (London, 1932), p. 325.

22. Lieutenant-General Sir (later Baron) Robert Baden-Powell, *My Adventures as a Spy* (London, 1915), pp. 11–12, 159.

23. Andrew, 'Mobilization of British Intelligence', p. 93.

24. See below, pp. 35–8.

25. Andrew, 'Mobilization of British Intelligence', pp. 94–7.

26. GC&CS was, however, initially suspicious of mathematicians, believing that 'the right kind of brain to do this work' was 'not mathematical but classical'. Christopher Andrew, 'Governments and Secret Services: A Historical Perspective', *International Journal*, XXXIV, no. 2 (1979), 167.

27. Hugh Trevor-Roper, *The Philby Affair* (London, 1968), p. 47.

28. 'John Whitwell' (Leslie Nicholson), *British Agent* (London, 1966), chapter 1.

29. The most recent study of the National Security Agency and Anglo-American cooperation in communications intelligence is James Bamford, *The Puzzle Palace* (Boston, Mass., 1982).

30. Christopher Andrew, 'Whitehall, Washington and the Intelligence Services', *International Affairs* (July 1977), 396–7.

31. Lord Vansittart, *The Mist Procession* (London, 1958), p. 597.

32. Andrew, 'Whitehall, Washington and the Intelligence Services', p. 395.

33. Cmnd. 8787 (1983), p. 85.

34. Michael Handel, 'Avoiding Political and Technological Surprise in the 1980s'; David S. Sullivan, 'Evaluating United States Intelligence Estimates'; R. Pipes, 'Recruitment, Training and Incentives for Better Analysis, Part 2', all in R. Godson (ed.), *Intelligence Requirements for the 1980s: Analysis and Estimates* (Washington, 1980).

35. Angelo Codevilla, 'Comparative Historical Experience of Doctrine and Organization', ibid., pp. 15–16.

36. Cmnd. 8787 (1983), p. 86.

37. William Colby, interviewed by Christopher Andrew in Part 5 of 'The Profession of Intelligence', first broadcast on BBC Radio 4 on 30 Aug 1981.

38. Sir Harold Wilson, *The Governance of Britain* (London, 1976), chapter 9.

39. House of Commons, *Parliamentary Debates*, 28 July 1977, col. 1223.

40. Chapman Pincher, *Inside Story* (London, 1978) pp. 15–21, 32–40.

41. David Owen, Alan Beith, Roy Hattersley, Robin Cook and Jonathan Aitken, interviewed by Christopher Andrew in 'File on Four', BBC Radio 4, 4 and 11 Aug 1982 (Producer Peter Everett).

42. House of Commons, *Parliamentary Debates*, 15 Dec 1924, col. 674.

43. DO (48)5, 5 July 1947, CAB 21/2554.

1. JAPANESE INTELLIGENCE AND THE APPROACH OF THE RUSSO-JAPANESE WAR
Ian Nish

N.B. Japanese names are shown in this essay with surnames preceding given names, according to normal Japanese convention.

1. Thanks are due for help in the preparation of this paper to Mr S. Boehncke, Mr M. Falkus, Dr J. Osterhammel and Dr S. Sugiyama.

2. See G. Kerst, *Jacob Meckel: sein Leben, sein Wirken in Deutschland und Japan* (Göttingen, 1970).

3. T. Takakura, *Tanaka Giichi denki*, 3 vols (Tokyo, 1958), vol. I, pp. 108–9.

4. Mutsu to Kurino, 15 Dec 1894, quoted in G. M. Berger (ed.), *Kenkenroku: A diplomatic record of the Sino-Japanese war, 1894–5* (Mutsu) (Tokyo, 1982), p. 271.

5. For the use made of Siebold by the prominent diplomat, Aoki Shūzō, see I. H. Nish, *Japanese foreign policy, 1869–1942* (London, 1977), pp. 45 and 270–2.

6. Tokutomi Iichirō, *Kōshaku Yamagata Aritomo den*, 3 vols (Tokyo, 1933),vol. III, pp. 98–109.

7. *Yamagata-den*, III, 100–1.

8. *Tanaka-denki*, I, 110.

9. Shimada Kinji, *Roshiya ni okeru Hirose Takeo*, 2 vols (Tokyo, 1976).

10. *Tanaka-denki*, I, p. 113.

11. *Tanaka-denki*, I, pp. 115–16.

12. *Tanaka-denki*, I, pp. 165–74.

13. *Tanaka-denki*, I, pp. 174–80.

14. *Tanaka-denki*, I, p. 115; *Komura gaikōshi* (Tokyo, 1953), vol. I, pp. 148–9.

15. *Tanaka-denki*, I, p. 181.

16. This is a précis of original materials taken from Tanaka's diary and memoranda to be found in *Tanaka-denki*, I, pp. 185–214.

17. *Tanaka-denki*, I, pp. 260–2.

18. Olavi Fält, 'Collaboration between Japanese intelligence and the Finnish underground during the Russo-Japanese war', in *Asian Profile*, IV/2 (1976) and 'Japan in Finnish underground newspapers during the Russo-Japanese war' in I. H. Nish and C. J. Dunn (eds), *European Studies on Japan* (Tenterden, 1979), pp. 130–1.

19. Michael Futrell, 'Colonel Akashi and Japanese contacts with Russian revolutionaries in 1904–5', in *St Antony's Papers, No. 2: Far Eastern Affairs* (1967), pp. 17–18.

20. *Tanaka-denki*, I, p. 181.

21. Kurobane Shigeru, *Nichi-Ro sensō to Akashi kōsaku* (Tokyo, 1976), pp. 73–4.

22. Kurobane, p. 74.

23. A. Hiratsuka, *Shishaku Kurino Shinichirō den* (Tokyo, 1942).

24. Kurobane, pp. 86–7.

25. *Rakka ryūsui* is reproduced in Kurobane, pp. 99–157. Akashi's exploits are dealt with in detail by Futrell, op. cit. and J. A. White, *The Diplomacy of the Russo-Japanese war* (Princeton, 1964), pp. 140–1.

26. Futrell, op. cit., p. 22; Kurobane, pp. 64–6. An important contribution is made in Jerzy J. Lerski, 'A Polish chapter of the Russo-Japanese war' in *Transactions of the Asiatic Society of Japan*, VII (Tokyo, 1959), 69–97.

27. Yamabe Kentarō, 'Gaikō bunsho to angō' in Berger, *Kenkenroku*, p. 264. Also

Foreign Office (Public Record Office, London) 800/134, MacDonald to Lansdowne, 30 June 1903.

28. *Nihon gaikō bunsho*, vol. 37/i, no. 53, Kurino to Komura, 15 Jan 1904; and G. P. Gooch and H. W. V. Temperley (eds), *British Documents on the Origins of the War, 1898–1914*, vol. ii (London, 1927), no. 281.

29. On Kokuryūkai, see M. B. Jansen, *The Japanese and Sun Yat-sen* (Cambridge, Mass., 1954). For one of the 'China adventurers', see Miyazaki Tōten, *My 33 Years Dream* (translated by S. Etō and M. B. Jansen, Princeton, 1982).

30. Ishimitsu recounts his experiences in a four-part work of which *Kōya no hana* is one. See Hashikawa Bunzō, *Nis-Shin Nichi-Ro no seneki* (Tokyo, 1970), pp. 108–35.

31. E.g. *Nihon gaikō bunsho*, vol. 34 (Tokyo, 1956), no. 533.

32. G. A. Lensen (ed.), *Korea and Manchuria between Russia and Japan* (Tokyo, 1966), pp. 246–7.

33. Morrison to Moberley Bell, 24 Nov 1903 in Lo Hui-min (ed.), *The Correspondence of G. E. Morrison*, 2 vols (Cambridge, 1976), vol. i, p. 239. My italics. The most detailed account of cooperation between Colonel Aoki and Yuan against Russian railways, telegraphs etc. is in Tani Toshio, *Kimitsu Nichi-Ro senshi* (Tokyo, 1966).

34. Papers of Sir John Jordan (Public Record Office, London), vol. iii, Jordan to F. A. Campbell (Foreign Office), 11 Jan 1904.

35. Jordan papers iii, Jordan to Campbell, 16 June, 1903.

36. Jordan papers iii, Jordan to Campbell, 15 Feb 1904.

37. Shimada, op. cit.; Tani, op. cit., *Kimitsu Nichi-Ro senshi*, underscores army-navy quarrels.

38. Tani, op. cit., suggests that between the two responsible commanders, Generals Matsukawa and Fukushima, there was rivalry over intelligence which led to mutual antagonism.

39. Shimada, op. cit.; F. S. G. Piggott, *Broken thread* (Aldershot, 1950), p. 46.

2. CODEBREAKERS AND FOREIGN OFFICES: THE FRENCH, BRITISH AND AMERICAN EXPERIENCE *Christopher Andrew*

1. R. de Billy, unpublished souvenirs, pp. 15 ff, Archives du Ministère des Affaires Etrangères, de Billy MSS 3.

2. M. Paléologue, *Journal de l'affaire Dreyfus 1894–1899* (Paris, 1955), p. 266. Cf. *Die Grosse Politik der Europäischen Kabinette (1871–1914)* (Berlin, 1922–7), vol. xiii, no. 3633.

3. O. Homberg, *Les coulisses de l'histoire* (Paris, 1938), p. 38.

4. M. Paléologue, *Au Quai d'Orsay à la veille de la tourmente. Journal 1913–1914* (Paris, 1947), p. 35.

5. Homberg, *Les coulisses*, pp. 38–9.

6. C. M. Andrew, 'Déchiffrement et diplomatie: le cabinet noir du Quai d'Orsay sous la Troisième République', *Relations Internationales* (1976), no. 5, 44 ff.

7. Ibid.; H. Guillemin, 'L'affaire Dreyfus. Le télégramme du 2 novembre', *Mercure de France*, cccxxxix (1960).

8. C. M. Andrew, *Théophile Delcassé and the Making of the Entente Cordiale* (London, 1968), pp. 98–100, also 'Déchiffrement et diplomatie', pp. 48–9.

9. Homberg, *Les coulisses*, pp. 38–9.

10. Haverna, 'Note sur l'organisation et le fonctionnement du service cryptographique de la Sûreté Générale', 7 Sept 1917, Archives Nationales, F⁷ 14,605.

11. R. Poincaré, 'Notes journalières', 16 Jan 1914, Bibliothèque Nationale cabinet des manuscrits (hereafter BN), n.a. fr. 16026.

12. A. Ferry, *Les carnets secrets 1914–1918* (Paris, 1957), p. 21.

13. Andrew, *Delcassé*, chapter 14.

14. Haverna, 'Note'; Andrew, 'Déchiffrement et diplomatie', pp. 51–3.

15. Andrew, 'Déchiffrement et diplomatie', pp. 53–5; J.-C. Allain, *Joseph Caillaux: le défi victorieux 1863–1914* (Paris, 1978), pp. 391–6.

16. Andrew, 'Déchiffrement et diplomatie', p. 54.

17. J. Chastenet, *Histoire de la Troisième Republique*, vol. IV (Paris, 1955), p. 94.

18. Haverna, 'Note'.

19. Poincaré, 'Notes journalières', 28 May 1914, BN n.a.fr. 16027.

20. Poincaré, 'Notes journalières', 14–16 Jan, 28 May 1914, BN n.a.fr. 16026–7.

21. Andrew, 'Déchiffrement et diplomatie', p. 57.

22. Poincaré, 'Notes journalières', 28 May, 23–25 June 1914, BN n.a.fr. 16027.

23. Poincaré, 'Notes journalières', 19–29 July 1914, ibid.

24. Rayner Heppenstall, *A Little Pattern of French Crime* (London, 1969), pp. 149–50.

25. Poincaré, 'Notes journalières', 22 July 1914, BN n.a.fr. 16027.

26. Ferry, *Carnets secrets*, p. 21.

27. Haverna, 'Note'; Andrew, 'Déchiffrement et diplomatie', pp. 57–8.

28. A. Ramm (ed.), *The Political Correspondence of Mr Gladstone and Lord Granville, 1876–1886*, vol. II (Oxford, 1962), pp. 33–5. Monson to Lansdowne, 21 Feb 1902, PRO FO 800/124.

29. F.O. to Treasury, 8 and 18 Dec 1911, PRO TI/11357/22713. The changes made brought only a limited improvement. See below, pp. 106ff.

30. C. M. Andrew, 'The British Secret Service and Anglo-Soviet Relations in the 1920s. Part I', *Historical Journal*, XX (1977), 678–9.

31. The best study of naval codebreaking is in Patrick Beesly, *Room 40* (London, 1982). On the broader context see C. M. Andrew, 'The mobilization of British Intelligence for the Two World Wars', in N. F. Dreisziger (ed.), *Mobilization for Total War* (Waterloo, Ontario, 1981).

32. A. G. Denniston, MS memoir on Room 40, n.d., Churchill College Archives Centre, Cambridge, Denniston MSS. Oliver to Admiralty, 7 March 1919; Oliver, 'Notes About Room 40 and Sir Alfred Ewing in the 1914–18 War', National Maritime Museum, Oliver MSS OLV/8.

33. F. H. Hinsley *et al.*, *British Intelligence in the Second World War*, vol. I (London, 1979), pp. 9–10. On the Zimmermann telegram see below, p. 141.

34. Denniston, MS memoir on Room 40.

35. Denniston, TS memoir on GC&CS, 2 Dec 1944. Denniston MSS. W. F. Clarke, 'The Years Between', Churchill College Archive Centre, Clarke MSS CLKE 3.

36. Andrew, 'The British Secret Service . . . Part I', pp. 683–7.

37. Ibid., pp. 692–5.

38. C. M. Andrew, 'British Intelligence and the Breach with Russia in 1927', *Historical Journal*, XXV, no. 4 (1982).

39. Ibid., p. 964.

40. Christopher Morris, Fellow of King's College, Cambridge, interviewed by Christopher Andrew on 'Timewatch', BBC2, 15 Dec 1982.

41. Andrew, 'The British Secret Service . . . Part I', p. 686.

42. Herbert Yardley, *The American Black Chamber* (New York, 1931), p. 21.

43. It was indeed 'Neptune'. David Kahn, *The Codebreakers* (New York, 1968), p. 351. R. S. Baker, *Woodrow Wilson, Life and Letters* (New York, 1928–39), vol. V, pp. 204ff, 307, 317–18; vol. VI, pp. 51–2, 143ff.

44. Kahn, *Codebreakers*, pp. 370ff. 'Historical Background of the Signal Security Agency', vol. II, chapter I, Washington National Archives, RG 457–77–1.

45. 'Historical Background of the Signal Security Agency', vol. III, pp. 39–55. Yardley refers to the breaking of British diplomatic codes in *The American Black Chamber*. He also claims various successes during the 1920s with some of the codes and cyphers of

Argentina, Brazil, China, Costa Rica, Cuba, Dominica, France, Liberia, Mexico, Nicaragua, Panama, Peru, Russia, El Salvador and Spain.

46. 'Historical Background of the Signal Security Agency', vol. III, pp. 69–118.

47. W. F. Friedman, 'A Brief History of the Signal Intelligence Service', pp. 9–10, 29 June 1942, National Archives RG 457–SRH–029.

48. R. Lewin, *The Other Ultra* (London, 1982), p. 33.

49. J. Bamford, *The Puzzle Palace* (Boston, Mass., 1982), pp. 18–26.

50. Friedman, 'Brief History', p. 12.

51. 'Historical Background of the Signal Security Agency', vol. III, pp. 169–70. Lewin, *Other Ultra*, p. 38. The SIS began work in 1930.

52. Lewin, *Other Ultra*, p. 25.

53. 'Historical Background of the Signal Security Agency', vol. III, pp. 288–9.

54. Ibid., p. 308.

55. Friedman, 'Brief History', pp. 13–14.

56. 'Historical Background of the Signal Security Agency', vol. III, p. 323.

57. Lewin, *Other Ultra*, p. 41.

58. Friedman, 'Brief History', p. 14.

59. Bamford, *Puzzle Palace*, p. 40.

3. BRITISH INTELLIGENCE IN IRELAND, 1914–1921   *Eunan O'Halpin*

1. Memorandum by Long, 19 May 1916, India Office Library, Curzon papers, MSS Eur. F112/176. For information concerning Major Price I am very grateful to Mr Norman Stewart Price CMG OBE. For their comments on an earlier draft of this article I would like to thank Dr Leon O'Broin, Emmet O'Connor, Dr C. S. Andrews and Colonel Dan Bryan.

2. Report by Basil Thomson on the organisation of intelligence in Ireland, September 1916, cited hereafter as 'Thomson report', p. 2. With Thomson to French, 8 May 1918 I[mperial] W[ar] M[useum], French papers, 75/46/12.

3. P[ublic] R[ecord] O[ffice], CO 904/157/1–2 contain the intelligence officers' reports from 1916 to 1918.

4. Kell to Hardinge, 13 May 1916, Cambridge University Library, Hardinge MSS 42/126–7.

5. Harrel had been dismissed from the DMP following the Bachelor's Walk shootings in 1914. Robert Brennan, *Allegiance* (Dublin, 1950), pp. 41–2, describes how he was approached by Harrel when a reporter in Wexford to act as an agent. Brennan was a known Sinn Feiner, and was struck by Harrel's ignorance of this. On p. 45 he mentions that Harrel's correspondence was routinely intercepted and read by Michael Collins's men in 1917 and 1918.

6. PRO, CO 904/23/4 has material on the political affiliations of dockyard employees. 'Thomson report', p. 3.

7. Admiral Sir Lewis Bayly, the senior naval officer in Ireland throughout the war, wrote a memoir, *Pull Together* (London, 1939), in which he gives an account of the navy's activities.

8. The army did prepare a list of suspects for deportation and detention in October 1915. If acted on 'there would *not* have been a *rebellion* & the consequent executions for all the leaders were included in these recommendations', wrote General Maxwell to Lord French, 7 Sept 1916, French papers, 75/46/11.

9. S[tate] P[apers] O[ffice, Dublin], CSO RP 1918, 18746.

10. Long to Gwynne, 19 Nov 1914, Bodleian Library, Gwynne MS 20.

11. Gwynne to Bonar Law, 28 Dec 1914, enclosing notes by J. D. Irvine dated 19 Dec 1914. H[ouse] of L[ords] R[ecords] O[ffice], Bonar Law papers, 36/5/59. The

disaster referred to was the sinking in October of the battleship *Audacious*, which struck a mine off the Donegal coast.

12. SPO, Crimes Branch Special carton no. 23, file on Casement.

13. Admiral Sir William James, *The Eyes of the Navy: a Biographical Study of Admiral Sir Reginald Hall* (London, 1955), pp. 45–53.

14. Draft of a chapter by Hall on 'The cruise of the *Sayonara*', Churchill College, Cambridge, Hall papers, 3/3. See Long to Bonar Law, 16 Jan 1917, on Lord Sligo, HLRO, Bonar Law papers, 81/2/16.

15. James, *Eyes of the Navy*, pp. 110–15. Hall circulated extracts from Casement's diaries during the latter's trial in 1916, in order to discredit him by proving him a homosexual. James, op. cit., pp. 112–15, and B. L. Reid, *The Lives of Roger Casement* (New Haven, Conn., 1976), pp. 382–4. Some writers maintained that the diaries were forgeries, but the evidence suggests that they were genuine.

16. PRO, CO 904/120/1–2 contain numerous police reports on the movements of suspects. Most of the leaders of the 1916 rebellion had been under observation for some years.

17. Royal commission on the rebellion in Ireland, *P*[arliamentary] *P*[apers] (1916) xi, p. 201. Unsigned note, 14 Apr 1916, PRO, CO 904/23/3 part 2.

18. 'Thomson report', p. 3; 'Royal commission', p. 199. For a sympathetic account of the Under-Secretary, Sir Mathew Nathan, see Leon O'Broin, *Dublin Castle and the 1916 Rising* (Dublin, 1966). It is worth noting that Nathan was not entirely inexperienced in intelligence matters: he gave evidence in 1902 to a secret War Office committee on 'permanent establishment of the mobilisation and intelligence division'. PRO, T1 10966/617.

I have located figures showing expenditure by the Irish government from the secret service vote, 1885–6 to 1921–2. They should be treated with caution: although accurate in themselves, they reflect only a proportion of expenditure on political intelligence in those years. The RIC and DMP evidently had some funds of their own for such work, and of course their staff costs would be met from the ordinary votes. Furthermore, naval intelligence and military intelligence had money for secret intelligence work other than that from the secret service vote.

Year	Amount	Year	Amount	Year	Amount
1885–6	17,487 11 11	1899–00	2,139 10 6	1913–4	869 6 2
1886–7	7,936 10 2	1900–1	1,945 0 6	1914–5	995 10 0
1887–8	4,248 18 4	1901–2	1,347 14 6	1915–6	981 0 0
1888–9	4,484 12 3	1902–3	1,962 11 9	1916–7	932 12 0
1889–90	4,423 17 2	1903–4	1,549 15 6	1917–8	1,803 5 0
1890–1	4,031 12 0	1904–5	1,502 7 7	1918–9	1,412 9 5
1891–2	4,505 18 9	1905–6	2,634 5 5	1919–20	8,499 4 0
1892–3	2,457 9 5	1906–7	837 6 3	1920–1	63,602 4 9
1893–4	1,303 14 3	1907–8	997 17 6	1921–2	36,308 10 4
1894–5	1,505 12 7	1908–9	813 1 0		
1895–6	1,536 18 4	1909–10	916 14 0		
1896–7	1,639 4 4	1910–11	984 4 2		
1897–8	1,758 17 7	1911–12	904 0 0		
1898–9	1,240 17 1	1912–13	807 0 0		

Source: PRO, T1 11689/25138 and T165/46 and 48.

19. See Maureen Wall, 'The background to the Rising' in K. B. Nowlan (ed.), *The Making of 1916: Studies in the History of the Rising* (Dublin, 1969), pp. 157–97.

20. 'Royal commission', p. 222.

21. Ibid.

22. Bayly, *Pull together*, p. 206. The sequence of events outlined here is given in some detail in O'Broin, *Dublin Castle*, *passim*.

23. James, *Eyes of the Navy*, p. 112.

24. Brian Inglis, *Roger Casement* (London, 1973), pp. 317–18. O'Broin, op. cit., p. 83.

25. Leon O'Broin, *Michael Collins* (Dublin, 1980), p. 15.

26. O'Broin, *Dublin Castle*, p. 83.

27. Ibid., p. 10. For his action in opening fire on the rebels, thereby causing them to retreat from the Castle, and for his general conduct during the Rising, Major Price was awarded the DSO. Information from Norman Stewart Price.

28. 'Royal commission', p. 250.

29. Ibid., p. 22. For Birrell's career, see Leon O'Broin, *The Chief Secretary: Augustine Birrell and Ireland, 1907–1916* (London, 1968). Birrell was somewhat unfortunate to be saddled with all the blame, given the vacillations of the cabinet on Irish policy, but he undoubtedly allowed his administration to become rather slack in its observation and treatment of separatist groups. After years of listening to nationalist hyperbole, he found it difficult to take the various extremist groups seriously. The same attitude appears to have pervaded the detective unit of the DMP.

30. See note 20 above.

31. In *The Scene Changes* (London, 1939), Thomson quotes from a diary he kept during the war. His grandson knows of no papers of any consequence that have survived.

32. 'Thomson report', pp. 1, 4 and 5.

33. Thomson to French, 8 May 1918, IWM, French papers, 75/46/12. See note 94 below.

34. Eunan O'Halpin, 'H. E. Duke and the Irish administration, 1916–18', *Irish Historical Studies*, XXII, no. 88 (September 1981), 364; Maxwell to French, 7 Sept 1916, IWM, French papers, 75/46/11.

35. MacDonogh (Director of Military Intelligence) to General Officer Commanding in Chief, Ireland, 2 Sept 1916, PRO, WO 35/69/8.

36. Ibid. Documents relative to the Sinn Fein movement, *PP* (1921) XXIX, 444–51.

37. Minute by Price, 4 Sept 1916, as in note 35 above.

38. MI5D to GHQ, Irish command, 25 Sept 1916, ibid.

39. As in note 36 above. Sean Cronin, *The McGarrity papers* (Tralee, 1972), pp. 64–5.

40. 'Documents', pp. 454–6.

41. O'Halpin, 'H. E. Duke', p. 366.

42. The Belfast man was R. J. Lynn, MP, editor of the *Northern Whig*. See Strachey to Lynn, 9 July 1918, HLRO, Strachey papers, S21/2/5. See also Carson to Lloyd George, 30 Oct 1917, enclosing material from Lynn warning of 'a repetition of 1641' in Ulster, with Sinn Fein using 'fire, poison and sword' in a new rebellion. HLRO, Lloyd George papers, F/6/2/18.

43. Unsigned [Thomson] to Strachey, 29 June 1918, HLRO, Strachey papers, S/21/2/5.

44. Strachey to Lynn, 9 July 1918, ibid. Strachey to Headlam, 17 Oct 1917, HLRO, Strachey papers, S/21/2/6. O'Halpin, 'H. E. Duke', p. 366.

45. Long had his own source of secret information on Irish affairs, as he was constantly in touch with the permanent head of the Irish local government board, Sir Henry Robinson, who produced capable reports from a strongly unionist perspective. They were concerned not with tales of mysterious foreigners and submarine landings, but with political conditions. Robinson occasionally sought confidential accounts of the state of the country from his subordinates stationed throughout Ireland. IWM, French papers, 75/46/12.

46. 'Documents', pp. 463–4. It transpired that the man in question, Robert

Monteith, was already back in Ireland. This slender evidence formed the basis for the claim that 'before the end' of 1917 'a secret headquarters had been set up in South America whence agents were sent to Ireland'. Draft memorandum on 'the story of the active links between the Sinn Fein movement and Germany', IWM, French papers, 74/46/12.

47. 'Documents', p. 467, says that on 2 Dec 1917 a man arrested in Mayo was found to be in possession of 'two pamphlets printed in Germany'. From this it was inferred that these had been sent by submarine. The Germans were notably reluctant to send even arms by those means, which makes it all the more unlikely that they would risk a U-boat simply to provide publicity material for Sinn Fein.

48. PRO, CO 904/92–114 contain the inspector general's monthly reports.

49. See note 3 above.

50. PRO, CO 904/23/5 contains papers on arms smuggling, 1916–17. Dissatisfaction with the intelligence agencies' failure to penetrate Sinn Fein and to find evidence of collusion with Germany was sometimes expressed in cabinet. See WC 186(1), 14 July 1917, PRO, Cab. 23/3.

51. WC 372(11), 25 Mar 1918, PRO, Cab. 23/5.

52. 'Documents', pp. 468–9. 'Précis of information re German help to Sinn Fein rebels' by Major Price, with Samuels to Lloyd George, Bonar Law and Long, undated, c. 13 May; telegram [from Hall?] on his interrogation of Dowling, with Mahon to French, 21 Apr 1918, IWM, French papers, 75/46/12.

53. Précis by Major Price, as in note 52 above.

54. H. C. Hoy, *40 OB or How the War was Won* (London, 1932), pp. 147–8. He claims that at the appointed time a handkerchief was waved in the prescribed manner, causing a submarine to surface and approach the shore: '. . . when she was close in two aeroplanes promptly appeared on the scene, and bombs, I am informed, put an end to that mission'. This is scarcely credible: from R. H. Gibson and Maurice Prendergast, *The German Submarine War* (London, 1932), it appears that no submarines were sunk off the Irish coast between 25 Apr and 10 July 1918, and none were destroyed by aircraft during the entire year.

55. Hoy, *40 OB*, p. 147.

56. French diary, 21 Apr 1918, IWM, French papers, 75/46/3.

57. Ibid., 19 and 25 Apr 1918.

58. Ibid., 5 May 1918.

59. Précis by Major Price, as in note 52 above. See also 'Documents', p. 469. The Cotters were keen sailors, and this probably explains the incident. Information from Dr C. S. Andrews, 8 June 1982. Richard Cotter was a brother-in-law of Mrs Eamon de Valera.

60. See 'Notes on the position in Ireland in the years 1917, 1918 and 1919', University College Dublin, Mulcahy papers, P7/D/35.

61. Précis by Major Price, and telegram [by Hall?], as in note 52 above.

62. French diary, 24 Apr 1918, IWM, French papers, 75/46/3.

63. Report from Irish command, 2 May; report from MI5D, 3 May 1918, conveying the substance of an Admiralty communication. IWM, French papers, 75/46/12. This report was cited in 'Documents', p. 472, but the date given was 4 May, and Copenhagen was not mentioned as its origin.

No arms appear to have reached Ireland, and it is unlikely that any were sent. From Dowling's admissions it seemed that no German landing could take place before mid-June.

64. French diary, 2 May 1918, IWM, French papers, 75/46/3.

65. Bonar Law to Carson, 25 Apr 1918, HLRO, Bonar Law papers, 84/7/25. WC 408(11), 10 May 1918, PRO, Cab. 23/6.

66. French diary, 8 and 12 May 1918, IWM, French papers, 75/46/3.

67. The proclamation also called for an increase in voluntary recruitment, warning that conscription would otherwise be enforced.

68. WC 408/A/2, 10 May 1918, PRO, Cab. 23/14.

69. French to Stamfordham, 18 May 1918, IWM, French papers, 75/46/3.

70. Leon O'Broin, *Michael Collins* (Dublin, 1980), pp. 30–1.

71. Long to Reading (ambassador in Washington), and Reading's reply, 17 and 20 May 1918, British Library, Balfour papers, MS 49741/178–9 and 186–8. I am grateful to Dr J. R. Fanning for this reference.

See Thomson's message to Long, 20 May 1918, that 'it is only possible . . . to give a rechauffé' of post-January 1917 material in order to avoid 'giving away sources of information'. W[iltshire] R[ecord] O[ffice], Long papers, 947/373. Long to French, 20 May 1918, WRO, 947/701; unsigned memorandum by Long on secret service organisation, undated, autumn 1918, WRO, Long papers, 947/672.

72. S. W. Roskill, *Hankey, Man of Secrets* (London, 1970–4), i, 554, diary of 21 May 1918. One draft of the proclamation asserted that 'an important feature in every plan for rebellion' was 'the establishment of submarine bases in Ireland to menace the shipping of all nations'. Draft memorandum, as in note 46 above.

73. WC 414/A, 22 May 1918, PRO, Cab. 23/14.

74. Charles à Court Repington, *The First World War 1914–1918* (London, 1920), ii, 311, diary for 29 May 1918. He later described it as 'a myth' to Donal O'Sullivan, author of *The Irish Free State and its Senate* (London, 1940), p. 42.

75. Sir Henry Robinson to French, 30 May 1918, IWM, French papers, 75/46/12, says the arrests took Sinn Fein supporters by surprise, but that if convincing evidence was forthcoming the separatist movement would never recover.

76. See A. W. Samuels to Lloyd George, 15 Dec 1920, PRO, PREM 1/7, in connection with the publishing of the 'Documents' White Paper. He had been Irish attorney general in 1918, and remained convinced that 'dangers' had then 'threatened not merely Ireland and the British Empire but the whole allied cause'. Samuels to French, 25 Apr 1921, IWM, French papers, 75/46/11.

77. James, *Eyes of the Navy, passim.*

78. Unfortunately there is nothing in Hall's papers in Churchill College, Cambridge, to throw fresh light on the 'German plot' affair.

79. French to Lloyd George, 19 May 1918, IWM, French papers, 75/46/11.

80. Minutes of viceroy's executive council, 1 July 1918, IWM, French papers, 75/46/13. See also Saunderson to Long, 12 Sept 1918, on military complaints that secret service information from London was never given in full. WRO, Long papers, 947/347.

81. Minutes of viceroy's executive council, 12 July 1918, as in note 80 above.

82. Inspector general's monthly reports, June 1918–Oct 1919. PRO, CO 904/106–10.

83. Unsigned memorandum by Long, as in note 71 above.

84. Hoy, *Room 40*, p. 268.

85. For the sequel to his removal, see Eunan O'Halpin, 'Sir Warren Fisher and the coalition, 1919–1922', *Historical Journal*, xxiv, 4(1981), 917–25.

86. The best account of events in Ireland from 1919 to 1921 is Charles Townshend, *The British Campaign in Ireland, 1919–1921* (Oxford, 1975).

87. Minutes of viceroy's executive council, 18 Jan, and French to Macpherson, 31 Jan 1919, IWM, French papers, 75/46/13. Major Price became county inspector in Cavan and Fermanagh, but he was frequently called to Dublin to advise on the situation generally. In October 1920 he was appointed assistant inspector general, and returned to work full time in Dublin Castle. In 1922 he received a warning that he was about to be shot, and was advised to walk out of his office and go straight to England 'leaving his hat on the door', so that the IRA would not realise he had left for good. This he did. He died there in 1931. Information from Norman Stewart Price.

88. Townshend, *British Campaign*, pp. 21–2. See French to Long, 5 June 1919, in which he complains that the navy no longer patrolled to prevent arms smuggling. IWM, French papers, 75/49/13. However, some form of naval intelligence seems to have continued: see A. W. Cope and B. G. Harwood to Sir Warren Fisher, 12 May 1920, HLRO, Lloyd George Papers, F/31/1/32.

89. O'Broin, *Michael Collins*, pp. 49–50.

90. Minutes of viceroy's executive council, 25 May, 2 and 10 June 1919, IWM, French papers, 75/46/13. On 10 Apr French had sought the services of Colonel Kell, 'the best man' to advise on how to set up 'a proper criminal investigation department'. Letter to Churchill, IWM, French papers, 75/46/11. This was symptomatic of the confusion which prevailed within the administration: Kell was head of MI5, which was an intelligence agency rather than a detective unit of the police.

91. French to Macpherson, 4 Nov 1919, IWM, French papers, 75/46/13.

92. Saunderson to Long, 19 Dec 1919, WRO, Long papers, 947/348.

93. Taylor was effectively head of the Irish administration, as his nominal superior had been cut out of all important decision-making by French.

94. Report of the committee of inquiry into the detective organisation of the Irish police forces, dated 7 Dec 1919. IWM, French papers, 75/46/12. In fact the copy cited was typed.

95. Ibid.

96. See French to Macpherson, 5 Mar 1920, IWM, French papers, 75/46/13. For the effects of the changes made on the RIC, widely seen within the force as sectarian and political in nature, see J. A. Gaughan, *Memoirs of Constable Jeremiah Mee, R.I.C.* (Dublin, 1975), pp. 77–9, 259.

97. Saunderson to Long, 17 Dec 1919, WRO, Long papers, 947/348.

98. Bell's report to French, undated, Jan 1920, PRO, CO 904/188/1.

99. Townshend, *British Campaign*, p. 91. Collins to William O'Brien, 6 July 1921, National Library of Ireland, O'Brien papers, MS 15687. I am grateful to Emmet O'Connor for this reference.

100. Bell to French, as in note 98 above.

101. Townshend, *British Campaign*, p. 65.

102. This assumption is based on Bell's report and notebook in the PRO, CO 904/188/1. On the inside cover of the notebook is written in Bell's handwriting, 'The Director of Intelligence, Scotland House, London SW1'. The director of intelligence was Sir Basil Thomson. For examples of Bell's activities, see the entries for 15 and 17 Feb 1920. He had 'just got in touch with a party in a prominent position in the Dublin Dockyard and am in hopes that some useful information may be obtained as I believe it is a happy hunting ground for S.F.', was 'on the track of one of the S.F. who escaped from M'Joy [Mountjoy Prison], and had noted an offer of information on the Ashtown ambush from a Mr Quigley, who unfortunately 'left phone box before any further information could be obtained'.

103. Townshend, *British Campaign*, p. 82.

104. Macready to Anderson, 8 Apr 1921, PRO, CO 904/188/2.

105. Townshend, *British Campaign*, p. 91.

106. Sturgis diary, 26 Sept 1920 and 13 Feb 1921, PRO, PRO 30/59/1–4.

107. See Montagu to Lloyd George, 29 June 1920, discussing the possible loan of agents from the Indian police to Irish command. HLRO, Lloyd George papers, F/40/3/11.

108. Sturgis diary, 26 Sept 1920, as in note 106 above.

109. One of Collins's informers, David Neligan, published an interesting but somewhat unreliable memoir, *The Spy in the Castle* (London, 1968). He and another agent, Eamon Broy, were well rewarded for their services, becoming senior police officers in the Irish free state.

110. Detective Hoey, for example, who was shot in 1919, had been bodyguard to H. E. Duke, the chief secretary from 1916 to 1918.

111. Tom Bowden, *The Breakdown of Public Security: the Case of Ireland 1916–1921, and Palestine 1936–1939* (London, 1977), p. 308. This book is confused, inaccurate and repetitious where Ireland is concerned.

112. This was Frank Teeling, who as an officer in the Free State army in 1923 'misconducted himself in such a way . . . as to run the danger of bringing serious discredit on us', as the army commander complained to the head of the government on 5 Feb 1923. The cabinet agreed to pay Teeling £250 to enable him to emigrate to Australia, but although the money was issued from a secret service fund it was not spent, as Teeling was detained after shooting a man dead in Dublin's Theatre Royal. SPO, S 2166.

113. Sturgis diary, 7 Dec 1920, as in note 106 above.

114. Collins was killed in an ambush in County Cork during the civil war which followed the treaty with Britain. Although the evidence seems straightforward enough, there has always been a slight air of mystery about his death. In *The Shooting of Michael Collins: Murder or Accident?* (Dublin, 1981), pp. 90–4, John M. Feehan put forward the bizarre theory that Collins was killed by one of his closest comrades, who was in reality an agent of 'the British secret service', a 'worldwide body' with 'millions of pounds of public money at their disposal'. This is scarcely credible.

In the autumn of 1922 one of the leading Republicans, Ernie O'Malley, got copies of British army intelligence documents, evidently sent to him 'by one of his agents from British General Headquarters'. These were appreciations of the situation rather than evidence of active intelligence operations, but the publication of extracts in a Republican newssheet greatly angered the Free State government, as they spoke of the murder by government forces of Republican prisoners. SPO, S 1784.

115. For the experiences of one army officer on intelligence duty in Ireland, see Major General Sir Kenneth Strong, *Intelligence at the Top* (London, 1968), pp. 1–5. He had £5 per month with which to pay informants, whom he would travel to meet disguised 'usually as the owner of a small donkey cart'. His sources were people such as railway workers and barmen who were well placed to notice any strangers or unusual occurrences in their districts. These were the sort of people, and this was the sort of intelligence, that would normally be the concern of the local police.

116. Neligan, *Spy in the Castle*, p. 78.

117. Nigel West, *M.I. 5: British Security Service Operations, 1909–1945* (London, 1981), p. 46, says all those killed were agents of the secret intelligence service (SIS). As already indicated in note 105 above, it is extremely doubtful whether all the victims were intelligence officers. Furthermore, it seems unlikely that they were SIS men, in that it was supposed to operate only outside the empire; within was the province of MI5. West is wrong also in dating Bloody Sunday in 1919, and in using the term 'Fenians' to describe IRA suspects detained in England in 1922. The book is not very authoritative on the early history of MI5, and it contains a good number of errors of fact.

118. See note 114 above. The woman concerned in Cork was engaged to Florence O'Donoughue, a leading IRA man in the area. Information from Dr C. S. Andrews, 8 June 1982.

119. See note 5 above.

4. BRITISH MILITARY AND ECONOMIC INTELLIGENCE: ASSESSMENTS OF NAZI GERMANY BEFORE THE SECOND WORLD WAR   *Wesley K. Wark*

1. See W. K. Wark, 'British Intelligence on the German Air Force and Aircraft Industry 1933–1939', *The Historical Journal*, xxv, 3 (1982), 627–48.

2. The first major pieces of intelligence arrived in May and November 1934: AI4 note, 22 May 1934, AIR 9/24; and air attaché, Paris, despatch 15 Nov 1934, C7802/31/18, FO 371/17713. For some insight into SIS activities in this period, see F. W. Winterbotham, *The Nazi Connection* (London, 1978). On the French Deuxième Bureau, see Georges Castellan, *Le Réarmament Clandestin du Reich 1930–1935* (Paris, 1954), pp. 174–5.

3. Wark, 'British Intelligence on the German Air Force', p. 631.

4. CID 1216-B, 4 Mar 1936, CAB 4/24.

5. Richard Overy, 'The German Pre-War Aircraft Production Plans: November 1936–April 1939', *The English Historical Review* (Oct. 1975), 778–97; Wilhelm Deist, *The Wehrmacht and German Rearmament* (London, 1981), chapter 4.

6. R. Overy, 'Hitler and Air Strategy', *Journal of Contemporary History*, xv, 3 (1980), 409.

7. CID 1265-B, 6 Oct 1936, CAB 4/25.

8. Air staff memo., 23 Oct 1936, AIR 9/24; D.P.(P)7, 'Progress of German Air Rearmament', 6 July 1937, CAB 16/182; AI3(b) est., 27 Oct 1938, AIR 40/2043.

9. Air staff to F.O., 11 Sept 1936, C6429/3925/18, FO 371/19946.

10. Sir Charles Webster and Noble Frankland, *The Strategic Air Offensive Against Germany 1939–1945* (London, 1961), I, pp. 91–6.

11. AI3 'Estimate of German Air Force Bombing Potential', 24 Aug 1938, AIR 9/90.

12. Ibid.

13. Karlheinz Kens and Heinz Nowarra, *Die Deutschen Flugzeuge 1933–1945* (Munchen, 1968).

14. ARP casualty estimates, see T. H. O'Brien, *Civil Defence* (London, 1955), pp. 15–16, 96, 144, 172.

15. See note 14 above. The file AIR 9/90, consisting of plans divisions' notes on the Munich crisis, contains much valuable material.

16. Newall to Kingsley Wood, 10 Sept 1938, AIR 8/248.

17. Moreover, there was some contradictory intelligence. MI5 reported from its German sources the warning that if Britain declared war, the Luftwaffe would launch an immediate attack on London: Hinsley, *British Intelligence*, I, 82. On the air power debate, see Barry Powers, *Strategy Without Slide Rule: British Air Strategy 1914–1939* (London, 1976).

18. Sir John Slessor, *The Central Blue* (London, 1956), p. 230. Slessor's memory was not quite accurate. The DCOS report was actually prepared by the Joint Planning Committee, of which he was a senior member.

19. Air attaché, Berlin, despatch, 6 Apr 1939, C5176/11/18, FO 371/22956.

20. Berlin embassy to FO, 27 July 1939, C10519/15/18, FO 371/22975.

21. On the British understanding of German air doctrine see Wark, 'British Intelligence on the GAF', 641–3.

22. CID 1182-B, 'The German Army: Its Present Strength and Possible Rate of Expansion in Peace and War', 2 July 1935, CAB 4/23.

23. WO 190/263, 18 July 1934. (WO 190 – the MI3 file of appreciation papers on the German army 1922–39 is an invaluable source for the study of military intelligence in the interwar years); CP 205(34), DRC report, secret appendix, 31 July 1934, CAB 16/110.

24. MI3, 30 Mar 1935, WO 190/315.

25. Ibid.; WO 190/324, 27 Apr 1935; WO 190/329, 9 May 1935.

26. Berlin embassy despatch, 9 Oct 1935, C6917/5023/18, FO 371/18883.

27. Military attaché, Berlin, despatch, 9 Feb 1938, C978/62/18, FO 371/18883; by July 1938 the MA was less certain of the army's autonomous power: C7648/1941/18, FO 371/21729.

28. CID 1182-B, 2 July 1935, CAB 4/23.

29. CID 1449-B, [July 1938], closed in file CAB 4/28, summarised in CID 1507-B, 19 Jan 1939, CAB 4/29.

30. WO 190/230, 11 Nov 1933.

31. WO 190/342, 23 July 1935; WO 190/344, 25 July 1935; CIGS paper, 16 June 1936, CAB 64/14; COS 698(revise) 28 Mar 1938, CAB 53/37; WO 190/644, n.d. [Aug 1938]; WO to F.O., 5 Sept 1938, C9306/65/18, FO 371/21668; WO to FO, 9 Sept 1938, C9451/65/18, FO 371/21668.

32. The exception was a WO study sent to the MA, Berlin, WO 106/5421. The lack of attention paid to the Czech army is confirmed by the memoirs of Brigadier H.C.T. Stronge (MA, Prague 1936–38), P226, The Imperial War Museum, London.

33. B. Bond (ed.), *Chief of Staff: The Diaries of Lt. Gen. Sir Henry Pownall* (London, 1972), ι, Appendix ιι, p. 383.

34. Gort to Lady Marjorie, quoted in J. R. Colville, *Man of Valour: The Life of Field Marshal the Viscount Gort* (London, 1972), p. 118; Diary entry for 22 Sept 1938 in Col. R. Macleod and D. Kelly (eds.), *The Ironside Diaries 1937–1940* (London, 1962), p. 62; Ismay memo., 20 Sept 1938, CAB 21/544.

35. WO and IIC estimates in CID 1507-B, 19 Jan 1939, CAB 4/29; and CID 1571-B, 24 July 1939, CAB 4/30.

36. COS 871(JP), 28 Mar 1939, CAB 53/47.

37. WO 190/751, 22 Feb 1939.

38. WO 190/752, 23 Feb 1939.

39. MI3(b) to FO 27 Feb 1939, C2501/32/18, FO 371/23001.

40. Military attaché, Berlin, telegram, 29 Mar 1939, C4399/13/18, FO 371/22958. See Ewan Butler, *Mason-Mac. The Life of Lt. Gen. Sir Noel Mason-Macfarlane* (London, 1972).

41. The accounts by Sidney Aster, *1939: The Making of the Second World War* (London, 1972), chapter 4, pp. 107–12 and N. H. Gibbs, *Grand Strategy* (London, 1976), ι, pp. 698–701 are somewhat misleading. In his reports to the COS and CID secretary, both of which were made available to the Cabinet, the Deputy Director of Military Intelligence emphasised that the German threat was one of military blackmail or, at most, a limited coup against Danzig. See: COS 286 Mtg., 30 Mar 1939, CAB 53/10; and DDMI to Ismay (this report went to Wilson and the PM), 'Germany's intentions regarding Danzig', 30 Mar 1939, PREM 1/331A.

42. Military attaché, Berlin, despatch, 23 Mar 1939, C3954/13/18, FO 371/22958.

43. David Dilks (ed.), *The Diaries of Sir Alexander Cadogan 1938–45* (London, 1971), 26 Mar 1939, pp. 163–4.

44. Military attaché, Berlin, despatch, 29 Mar 1939, C4760/13/18, FO 371/22958; Cadogan min., 31 Mar 1939, ibid.

45. Group Captain Goddard to FO, 24 Apr 1939, AIR 40/1487.

46. Geyr von Schweppenburg, *The Critical Years* (London, 1952), p. 81.

47. The MI3 collation file on Germany (WO 190) includes 36 reports on mechanisation and motorisation in the German army between 1933–9. This evidence flatly contradicts Hinsley's statement that the War Office paid no attention to the matter, *British Intelligence*, ι, p. 76. On the study of German military doctrine, see WO 190/640, 15 July 1938; WO 216/189, 16 Mar 1938; and military attaché, Berlin, despatch, 12 Oct 1937, C 7105/136/18, FO 371/20732.

48. WO 190/675, 23 Sept 1938; WO to FO, 24 Sept 1938, C11000/65/18, FO 371/21670.

49. Bond (ed.) *Chief of Staff*, ι, 221.

50. See W. K. Wark, 'Baltic Myths and Submarine Bogeys: British Naval Intelligence and Nazi Germany 1933–1939', *The Journal of Strategic Studies*, νι, no. 1 (1983).

51. See the works by Patrick Beesly: *Room 40: British Naval Intelligence 1914–18*

(London, 1982); *Very Special Admiral: The Life of Admiral J. H. Godfrey* (London, 1980); *Very Special Intelligence* (London, 1977). Also Donald McLachlan, *Room 39* (London, 1968) and Anthony Wells, 'Naval Intelligence and Decision-Making in an era of Technical Change', in B. Ranft (ed.) *Technical Change and British Naval Policy 1860–1939* (London, 1977).

    52. Major General Sir Kenneth Strong, *Intelligence at the Top* (London, 1968), p. 18.

    53. Wark, 'Baltic Myths', pp. 64–70.

    54. Quoted in Gibbs, *Grand Strategy*, I, p. 166.

    55. Wark, 'Baltic Myths', pp. 66–7.

    56. CID 1252-B, 'German Naval Construction', 22 July 1936, CAB 4/24; 'Estimate of German Naval Forces 1939 and 1942', 9 Jan 1935, ADM 116/3373 and minute, 21 Dec 1934, ibid.

    57. FO minute, 30 Nov 1933, C10777/404/18, FO 371/16730; Naval attaché, Berlin, despatch, 27 Nov 1934, C8066/2134/18, FO 371/17765.

    58. This was the 'Baltic myth'. See Wark, 'Baltic Myths', pp. 65, 72–3.

    59. The 35 per cent ratio only offered some hope to the British of securing a two-power standard provided the Japanese fleet did not exceed the Washington Treaty limits of 1922 (in effect a fleet 60 per cent the size of the Royal Navy). However, Japan had already indicated her decision to terminate her adherence to the Washington Naval Treaty. See Gibbs, *Grand Strategy*, I, pp. 155–6.

    60. For example, Chatfield memo., 22 Dec 1936, ADM 116/3378.

    61. Admiral J. H. Godfrey, *Naval Memoirs*, typescript, privately printed, copy in Imperial War Museum, London, Vol. v, 251.

    62. Hinsley, *British Intelligence*, I, pp. 52–5. See also the papers of codebreakers Clarke and Denniston, Churchill College Archives, Cambridge.

    63. Wark, 'Baltic Myths', pp. 73–5.

    64. 'Revised draft of naval intelligence report – Section 2 – Strategy and Tactics', 29 Aug 1936, ADM 178/137.

    65. On the Admiralty's interwar neglect of trade defence matters, see Stephen Roskill, *Naval Policy Between the Wars* (London, 1976), II, pp. 226–9.

    66. H. Rosinski, *The Development of Naval Thought* (Newport, 1977), essays reprinted from *Brassey's Naval Annual*, pp. 53–101.

    67. Naval attaché to DNI, 15 May 1939, ADM 1/9956.

    68. DNI minute, 30 May 1939, ibid.

    69. See Wark, 'Baltic Myths', pp. 75–6.

    70. G. C. Peden, *British Rearmament and the Treasury 1932–1939* (Edinburgh, 1979), esp. pp. 160–7.

    71. CID 1090-B, 6 May 1932, CAB 4/21. (For unfathomable reasons, the records of the IIC remain mostly under extended closure in CAB 48.)

    72. Hinsley, *British Intelligence*, I, p. 33.

    73. For a discussion of these, see ibid., chapter 1.

    74. Ibid. Hinsley's discussion of the IIC's reporting is seriously marred by the author's supposition that the German economy was being geared for a 'Blitzkreig'. See note 88 below.

    75. These are not discussed in Hinsley, *British Intelligence*, I, chapter 2. CID 1134-B, 'Germany's Industrial Measures for Rearmament and for Aircraft Production', 22 Mar 1934, CAB 4/22; CID 1426-B, 'Germany: Export of Armaments', 2 May 1938, CAB 4/27.

    76. CID 1134-B, 22 Mar 1934, CAB 4/22.

    77. 'Germany and Industrial Mobilisation', 9 June 1935, C4687/4687/18, FO 371/18882.

    78. ICF/322, 'Germany: Theory of Industrial Mobilisation', 18 May 1937,

C3792/78/18, FO 371/20727 (extracts); ICF/322 (full translation), 15 Sept 1937, C6702/78/18, FO 371/20729.

79. CP 316(37), 15 Dec 1937, CAB 24/273. For an extended discussion see Gibbs, *Grand Strategy*, I, pp. 282–95.

80. FO to Morton, 14 Feb 1938, C542/65/18, FO 371/21666.

81. Morton preliminary notes to FO, 25 Jan 1939, C542/65/18, FO 371/21666; CID 1426-B, 2 May 1938, CAB 4/27.

82. Nicholls minute, Apr 1938, C1801/65/18, FO 371/21666; Halifax to Inskip, 27 Apr 1938, ibid.

83. CAB. CONS. 24(38), 18 May 1938, CAB 23/93.

84. Chamberlain comments, ibid.

85. CID 330 Mtg, 21 July 1938, CAB 2/7. The IIC paper was quietly shelved after a discussion in this committee.

86. Morton contemptuously dismissed an Air Ministry suggestion that the German economy might not be mobilising for total war, Morton to Webb, 19 July 1938, CAB 104/35.

87. Berlin embassy minute, 31 Dec 1935, C61/4/18, FO 371/19883.

88. On German war preparations see the revisionistic essay, arguing against the notion of economic 'blitzkrieg' planning, by Richard Overy, 'Hitler's War and the German Economy: A Reinterpretation', *The Economic History Review*, xxxv, 2 (May 1982), 272–91.

89. For intelligence on the comparison of German and British aircraft production figures in 1939, see Morton to FO, 1 Feb 1939, C2382/11/18, FO 371/22956. An example of the numerous reports on declining quality in German arms manufacture is CID 1571-B, 24 July 1939, CAB 4/30.

90. The series consists of: COS 401(JP), 2 Oct 1935, CAB 53/25; COS 513(JP), 26 Oct 1936, CAB 53/29; COS 747 (JP), 15 July 1938, CAB 53/40; and COS 831 (JP), 26 Jan 1939, CAB 53/44.

91. The Oct 1936 appreciation was censored by Sir Maurice Hankey as Chairman of the DCOS in the winter of 1936–7: see DCOS 8, 9, 11, 12 Mtgs, Nov 1936, CAB 54/1 and DCOS 24, Dec 1936, CAB 54/3. The July 1938 paper was stopped by Hankey and Chatfield in the COS committee, principally because it was based on the supposition of British involvement in a war over Czechoslovakia: COS 245 Mtg, 25 July 1938, CAB 53/9.

92. The COS considered the JPC draft, COS 831(JP) at three meetings in Feb 1939: COS 274–276 Mtgs, CAB 53/10. The COS final version was circulated as COS 843, 'European Appreciation 1939–40', 20 Feb 1939, CAB 53/45. It went to the Cabinet as D.P.(P)44, 20 Feb 1939, CAB 16/183.

93. D. Dilks (ed.), *The Diaries of Sir Alexander Cadogan*, 9 Feb 1939; Neville Chamberlain to Hilda, 5 Feb 1939, Neville Chamberlain papers, Birmingham University Library.

94. COS support for an Eastern front was indicated in COS 285 Mtg, 28 Mar 1939, CAB 53/10 and in COS 872, 'Military Implications of an Anglo-German Guarantee of Poland and Roumania', 3 Apr 1939, CAB 53/47. On the staff talks see COS 927, 'Anglo-Polish Staff Conversations, 1939', 15 June 1939, CAB 53/50 and COS 914, 'Staff Conversations with the French', 25 May 1939, CAB 53/49.

95. See Gibbs, *Grand Strategy*, I, chapter xix.

96. Sir John Slessor, *The Central Blue*, 235.

5. FLASHES OF INTELLIGENCE: THE FOREIGN OFFICE, THE SIS AND SECURITY BEFORE THE
    SECOND WORLD WAR   *David Dilks*

1. To the committee under the late Sir Duncan Wilson investigating the working of the Public Records Acts of 1958 and 1967; it reported in 1981.

2. D. N. Dilks (ed.), *The Diaries of Sir Alexander Cadogan* (London, 1971), p. 155.

3. O. G. Sargent to B. C. Newton, 16 Nov 1931 and SIS to C. J. Norton, 29 Oct 1931, C8074/8074/62, FO 371/15208, PRO (all further references to official papers are from PRO files); for the supply of SIS reports to Kabul, see minute by H. J. Seymour, 13 Oct 1930, N6980/6980, FO 371/14801.

4. Minutes by Sargent and Sir R. Vansittart, 10 July 1933, C5997/245/18, FO 371/16707.

5. D. Dilks, 'Appeasement and "Intelligence" ', in Dilks (ed.), *Retreat from Power*, vol. I (London, 1981), p. 149; D. Kahn, *Hitler's Spies* (New York, 1978), p. 183; E. L. Woodward and R. d'O. Butler (eds.), *Documents on British Foreign Policy*, 3rd ser., vol. v, pp. 489–90; minute by Sir A. Cadogan, 16 Aug 1939, R6472/6472/22, FO 371/23827; Cadogan to Sir P. Loraine, 19 Aug, and reply 23 Aug 1939, Loraine papers. I am indebted to Mr Gordon Waterfield for this last reference.

6. Minute by Sir R. Vansittart, 27 Jan 1931, V157/3/750, FO 627/29.

7. SIS to N. Bland, FO, 10 Aug 1927, E3581/6/34, FO 371/12282.

8. See, for example, a minute by C. Howard Smith, 26 May 1926, C6024/6024/12, FO 371/11233.

9. Lord Vansittart, *The Mist Procession* (London, 1958), p. 516.

10. M. Toscano, *Designs in Diplomacy* (Baltimore, 1970) pp. 412–13, and *The History of Treaties and International Politics* (Baltimore, 1966) pp. 29–30.

11. I am indebted for this information to the late Major-General R. F. K. Belchem, who served in Egypt and Palestine from 1936; cf. F. H. Hinsley *et al.*, *British Intelligence in the Second World War* (London, 1979), vol. I, pp. 52–3, 199, and *Foreign Relations of the United States, 1937*, vol. I, pp. 393–4.

12. The report of 20 Feb 1937, with Vansittart's marginal comments, is Y775/775/650, FO 850/2.

13. R. B. Howorth to Sir M. P. A. Hankey, 20 Feb 1936, FA/H/13, CAB 21/421.

14. Toscano, *Designs in Diplomacy*, pp. 412–13.

15. R. B. Howorth to Sir M. P. A. Hankey, 20 Feb 1936, FA/H/13, CAB 21/421; W. N. Medlicott, D. Dakin and M. E. Lambert (eds), *Documents on British Foreign Policy*, 2nd ser., vol. xv, p. 688.

16. C. Campbell (Managing Director of the Marconi Company in Egypt) to Sir M. Lampson, 9 Dec 1936; Lampson to the Secretary of State (Eden), 21 Dec 1936; FO minutes on these papers, especially those by R. I. Campbell and H. E. Eastwood, 6 and 7 Jan 1937, J49/49/16, FO 371/20897.

17. See note 12 above.

18. *Documents on British Foreign Policy*, 2nd ser., vol. xv, p. 693.

19. Y832/7/5/650, dated 22 July 1937, FO 850/2.

20. Sir R. H. Campbell to Eden, 10 Mar 1937, R. 1687/224/92, FO 371/21198.

21. Minute by Sir O. Sargent, 25 Jan 1937 and memorandum by Eden, 23 Jan 1937, R650/224/92, FO 371/21197; Eden to Sir R. H. Campbell (Belgrade), despatch, 4 Feb 1937, R889/224/92, ibid.

22. See note 20 above.

23. Sir R. H. Campbell to Eden, 11 Mar 1937, R1688/224/92, FO 371/21198.

24. Minutes by O. O'Malley, Sir O. Sargent, Sir A. Cadogan, 11 Mar 1937, on R1687/224/92, FO 371/21198.

25. Minutes by O. O'Malley and C. J. Norton, 19 and 24 Mar 1937, ibid.

26. Minute by C. J. Norton, 16 Mar 1937, ibid.
27. Minute by C. J. Norton, 12 Apr 1937, and Eden to Sir R. H. Campbell, 12 Mar 1937, ibid.
28. M. Muggeridge (ed.), *Ciano's Diary 1937–1938* (London, 1952), pp. 31, 44, 49, 63.
29. M. Muggeridge (ed.), *Ciano's Diary, 1939–1943* (London, 1947), pp. 101–2.
30. J. B. Hoptner, *Yugoslavia in Crisis 1934–1941* (New York, 1962), p. 125; Sir R. H. Campbell to Lord Halifax, and to Sir A. Cadogan, 21 Jan 1939, R1080/111/67, FO 371/23738.
31. Hoptner, *Yugoslavia in Crisis*, p. 125.
32. M. Muggeridge (ed.), *Ciano's Diplomatic Papers* (London, 1948), p. 46; H. McG. Smyth, *Secrets of the Fascist Era* (Illinois, 1975), p. 19.
33. K. von Schuschnigg, *Austrian Requiem* (London, 1947), pp. 111–13.
34. *Hansard*, HC, 5th Ser.: vol. 445, cols. 758–9.
35. M. Toscano, *Origins of the Pact of Steel* (Baltimore, 1967), p. 143.
36. C14471/42/18, Flag G, FO 371/21659; for a reference to this memorandum see Cadogan's minute of 9 Nov 1938 in the same file. I refrain from dealing here with intelligence about Germany's military strength, treated in detail in chapter 4 of this volume by Dr Wark.
37. Hinsley *et al.*, *British Intelligence*, p. 56.
38. See the record of a conservation with Goerdeler in Switzerland on 4 Dec 1938, C938/15/18, and a memorandum by F. K. Roberts, 21 Jan 1939, C864/15/18, FO 371/22961; Sir I. Kirkpatrick, *The Inner Circle* (London, 1959), pp. 137–9; memoranda by G. J. Jebb, 19 Jan 1939, CAB 27/627, and 6 Jan 1939, C939/15/18, FO 371/22961.
39. His identity is clear from documents in the Christie papers at Churchill College, Cambridge; 'Knight', being a translation of 'Ritter', would have deceived the serious investigator little longer than President Wilson's 'Neptune' and 'Mars'.
40. For examples, see a report by Vansittart to Halifax, 6 Jan 1939, Christie to Vansittart, 20 Jan 1939, and a memorandum by Vansittart 25 Jan 1939, in Christie papers 180/1/29.
41. Hinsley *et al.*, *British Intelligence*, p. 42; Christie to Vansittart, 20 Jan 1939, Christie papers 180/1/29.
42. Cadogan to Henderson, 28 Feb 1939, 39/9, FO 800/270.
43. Minute by Cadogan, 14 Feb 1939, W793/793/50, FO 371/23994.
44. Minute by Col. S. G. Menzies, 14 Dec 1938, ibid.
45. Sir L. Oliphant to Brig-Gen. F. G. Beaumont-Nesbit, 15 Feb 1939, ibid.

6. ENIGMA, THE FRENCH, THE POLES AND THE BRITISH, 1931–1940 *Jean Stengers*

1. P. Paillole, 'France: le contre-espionnage s'est heurté au scepticisme du Commandement', *Le Crapouillot*, new series, 52 (Autumn 1979), 55.
2. The precise figure, calculated by Colonel Tadeusz Lisicki, is 5,172,165,503,971, 832,752,302,775,832,450,732,675,000,000,000,000,000,000,000,000,000,000, 000,000,000,000,000,000: see J. Garlinski, *Intercept. The Enigma War* (London, 1979), p. 23. The fullest descriptions of the Enigma will be found in Garlinski, pp. 192 ff. (Appendix by T. Lisicki) and in Gordon Welchman, *The Hut Six Story: Breaking the Enigma Codes* (New York, 1982), pp. 38 ff. Photographs of the machine are in J. Rohwer and E. Jäckel (eds.), *Die Funkaufklärung und ihre Rolle im Zweiten Weltkrieg* (Stuttgart, 1979), pp. 36, 56; Garlinski, *Intercept*, plate 23; Francis Russell, *The Secret War* (Alexandria, Va, 1981), p. 92. One of the best preserved Enigmas is on exhibition at the Museum of the Polish Army (Muzeum Wojska Polskiego) at Warsaw. Another

Enigma belongs to the collections of the General Sikorski Historical Institute in London; there are numerous photographs of this machine, e.g. in Brian Johnson, *The Secret War* (London, 1978), pp. 311, 318; Garlinski, *Intercept*, plate 5; *Dictionnaire de la Seconde Guerre Mondiale*, vol. II, (Paris, 1980), p. 1833; Peter Calvocoressi, *Top Secret Ultra* (London, 1980), pp. 54 ff. But this is not a German Enigma; it is a Polish or French reconstruction of unknown origin. The two main differences between the German machine and the replica are that in the original machine, the plugboard is in front and the keyboard is arranged as that of a German typewriter (QWER. . . .), whereas in the replica the plugboard is in the rear and the keyboard is arranged alphabetically.

3. Colonel Gwido Langer, Report (in Polish) written probably at the end of 1940; property of Colonel Lisicki, London (extracts kindly communicated by Colonel Lisicki to the author).

4. Gustave Bertrand, *Enigma ou la plus grande énigme de la guerre 1939–1975* (Paris, 1973), 298 pp.

5. They are now in the hands of the general's widow, at Théoule-sur-Mer, in the south of France; we wish to thank Madame Bertrand very respectfully.

6. A few years before however, Colonel Michel Garder had devoted to the subject two or three pages which gave a completely erroneous and twisted version (M. Garder, *La Guerre Secrète des Services Spéciaux francais (1935–1945)* (Paris, 1967), pp. 77–9). Garder's source was what General Navarre had told him in a short conversation and that he had distorted (my interview with General Navarre, 1979). From Garder, this version has passed to Anthony Cave Brown (*Bodyguard of Lies* (London, 1976), pp. 16–17, based upon Garder but without reference to his book). Colonel Garder's errors had at least one happy consequence: they so infuriated Bertrand that he decided to break silence so as to put things right (Bertrand, *Enigma*, pp. 13–14, 265–71).

7. The book was not reviewed in any important periodical and it sold very badly. By the beginning of 1975, the publisher, the Librairie Plon, had already sold a part of the stock at bargain prices (Bertrand Papers). The well-known French historian Max Gallo told me that in 1976, when he published in a collection of which he was the editor a French translation of Winterbotham, he had no idea of the existence of Bertrand's book. The French intellectual paper *Le Monde,* when commenting in 1977 upon the *Ultra* question, did not mention it either; it referred only to Winterbotham's version (*Le Monde*, 20 Oct 1977). However, Bertrand found better echoes among the limited number of specialists in Poland and in Britain.

8. In a strange way, for instance, a man frequently mentioned under the name of *Rex* is suddenly called *Lemoine* (pp. 250–3), without any warning as to the change of name.

9. P. Paillole, *Services Spéciaux, 1935–1945* (Paris, 1975); H. Navarre, *Le Service de Renseignements, 1871–1944* (Paris, 1978).

10. October 1932 in Bertrand, *Enigma*, pp. 21, 23. This is either a typographical error or a slip of the pen.

11. Interview given to *Nice-Matin*, 16 Aug 1973.

12. The identification of *Asché* as Hans-Thilo Schmidt was revealed for the first time by David Kahn in his review of Winterbotham in the *New York Times* of 29 Dec 1974; it was confirmed by Paillole (*Services Spéciaux*, p. 63). The source of the identification was Bertrand himself, who had been interviewed by Kahn. On *Asché*-Schmidt, see Bertrand, pp. 23 ff., 250–2; Paillole, pp. 33, 63–4; Navarre, *Service de Renseignements*, pp. 54–6, 69–73, 81; H. Navarre, *Le temps des vérités* (Paris, 1979), pp. 57–8, 69. *Asché* was the best paid and most important 'agent' of the French Intelligence Service. He was so bold that he still went to meet Navarre near Lugano at the beginning of 1940 (Navarre, *Le temps des vérités*, p. 69; my interview with General Navarre, 1979). In 1943, he was exposed, convicted and executed. On his brother, General Rudolf Schmidt, who seems to have been the source – the involuntary source certainly – of some of the most

meaningful information he communicated to the French, see a short notice in the *Bulletin trimestriel de l'Association des Amis de l'Ecole Supérieure de Guerre*, No. 81 (1979), 65–6.

13. Bertrand Papers.

14. Ibid.

15. The assertion of Colonel Garder (*La Guerre Secrète*, p. 79), followed by Cave Brown (*Bodyguard of Lies*, p. 16), that the French had succeeded in reconstructing an Enigma, is complete nonsense. Paillole is also wrong in what he writes in his book on that subject (*Services Spéciaux*, p. 64).

16. Bertrand, *Enigma*, p. 37, fully confirmed by the data of the Bertrand Papers. The date of this mission later became a source of total confusion. Marian Rejewski, in his correspondence with General Bertrand, observed that Bertrand could not have come to Warsaw with *Asché* documents in Dec 1931 if, as he had stated in his book, *Asché's* treason dated from October 1932 (Rejewski to Bertrand, 24 July 1974; Bertrand Papers). Bertrand, in his answer, made the wrong correction; instead of confirming Dec 1931 and correcting Oct 1932 to Oct 1931, he corrected Dec 1931 to Dec 1932, in contradiction with the precise data of his own papers, which he overlooked at the time (Bertrand to Rejewski, 5 Aug 1974; copy ibid.). From then on, Rejewski disseminated the wrong date of Dec 1932, which is found in many publications.

17. Bertrand Papers.

18. Bertrand, *Enigma*, p. 38.

19. Bertrand, *Enigma*, p. 38; F. H. Hinsley, with E. E. Thomas, C. F. G. Ransom and R. C. Knight, *British Intelligence in the Second World War*, vol. I (London, 1979), p. 488.

20. The legend can be traced to Brian Johnson, *The Secret War*, pp. 311–12, who quoted the testimony of Colonel Lisicki. From there, it passed to publications as serious as Ronald Lewin, *Ultra goes to War: The Secret Story* (London, 1978), p. 30, or Jürgen Rohwer, 'Der Einfluss der alliierten Funkaufklärung auf den Verlauf des Zweiten Weltkrieges', *Vierteljahrshefte für Zeitgeschichte*, XXVII (1979), 335. Johnson had misunderstood Lisicki, who had spoken of a *commercial* Enigma (author's conversation with Colonel Lisicki). For Lisicki's own source of information, see Garlinski, *Intercept*, pp. 2–3.

21. F. W. Winterbotham, *The Ultra Secret* (London, 1974), pp. 10–11.

22. These were often only short hints. Professor Jack Good, who worked in Hut 8 at Bletchley from May 1941 to Oct 1943, wrote: 'My first boss, the famous mathematician A. M. Turing, only once mentioned the Poles, and that evasively' (review of Gordon Welchman, *New Scientist*, 7 Oct 1982, p. 42).

23. Jones was told that the Poles 'had stolen the wheels of an actual machine' (R. V. Jones, *Most Secret War* (London, 1978), p. 63). For brevity's sake, we do not mention the story told in William Stevenson's *A Man called Intrepid* (London, 1976) about an ambush organised by the Poles to gain hold of an Enigma. Like almost everything else concerning Enigma in the book, it is pure rubbish (see the devastating reviews of Stevenson by H. R. Trevor-Roper in the *New York Review of Books*, 13 May 1976, and by David Hunt in the *Times Literary Supplement*, 28 May 1976; also S. Freeman in the *Sunday Times*, 20 Sept 1981).

It must be observed that Gordon Welchman still believes on rational grounds that the Poles must have obtained the most elaborate version of the German Enigma 'by capture or some other nefarious means' (*The Hut Six Story*, p. 16). For a refutation of his reasoning, see the review in *Cryptologia*, VI, 2 (April 1982), 164–5.

24. T. Rakusa-Suszczewski,, 'Marian Rejewski' (in Polish), *W. T. K. Tygodnik Katolikow* (Warsaw), 6 July 1980; Christopher Kasparek and Richard A. Woytak, 'In memoriam Marian Rejewski', *Cryptologia* VI, 1 (Jan 1982), 19–25.

25. The revelation of his achievements appeared for the first time in an interview given by Colonel Wladyslaw Kozaczuk, a Polish military historian, to the *Express*

Wieczorny (of Warsaw) on 20 Dec 1973. Kozaczuk had read Bertrand's book and had established a link between his data and those of a memorandum which Rejewski had written some years before and had deposited in the archives of the Military Historical Institute. This was actually the first time the name of Rejewski was mentioned publicly.

26. Quoted as 'Rejewski, Report'. The text was found in England after the war and sent to Rejewski in Warsaw; I obtained a copy from Rejewski. After my discussion with him, there can be no doubt about the date of the document.

27. (a) 'An application of the theory of permutations in breaking the Enigma Cipher', *Zastosowania Matematyki — Applicationes Mathematicae* (Warsaw), XVI, 4 (1980), 543–59; published in Polish as an appendix to W. Kozaczuk, *W Kręgu Enigmy* (Warsaw, 1979), pp. 369–93; English translation of this Polish version by C. Kasparek in *Cryptologia*, VI, 1 (Jan 1982), 1–18; (b) 'Jak matematycy polscy rozszyfrowali Enigmę', *Annales Societatis Mathematicae Polonae*, 2nd series, *Wiadomosci Matematyczne*, XXIII, 1 (1980), 1-28; English translation, 'How Polish Mathematicians deciphered the Enigma', *Annals of the History of Computing*, III, 3 (July 1981), 213–34; (c) although it is not really an article, I count also Rejewski's remarks on Hinsley's *British Intelligence in the Second World War*, dating from 1979; the original Polish text was very kindly communicated to me by Colonel Lisicki; English translation in *Cryptologia*, VI, 1 (Jan 1982), 75–83.

28. A journalist of the East Berlin weekly *Horizont* in 1975 (*Horizont*, VIII (1975) No. 49); the BBC researcher Susan Bennett in 1976 (see Brian Johnson, *The Secret War*, pp. 312, 351); Jean Stengers during a full week in Warsaw in June 1978 (see J. Stengers, 'La guerre des messages codés, 1930–1945', *L'Histoire*, No. 31 (Feb 1981), 19–31, with supplements in No. 33 (April 1981), 100–1); Richard Woytak in July 1978 ('A Conversation with Marian Rejewski', *Cryptologia*, VI, 1 (Jan 1982), 50–57). There were certainly many other interviews.

29. He was a great help in Poland to Colonel Wladyslaw Kozaczuk (see his series of articles on 'Enigma' in the Polish weekly *Stolica*, XXX (1975) Nos. 1–27, partly translated into German in *Horizont*, VIII (1975), Nos. 41–48; 'The war of wits' in *Poland* (1975), Nos. 6 and 7, and the French version in *La Pologne* (1975), Nos. 6 and 7; and his books *Zlamany Szyfr* (Broken Cypher) (Warsaw, 1976) and *W Kręgu Enigmy* (Around the Enigma) (Warsaw, 1979) and to Stanislaw Strumph Wojtkiewicz, *Sekret Enigmy* (Warsaw, 1978). Marian Rejewski definitely told me however that he was far from approving all that these two authors had written, often with too much enthusiasm or imagination. Rejewski also had a very active correspondence with his friend Colonel Lisicki in London (Lisicki was his former superior in the Polish army in Britain); see Lisicki's contribution to Rohwer and Jäckel (eds), *Die Funkaufklärung*, pp. 66–86, and above all his help and collaboration in the book by J. Garlinski.

30. Interview of Mr C. Gaca, a former Polish cryptologist, now living in France, who took part in the operation. 'We buried six *bombas* and more than seventy Enigmas', Mr Gaca recalls; 'it was an extremely hard task.'

31. As we have said before, the origin of the Enigma preserved at the Sikorski Historical Institute in London cannot be traced with certainly (see note 2).

32. A sketch of a *bomba* drawn by Rejewski himself in 1976 is in Brian Johnson, *The Secret War*, p. 316; drawings of the cyclometer and of the perforated sheets are in the articles quoted above, note 27.

33. He entered the service in Warsaw on 1 Sept 1932. Before that date, while a teaching assistant at the University of Poznan, he had already worked for some time in a branch office of the Cypher Bureau in Poznan; this was only a part-time job.

34. Rejewski repeatedly said: on 8 Dec 1932. But I am afraid that precise date was only a deduction. He deduced it from the fact (which was not a fact, as we have seen) that Bertrand had arrived for the first time in Warsaw with the Asché documents on 7 Dec 1932 (see note 16).

35. Rejewski, Report (see note 26). Later on, Rejewski gave the date of the keys as 1932 instead of 1931. But this was again a deduction based upon his false assumptions as regards Bertrand's first arrival in Warsaw. We have every reason to stick to the dates of his first report.

36. There is a widespread version according to which the initial success was not due to Rejewski alone, but to the Rejewski–Rozycki–Zygalski team, which we will find at work immediately afterwards. This is contradicted by Rejewski's very firm statements, which seem to be unimpeachable. 'Le chiffre Enigma fut rompu par moi seul en décembre 1932', he wrote to Bertrand in 1975 (letter of 19 Mar 1975, Bertrand Papers). See also the article (b) quoted in note 27. It was also one of the main objects of my questions when I met him.

37. 'Sans eux, la solution aurait été différée pour longtemps, ou même, qui le sait, pour jamais' (Rejewski to Madame Bertrand, 8 Aug 1976; Bertrand Papers). He had written in 1941–2: 'Without these documents, the decipherment of the Enigma would have been delayed by several years' (Rejewski, Report).

38. Both Rozycki and Zygalski were, like Rejewski, young mathematicians who had studied at the University of Poznan. Rozycki (born 1909) died accidentally in Jan 1942; see a letter about him by Rejewski of Nov 1979 quoted in *Cryptologia*, VI, 1 (Jan 1982), 59. Zygalski (born 1907) during the war had the same destiny as Rejewski; he went first to *Bruno*, then to the south of France and finally to England. But he remained in Britain after the war and became a lecturer in mathematics at the Polish University College (incorporated into the Battersea College of Technology). At the end of his life, he was an invalid, so he was unable to provide any useful information on Enigma. He died on 30 Aug 1978. No obituary appeared in *The Times*.

39. On the AVA factory, see J. Garlinski, *Intercept*, pp. 20 ff., and Maria Danilewicz-Zielinska, 'Zanim doszlo du rozszyfrowania Enigmy' (Before one succeeded in deciphering Enigma), *Orzel Bialy* (London) Dec 1974.

40. This was one of the strongest assertions by Rejewski during our meetings with him in June 1978: he never received any other *Asché* documents than those he got in Dec 1932. Bertrand went on bringing new *Asché* material to Warsaw, but this material was no longer essential for the work of the Polish cryptologists.

41. Rejewski, Report. This is confirmed by Colonel Stefan Mayer, the former chief of military intelligence, who recalls: 'In January 1938, a two-week test was conducted regarding the deciphering of the intercepted Enigma material. About 75 per cent of this material was then deciphered. To check this, one day I myself selected radiograms from the intercepted material and ordered them to be deciphered in my presence. The result was perfect' (Mayer, memorandum of 1974 quoted by Richard A. Woytak, *On the Border of War and Peace. Polish Intelligence and Diplomacy in 1937–1939 and the origins of the Ultra Secret* (Boulder, 1979, p. 9). Hinsley's doubts as to the value of this test (*British Intelligence*, p. 490) are dispelled by Rejewski's remarks on Hinsley (see *Cryptologia*, VI, 1 (Jan 1982), 79; also M. Rejewski, 'How Polish Mathematicians . . .', p. 225).

42. Rejewski's remarks on Hinsley, in *Cryptologia*, note 41 above, p. 78.

43. Mayer to Bertrand, 9 May 1976; Bertrand Papers. General Bertrand was at that time near the end of his life and he was not able to read this letter. He died on 23 May 1976. On Mayer, see his obituary in *The Times* of 1 April 1981.

44. Both Bertrand and Rejewski said with a smile that Braquenié was not in his field a first-class man ('Il n'était pas très fort').

45. See on him Penelope Fitzgerald, *The Knox Brothers* (London, 1977).

46. This 'third man' has given rise to much speculation. He had been introduced in Warsaw as a 'Mr (or Professor) Sandwich'. Colonel Mayer claims that he was actually Stewart Menzies; he met Menzies six years later, he says, and he recognised him as the 'Sandwich' of July 1939 (Garlinski, *Intercept*, p. 46, n. 30). This identification has generally been accepted (Brian Johnson, *The Secret War*, p. 319, with some reservations;

R. Lewin, *Ultra goes to War*, p. 43; F. Russell, *The Secret War*, p. 71; Basil Collier, *Hidden Weapons. Allied Secret or Undercover Services in World War II* (London, 1982), p. 51). But General Bertrand wrote with indignation that it was all nonsense: the 'third man' was simply Commander Sandwith, of the Admiralty. 'Le Commander Sandwith qui est venu à Varsovie et qui était le Chef du Service d'Interception de l'Amirauté, m'était connu avant de venir à Pyry (the out-station where the July 1939 meeting took place) et n'avait aucune possibilité de ressemblance avec Menzies, que je connaissais encore mieux' (letter to Rejewski, 10 Mar 1976; copy in the Bertrand Papers). This is a decisive statement for the Bertrand Papers show that Bertrand met both Menzies and Commander Sandwith in London on 16–17 Aug 1939, just one month after the Warsaw session. Mrs Caroline Oliver, who was attached to the GC&CS before the war (she entered it in 1937) remembers that Commander Sandwith was a frequent visitor to the offices of the 'School'.

Contrary to what Brian Johnson says (*The Secret War*, p. 324 – but see a different view p. 319), Alan Turing was certainly not a member of the British group. Marian Rejewski clearly remembers meeting him for the first – and also last – time at *Bruno* (Kozaczuc, *W Kręgu Enigmy*, p. 357; my conversations with Rejewski).

47. Bertrand, *Enigma*, pp. 60–1.

48. Malcolm Muggeridge, 'The Lucy Spy Mystery', *The Observer*, 8 Jan 1967. After that came short allusions by David Kahn in *The Codebreakers* (New York, 1967), p. 484, by Hugh Trevor-Roper in *The Philby Affair* (London, 1968), pp. 73–4, by Page, Leitch and Knightley in their *Philby* (London, 1968; 2nd ed., 1969), see paperback edition, 1977, pp. 182–5; by Richard Deacon in his *History of the British Secret Service* (London, 1969), pp. 363–4); by Ladislas Farago in his *Game of the Foxes* in 1972 (see paperback edition, 1973, pp. 226–9, 319, 571) and again by Malcolm Muggeridge in 1973 (*Chronicles of Wasted Time* vol. II, *The Infernal Grove* (London), pp. 127–32, 150, 162, 176, 187, 188, 201, 204).

49. Calvocoressi, *Top Secret Ultra*, p. 14.

50. Some believe that Winterbotham 'braved the Official Secrets Act' (Ian McEwan, 'Enigma Machine', *New Statesman*, 19 May 1978, p. 675). He dutifully obeyed in fact all the rules (see the 'Londoner's Diary' in the *Evening Standard* of 22 Nov 1976).

51. Reprinted in N. Metropolis, J. Howlett and Gian-Carlo Rota (eds), *A History of Computing in the Twentieth Century. A collection of essays* (New York, 1980), pp. 31–45. Also with slight changes in *Annals of the History of Computing*, I, 1 (July 1979), 38–48, and in *Cryptologia*, III, 2 (April 1979), 65–77. See also I. J. Good, 'Studies in the History of Probability and Statistics. XXXVII. A. M. Turing's statistical work in World War II', *Biometrika*, LXVI, 2 (1979), 393–6.

52. *Hansard*, vol. 941 no. 36; see also Hinsley, *British Intelligence*, vol. I, pp vii–viii, and vol. II (London, 1981), p. x.

53. Welchman, *The Hut Six Story*.

54. See note 19. Marian Rejewski knew – most probably through Bertrand – that the British Cypher Bureau had had some essential *Asché* documents at its disposal (Rejewski, Report). So, he remarked, the initial conditions of the French, the British and the Poles, as regards the decipherment, were not dissimilar.

55. Hinsley, *British Intelligence*, vol. I, pp. 54, 491.

56. 'Ci inclus des petits batons' (Knox to Rejewski, 1 Aug 1939; reproduction in Kozaczuk, *W Kręgu Enigmy*, plate between pp. 128 and 129). Rejewski explained to me what it meant.

57. Hinsley, *British Intelligence*, vol. I, p. 54.

58. Letter from Dr Peter Twinn to the author of 15 Dec 1981.

59. Hinsley, *British Intelligence*, vol. I, p. 54.

60. Welchman, *The Hut Six Story*, p. 89.

61. Rejewski, Report.

62. Welchman, *The Hut Six Story*, pp. 71, 76, 87, 89. The British, Rejewski notes, adopted our methods. 'The only difference was that we used millimeter-ruled paper and they used paper divided into inches, that our paper was white and theirs was creamcolored, that we cut the holes out toilsomely with razor blades and they used a perforator' (Rejewski's remarks on Hinsley, in *Cryptologia*, note 41 above, p. 82).

63. Langer report of the end of 1940 (see note 3); Hinsley, *British Intelligence*, vol. I, p. 493; T. Lisicki, 'Pogromcy Enigmy we Francji' (The conquerors of the Enigma in France), *Orzeł Biały* (Sept 1975). The key broken on 17 Jan 1940 was that of 28 Oct 1939. This has led to a confusion by Bertrand, who writes that the breaking itself occurred on 28 Oct 1939 (*Enigma*, p. 76). From Bertrand the error has spread to other publications (e.g. P. Paillole, v° *Ultra* in *Dictionnaire de la Seconde Guerre Mondiale*, vol. II (Paris, 1980), p. 1833).

64. Langer Report (see note 3 above).

65. Welchman, *The Hut Six Story*, pp. 98–101, 104–10, 165. This is one of the most important revelations of Welchman's book.

66. Exactly on 21 May 1940 according to the Langer Report.

67. Welchman, *The Hut Six Story*, pp. 77–82, 295 ff. Welchman does not remember when exactly the first *bombe* was put into use. He places it around Sept 1940 (see pp. 101, 119). This is approximately consistent with the month of August given by Hinsley for the introduction of 'the first of the machines developed for finding the Enigma settings' (*British Intelligence*, vol. I, p. 184). But it is in contradiction with Hinsley's date for the first *bombe*, which is the end of May 1940 (p. 494). The whole story told by Welchman cannot be reconciled with this last date.

68. R. Lewin, *Ultra goes to War*, pp. 129–33; B. Randell, 'Colossus: godfather of the computers', *New Scientist*, 10 Feb 1977, pp. 346–8; the same author's, 'The Colossus', in Metropolis, Howlett and Gian-Carlo Rota (eds), *A History of Computing*, pp. 47–92.

69. 'The Profession of Intelligence', presented by Christopher Andrew, BBC, Radio 4, 16 Aug 1981; BBC transcript.

70. Bertrand, *Enigma*, p. 256.

71. Letter to the author, 15 Dec 1981.

72. Welchman, *The Hut Six Story*, p. 164–5.

73. 'We were lucky': this is also Welchman's opinion (p. 169). But he refers to another aspect of that luck. A very small change to the construction of the Enigma, he remarks, would have made it practically impregnable. Luckily, the Germans did not have the idea (see pp. 168–9).

7. CODEBREAKING IN WORLD WARS I AND II: THE MAJOR SUCCESSES AND FAILURES, THEIR CAUSES AND THEIR EFFECTS *David Kahn*

This paper was originally delivered as the opening speech at a conference of the Arbeitskreis für Wehrforschung, joined by the Clausewitz-Gesellschaft and the Deutsche Gesellschaft für Wehrtechnik, on 'Modern technology and its consequences for the conduct of war: the example of radio intelligence', in Bonn, 15 Nov 1978. Since the publication of an earlier version of this article in the *Historical Journal* in 1980, I have made a few changes in the text to include new information and correct errors, and have updated the notes. A few passages on subjects discussed at greater length elsewhere in this volume have been deleted by the editors.

1. Georges Dossin, 'Signaux lumineux au pays de Mari', *Revue d'Assyriologie et d'Archéologie Orientale*, XXXV (1938), 174–86.

2. Livy XXVII, xliii, 1–8.

3. (1851).

4. David Kahn, *The Codebreakers: the story of secret writing* (New York, 1967), *passim*.

5. Ibid., pp. 298–9.

6. Christopher Andrew, 'Déchiffrement et diplomatie: le cabinet noir du Quai d'Orsay sous la Troisième République', *Relations Internationales*, III (1976), 37–64; Marcel Givierge, 'Etude historique sur la Section du Chiffre', Epoques 1–4, N.A.F. 2453, Département des Manuscrits, Bibliothèque Nationale, Paris. See above, pp. 34ff.

7. François Cartier, 'Le service d'écoute pendant la guerre', *Radio-Electricité*, IV (1923), 453–60, 491–8 at p. 498.

8. Maximilian Ronge, *Kriegs- und Industrie-spionage* (Zurich, 1930), pp. 58–60; August von Urbanski, 'Wie unsere Chiffren-Gruppe entstand' (Oktober 1924), Nachlass B-58, Kriegsarchiv, Vienna. See also Harald Hubatschke, 'Die amtliche Organisation der geheimen Briefüberwachung und des diplomatischen Chiffrendienstes in Osterreich', *Mitteilungen des Instituts für Osterreichische Geschichtsforschung*, LXXXIII (1975), 352–413 at pp. 412–13.

9. Russia (1923–, USSR), Kommissia po izdaniu dokumentov epokhi imperializma, *Die Internationalen Beziehungen im Zeitalter des Imperialismus: Dokumente aus den Archiven der Zarischen und der Provisorischen Regierung*, ed. M. N. Pokrowski, German ed. Otto Hoetzsch (Berlin, 1931–42), *passim*, shows that Russia intercepted and solved diplomatic messages of England, France, Germany, Austria, Italy, Bulgaria, Turkey, Persia, and Greece before World War I. For police codebreaking, Richard J. Johnson, 'Zagranichaia Agentura: the tsarist political police in Europe', *Journal of Contemporary History*, VII (1972), 221–42; Kahn, *The Codebreakers*, pp. 618–21.

10. Erich Ludendorff, *Ludendorff's own story* (New York, 1919), I, 57–8.

11. Major [Kunibert] Randewig, 'Die deutsche Funkaufklärung in der Schlacht bei Tannenberg', *F-Flagge* (magazine of German army signal troops) (1936), pp. 135–8, 154–7 at p. 135.

12. Arthur Schuetz (pseud. Tristan Busch), *Secret Service Unmasked*, trans. Anthony V. Ireland (London, [1948]), p. 58; Nicholas N. Golovine, *The Russian Campaign of 1914*, trans. A. G. S. Muntz (Fort Leavenworth, 1933), pp. 171–2; Germany, Reichsarchiv, *Der Weltkrieg: 1914 bis 1918*, II (Berlin, 1925), p. 351.

13. Max Hoffmann, *War Diaries and other Papers*, trans. Eric Sutton (London, 1929), II, 267.

14. Ibid., I, 41, 18.

15. Ronge, *passim*; Yves Gylden, *The contribution of the Cryptographic Bureaux in the World War*, trans. Military Intelligence Division (Washington, 1935), pp. 60–77.

16. Max Hoffmann, *The War of Lost Opportunities* (London, 1924), p. 132.

17. Odoardo Marchetti, *Il servizio informazione dell'esercito italiano nella grande guerra* (Roma, 1937), p. 181.

18. Intercepts dated 14, 21, and 27 Dec 1916, 5 N 83, Service Historique, Etat-major de l'Armée de terre, Château de Vincennes; Givierge, 'Etude historique sur la Section du Chiffre', Epoque 15, pp. 98–9; Sam Wagenaar, *Mata Hari*, adaptation de Jacques Haubart (Paris, 1965), pp. 198–203.

19. 'Conference de M. Georges Jean Painvin', *Bulletin de l'A.R.C.* (*Amicale des Reservistes du Chiffre*), new series, VIII (1961), 5–47, at pp. 17–45; Kahn, *The Codebreakers*, pp. 339–47.

20. Henri Morin, *Service secret: à l'écoute devant Verdun*, ed. Pierre Andrieu (Paris, 1959), *passim*; Hermann Cron, *Die Organisation des deutschen Heeres im Weltkrieg*, Forschungen und Darstellungen aus dem Reichsarchiv, V (Berlin, 1923), 112; Albert Praun, *Soldat in der Telegraphen- und Nachrichtentruppe* (Wurzburg, [c. 1965]), pp. 18–20, 26; Maximilian Ronge, 'Der Telephon-Abhorchdienst', pp. 670–729, and Beilagen, Nachlass B/126: F.2, Kreigsarchiv.

21. R. E. Priestley, *The Signal Service in the European War of 1914 to 1918* (France) ([London?], 1921), p. 106.

22. Sir Alfred Ewing, 'Some special war work', in R. V. Jones, 'Alfred Ewing and

"Room 40" ', *Notes and Records of the Royal Society of London*, xxxiv (July 1979), 65–90; Winston S. Churchill, *The World Crisis* (New York, 1923), i, 503–4; Admiral Sir William James, *The Eyes of the Navy: a biographical study of Admiral Sir William Hall* (London, 1956), passim.

23. Barbara Tuchman, *The Zimmermann Telegram* (New York, 1958); William F. Friedman and Charles J. Mendelsohn, *The Zimmermann Telegram of January 16, 1917 and its Cryptographic Background* (1938, reprinted Laguna Hills, Calif. 1977); Kahn, *The Codebreakers*, pp. 282–97. Patrick Beesly, *Room 40: British Naval Intelligence 1914–18* (London, 1982).

24. David Kahn, *Hitler's Spies: German military intelligence in World War II* (New York, 1978), pp. 185, 190–91, 214; F. H. Hinsley with E. E. Thomas, C. F. G. Ransom and R. C. Knight, *British Intelligence in the Second World War: its influence on strategy and operations* (London, 1979–), i, 20; Christopher Andrew, 'The British Secret Service and Anglo-Soviet relations in the 1920s. Part I: From the trade negotiations to the Zinoviev letter', *Historical Journal*, xx (1977), 673–706 at p. 680; Herbert O. Yardley, *The American Black Chamber* (Indianapolis, 1931), pp. 239–40.

25. Kahn, *The Codebreakers*, pp. 394–426.

26. U.S. Patent 1,657,411; Siegfried Türkel, *Chiffrieren mit Geräten und Maschinen* (Graz, 1927), pp. 71–94 and plates M–P; *Handbuch der Deutschen Aktien-Gesellschaften* (Berlin, 1935), v, 6610.

27. [Marian Rejewski], 'Enigma 1930–1940; Metodi i historia rozwiazania niemieckiego szyfru maszynowego (w zarysie)' (unpublished; in private collection), p. 1; Jürgen Rohwer, *The Critical Convoy Battles of March 1943: the battle for HX. 229/SC122*, trans. Derek Masters (London, 1977), p. 231.

28. Kahn, *The Codebreakers*, pp. 426–7; memorandum, Y7858/437/G/39, signed E.N.T. (Edward N. Travis), 21 July 1939, FO 850/4/XJ3968, Public Record Office, London, mentions the Royal Air Force's Typex machine.

29. Memorandum of 29 Nov 1937 in OKW: Wi/IF 5.2150, Bundesarchiv/Militärarchiv, Freiburg-im-Breisgau; Thomas H. Dyer (U.S. Navy cryptanalyst), interview, 12 Dec 1963.

30. Willi Jensen, 'Hilfsgeräte der Kryptographie', Dissertation (withdrawn), Flensburg, 1955; Brian Randall, *The Colossus*, Technical Report Series, no. 90, Computing Laboratory, University of Newcastle-upon-Tyne (Newcastle, 1976); Brian Johnson, *The Secret War* (London, 1978), pp. 327–49.

31. Among the better known are those recounted in Yardley, *The American Black Chamber*, pp. 289–317, and Richard H. Ullman, *The Anglo-Soviet Accord* (Princeton, 1973), pp. 267–310.

32. Hinsley *et al.*, *British Intelligence*, ii, 65, tells of the acquisitions of Enigma machines by the Soviet Union but states that during the war Britain remained 'uncertain of the extent of their Sigint [signal intelligence] achievements' and could not determine 'whether and, if so, from what dates they succeeded in reading Enigma keys'.

33. Shiro Takagi, 'Nippon No Black Chamber', *All Yomimono* (Showa 27, Juichigatsu (November 1952)), 157–75 (unpublished translation, 'The Black Chamber of Japan', by Flo Morikami); Interrogation of Lt-Gen. Seizo Arisue (chief of Army intelligence), United States Strategic Bombing Survey, interrogation no. 238, p. 10, Record Group 43, National Archives, Washington.

34. Kurt Vetterlein (engineer in charge of the intercept post), interview, 1 Sept 1967; transcripts of intercepts in Inland II geheim, Vol. 477 f, Politisches Archiv, Auswärtiges Amt, Bonn; Germany, Oberkommando der Wehrmacht, Wehrmachtführungsstab, *Kriegstagebuch . . . 1940–1945*, ed. Percy Ernst Schramm (Frankfurt, 1961–9), iii, 854; Walter Schellenberg, *The Labyrinth: memoirs of Walter Schellenberg*, trans. Louis Hagen (New York, 1956), p. 366.

35. [Kunibert] Randewig, 'Taktische Funkpeiling', *Wehrtechnische Hefte*, 52 (1955),

pp. 104–10; Randewig, 'Verfahren der Funkaufklärung-Empfangs- und Peildienst-Auswertung', in Albert Praun (ed.), 'Eine Untersuchung über den Funkdienst des russischen, britischen und amerikanischen Heeres im zweiten Weltkrieg vom deutschen Standpunkt aus, unter besonderer Berücksichtigung ihrer Sicherheit', 18 Feb 1950 (unpublished; in private collection); reports of radio reconnaissance units in Heeresgruppe Nord, 74130/28, Bundesarchiv/Militärarchiv; Herbert Schmidt (radio direction finder), interview, 30 Jan 1970; Fritz Neeb (operating head of Army Group Centre radio intelligence), interview, 30 Dec 1972.

36. Report of 14 Mar 1942, Armeeoberkommando 11, 22279/3, Bundesarchiv/Militärarchiv; report of 19 Jan 1942, 24. Infanterie Division, 22006/11, Bundesarchiv/Militärarchiv; report of 25 Feb 1944, III. Panzer Korps, 53975/5, Bundesarchiv/Militärarchiv.

37. Report of 1 Mar 1944, p. 9, Heeresgruppe Nord, 75130/31, Bundesarchiv/Militärarchiv.

38. Reports at pp. 107 and 110, Heeresgruppe D, 85459, Bundesarchiv/Militärarchiv; United States, War Department, Military Intelligence Division, *German Operational Intelligence: a study of German operational intelligence*, produced at German Military Documents Section by a combined British, Canadian, and US Staff, (n.p., April, 1946), pp. 8–9, 24.

39. Kahn, *The Codebreakers*, p. 472, errs in saying that the Germans obtained the code from the Italians, who had stolen it from the American embassy in Rome and were reading Feller's messages themselves (General Cesare Amè, *Guerra segreta in Italia 1940–43* [Rome, 1954], pp. 96–8). The Germans solved it themselves.

40. Wilhelm F. Flicke, *War Secrets in the Ether*, trans. Ray W. Pettengill (Washington, 1953, reprinted with emendations, Laguna Hills, Calif., 1977), II, 192–8; Herbert Schaedel (archivist for the Chiffrierabteilung of the Oberkommando der Wehrmacht), interview, 29 July 1969; Anton Staubwasser (British specialist in the German army high command's Foreign Armies West), interview, 9 Mar 1970.

41. Hans-Otto Behrendt (assistant intelligence officer to Rommel at the time), interview, 18 Nov 1978. Hans-Otto Behrendt, *Rommels Kenntnis vom Feind im Afrikafeldzug: Ein Bericht über die Feindnachrichtenarbeit, insbesondere die Funkaufklärung* (Freiburg, 1980), pp. 175–8, 188–204.

42. [Adolf Hitler], *Hitlers Tischgespräche im Führerhauptquartier 1941–1942*, ed. Henry Picker, new ed. Percy Ernst Schramm (Stuttgart, 1963), transcript for 29 June 1942.

43. Flicke, *War Secrets in the Ether*, p. 197.

44. Ulrich Liss, 'Der entscheidende Wert richtiger Feindbeurteilung – I: Beispiele aus der neueren Kriegsgeschichte', *Wehrkunde*, VIII (Nov. 1959), 584–92 at p. 585; Reinhard Gehlen *et al.* 'The German G-2 Service in the Russian Campaign (Ic-Dienst Ost)', 1st Special Intelligence Interrogation Report, Interrogation Center United States Forces European Theater (22 July 1945), p. 16.

45. Karl Dönitz, letter, 27 Jan 1970.

46. Heinz Bonatz, *Die deutsche Marine-Funkaufklärung 1914–1945* (Beiträge zur Wehrforschung, XX/XXI (Darmstadt, 1970), p. 138; Jürgen Rohwer, 'La Radiotelegraphie: Auxiliare du commandement dans la guerre sous-marin', *Revue d'histoire de la deuxième guerre mondiale*, XVIII (Jan 1968), 41–66 at p. 52.

47. *B-Dienst* war diary, p. 78, III M 1006/6, Bundesarchiv/Militärarchiv; Wilhelm Tranow (technical head of the *B-Dienst*), interview, 1 July 1970.

48. Rohwer, *The Critical Convoy Battles of March 1943*, pp. 240, 51, 61. See also Heinz Bonatz, *Seekrieg im Äther* (Herford, 1981).

49. *B-Dienst* war diary, p. 169, III M 1006/6, Bundesarchiv/Militärarchiv.

50. Walther Seifert (head of evaluation for the *Forschungsamt*, Göring's codebreaking and wiretapping agency), interview, 19 Aug 1970; 'Die Vernehmung von Generaloberst Jodl durch die Sowjets', trans. Wilhelm Arenz, *Wehrwissenschaftliche*

Rundschau, II (Sept 1961), 534–42 at p. 539. Hinsley *et al.*, *British Intelligence*, II, 640–2.

51. Report of 10 Oct 1944, p. 1, in Heeresgruppe C, 75138/31, Bundesarchiv/Militärarchiv.

52. Dyer interview; Wesley A. Wright (navy cryptanalyst in Pearl Harbor), interview, 12 Dec 1963. Additional first-person material in W. J. Holmes, *Double-edged Secrets: U.S. naval intelligence operations in the Pacific during World War II* (Annapolis, 1979), and Edward Van Der Rhoer, *Deadly Magic: a personal account of communications intelligence in World War II in the Pacific* (New York, 1978).

53. Dyer interview.

54. Chester W. Nimitz and E. B. Potter (eds), *The Great Sea War: the story of naval action in World War II* (Englewood Cliffs, NJ, 1960), p. 245.

55. Letter to presidential candidate Thomas E. Dewey, 27 Sept 1944, in United States, Congress, Joint Committee on the Investigation of the Pearl Harbor Attack, *Pearl Harbor Attack*, Hearings, 79th Congress, 1st and 2nd Sessions (Washington, 1946), part 3, pp. 1132–3 at p. 1132.

56. Charles A. Lockwood (commander of US submarines in the Pacific), letter, 25 Nov 1964. See also United States, Navy, Chief of Naval Operations, OP-20-G-7, 'The role of communications intelligence in submarine warfare in the Pacific (January 1943–October, 1943)', 19 Nov 1945, SRH-011, Record Group 457, National Archives, Washington, D.C. and Clay Blair, Jr., *Silent Victory: The U.S. submarine war against Japan* (Philadelphia, 1975).

57. Cited in Nimitz and Potter, *The Great Sea War*, pp. 422–3.

58. Burke Davis, *Get Yamamoto* (New York, 1969); Holmes, *Double-edged Secrets*, pp. 135–6.

59. Various sources. Kahn, *The Codebreakers*, p. 19, errs in implying that the Purple machine used rotors. The suggestion that Purple was similar cryptographically to the Enigma and thus owed its solution to the Enigma solution has been educed from this Kahn error and is itself false. The solutions were entirely independent of one another.

60. *Pearl Harbor Attack*, part 36, p. 312, part 34, p. 84.

61. United States, War Department, Office of Assistant Chief of Staff, G-2, 'Magic Summaries', 20 Mar to 31 Dec 1942, NC3-457-78-4, and 'Magic Diplomatic Summaries', 1943, NC3-457-78-7, both Record Group 457, National Archives. These have been published on microfilm by University Publications of America, accompanied by *A Subject and Name Index to the Magic Documents: Summaries and Transcripts of the Top-Secret Diplomatic Communications of Japan, 1938–1945*, ed. Paul Kesaris, index compiled by David Wallace (Frederick, Maryland, 1982). Ronald Lewin, *The American Magic: Codes, Ciphers and the Defeat of Japan* (New York, 1982), chapter 11.

62. ' "Magic" Summary', no. 562 of 9 Oct 1943 in 'Magic Diplomatic Summaries'. This meeting, incidentally, is not included in Andreas Hillgruber (ed.), *Staatsmänner und Diplomaten bei Hitler; Vertrauliche Aufzeichnungen über Unterredungen mit Vertretern des Auslandes*, 2. Teil, 1942–1944 (Frankfurt, 1970). The intercepts thus constitute a useful new source for the history of Hitler's Reich.

63. ' "Magic" Summary' of 17 Dec 1943, in 'Magic Diplomatic Summaries'.

64. *Pearl Harbor Attack*, part 3, p. 1132.

65. See the account by Jean Stengers, above, chapter 6.

66. Penelope Fitzgerald, *The Knox Brothers* (New York, 1977), *passim*.

67. Ronald Lewin, *Ultra Goes to War* (New York, 1978), pp. 112–13 and Wladyslaw Kozaczuk, *Enigma* (Frederick, Maryland, 1984), chapters 1–4, 5, appendices C, D, E. Gordon Welchman, *The Hut Six Story: Breaking the Enigma Codes* (New York, 1982), pp. 77–81, 295–307; Peter Calvocoressi, *Top Secret Ultra* (London, 1980), pp. 10–13; I.J. Good, 'Early work on computers at Bletchley', *Cryptologia*, III (April, 1979), 65–77; Andrew Hodges, *Alan Turing: The Enigma* (New York, 1983), especially chapter 4.

68. Hinsley *et al.*, *British Intelligence*, I, 178–9.

69. Ibid., pp. 528–48; N. E. Evans, 'Air intelligence and the Coventry raid', *Royal United Services Institution Journal* (Sept 1976), 66–73.

70. H. R. Trevor-Roper (a solver with E. W. B. Gill of the hand cyphers), interview, 1972; Werner Trautman (head of Abwehr radio station in Hamburg), interview, 20 Aug 1970; Kim Philby, *My Private War* (New York, 1968), p. 65; Hinsley *et al.*, *British Intelligence*, I, p. 120.

71. John Masterman, *The Double-cross System in the War of 1939 to 1945* (New Haven, 1972), *passim*; Kahn, *Hitler's Spies*, ch. 26.

72. Rohwer, *The Critical Convoy Battles of March 1943*, p. 238; Patrick Beesly, *Very Special Intelligence* (London, 1977), pp. 70–1; Hinsley *et al.*, *British Intelligence*, I, 336–7.

73. Hinsley *et al.*, *British Intelligence*, II, 229, 667. The original version of this paper followed Beesly, *Very Special Intelligence*, pp. 110–11, in saying that the change to the four-rotor Enigma took place on 8 March 1943 and that Bletchley solved it in a few days. This is wrong. Beesly was apparently thinking of a new U-boat code for short-signal weather reports put into use on 10 March 1943 that Bletchley at first feared would be 'fatal' to its work but that it in fact recovered in nine days (Hinsley *et al.*, *British Intelligence*, II, 750).

74. Beesly, *Very Special Intelligence*, pp. 64–5; Jürgen Rohwer, diagram 'Development of German cipher-circles for Funkschlüssel M (naval Enigma)', in *Newsletter of the American Committee on the History of the Second World War*, no. 17 (May 1977), 5.

75. Hinsley *et al.*, *British Intelligence*, II, 229–30, 547–67, 747–52.

76. Ibid., 572; Beesly, *Very Special Intelligence*, pp. 200–1; Jürgen Rohwer, 'Die alliierte Funkaufklärung und der Verlauf des Zweiten Weltkrieges', *Vierteljahrshefte für Zeitgeschichte*, XXVII (1979), 325–69 at 356–62; Günter Böddeker, *Die Boote im Netz* (Bergische Gladbach, 1981), *passim*; Alberto Santoni, *Il Vero Traditore: Il ruolo documentato di Ultra nella guerra del Mediterraneo* (Milano, 1981). For a more detailed analysis of the Battle of the Atlantic see chapter 8 in this volume by Jürgen Rohwer.

77. United States, Army, 6824 Detailed Interrogation Center, (MIS)M. 1121, 'Information on German Secret Teletypewriters', Record Group 165, National Archives; U.S. Patent No. 1,912,983; Hans Rohrbach, 'Chiffrierverfahren der neusten Zeit', *Archiv der elektrischen Übertragung*, 2 (Dec 1948), 362–9 at § 13.

78. Randall, *The Colossus*.

79. Lewin, *Ultra Goes to War*, pp. 325–6; [United States, Army], Memorandum for Colonel [Telford] Taylor, 'Ultra and the U.S. Seventh Army', 12 May 1945, SRH-022, Record Group 457, National Archives; US Army Air Force, *Ultra and the History of the United States Strategic Air Force in Europe vs. the German Air Force* (written 1945; published Frederick, Md., 1980).

80. Memorandum for Colonel Taylor, 'Ultra and the U.S. Seventh Army', p. 2. Hinsley *et al.*, *British Intelligence*, II, chapter 19.

81. Lewin, *Ultra Goes to War*, pp. 336–40. Ralph Bennett, *Ultra in the West* (London, 1979), pp. 112–24.

82. According to records in the Berlin Document Center, the technical heads of the OKW *Chiffrierabteilung* (Wilhelm Fenner) and of the *B-Dienst* (Wilhelm Tranow) were not party members; Tranow wrested this post from an old party member (Lothar Franke, membership no. 19,852). The Foreign Office codebreaking unit's administrative head (Kurt Selchow) joined after the start of the war (1 Jan 1940, membership no. 7,910,928); of his three main assistants, two were party members, one early (Adolf Paschke, 1 May 1933, 2,649,870), and one late (Rudolf Schauffler, 1 Jan 1942, 8,743,951), and one was not (Werner Kunze). The leading officials of the *Forschungsamt*, Göring's wiretapping and codebreaking agency, were all Nazis.

83. Seifert, interview.

84. Leo Hepp, 'Das Grösste Geheimnis des Zweiten Weltkrieges?', *Wehrkunde* (1976), pp. 86–9 at 88–9; Dr Erich Hüttenhain (in charge of German cipher systems in OKW *Chiffrierabteilung*), letter, 15 Feb 1979.

85. This section, especially the part dealing with the technical reasons, owes a great deal to Dr C. A. Deavours, professor of mathematics at Kean College of New Jersey, who has thoroughly investigated the cryptology of the Enigma. I am deeply grateful to him for his help. The section has also benefited from the following people, who read it in draft and commented upon it: Dr I. J. Good, one of the team who worked with Newman at Bletchley on the electronic cryptanalytical machines and is now University Distinguished Professor of Statistics at the Virginia Polytechnic Institute and State University; Dr Karl-Heinz Ludwig, professor at the University of Bremen and author of *Technik und Ingenieure im Dritten Reich* (Düsseldorf, 1974); Dr Henry A. Turner, professor of history at Yale University specialising in twentieth-century German economics; Dr Andreas Hillgruber, professor of history at Cologne University and a leading World War II historian; Heinz Bonatz, retired Kapitän zur See, head of the *B-Dienst* from 1934 to 1936 and from 1942 to 1944; Dr Erich Hüttenhain, and Dr Alan Beyerchen, professor of history at the Ohio State University and author of *Scientists under Hitler: politics and the physics community in the Third Reich* (New Haven, 1977).

86. Hinsley *et al.*, *British Intelligence*, ii, 631, 639. Alan S. Milward, *War, Economy and Society 1939–45* (Berkeley, 1977), pp. 169–193, discusses similar problems in a broader context.

87. Tadeusz Lisicki, 'Die Leistung des polnischen Entzifferungdiensten bei der Lösung des Verfahrens der deutscher "Enigma" – Funkschlüsselmaschine', in Jürgen Rohwer and Eberhard Jäckel (eds), *Die Funkaufklärung und ihre Rolle im Zweiten Weltkrieg* (Stuttgart, 1979), pp. 71–5; Kozaczuk, *Enigma*, pp. 48–9, 53–4, 251–4, 265–9, 274–5.

88. Another general reason might seem to be that the Allies' larger population would have given them more, and probably better, people for codebreaking. But it is not known how many of the approximately 10,000 people at Bletchley were solving cyphers other than German at any particular time or how many in the German agencies were solving Soviet, Italian, Japanese, Turkish, Swedish, and other non-US and non-UK systems at the same time. Moreover, the contributions of other governments – Canadian, Free French, Dutch, Italian, Japanese, Hungarian – to their respective allies cannot readily be measured in terms of manpower. Finally, the number of persons in field units, both Allied and German, is not known with precision. I myself have the feeling that more people in the West attacked German cyphers than worked in Germany on Allied cyphers and so I think that greater Allied population probably did contribute to greater success. But, lacking the figures that would prove or disprove this conjecture, I do not advance it. A corollary to this would be that the Allies' greater industrial capacity enabled them to help both their codebreakers and their codemakers more. But this help would have been so small in relation to either the Allied or the Axis war effort as to be insignificant. So this cannot be adduced as a factor, either.

89. Kahn, *Hitler's Spies*, pp. 172–222, esp. p. 176.

90. Ibid., pp. 534–6.

91. This is developed in more detail in ibid., pp. 528–31.

92. Carl von Clausewitz, *On War*, trans. and ed. Michael Howard and Peter Paret (Princeton, 1976), book vi, chapter 1.

93. Ibid., book vii, chapter 2.

94. Georges Castellan, *Le réarmament clandestin du Reich, 1930–1935, vu par le 2ᵉ bureau de l'état-major français* (Paris, 1954); Bonatz, *Die deutsche Marine-Funkaufklärung*, p. 93; David Kahn, *Kahn on Codes* (New York, 1984), pp. 76–88. Cf above, pp. 127ff.

95. Hinsley *et al.*, *British Intelligence*, i, 12–13, 36–43; Kahn, *Hitler's spies*, pp. 54, 387–8, 393–8.

96. Solomon Kullback, telephone interview, 2 Oct 1978.

97. Tranow, interviews. The book was Roger Baudouin's *Elements de cryptographie* (Paris, 1939).

98. W. Preston Corderman (a first student in this school, later wartime head of the US Army codebreaking agency), interview, 2 Nov 1976; W. F. Friedman, *Military Cryptanalysis* (Washington, 1938–42).

99. United States, War Department, Technical Manual 11–380, *Converter M-209* (27 Apr 1942), § 5 b.

100. See, for example, Germany, Oberkommando der Wehrmacht, Heeresdienstvorschrift geheim 7 (also Marinedienstvorschrift 534, Luftwaffedienstvorschrift geheim 7), *Allgemeine Schüsselregeln für die Wehrmacht*, 1 Apr 1944, and Germany, [Reichswehrministerium], Heeresdienstvorschrift geheim 13 (also Luftwaffedienstvorschrift geheim 13), *Gebrauchsanleitung für die Chiffriermaschine Enigma*, 12 Jan 1937).

101. Beyerchen, letter, 13 Apr 1979, says that urgency stimulated the Allies to break down the barrier between theoretical and applied mathematicians and scientists and that the lack of urgency in Germany 'left their peacetime barrier intact'.

102. T. H. Flowers, letter, 13 Feb 1979. I am deeply grateful to Mr Flowers for this letter and one of 18 Apr 1979, which explain how the British advanced from electromechanical to electronic machines.

103. Ibid.; I. J. Good, 'Early work on computers at Bletchley', *Cryptologia*, 3 (April, 1979), 65–77 at p. 73; Hodges, *Turing*, pp. 225–7, 267–8.

104. Konrad Zuse (German computer pioneer), letters, 22 Nov 1976 and 5 Jan 1977.

105 Bonatz, interview, 15 Nov 1978.

106. See, for example, Max Pinl and Lux Furtmuller, 'Mathematicians under Hitler', Leo Baeck Institute, *Year Book XVIII* (London, 1973), 129–82.

107. An attempt to trace the roots of German arrogance in Kahn, *Hitler's Spies*, pp. 525–8.

108. Beesly, *Very Special Intelligence*, pp. 57–8; Kahn, *Hitler's Spies*, p. 533.

109. Kullback, interview.

110. Harold Deutsch, talk at colloquium on 'What role did radio intelligence play in the course of the Second World War?', Stuttgart, 17 Nov 1978.

111. See also David Kahn, 'The Ultra conference', *Cryptologia*, 3 (January, 1979), 1–8 at pp. 5–6.

112. Preface to Praun, 'Eine Untersuchung . . . '.

113. Eisenhower to Menzies, 12 July 1945, Eisenhower Library, Abilene, Kansas.

114. *Pearl Harbor Attack*, part 3, p. 1133.

8. RADIO INTELLIGENCE AND ITS ROLE IN THE BATTLE OF THE ATLANTIC
Jürgen Rohwer

1. The most important sources about radio-intelligence in the Battle of the Atlantic are as follows.

National Archives, Washington: SRS-548: B-Berichte and xB-Berichte, 18 Sept 1939–23 May 1945 (excluding 23 April 1944–6 Jan 1945). Original German Naval Intelligence Summaries, 18 vols, 11861 pp. SRS-1166: TICOM-B-Berichte, Vol. 19 (5 May 1944–20 Aug 1944), vol. 20 (20 Aug 1944–24 Dec 1944). German Naval Intelligence Summaries (reproductions of originals held by the British), 1457 pp.

Public Record Office, London – Kew: ADM 223: War of 1939–1945: Naval Intelligence Papers. DEFE 3: Intelligence from Enemy Radio Communications 1939–1945. Vol. 1–4, 20–34, 66–82, 705–44.

2. This reconstruction is based mainly on the Reports of Proceedings with Convoys by the Convoy Commodores and the Senior Officers Escort, to be found in the PRO

Series ADM 199 and in the Directorate of History, Dept. of Defence in Ottawa and in the Convoy Folders for HX-, SC-, ON- and ONS-Convoys in the Operational Archives, US Navy Yard, Washington. In addition I have used the Daily Operation Maps of the US Atlantic Fleet, O.A., Navy Yard, Washington.

3. Hinsley F. H. with Thomas, E. E., Ransom, C. F. G. and Knight, R. C., *British Intelligence in the Second World War, Its Influence on Strategy and Operations.* Vol. ii (London 1981). Appendix 1: British Cypher Security During the War, pp. 631–42.

4. Information from the weekly xB-Berichte-Series, See note 1 above, SRS-548. Also Bonatz, Heinz, *Seekrieg im Äther*, Die Leistungen der Marine-Funkaufklärung 1939–1945 (Herford, Mittler, 1981).

5. Main source: Kriegstagebuch des Befehlshabers der U-Boote 1939–1945. (Original in the Bundesarchiv-Militärarchiv, Freiburg.) Also, Dönitz, Karl, *10 Jahre und 20 Tage*, 7.Aufl. (München, 1980). Mit einem Nachwort über die Schlacht im Atlantik in der historischen Forschung 1980. Rohwer, Jürgen, *The Critical Convoy Battles of March 1943: The Battle HX.229 and SC.122* (London, Ian Allan, 1977); Douglas, W. A. B. and Rohwer, J., 'The Most Thankless Task Revisited: Convoys, Escorts and Radio Intelligence in the Western Atlantic 1941–1943', in *The RCN in Retrospect* (ed. James Boutilier, Vancouver, Univ. of British Columbia Press, 1982) pp. 175–234.

6. Roskill, Stephen W., *The Secret Capture* (London, 1959); Beesly, Patrick, *Very Special Intelligence: The Story of the Admiralty's Operational Intelligence Centre 1939–1945* (London, Hamish Hamilton, 1977); Hinsley *et al.*, op. cit., Vol. i (London, HMSO, 1979), pp. 115–36,330–46, app. 12., Vol. ii, pp. 163–234, 525–72, app. 8, 9, 10 and 19.

7. Rohwer, Jürgen, 'La radiotélégraphie, auxiliaire du commandement dans la guerre sousmarine', in *Revue d'Histoire de la Deuxième Guerre Mondiale* (1966), pp. 42–66.

8. Personal information from the British, American and Canadian experts P. Beesly, E. E. Thomas, P. Calvocoressi, Sir H. Marchant, M. Pain, K. Knowles and P. McDiarmid. Also, Rohwer, J. and Jäckel, E., *Die Rolle der Funkaufklärung im Zweiten Weltkrieg* (Stuttgart, Motorbuch, 1979).

9. Rohwer and Jäckel, op. cit., pp. 388.

10. Rohwer, Jürgen, 'Special Intelligence und die Geleitzugsteuerung im Herbst 1941', in *Marine-Rundschau* 76 (1978), 711–19; Rohwer, Jürgen, 'Die USA und die Schlacht im Atlantik', in *Kriegswende Dezember 1941*, Rohwer, Jürgen and Jäckel, Eberhard (eds) (Koblenz, Bernard & Graefe, 1983).

11. Beesly, Patrick, Rohwer, Jürgen and Knowles, Kenneth, 'Special Intelligence and the Battle of the Atlantic. The British, the German, the American View', in *Changing Interpretations and New Sources in Naval History*, Papers from the Third Naval Academy History Symposium, Robert W. Love (ed.) (New York, Garland 1980), pp. 413–49.

12. Hinsley, op. cit., Vol. ii, appendix 19, 'The Breaking of the U-boat Enigma (Shark)', pp. 747–52.

13. Bonatz, op. cit., pp. 245–57.

14. Gretton, Sir Peter, *Crisis Convoy. The Story of the Atlantic Convoy HX.231* (London, Davies, 1974).

15. Roskill, Stephen W., *The War at Sea, 1939–1945*, vol. ii. (London, HMSO, 1956), pp. 367–9; Rohwer, *The Critical Convoy Battles*, op. cit., pp. 195–200; Hinsley, op. cit., Vol. ii, pp. 525–72; *The RCN in Retrospect*, op. cit., pp. 221–34.

9. THE CAMBRIDGE COMINTERN · *Robert Cecil*

The writer claims good authority for all unqualified statements; he has not in all cases been able to disclose what it is. He wishes to express his thanks to all those, named and unnamed, who have helped him in verifying a series of events, some of which necessarily remain shrouded in darkness.

1. Kim Philby, *My Silent War* (London, 1968), p. xix.
2. P. Seale and M. McConville, *Philby: The Long Road to Moscow* (London, 1978), pp. 66–8.
3. M. Straight, *After Long Silence* (London 1983).
4. Ibid., p. 144.
5. G. Rees, *A Chapter of Accidents* (London, 1972), p. 149.
6. Ibid., p. 118.
7. Philby, *My Silent War*, p. 74.
8. The author is indebted to Mr John Reed for this account.
9. A more detailed account will be found in B. Page, D. Leitch and P. Knightley in *Philby: The Spy Who Betrayed a Generation* (London, 1977), pp. 211–15.
10. F. Giles, *From Russia with Love, Sunday Times Weekly Review*, 6 Jan 80.
11. Rees, *A Chapter of Accidents*, p. 187.
12. *Hansard*, 7 Nov. 55, col. 1495.
13. Rees, *A Chapter of Accidents*, p. 191.
14. Philby, *My Silent War*, p. 127.
15. Lord Greenhill, *The Times*, 7 Sept 77.
16. Straight, *After Long Silence*, p. 251.
17. A. Boyle, *The Climate of Treason* (London, 1979), p. 383.
18. D. D. Maclean, *British Foreign Policy Since Suez* (London, 1970).
19. Z. K. Brzezinski, *Ideology and Power in Soviet Politics* (London 1962), p. 5.
20. L. Frank, *Der Mensch ist Gut* (Zurich 1917).

10. SECRET INTELLIGENCE IN THE UNITED STATES, 1947–1982: THE CIA'S SEARCH FOR LEGITIMACY   Harry Howe Ransom

1. Harry Howe Ransom, 'Don't Make the CIA a KGB', *The New York Times*, Op-Ed page, 24 Dec 1981, p. A23.
2. Harry Rositzke, *The CIA's Secret Operations* (New York, 1977), p. 17.
3. US Senate, Select Committee on Intelligence. *Final Report Book* IV, 'History of the Central Intelligence Agency', by Anne Karalekas. Senate Report No. 94–755. 94th Congress, 2nd Session (Washington DC, 1976), pp. 1–102. In 1949 the covert operations budget was $4.7 million; in 1952, $82 million. The number of CIA foreign stations in 1949 was seven; by 1952 it was forty-seven.
4. For coverage of the founding years of the CIA, see, among others: Ray Cline, *Secrets, Spies and Scholars* (Washington, DC, 1976); William R. Corson, *The Armies of Ignorance* (New York, 1977); Harry Howe Ransom, *The Intelligence Establishment* (Cambridge, Mass., 1970); and Thomas F. Troy, *Donovan and the CIA* (Washington, DC, 1982).
5. Quoted in US Senate Select Committee, Book IV, p. 42.
6. For detailed accounts of these episodes, see Kermit Roosevelt, *Countercoup: The Struggle for the Control of Iran* (New York, 1979); Richard H. Immerman, *The CIA in Guatemala* (Austin, Texas, 1982); and Stephen Schlesinger and Stephen Kinzer, *Bitter Fruit: the Untold Story of the American Coup in Guatemala* (Garden City, New York, 1982).
7. Quoted in US Select Committee, Book IV, pp. 52–53.
8. Ibid., p. 63.
9. Philip Agee, *Inside the Company: CIA Diary* (London, 1975).
10. 'Text of Reagan Statement on Order', *The New York Times*, 5 Dec 1981, p. 11.
11. In another essay covering this same historical period, I have analysed the

interaction of domestic and international politics as they affected intelligence policy. See: 'Strategic Intelligence and Intermestic Politics', in Charles W. Kegley, Jr and Eugene R. Whittkopf (eds), *Perspectives on American Foreign Policy: Selected Readings* (New York, 1983), pp. 299–319.

Bibliographical Note

A burgeoning bibliography confronts those seeking to understand the evolution of the modern United States intelligence system. No other nation has seen its intelligence secrets bared in such abundant detail. Published items fall into five categories: bibliographies; government documents; subjective memoirs by, or biographies of, intelligence professionals; 'whistle-blowing' polemics; and scholarly works by historians and social scientists.

A growing number of bibliographies are available, including Paul W. Blackstock and Frank L. Schaf, Jr, *Intelligence, Espionage, Counterespionage, and Covert Operations: A Guide to Information Sources* (Detroit, Michigan, 1978); George C. Constantinides, *Intelligence and Espionage: An Analytical Bibliography* (Boulder, Colorado, 1983); Myron J. Smith, Jr, *The Secret Wars*, Vol. II (1945–1980) (Santa Barbara, California, 1981).

With the creation of permanent, select committees in the US House of Representatives and Senate, a large flow of public hearings and reports on intelligence activities began. Undergirding these are the numerous hearings, studies and reports published by the select investigative committees in the House (Otis Pike, chairman) and the Senate (Frank Church, chairman) in 1975–6. In June 1975 the *Report to the President* of the Commission on CIA Activities Within the United States (Nelson A. Rockefeller, chairman) was published (Washington DC). Also useful is Volume 7 of the *Appendices*, Commission on the Organization of the Government for the Conduct of Foreign Policy (Robert D. Murphy, chairman) (Washington, DC, June 1975). A very useful selection of the most significant sections from the above-listed sources can be found in Tyrus G. Fain (ed.), *The Intelligence Community: History, Organization and Issues* (New York and London, 1977).

In the memoir-biography category, the most revealing work is Thomas Powers, *The Man Who Kept the Secrets: Richard Helms and the CIA* (New York, 1979). Also providing insights are David D. Martin, *Wilderness of Mirrors* (New York, 1980); William E. Colby, *Honorable Men, My Life in the CIA* (New York, 1978); and Ray S. Cline, *The CIA Under Reagan, Bush and Casey* (Washington, 1981).

Among the most notable polemical works are: Philip Agee, *Inside the Company, CIA Diary* (New York, 1975); Morton H. Halperin, *et al.*, *The Lawless State: The Crimes of the U.S. Intelligence Agencies* (New York, 1976); Victor Marchetti and John Marks, *The CIA and the Cult of Intelligence* (New York, 1974); John Stockwell, *In Search of Enemies* (New York, 1978); and Frank Snepp, *Decent Interval: An Insider's Account of Saigon's Indecent End* (New York, 1977).

Representative scholarly works include Roy Godson (ed.), *Intelligence Requirements for the 1980s*, 5 volumes (Washington, DC, 1979–82); Harry Howe Ransom, *The Intelligence Establishment* (Cambridge, Mass., 1970); Richard E. Morgan, *Domestic Intelligence, Monitoring Dissent in America* (Austin, Texas, 1980); Stafford T. Thomas, *The U.S. Intelligence Community* (Lanham, Md., 1983); Robert L. Pfaltzgraff, Jr., Uri Ra'anan and Warren Milberg (eds), *Intelligence Policy and National Security* (Hamden, Conn., 1981); and Lawrence Freedman, *U.S. Intelligence and the Soviet Strategic Threat* (Boulder, Colo, 1977).

11. THE HISTORY OF THE D-NOTICE COMMITTEE   *Alasdair Palmer*

* My thanks are due to Peter Hennessy and Christopher Andrew, both of whom provided a great deal of help, knowledge and encouragement. Without Peter Hennessy, the chapter would never have been started. Without Christopher Andrew, it would never have been finished – or published. Duncan Campbell, Admiral Ash, and Sir Frank Cooper shared their views of the system with me, for which I am also very grateful. Unfortunately, virtually all of the committee's records since 1918 have gone 'missing'.

1. WO 32/6381. All numbered references, unless otherwise stated, are to the PRO papers at Kew.

2. Ibid.

3. See Philip M. Towle, 'The Debate on Wartime Censorship in Britain', in B. Bond and I. Roy (eds), *War and Society*, vol. I (London, 1975).

4. Cab 4/1, CID Paper 39B.

5. Cab 17/91.

6. Cab 17/91. For the *Guardian*, such 'power in the hands of government would be a dangerous weapon', while *The Times* claimed that 'the natural attitude of every government is to try and make out that everything is being well done, and to conceal its faults as much as possible' and viewed 'with apprehension any system which made penal the publication of all military and naval news except as authorised by the government'.

7. Cab 17/91. The quotations from Leng and Robbins also come from this file.

8. Cab 17/91.

9. The quotations are from one he published – anonymously – in the *Fortnightly*, March 1906.

10. ADM 116/1058. The Admiralty reaction to the offending article in the *Daily Express* is also to be found here, as is my quotation from *The Times*.

11. Ibid.

12. Ibid.

13. Cab 4/5.

14. See David French, 'Spy Fever in Britain 1900–1915'. *The Historical Journal*, XXI, (1978) and Christopher Andrew, 'The Mobilization of British Intelligence for the Two World Wars', in *Mobilization for Total War*, ed. N. F. Dreisziger (Waterloo, Ontario, 1981).

15. Cab 3/2, Paper 47B.

16. Quoted in Towle, 'The Debate on Wartime Censorship'.

17. Cab 17/91.

18. Ibid.

19. Ibid.

20. Cab 4/5.

21. Ibid.

22. Appendix to Paper 167B, Cab 5/3.

23. Suppressing, amongst other items, the trials of HMS *Edinburgh*, 'acceleration of certain works in government and private dockyards', and embarkation practice for a putative expeditionary force.

24. Cab 4/5.

25. Quotation in Colin Lovelace, 'British Press Censorship during the First World War' in *Newspaper History from the 17th Century to the Present Day*, G. Boyle, J. Curran and P. Wingate (eds) (London, 1978).

26. Cab 24/5.

27. Quoted in Lovelace, 'British Press Censorship'.

28. Cab 14/15.

29. For the full details of how the Foreign Office did this, see Philip M. Taylor, *The Projection of Britain: British Overseas Propaganda 1918–1939* (Cambridge, 1980).

30. Cab 4/8.

31. ADM 116/4082.

32. At 169th meeting of the CID, 20 Feb 1923 – see Cab 4/8.

33. ADM 116/4082.

34. ADM 116/4082. Robbins maintained that 'if an editor has . . . Communistic sympathies, he would keep them in check when his journalistic career and reputation were at stake'.

35. See Christopher Andrew's chapter in this volume.

36. A policy exactly opposite to that advanced by the Americans, who went out of their way to feed the public appetite for information on the terrifying new discovery. For examples of the ludicrous lengths the British government was prepared to go to try to ensure atomic research was shrouded in secrecy, see M. Gowing, *Independence and Deterrence* (London, 1974), Vol. 2: *Policy Execution*, pp. 126–37. It is worth noting that once again, the comic fastidiousness was a total flop: the Russians got much more secret information from the spies Klaus Fuchs and Donald MacLean. Gowing notes that 'the men in charge of the project – Portal and then Morgan as controllers, Cockcroft, Hinton, Penney and Perrin . . . believed the extreme security surrounding the project was irrational and counter productive' (p. 134).

37. G. M. Thomson, *The Blue Pencil Admiral* (London, 1947), p. 30.

38. Ibid., p. 136.

39. ADM 1/20905.

40. An example of this is a reply in 1951 by the Deputy Editor of the *Daily Telegraph* – then Malcolm Muggeridge – to a complaint from the Chairman of the committee that an article on August 1 had mentioned a bomb test in Australia, contravening a D-notice ban. Muggeridge was 'most distressed . . . you may be sure the lapse was unintentional and that all requisite steps will be taken to avoid any further repetition of the offence'. Quoted in Gowing, *Independence and Deterrence*, Vol 2, p. 137.

41. Chapman Pincher's fascinating evidence to the 1980 Select Committee on Defence HC773 provides much of the basis for this and subsequent remarks.

42. Aitken's book documenting his experiences is *Officially Secret* (London, 1971).

43. See his submission to the 1980 Select Committee, HC773, reiterated in conversation in December 1982.

44. Press evidence, HC773.

45. Official documents explaining the system stress this.

46. The details are from Chapman Pincher's book, *Inside Story* (London, 1978) and the relevant government publications, Cmnd 330d and 3312.

47. Nigel West, *A Matter of Trust: MI5, 1945–72* (London, 1982).

48. Pincher, in *Inside Story*, p. 69, alleges that MI5 put the name on a D-notice, which was then communicated by the Press Association's teleprinter, to punish the *Telegraph*, on the assumption that the rest of the press, on seeing it there, would think that anything MI5 thought safe enough to share with journalists was safe enough to publish.

49. HC773, p. 122.

50. See the submissions of the editors of such papers as the *Guardian* and the *Financial Times*, and programmes such as 'World in Action', in HC773.

51. Both the Assistant Director-General at the BBC (Alan Protheroe) and the Deputy Editor at ITN (Don Horobin) sit on the D-notice committee. Both are basically in favour of the system, though both agree that it does not play much of a role in their lives – and that there may be a causal connection between those two evaluations.

52. See A. Protheroe's article in the *Listener*, May 1982. Robert Harris, *Gotcha! The Media, the Press and the Falklands Crisis* (London, 1983) documents the shortening tempers and growing suspicions of *mauvaise foi* in detail.

List of Contributors

CHRISTOPHER M. ANDREW is Fellow and Senior Tutor of Corpus Christi College, Cambridge and editor of the *Historical Journal*. He has written and broadcast widely on modern history and international relations. His most recent book, written jointly with A. S. Kanya-Forstner, is *France Overseas* (1981). His next book, *Secret Service: The Making of the British Intelligence Community*, will be published in 1985.

ROBERT CECIL, CMG, served for over thirty years in the British diplomatic service before becoming Reader in Contemporary German History at the University of Reading. His books include *The Myth of the Master Race* (1972) and *Hitler's Decision to Invade Russia* (1975).

DAVID N. DILKS is Professor of International History, University of Leeds and author of *Curzon in India* (2 vols, 1969, 1970); editor of the *Diaries of Sir Alexander Cadogan* (1971) and *Retreat from Power* (2 vols, 1981). The first volume of his *Life of Neville Chamberlain* will be published in 1984.

DAVID KAHN is the author of *The Codebreakers*, *Hitler's Spies* and *Kahn on Codes* and of numerous articles on cryptology and military intelligence and is editor of *Cryptologia* magazine. He is assistant Viewpoints editor at *Newsday*, the Long Island daily, and has a D.Phil. in modern history from Oxford University.

IAN NISH is Professor of International History, London School of Economics and Political Science. He is the author of *The Anglo-Japanese Alliance* (1966); *Alliance in Decline* (1972) and *Japanese Foreign Policy (1869–1942)* (1977).

EUNAN O'HALPIN is Lecturer in Public Administration, National Institute for Higher Education, Dublin. He is the author of articles published in the *Historical Journal* and *Irish Historical Studies* and of *British Government in Ireland 1891–1922* (forthcoming from Gill and Macmillan).

ALASDAIR PALMER is research student at Corpus Christi College, Cambridge, working on liberal political theory. He has written articles for *The Times* and *The Economist*.

HARRY HOWE RANSOM is Professor of Political Science at Vanderbilt University, Nashville, Tennessee. He has taught at Princeton and Harvard Universities and at the University of Leeds. He is the author of *The Intelligence Establishment* (1970) *Can American Democracy survive Cold War?* (1963) and numerous articles and essays.

JÜRGEN ROHWER is Professor of Contemporary History at the University of Stuttgart.

JEAN STENGERS is Professor of Contemporary History at the University of Brussels and a Member of the Belgian Royal Academy. He has written extensively on Leopold II and the Congo, Belgian history and international relations. His most recent book is *Leopold III et le Gouvernment: les deux politiques belges de 1940* (1980).

WESLEY K. WARK is Lecturer in European History, University of Calgary. He is the author of a forthcoming book on British intelligence and Nazi Germany in the 1930s and of articles for the *Historical Journal* and the *Journal of Strategic Studies*.

Index